Enabling Access

Access

Effective Teaching and Learning
for Pupils with Learning Difficulties

Second Edition

Edited by
**Barry Carpenter, Rob Ashdown
and Keith Bovair**

David Fulton Publishers
London

David Fulton Publishers
2 Park Square, Milton Park, Abingdon, Oxon OX14 4RN

270 Madison Avenue, New York, NY 10016

First published in Great Britain in 1996 by David Fulton Publishers
Transferred to digital printing

David Fulton Publishers is an imprint of the Taylor & Francis Group, an informa business

Copyright © David Fulton Publishers Ltd, 2001

British Library Cataloguing in Publication Data
A catalogue record for this book is available from the British Library.

ISBN 1-85346-676-X

Typeset by Book Production Services, London

Contents

Part II: Access and Entitlement to the Whole Curriculum

Part III: The Context for the Whole Curriculum

The Contributors

Rob Ashdown is head teacher at St. Luke's School for pupils with severe learning difficulties in Scunthorpe and a regional (distance-learning) tutor for the University of Birmingham. He has published widely and is co-editor of *The Curriculum Challenge* and *Enabling Access*.

Sally Beveridge is senior lecturer at the University of Leeds where she teaches on initial teacher education and continuing professional development. She has taught in primary and secondary schools and directed an inclusive pre-school project for children and families.

Keith Bovair is head teacher of a school for pupils with complex needs in Enfield. He lectured for the University of Birmingham, and is president of the European Association for Special Education. He has published seven books and numerous contributing chapters and articles.

Erica Brown is head of research and development at the International Education and Training Centre, Acorns Children's Hospices Trust in Birmingham, a trained bereavement counsellor, a school inspector and school governor. She has published and lectured nationally and internationally in religious education, special education and bereavement.

Richard Byers lectures in inclusive and special education at the University of Cambridge, and edits the *British Journal of Special Education*. His recent publications focus on the curriculum for pupils with special educational needs and the development of inclusive policy and practice.

Barry Carpenter is Chief Executive of Sunfield, a residential school for children with severe and complex learning needs, and honorary professor at the University of Northumbria. He writes and lectures nationally and internationally and represents Europe on the World Council for Early Intervention.

Tina Detheridge is a director of Widgit Software Ltd, and she has worked, lectured and written for many years on the development and application of information and communications technology (ICT) for pupils with special needs. She is co-author of *Literacy through Symbols* (1997, Fulton).

Ann Fergusson works on the special needs team at University College, Northampton, and has worked on projects for the National Curriculum Council and the Qualifications and Curriculum Authority. She co-edited *Implementing the Whole Curriculum for Pupils with Learning Difficulties* (1996, Fulton).

Bernard Gummett is head teacher at George Hastwell School in Cumbria for pupils with severe/profound and multiple learning difficulties. He was a major contributor to *Extending Horizons* (NCET), and advised online as part of a regional National Grid for Learning initiative.

Penny Lacey is a lecturer in education at the University of Birmingham, specialising in severe and profound learning difficulties. She is a co-director of Special Music Courses, a not-for-profit organisation that provides short courses in music and related arts.

Hazel Lawson is senior lecturer in special educational needs at Middlesex University, and has taught in primary and special schools. She wrote *Practical Record Keeping* (1998, Fulton), and has worked on curriculum guidelines for the Qualifications and Curriculum Authority.

Ann Lewis is professor of special education and educational psychology at the University of Birmingham. Her extensive writing includes the books *Primary Special Needs and the National Curriculum* (1995, Routledge) and, with Geoff Lindsay, *Researching Children's Perspectives* (2000, Open University Press).

Clare Martin is deputy head at George Hastwell School in Cumbria for pupils with severe/profound and multiple learning difficulties. She was a major contributor to *Extending Horizons* (NCET), and was involved in the Schools Curriculum and Assessment Authority project on whole-curriculum access.

Peter Mittler is emeritus professor of special education at the University of Manchester. He has served on national and international committees and undertaken consultancies to international organisations. His most recent book, *Working Towards Inclusive Education* (2000, Fulton), was highly commended in the NASEN/*TES* 2000 book awards.

Denise Morris is special-schools consultant to Bristol LEA and has worked in special schools and as a special-needs LEA adviser. She is co-author of *Implementing the Literacy Hour in Special Schools* and *Implementing the Numeracy Hour in Special Schools* (2000, both Fulton).

Brahm Norwich is professor of educational psychology and special educational needs at the University of Exeter. He was previously a professor of special-needs education at London University. He has worked as a teacher, professional educational psychologist, teacher trainer and educational researcher.

Carol Ouvry is a course coordinator (distance) in learning difficulties for the University of Birmingham. She edits *PMLD–Link*, is author of *Educating Children with Profound Handicaps*, and recently co-edited (with Penny Lacey) *Working with People with Profound Learning Difficulties* (2001, Fulton).

Sue Panter is assistant head teacher at Sheredes School in Hertfordshire, and an honorary tutor (distance-learning) and course unit writer for the University of Birmingham. A new edition of her book, *How to Survive as a Special Educational Needs Coordinator* (1995, Q.Ed.) is forthcoming.

Melanie Peter lectures for several universities on special education. She is a freelance consultant on arts education and special educational needs. Her most recent book (with Dave Sherratt) is *Developing Play and Drama in Children with Autism Spectrum Disorders* (2002, Fulton).

Jill Porter is a senior lecturer and senior doctorate tutor at the University of Birmingham. She has been involved in initial and in-service teacher training in special educational needs and, before entering higher education, taught pupils with moderate, severe and profound learning difficulties.

Ron Ritchie is Associate Dean at the Faculty of Education, University of the West of England, Bristol. He has held secondary and primary teaching and LEA advisory posts. His publications include *Primary Science* (with Chris Ollerenshaw, 1997, Fulton) and *Effective Subject Leadership* (1999, Open University Press).

Philippa Russell is director of the Council for Disabled Children. She advises on policy development at the Department of Health and the Department for Education and Employment, and she has been appointed as Disability Rights Commissioner. She has served on the National Advisory Group for Special Educational Needs.

Suzanne Saunders combines teaching children with dyslexia with raising a family. She worked for ten years as head of education in a residential school for children with profound and multiple learning difficulties, and she was a researcher and lecturer at Westminster College, Oxford.

Chris Stevens is head of special educational needs and inclusion at BECTa. He was professional officer for special educational needs at the National Curriculum Council (now QCA), and a head teacher of a special school for pupils with severe learning difficulties.

David Sugden is pro vice chancellor and professor of special needs in education at the University of Leeds. He has taught in primary, special and secondary schools. He is the author of five books, numerous articles, and many national and international conference papers.

Christina Tilstone is senior lecturer in special education at the University of Birmingham. She has taught children with severe learning difficulties and worked in teacher education. She publishes widely and was, until recently, editor of the *British Journal of Special Education*.

Helen Wright is associate professor of physical education at Nanyang Technological University, Singapore. She has published articles and a book in the areas of physical education and developmental coordination disorder, and is a regular presenter at national and international conferences.

Acknowledgements

We would like to acknowledge our debt to all of the contributors to the second edition of this book. They approached their task with enthusiasm and commitment, and we are grateful that they gave so freely of their time. Each one has been dedicated to ensuring that entitlement and access to the curriculum for pupils with learning difficulties is not rhetoric but reality. The fact that they did such a good job for the first edition ensured that it received the National Association of Special Educational Needs/*Times Educational Supplement* Academic Book Award for 1996.

For her knowledge and skills in editorial work and her boundless patience, we are indebted to Jo Egerton. We are especially grateful for the support and advice of Dr. Christina Tilstone. We would also like to thank David Fulton and his team, who recognised the value of producing a second edition of this book and who continue to make such a significant contribution to the education of pupils with special educational needs.

Foreword

I am very pleased to write the foreword for the second edition of *Enabling Access*. The first edition of the edited book won the National Association for Special Educational Needs/*Times Educational Supplement* Book Award for books in the field of special educational needs (SEN) in 1996. I chaired the committee that selected this book for the award. This was the first time that an edited book had won the award since its inception in the early 1990s. The committee came to its decision because of the book's relevance, breadth and quality. It has become a key text for those involved in the field of teaching children and young people with a range of learning difficulties. It is in this context that I was very keen to accept the request to write a brief foreword for the second edition.

Since the first edition, there have been changes in the schools system and the National Curriculum, both of which have a bearing on teaching and the systems that support the process of educating children and young people with difficulties in learning and disabilities. Since 1996, when the first edition was published, we have had a new government in the UK – one that has reviewed provision for SEN and instigated a programme of action. The government has established 'inclusion' as a key policy principle across all its social policies. More specifically, SEN inclusion has become one of the pillars of the government's education policy.

This new focus in policy has been translated into particular developments in several ways, and it is in this context that a second edition of the original book has much to contribute. These developments include the National Curriculum 2000. The statements of values, aims and purposes in this new version of the National Curriculum give inclusive values a central role. As Barry Carpenter and Rob Ashdown state in the first chapter, the debates about and commitments to inclusion now need to be converted into curriculum practice. But, as the various chapters in this new edition show, this task continues to be challenging, both at conceptual and practical levels. It is not made easier by the complexity of balancing inclusive values with those of raising standards and meeting individual needs within available 'real world' resources and know-how.

I am confident that those who have found the first edition useful will find new ideas and practices in the second edition. Those not familiar with the first edition will come to find this new version very useful. The second edition makes a significant contribution to enabling access; I welcome it and recommend it to you.

Professor Brahm Norwich
School of Education, University of Exeter
January 2001

Chapter 1

Enabling Access

Barry Carpenter and Rob Ashdown

This second edition of *Enabling Access* seeks not only to reappraise the earlier debates in relation to the National Curriculum and its application to pupils with special educational needs (SEN), but also to set into the current contexts the debates that surround the 2000 version of the National Curriculum. At the point of the introduction of the National Curriculum in 1989, the dialogue was about 'entitlement'. Teachers rose to the challenge and demonstrated how, through a variety of innovative teaching approaches, pupils with moderate, severe and profound learning difficulties could receive their entitlement to the statutory curriculum. Over a decade later, the National Curriculum is the bedrock upon which all teachers now plan, implement and evaluate their teaching and pupils' learning.

While the affirmation of entitlement was the first step in the implementation of the development of a National Curriculum for all, it was not the solution. Entitlement alone does not meet needs, nor does entitlement mean that the curriculum is appropriately designed or delivered to meet the diversity of SEN that exist within our pupil population. The debate moved then to access. In the first edition of *Enabling Access*, a range of quality classroom practices were articulated that demonstrated how children of all abilities could be engaged as learners in the dynamic process of teaching and learning.

Throughout the last decade the evolution of the school curriculum has been informed by two overarching principles. As set out in the Education Reform Act 1998 and later legislation, there have always been the aims that the curriculum in all schools should be balanced and broadly based, and that it should:

- promote the spiritual, moral, cultural, mental and physical development of pupils school and in society;
- prepare pupils for the opportunities, responsibilities and experiences of adult life.

These are significant goals for which no quick-fix solution is possible. Hence the latest version of the National Curriculum is prefaced by another major stepping stone, which will enable us to satisfy these principles – that of 'inclusion'.

In this second edition of *Enabling Access*, the contributors seek not only to stimulate teachers into designing learning activities that are appropriate to the needs of all pupils, but also to show how such activities can contribute to inclusive practices. The societal debates around inclusion over the last ten years or more (Tomlinson 1982; Skrtic 1991) now need to be translated into dynamic curriculum practice if they are to truly impact on the lives of children and subsequently upon our future society. We would adopt the same pragmatic line as that of Florian *et al.* (1998, p. 1) that:

> special educators, meaning those with expertise in the education of pupils who experience difficulty in learning at school, are important players in promoting more inclusive practice.

Central to this debate should be the rights of the child as a learner. How do we design learning environments and learning activities that will ensure that each child is an active participant in the learning process and not a bystander, a peripheral participant, watching the activity of others? Throughout this book the contributors strive to articulate how pupils with learning difficulties can be included in all aspects of the curriculum, and how those closest to them – particularly their families, teachers and other professionals – can be supported in achieving this goal. We must together seek to build an inclusive curriculum.

Who are the children?

The pupil group debated in this book mainly comprises those pupils with moderate learning difficulties (MLD) or severe learning difficulties (SLD). The discussion around curriculum adaptation, modification and design will also be relevant to those among such pupils who have moderate to severe physical and/or sensory disabilities, delays or disorders of language and communication, an autistic spectrum disorder or behavioural, social and emotional difficulties. A significant and challenging minority of these pupils have profound and multiple learning difficulties (PMLD). The Department for Education and Employment (DfEE) and the Qualifications and Curriculum Authority (QCA) in the excellent *Planning, Teaching and Assessing the Curriculum for Pupils with Learning Difficulties* (DfEE/QCA 2001) clearly state that no pupils should be regarded as having too great a degree of disability or learning difficulty to be included in the nation's curriculum framework. Social exclusion is a constant threat to some children with significant degrees of learning difficulty; their challenging behaviour may lead some schools to decide that such pupils can no longer be effectively educated in that school; disenfranchisement from the education system may loom large. Thus, it is important in our definition of inclusion to think of children with MLD, SLD and PMLD remaining within the education system regardless of the setting.

The target audience for this book includes not only the teachers of these pupils, who may work in nurseries, primary and secondary schools or special schools, but also other education specialists working for various national and local government organisations and agencies, as well as people in voluntary and charitable organisations and schools. We have endeavoured to recognise that, in giving access to inclusion for all, there are many challenges that teachers face, not least of which is how to promote inclusive learning styles (Read 1998). Without considering the aetiology or specific settings of pupils, we would hope that this book would be relevant to all teachers of pupils with learning difficulties. We recognise the increasing diversity of many classroom situations, and the ever-widening ability ranges within these classrooms – whether in special or mainstream schools. We hope that, at a time of critical re-examination of pedagogy and even the very framework of schools, this book will enable teachers to remain focused on the needs of their pupils and to ensure that equality of education opportunity exists for all at a time of rapid change. Our goal is that children learn and learn well, and this can only be achieved through a curriculum of the highest quality and teachers with the skills and convictions to deliver it effectively.

In the context of this book, the pupils in focus are those who require particular learning pathways to be charted for them if they are to be given access to the statutory curriculum. They are pupils for whom imaginative and creative programmes of study (PoS) are necessary to enable them to receive their curriculum entitlement; pupils who, without a well-differentiated curriculum, would be alienated from the flow of learning experience in the classroom, pupils who need the employment of specific engagement strategies so as to ensure their participation in the curriculum; and pupils who, without learning routes that mirror their learning styles, would remain on the periphery of curriculum activity when their right is to be active participants at the heart of the learning process. Alongside access to the curriculum now comes access to inclusion. This relies still upon the innate creativity and personal skills of the teacher working with pupils with learning difficulties. We are still seeking to *enable access.*

Articulating purposes and values

A criticism of the National Curriculum since its inauguration has been that it is a 'top down' model of curriculum development. As such, it has been in direct opposition to the style of pupil-centred and school-based curriculum development that had been a feature of special education. The phased implementation of the National Curriculum originally made it feel very fragmented. However, teachers have responded and have added to their repertoire the skills of interpretation, of working from a common curriculum spine, and of differentiating such material until it touches pupils at their point of learning.

A further criticism, voiced by us in the first edition of this book, has been that the National Curriculum as a whole has suffered from a lack of underpinning philosophy. However, the handbooks for both primary and secondary schools for the 2000 version (DfEE/QCA 1999a, 1999b) begin with a clear statement of values, aims and purposes. There is recognition that the school curriculum comprises all learning and other experiences that each school plans for its pupils, and that the National Curriculum is an important element of the school curriculum but not the *whole* curriculum. There is clear acknowledgement from the outset of the educative role of families alongside teachers, with the laudable aim that education should reflect certain 'enduring values'. A statement of values, which is included in a final section in each of the handbooks mentioned above, talks about helping pupils to value themselves as unique human beings, to value their relationships with others (including their families), to value and respect others, to value the diversity in our society, to value the laws and customs that recognise human rights and responsibilities, and to value both natural and man-made environments.

Education is the means by which society can prepare its future generations to respond to a rapidly changing world. If there are significant changes facing our typically developing children, then these changes are even more magnified for children with learning difficulties. For them, what will be the impact of continued globalisation of the economy and society, the new work and leisure patterns, and the rapid expansion of communication technologies? The latter may bring welcome breakthroughs for many people with learning difficulties through greater access to areas of society that, to date, have been closed to them. What is important is that the citizenship of all children is recognised, and in this regard the inclusion of citizenship within the National Curriculum framework is welcome. An awareness of citizenship, and Personal, Social and Health

Education (PSHE) are key to the holistic development of all of our children. The formal addition of these two areas of study to the curriculum brings a welcome balance to the National Curriculum, as previous criticisms have centred upon its heavy academic bias.

The guidance to schools in the handbooks for the 2000 version of the National Curriculum reiterates the two broad aims through which values and purposes can underpin the curriculum: firstly, that the school curriculum should provide opportunities for all pupils to learn and to achieve; and, secondly, that it should promote pupils' spiritual, moral, social and cultural development and prepare them for the opportunities, responsibilities and experiences of life. The four main purposes of the National Curriculum are set out too:

• to establish an entitlement for all pupils to a number of areas for learning and to develop knowledge, understanding, skills and attitudes that are deemed to be necessary for self-fulfilment and development as active and responsible citizens;
• to establish national standards, or expectations, for the performance of all pupils;
• to promote curriculum continuity and ensure sufficient flexibility to ensure progress in the learning of all pupils across the nation; and
• to promote public understanding of, and confidence in, what schools teach. There is also helpful elaboration of the four major curriculum principles – breadth, balance, relevance and differentiation.

The specific guidance offered for curriculum planning for pupils with learning difficulties (DfEE/QCA 2001) takes these aims and purposes further and suggests that the school curriculum for pupils with learning difficulties might, therefore, aim to:

• enable pupils to interact and communicate with a wide range of people;
• promote self-advocacy or the use of a range of systems of supported advocacy;
• enable pupils to express preferences, communicate needs, make choices, take decisions and choose options that other people act upon and respect;
• prepare pupils for an adult life in which they are enabled to exercise the greatest possible degree of independence and autonomy;
• increase pupils' awareness and understanding of their environment and of the world;
• encourage pupils to explore, to question and to challenge;
• provide a wide range of learning experiences in age-appropriate contexts for pupils in each key stage.

The building blocks available to teachers to implement the 2000 version of the National Curriculum are much better than before. These principles should inform curriculum planning for the whole curriculum and enable all professionals in schools – including therapists, who may have been alienated by the style of the National Curriculum to date – to feel that their contribution is once more valued within a holistic overview. Common, group and individual needs can comfortably sit alongside each other in the knowledge that a range of curriculum experiences will be available through which one or more of these needs can be met. What is clear is the recognition that the curriculum cannot remain static: it must be responsive to change, and it is therefore a dynamic process in which teachers engage; and the outcomes of this process must be ultimately empowering to children as learners.

What are the needs of pupils with learning difficulties?

Regardless of the structure or content of the curriculum, each child as a learner (or that child's advocate) has the right to ask of the child's teachers, 'What do I get out of this?' The latest version of the National Curriculum, with the explicit inclusion of PSHE and citizenship, is better able to articulate a response to this question. Six skill areas, described as key skills, are embedded in the National Curriculum and are designed to permeate all educational experiences across the whole curriculum, and in life outside and beyond school. These cross-curricular skills are crucial to the design of learning opportunities for children with learning difficulties because they will enable specific experiences to be designed in response to each child's unique needs. They will also increase the level of relevance in the curriculum experience. The six key skills are:

- communication;
- application of number;
- information and communication technology (ICT);
- working with others;
- improving own learning and performance;
- problem-solving.

The guidance on planning the curriculum for pupils with learning difficulties illuminates how these six key skill areas potentially can be applied to children at any particular level of ability (DfEE/QCA 2001).

Thinking skills are covered in this guidance and also in the handbooks for the National Curriculum under *Promoting Skills across the National Curriculum* (DfEE/QCA 1999a, p. 20; 1999b, p. 22). The clearer acknowledgement of thinking skills, and of the six key skill areas, is far more consonant with the fundamental beliefs of teachers working with children with learning difficulties than has previously been the case.

The promotion of thinking skills very much focuses upon 'learning how to learn'. The guidance from DfEE and QCA on curriculum planning for pupils with learning difficulties further elaborates the nature of thinking skills. It pinpoints how success in thinking is determined by effectiveness in three combined operations:

- acquiring and organising knowledge through sensory awareness and perception;
- thinking through situations and making meaningful what is done (e.g. planning, decision-making and evaluating); and
- strategies for using knowledge and solving problems (e.g. remembering, reflecting, generating ideas).

Other priority skills in addition to the key skills and thinking skills are also articulated; examples given relate to physical orientation and mobility, learning, organisation and study, personal care, self-control, daily living and leisure, and recreation.

This critical analysis of the process of thinking, linked with the defined facets of thinking skills in the National Curriculum handbooks (e.g. information processing skills, reasoning skills, enquiring skills, creative thinking skills, evaluation skills), enables teachers to concentrate on the learning process as much as on learning content. In turn, this may provide teachers with a clearer overview of progression within the curriculum. To some pupils this may not always be hierarchical and, as a result, lateral progression is given much emphasis in the guidance for planning the curriculum for pupils with learning difficulties. This type of progression focuses upon learning to perform the same skill in a variety of contexts involving different people, settings, equipment, activities and so on. Such scope for recording and celebrating achievement is crucial, particularly for some children with very profound and complex learning difficulties. Ultimately, the careful planning of curriculum content and experiences, interwoven with cross-curricular skills, should enable previous learning and achievements to be built upon and should take pupils forward. If the curriculum is to be a truly worthwhile experience for these children, then it should be relevant and appropriate – *enabling access*, promoting empowerment, facilitating achievement, meeting individual needs and allowing the attainment of personal goals.

Planning mechanisms must address long- and medium-term planning, short-term planning, and particularly the interface with individual education plans (IEPs; for more details see Ashdown 1996; Carpenter 1998). The context for the planning and delivery of the curriculum experience of pupils is now an inclusive classroom. Whether this is in a mixed-ability classroom in a primary or secondary school, or a classroom in a special school where children with a range of learning difficulties are in one classroom, the principles of an inclusive curriculum apply.

What are the elements of an inclusive classroom that a teacher should identify? Inclusion:

- is premised on diversity;
- is multidimensional;
- applies to individuals;
- applies to all learners;
- is diagnostic;
- challenges expectations;
- challenges classroom relationships;
- is an integral aspect of effective learning;
- is relevant to all teachers;
- requires a long-term, whole-school strategy.

Mittler (2000) clearly articulates the challenges arising from the development and implementation of inclusive policies and provision (p. vii): 'Inclusion is not about placing children in mainstream schools. It is about changing schools to make them more responsive to the needs of all children.' An inclusive curriculum is fundamentally a framework for enabling pupils of all abilities to show what they know, understand and can do. It should enable a celebration of achievement for all pupils and provide, through careful monitoring and evaluation of pupil performance, information on continuity and progression. Most of all, if we are to value the individual qualities and abilities of each and every one of our pupils, the classroom must be pervaded by an atmosphere in which there is an expectation of success.

To achieve this, the most successful curriculum planning will have sought the input of the pupils. They may have expressed their choices and preferences through the spoken word, through signing and symbols, objects of reference, picture-exchange systems or other augmentative forms of communication, but partners in planning they should be – as, indeed, their families should be. These viewpoints will ensure that curriculum planning is genuinely based on an holistic overview of pupil needs, and that, outside the school context, there will be maximum opportunity for the transference of skills into the key environments experienced, over time, by such a pupil. The true test of the quality of any curriculum remains the ability to ensure that learners can have their individual needs met and to use what they have learned in the naturalistic settings that they encounter each day of their life. It is a blending of the negotiated goals, mediated through the curriculum, with the pupil's life-style. As Senge (2000, p. 4) states:

> Learning is at once deeply personal and inherently social; it connects us not just to knowledge in the abstract, but to each other. Why else would it matter so much when a teacher notices something special about a student? Throughout our lives, as we move from setting to setting, we encounter novelty and new challenges, small and large. If we are ready for them, living and learning become inseparable.

Significant developments since 1995

Since the publication of the first edition of this book, there have been major changes in the requirements on schools and a plethora of non-statutory guidance has been published. We must begin by acknowledging the outcomes of a review of the National Curriculum in England conducted by Sir Ron Dearing, Chairman of the now-defunct School Curriculum and Assessment Authority (SCAA). The so-called Dearing Report recognised that aspects of the National Curriculum had not served the interests of some pupils with SEN (SCAA 1994). The resulting 1995 version of the National Curriculum significantly included *common requirements* applying to the statutory orders for each subject. They stressed that the PoS for each key stage should be taught to the great majority of pupils in that chronological age-band, in ways appropriate to their abilities. For the small number of children who may need the provision, it was stated that material might be selected from PoS for earlier key stages where this is necessary for individual pupils to progress and demonstrate achievement. This development was significant because it legitimised the fact that, say, pupils with SLD/PMLD may need to continue to follow elements of the Key Stage 1 PoS well after seven years of age. The common requirements also stressed the need to use augmentative means of communication, non-sighted methods, technological and other aids or adapted equipment, as appropriate. The common requirements have since been enshrined within the all-important statement on inclusion contained in the handbooks for the 2000 version of the National Curriculum.

The QCA, as the successor to the SCAA, has overseen a number of significant developments since 1995. As regards assessment, national Level 1 and Level 2 assessment tasks were introduced as an alternative to written tests at the end of key stages, initially by SCAA and refined in subsequent years by the QCA. So-called 'P' scales were produced, providing performance criteria for eight levels, leading to Level 1 in mathematics and English, as well as for aspects of personal and social development (DfEE/QCA 1998). These have been revised and include performance criteria for science instead of personal and social development (DfEE 2001). They were developed to aid the target-setting process in schools where there are pupils who achieve significantly below age-related expectations. A renewed focus on target setting and measuring pupils' learning has been a significant development of recent years. Schools have been encouraged to set SMART targets (specific, measurable, achievable, realistic, time-related) for pupils and to use measures of pupil achievement when evaluating the success of the school in terms of progress towards achieving whole-school development targets, the effectiveness of schemes of work, and even the quality of work of each individual teacher through a reinvigorated performance-management process.

The QCA has also published exemplar schemes of work for each National Curriculum subject and for religious education for Key Stages 1–3, which may be adopted or modified to suit each individual school. These documents include important non-statutory guidance for schools that wish to develop their own schemes of work rather than use the models provided. The QCA also commissioned the development of the very important guidance on planning the curriculum for pupils with learning difficulties, mentioned above (DfEE/QCA 2001).

Schools were promised in the Dearing Report (SCAA 1994) a period of relative stability and autonomy as regards the curriculum, but this was barely noticeable. A change of government and an increasing emphasis on raising standards led to a large number of initiatives to which schools were required to respond, notably the National Literacy and Numeracy Strategies. Also, there has been an insistence upon introducing more rigour into the process of curriculum planning and a greater degree of breadth and balance in the curriculum, even though new flexibilities in the curriculum have been introduced. Nevertheless, we remain confident that schools have considerable freedom as regards the content of the whole-school curriculum and teaching approaches. Since 1995, first SCAA and then the QCA have made plain that the PoS for each subject and key stage should be regarded as a minimum entitlement that serve as a basis for planning the curriculum. The fundamental message has been that it is for schools to decide how and in what depth to teach the material contained in the PoS. No methodology is mandated; teaching methodology remains a matter for schools to determine. Moreover, there is no insistence that all individual priorities for pupils can be met entirely through the statutory PoS, and it is recognised that they may have to be met through additional activities that occur alongside the PoS. The significance for teachers of all pupils with learning difficulties of the comprehensive guidance on planning the curriculum for all pupils with learning difficulties (DfEE/QCA 2001) cannot be overstated. This document endorses every school's right to determine an appropriate curriculum for its pupils and its responsibilities for enabling access for all pupils to the whole-school curriculum.

What remains to be achieved?

The Office for Standards in Education (OFSTED) has produced handbooks for the inspection of primary and secondary schools and special education provision (OFSTED 1999a), which make plain the responsibilities of each school. The handbooks emphasise the need for a structure and organisation to the school curriculum that is efficient, and for unambiguous policy statements and schemes of work for each curriculum area (whether these be National Curriculum subjects, religious education, or other aspects of the whole curriculum). It is expected that schools will closely scrutinise the effectiveness of the teachers and that there should be strategies for monitoring and supporting curriculum developments that are used by the school's leadership group.

The findings from inspections of schools are now reported annually by Her Majesty's Chief Inspector of Schools (HMCI) and these reports have much to say about the curriculum for pupils with SEN in general. As regards the curriculum for pupils in special schools and units, the clearest indicators of progress in curriculum planning come from an OFSTED analysis of the outcomes of inspections in special schools during the period 1994–8 (OFSTED 1999b). As regards special schools, the proportion of schools where pupils are deemed to make good or very good progress has increased considerably. This is against a background of an increase in the range and complexity of disabilities in many schools – for instance, many schools for pupils with MLD include a higher proportion of pupils with behavioural problems and pupils who would formerly have attended schools for pupils with SLD. The quality of teaching has similarly improved. For instance, HMCI noted that schools are making increasing use of pupils' IEPs to identify personal targets in English and mathematics for pupils and to highlight their progress (OFSTED 2001). The quality of teaching is said to be lowest in ICT lessons and in the use of ICT in other subjects, reflecting a continuing lack of confidence among many teachers in their own use of ICT and a lack of awareness of the potential uses of ICT across the curriculum.

As regards the curriculum, HMCI has noted an encouraging improvement in curriculum coverage by special schools, but cautions that many schools still need to make further improvements to ensure that all pupils have access to the full National Curriculum and religious education (OFSTED 2001). Many special schools were seen to be struggling to achieve a satisfactory balance between subjects for all of their pupils. The subjects that are most likely to receive insufficient allocations of teaching time have been shown to be religious education, science and music while English is often allocated an unduly large amount of space on the timetable.

Many special schools have been found to be short of the recommended teaching time, especially at Key Stages 3 and 4, but this is not the only relevant factor. OFSTED (1999b) also states that other factors, which have worked against the achievement of a satisfactory balance in the curriculum, include:

• weak curricular leadership that fails to monitor the balance for classes, groups and individual pupils;
• timetabling being left entirely to individual teachers;
• complex patterns of pupil groupings;
• the introduction of changes in the timetable and groupings during the year in response to unforeseen circumstances;
• intrusion into pupils' personal timetables by therapies and activities such as horse riding, especially when these involved locations away from the school.

In short, some key issues in many special schools at the end of the twentieth century were that sufficiently detailed schemes of work were not in place for all subjects and that there was insufficient guidance for teachers from the governing body, head teacher and subject coordinators about what to teach and how to teach it. HMCI argued that schools showed awareness of the value of monitoring and evaluating quality of teaching and the impact of initiatives, but they were failing to put appropriate strategies for achieving this into practice for various reasons: many schools are still developing their systems for pupil assessment; the monitoring roles of curriculum coordinators are undeveloped in many schools; and coordinators often lack timetabled opportunities during taught time to observe colleagues at work and to advise them (OFSTED 2001).

Indications of key factors in the development of effective curricular leadership may be found in the OFSTED report on special school inspections (OFSTED 1999b). They can be summarised as:

• the identification of a senior teacher with a responsibility for the oversight of all planning and documentation, including auditing of teachers' timetables;
• clear curriculum policy;
• schemes of work written to similar formats that permit comparisons of curriculum content and teaching approach;

- schemes of work that document the links between subjects and the particular contribution of cross-curricular subjects such as ICT;
- clear and detailed job descriptions for subject coordinators;
- regular curriculum-development meetings, at which subject coordinators can exchange ideas about planning;
- classroom monitoring by the subject coordinators and the overall curriculum coordinator.

OFSTED inspection reports have also noted that: there have been substantial improvements in pupils' progress and the quality of teaching; teachers have taken various steps to improve their personal knowledge; subject coordinators have supported non-specialist colleagues through giving advice and developing detailed schemes of work; subject coordinators are increasingly involved in monitoring their colleagues' teaching; and schools have received much additional financial support to acquire further resources for teaching and learning to support the National Curriculum, particularly in relation to ICT and books, as a result of government initiatives that targeted these developments through the Standards Fund. Nevertheless, the above summary shows that there are some clear messages from OFSTED inspections about inadequacies in the processes of curriculum construction and delivery in many schools. There are remedies to these problems: there is guidance for schools seeking to develop a systematic and rigorous approach to school self-evaluation, and guidance in the OFSTED handbooks (OFSTED 1999a), in courses designed by OFSTED about self-evaluation, in the course leading to the National Professional Qualification for Headship, in the Leadership Programme for Serving Heads, and in other courses for other school leaders. These will thoroughly familiarise the leadership group of schools with the major accountabilities and potential strategies.

Despite the new guidance and training for schools' self-evaluation, significant problems remain for schools that have pupils with MLD, SLD and PMLD. For the first ten years of existence of the National Curriculum, schools struggled to come to grips with it and to develop realistic schemes of work that would have benefit for all their pupils. They had to do so without any clear models for their schemes of work or models for short-term planning. The published guidance from SCAA (1995, 1996) for planning the curriculum was helpful, but only contained fragmentary examples of planning documents and activities. It was only in the late 1990s that the QCA significantly stimulated curriculum development by producing model schemes of work in the various subject areas for primary and secondary schools. Also, a voluntary organisation called EQUALS produced its own models for long-term plans and schemes of work for teachers of pupils with PMLD, SLD and MLD (EQUALS 1999a, 1999b, 2000). Eventually – and long overdue – the non-statutory guidance on planning the curriculum for pupils with learning difficulties was produced, and this includes more concrete examples of the opportunities afforded by teaching the different subjects at each key stage (DfEE/QCA 2001). Even so, much work remains to be done to achieve a national consensus about what should be taught, how it should be taught, how much time should be spent teaching it, and how the attainments of pupils with complex learning difficulties should be measured. The exemplar schemes of work described above are not without their flaws, although they provide useful pointers for all kinds of schools that are seeking to improve or develop the whole-school curriculum.

An allied problem lies in demonstrating unequivocally the achievements of pupils. OFSTED reported that too many teachers do not make sufficient use of assessment information on pupils in planning lessons (OFSTED 1999b, 2001). Typically, the lack of an agreed policy on assessment and a clear system for monitoring implementation is cited as resulting in inconsistency in practice. Teachers' records focus too often on experiences and changes in attitudes rather than on what pupils actually learn, and the process of SMART target-setting is not securely established. Often, teachers are overburdened with paperwork as a result of the failure to overhaul existing systems. Improvements are essential if assessment is truly going to inform teachers' planning and demonstrate added value.

It is not always a simple matter to generate meaningful SMART targets, particularly for pupils who cannot or will not engage readily with the learning process. In the case of pupils with PMLD, much learning could be going on in the absence of demonstrable changes in behaviour; the observable evidence for learning may be fleeting or inconsistently shown; reductions in challenging behaviour that is a block to learning may be the only evidence of progression; and, for some pupils with progressive deterioration because of a physical condition, maintaining existing skills is targeted rather than actual progression. In the case of pupils who present challenging behaviours, progress may be evident only in small changes in attitudes to work and interaction with others. However, the DfEE and QCA have provided the developing framework of 'P' level descriptions (DfEE/QCA 1998; DfEE 2001), which extends the level descriptions for aspects of English and mathematics back to the earliest developmental levels of response and achievement wherever possible. Subsequently, to support assessment of pupils' progress, performance descriptions of the attainments of pupils working towards Level 1 were developed as eight levels in relation to all subjects (DfEE/QCA 2001). Significantly, the earliest levels are generic; that is, they have not been fully developed in subject-specific ways, although subject-focused descriptions are offered from the fourth level upwards. Of course, this is because any one behaviour may be viewed as a precursor to further learning in more than one subject area in the case of pupils who are developmentally so very delayed.

It is important to remind ourselves that there is simply not enough evidence about the most effective ways of developing knowledge, skills and understanding in the various subject areas with pupils with learning difficulties. Our knowledge about the psychological reality of learning difficulties is very sketchy and few of the accepted elements of teaching methodology have been empirically demonstrated to be effective. The level of detail in the guidance for the National Literacy and Numeracy Strategies gives a false impression that the best methods for teaching literacy and numeracy to all pupils are well established – but this is far from the truth. OFSTED (2001) has reported on the National Literacy and Numeracy Strategies in special schools and noted that some of the methodologies indeed seem to be beneficial. Nevertheless, much more experience of using the recommended methodologies has to be garnered.

In this context, it is worth briefly summarising potential targets for educational research:

- developing effective styles of teaching that are interactive, moving away from the prescriptive and teacher-led activities that do little to empower pupils and encourage personal autonomy;
- developing teaching methodologies that take into account the implications of findings about the learning and development of children with different disabilities and learning difficulties;
- developing activities that are likely to engage all learners and developing positive approaches to teaching self-control to pupils who present seriously challenging behaviours;

● developing new ICTs that have the potential for transforming the curriculum for pupils with a range of disabilities and learning difficulties.

The content of this book

Part I: Perspectives on the National Curriculum

The first section of the book consists of chapters about every National Curriculum subject. At the time of writing, brand-new subject-specific guidance on the curriculum for pupils with learning difficulties (DfEE/QCA 2001) was being developed, and the contributors have taken that guidance into account, making appropriate alterations to their text. Most of the contributors to the first edition of this book were able to contribute substantially revised chapters to this second edition. For some subjects, entirely new chapters have been written. The contributors do not necessarily treat every aspect of the statutory PoS for every key stage for their assigned subject; also, they do not describe the whole range of activities and experiences which are possible. There simply is not the space to do so within the confines of a chapter of only twenty pages or so. Therefore, readers will find some obvious omissions – for instance, there is nothing specific about teaching drama, although this was covered well by Hinchcliffe (1996) in the first edition.

Part II: Access and entitlement to the whole curriculum

The next section begins with an insightful chapter by Erica Brown that demonstrates the importance of religious education for all pupils and offers suggestions about the range of activities that are possible. This is followed by a brand-new chapter by Hazel Lawson and Ann Fergusson on PSHE and citizenship, which reflects the status given to these important areas in the 2000 revision to the National Curriculum. The chapter by Carol Ouvry and Suzanne Saunders specifically tackles questions concerning access and entitlement to the whole curriculum for pupils with PMLD. The curriculum model that they describe has considerable relevance for teachers of all pupils with SEN. Of course, a school curriculum is more than the actual content of skills, knowledge and understanding that teachers aim to impart; it is also very much to do with the classroom processes of teaching and learning, which are effectively explored in the chapter by Richard Byers. Equally important is the need for teachers to have a clear understanding of what each pupil can do; hence the inclusion of a chapter by Ann Lewis that deals with what makes for effective assessment and that identifies important issues and principles. It is essential that teachers be prepared to reflect on their own practice and modify it in the light of pupils' learning and the availability of new models of learning and teaching, which is why there is a chapter by Sally Beveridge on action research in the context of the classroom.

Part III: The context for the whole curriculum

Schools depend for their success on having the active support and cooperation of parents who interact with the pupils for far more of their waking hours than the school staff do. In the past, all too often, schools have paid much lip service to the concept of partnership with parents without doing enough to create the conditions for this to develop. In his chapter, Barry Carpenter explores the problems experienced by families who have a child with learning difficulties. He shows how much can be done, and is being done, to realise the ideal of a home–school partnership. The theme is continued by Philippa Russell in a chapter that explores the roles and responsibilities of the various agencies, the rights and the responsibilities of parents, and the need for the involvement of the children themselves.

Schools also need well-qualified staff who are equipped to meet the demands of a complex curriculum and a complex role. For more than a decade there have been many indications that the country is not keeping pace with demand for a supply of well-trained teachers of children with SEN. Partly in response to such concerns, the Teacher Training Agency has produced teacher standards for SEN specialist teachers and SEN coordinators in schools. Jill Porter's chapter discusses the nation's requirements, how training was provided in the past and how it might be provided in the future.

Christina Tilstone reminds us that schools have huge obligations to their pupils, which must be reflected in their development of an inclusive curriculum. There is a life beyond school, and schools must ensure that any obstacles are removed so that they can participate fully in society at levels and in ways that are appropriate for each individual. This goal has profound implications for schools, because at every step of curriculum planning there needs to be careful consideration as to whether it limits or extends opportunities. The extent to which the curriculum of a school permits its pupils to participate in normal community activities (e.g. education, leisure, work, living in one's own home) can have a pervasive effect on the lives of the pupils, as children and as adults, as well as on the attitudes of the general public towards all children and adults with learning difficulties and disabilities.

Peter Mittler is the final contributor to this book. He brings the focus back to the personal and social development of the maturing child and young adult, and he reflects on the important theme of developing pupils' skills of self-advocacy and its implications for schools.

In conclusion ...

In 1995, there were promises of a period of stability for schools, but these promises were not fulfilled. Since then, schools and Local Education Authorities have been buffeted by the forces set in motion by the radical political agenda of central government, and we expect that there will continue to be rapid educational change. The governors, head teachers and others with responsibility for leadership in each school have to become more rigorous in developing and sustaining their school's systems of self-evaluation. Teachers should prepare themselves for these changes, not least of which is the fresh focus on their individual responsibilities for raising pupils' attainments.

In the first edition of this book, we stated that teachers badly need opportunities for an effective debate about the nature and content of the whole curriculum. We still feel that this is the case. The debate needs to be widened beyond the present narrow concentration on a circumscribed set of pupil competencies and a relatively small number of teaching methodologies that happen currently to be in favour. There needs to be a much clearer understanding of what is meant by inclusion and what makes for inclusive schools and classrooms. We feel that the DfEE, QCA, OFSTED and other governmental agencies have not even begun to scratch the surface when it comes to exploring appropriate teaching methodologies for the diverse group of pupils with complex learning difficulties, although we find comfort in the burgeoning literature on good practice in the classroom and the non-statutory guidance on planning the curriculum for such pupils (DfEE /QCA 2001). Although it raises many questions as well as providing answers, we believe that the new edition of this book also makes an effective contribution to the debate on the curriculum.

References

Ashdown, R. W. (1996) 'Coordinating the whole curriculum', in Carpenter, B., Ashdown, R. and Bovair, K. (eds) *Enabling Access: Effective teaching and learning for pupils with learning difficulties*, London: David Fulton.

Carpenter, B. (1998) 'The interface between the curriculum and the code', *British Journal of Special Education* **24**(1), 18–21.

DfEE (2001) Supporting the Target-Setting Process: Guidance to effective target setting for pupils with special educational needs (Revised edition). London: DfEE.

DfEE/QCA (1998) *Supporting the Target Setting Process: Effective target setting for pupils with special educational needs.* London: DfEE /QCA.

DfEE/QCA (1999a) *The National Curriculum: Handbook for primary teachers in England.* London: DfEE /QCA.

DfEE/QCA (1999b) *The National Curriculum: Handbook for secondary teachers in England.* London: DfEE/QCA.

DfEE/QCA (2001) *Planning, Teaching and Assessing the Curriculum for Pupils with Learning Difficulties.* London: DfEE/QCA.

EQUALS (1999a) *Scheme of Work for Pupils with PMLD.* North Shields, Tyne and Wear: EQUALS.

EQUALS (1999b) *Scheme of Work for Pupils with SLD.* North Shields, Tyne and Wear: EQUALS.

EQUALS (2000) *Scheme of Work for Pupils with MLD.* North Shields, Tyne and Wear: EQUALS.

Florian, L. *et al.* (1998) 'Pragmatism not dogmatism: promoting more inclusive practice', in Tilstone, C., Florian, L. and Rose, R. (eds) *Promoting Inclusive Practice.* London: Routledge.

Hinchcliffe, V. (1996) 'English', in Carpenter, B., Ashdown, R. and Bovair, K. (eds) *Enabling Access: Effective teaching and learning for pupils with learning difficulties.* London: David Fulton Publishers.

Mittler, P. (2000) *Working Towards Inclusive Education: Social contexts.* London: David Fulton Publishers.

OFSTED (1999a) *Handbook for Inspecting Special Schools and Pupil Referral Units.* London: The Stationery Office.

OFSTED (1999b) *Special Education 1994–1998: A review of special schools, secure units and pupil referral units in England.* London: The Stationery Office.

OFSTED (2001) *Annual Report of HM Chief Inspector of Schools 1998/99.* London: The Stationery Office.

Read, G. (1998) 'Promoting inclusion through learning styles', in Tilstone, C. *et al.* (eds) *Promoting Inclusive Practice*, London: Routledge.

SCAA (1994) *The National Curriculum and its Assessment: Final report.* London: SCAA.

SCAA (1995) *Planning the Curriculum at Key Stages 1 and 2.* London: SCAA.

SCAA (1996) *Planning the Curriculum for Pupils with Profound and Multiple Learning Difficulties*, London: SCAA.

Senge, P. (2000) *Schools that Learn.* London: Nicholas Brearley.

Skrtic, T. (1991) 'Students with special educational needs: artefacts of the traditional curriculum', in Ainscow, M. (ed.) *Effective Schools for All.* London: David Fulton Publishers.

Tomlinson, S. (1982) *A Sociology of Special Education.* London: Routledge and Kegan Paul.

Part I:
Perspectives on the National Curriculum

Chapter 2

English

Barry Carpenter and Denise Morris

In the Foreword to the National Curriculum document for English, David Blunkett (1999) writes: 'An *entitlement* to learning must be an entitlement for all pupils.' The document contains, for the first time, a detailed, overarching statement on inclusion, which makes clear the principles that schools must follow right across the curriculum to ensure that all pupils have a chance to succeed whatever their individual needs and the particular barriers to their learning.

In recent years, the English curriculum for all children – but particularly those with learning difficulties – has undergone a radical reappraisal. With the advent of the National Literacy Strategy in 1998, closely followed by Curriculum 2000 containing the statutory requirements for teaching English, and, most recently, *Planning, Teaching and Assessing the Curriculum for Pupils with Learning Difficulties: English* (QCA 2001), the very structure and content of teaching English to children with special educational needs has been transformed.

The importance of English within the curriculum is self-evident. As Hinchcliffe (1996, p. 15) writes:

> Speaking and listening, reading and writing, represent the channels through which the whole-school curriculum is taught and by which children's knowledge, skills and understanding are demonstrated.

If we also consider 'English' as a subject, and the expectations of achievement, it is important to identify a clear way forward for pupils with severe and complex learning difficulties. If children with such problems are to be able to make sense of their world and demonstrate their knowledge, it is essential that we as practitioners find ways of enabling them to communicate in whatever way is possible for them. This has been the essence of some very creative curriculum development in English and communication (Park 1998a and1998b; Slinger *et al.* 1999; Smith 2000).

The United Nations Educational, Scientific and Cultural Organisation (UNESCO; 1997) states that basic literacy is the capacity to read and write, with understanding a short statement about everyday life. Watson and Giorcelli (1999) argue that there is a need to face 'the literacy challenge': firstly, through the need to raise the extent of basic literacy internationally from 77 per cent towards 100 per cent (and in the least developed nations the average rate is 48 per cent); secondly, to avoid complacency in Western societies where literacy is around 95 per cent. Watson and Giorcelli report declines in reading levels, from both Australian and American studies, among secondary-age pupils. This has certainly been a concern of the present UK government, resulting in the introduction of the National Literacy Strategy, currently being extended from primary to secondary schools.

In this chapter, we intend to explore some of the ways in which pupils with severe, profound and complex needs can develop English skills by focusing on communication. We will also show the importance of Attainment Target 1 (ATI) English for such pupils in the development of their own ability to make choices. Such choices will eventually enable them to control their own environment, and also to assimilate knowledge so that they learn to understand the world around them. We will use the work of the Bristol Literacy Project for Pupils with Special Needs to show how access to the literacy framework for children with SEN can be enabled, and how achievements can be planned for and celebrated through their 'small steps to success' approach. We will also discuss the potential of the multimodal approach to literacy developed at Sunfield School, Worcestershire.

The literacy challenge

Loretta Giorcelli and Alan Watson suggest that we should strive for more than basic literacy. They present two concepts, 'functional literacy' and 'active literacy', both of which have applied relevance to teaching literacy to children with learning difficulties. Functional literacy is a level of literacy required for effective functioning in one's own group and community and is often the benchmark set for children with learning difficulties. But is it enough? Active literacy takes requirements a step further, and refers to 'the use of language to enhance thinking, creativity and questioning in order to promote personal growth and to produce more effective participation in society'. (Watson and Giorcelli, 1999, p. 13). As we move towards more inclusive forms of education, we are preparing our children for life in (hopefully) more inclusive societies (Carpenter 2001); and thus this statement gives us an inclusive literacy stance that is keenly allied to the goals of the new citizenship curriculum (see Chapter 14 of this book).

New challenges face children and adults with learning difficulties. Their future is one of 'inclusion': a life as part of the community, not separate from it. With these challenges come higher expectations of the person with learning difficulties. New situations in society demand that people with learning difficulties use and apply their social skills, and also that these skills become an integral part of their daily functional behaviour. Literacy is a daily part of life in the community. Those with learning difficulties will need to decode, comprehend and act appropriately to the printed word surrounding them in a community-based environment. The onus for the development of functional and active literacy skills rests with the school as the main educational agent.

Finding the foundations

In the 1980s, many researchers were advocating an interactive approach combined with multisensory learning styles, to encourage pupils with severe and complex needs to make a response to stimuli. Flo Longhorn (1988, p. 6) wrote: 'A multisensory approach aims to use the child's senses to break through the barriers of the child's handicap, and aims to aid communication with the child.' Longhorn was a great advocate of the sensory approach for children with very special needs. In her view, the road to learning is very long when children have to cope with a wide range of impairments. She believed that we should try to interpret the environment for the child by focusing on whatever strengths the child has and by using those strengths to help them understand and learn through the schools' own curriculum. Longhorn (1991, p. 79) observed further:

A sensory curriculum provides a rich sensory tapestry for the very special child to weave his or her own unique patterns of learning. Now the golden threads of a National Curriculum can be woven into the tapestry, enhancing the learning experiences of the very special child.

Many researchers at that time were advocating interactive approaches. Bozic and Murdoch (1995) commented on the way in which curriculum development for multisensory-impaired children should aim to help them make sense of their perceptions of the world, through interacting with others and forming relationships. They claimed that only when this happens would these children wish to both participate and influence events. Interactions with others would encourage them to *want* to communicate. Mercer (1988) discussed how Vygotsky had shown that the communication of infants does not develop in isolation but, rather, through interaction with more competent others such as parents, teachers and peers. He discusses how the acquisition of language is mastered first in collaboration with an adult and a more competent peer, solely with the object of communicating. Once mastered in this way, it can then become internalised and serve under conscious control as a means of carrying out inner speech dialogue.

Mercer (1988) also drew several conclusions from past work on literacy development in early childhood – for example, that literacy development begins long before children start formal instruction and that it develops in real-life settings from birth to six years old. The earlier results describe how children learn written language through active engagement with their world, and profit from the modelling of literacy by significant adults. Goodman (1984) found that even children who would be described as 'at risk' for becoming competent readers had knowledge about many aspects of reading. They knew how to handle books, and they understood the directionality of written language and the function of print in a book.

However, while, in a typically developing child, pre-literacy learning occurs without additional scaffolding by families or professionals, children with severe and complex learning needs may require extra support if they are to form interactive and responsive relationships with others. Glenn *et al.* (1995, p. 106) reflect:

Children with profound learning difficulties present a particular challenge to those who work with them. Profound motor sensory and intellectual disabilities may result in an apparent lack of responsiveness towards people and objects.

Psychological researchers, such as Bruner (1978) and Snow (1989), have investigated the right conditions for learning to take place with such pupils. They have illustrated how joint activities between children and adults promote a real and positive context for the acquisition of early communication and language. These kinds of activities, which are often based on turn-taking play activities such as peek-a-boo, are fundamental and important areas for children at the very earliest levels of development. Bozic *et al.* (1995)

have also shown how these features can often be exploited in language and communication-intervention work with children who have learning difficulties.

Learning styles

To appreciate fully how some children with learning difficulties may access the English curriculum, we need to consider what we know about their learning styles, particularly in relation to literacy. There has been considerable emphasis on the early identification of individual patterns of strengths and weaknesses in the area of reading skills for children with reading difficulties (Clay 1985; Sylva and Hurry 1995). A common theme emerging across many of the disability areas that give rise to moderate, severe and profound learning difficulties is the need for strong visual models (see, for Down's Syndrome, Buckley 1985; for autistic spectrum disorder (ASD), Jordan and Powell 1995 and Peeters 2000; for PMLD, Aird 2001; for multisensory impairment, McClarty 1995; for physical impairments, Clarke *et al.* 2001; and for dyspraxia, Portwood 2000). To augment, to support, to supplement the dominant auditory–vocal teaching style of most classrooms with significant visual inputs would appeal to a large number of children with diagnosed learning difficulties.

Research on children with Down's Syndrome and short-term auditory memory can help us to understand the problems experienced by other children with learning disabilities in this area. Short-term auditory memory is just one of the memories that the brain possesses (Bristow *et al.* 1999), but it is the one that helps us to make sense of language. We use this memory to hold, process, understand and assimilate spoken language long enough to respond to it. Not only does short-term memory directly relate to the speed with which individuals can articulate words (Jarrold *et al.* 1999), but research also shows that this efficiency influences the speed at which children learn new words and learn to read.

Many children with Down's Syndrome have poor short-term auditory memories. Generally, long-term memory is not impaired and neither is short-term memory for visual and spatial material. The reasons for children with Down's Syndrome having poor short-term auditory memory is still the subject of debate (Alton 2001). Whatever the cause of the brain's difficulty in functioning, the most successful intervention, as the ongoing work of Sue Buckley has illustrated (Buckley and Bird 1994) is to reinforce verbal information through visual means. This is why signing has been so successful with this pupil group, as well as other strategies such as symbols and whole-word approaches (Carpenter 1991).

Through appropriate differentiation, it is possible to employ teaching strategies that mitigate against the difficulties caused by short-term auditory memory. Various writers in the field recommend strategies to bypass some of these difficulties. Laws *et al.* (1996) suggest the use of pictures and words to encourage the use of rehearsal strategy; Kumin (1994) recommends teaching grammar visually through concrete objects, symbols or signs; Alton (2001) describes how a child can be helped to link letter sounds with letter names by providing a clue or connection such as an icon or pictogram; Carpenter (1991) talks of symbol clues in a small box-file spelling dictionary to aid independent writing; and Hinchcliffe (1996) shows how drama (as a visual–spatial medium) can aid access to text narrative as well as improve communication skills.

Indeed, teaching reading itself to children with Down's Syndrome – even before speech (accepting sign, vocalisation or verbal approximation as a response) – has been strongly advocated over the last two decades (Alton 2001; Buckley 1985; Buckley and Bird 1994). Reading is a visual tool that can be used to compensate for poor auditory short-term memory, and to reinforce and develop language skills. However, learning phonetic strategies can be problematic for any child with poor short-term memory because the ability to learn letter names and sounds, to break down and build up sounds into words, and generally to remember sets of phonic rules all rely on good memory skills (Bristow *et al.* 1999). In contrast, children with Down's Syndrome are often able to develop a sight vocabulary by relying on their stronger visual skills and associating the visual form of a word with the corresponding verbal response.

What is stressed here for children with Down's Syndrome is the visual medium. This is a common approach across all forms of learning difficulty, and strategies such as pictures, objects, photographs, symbols, signs and words have all been reported as successful, whether used to compensate for, supplement or complement auditory–vocal teaching methods. This is so across ASD (Jordan and Powell 1995), multisensory impairment (Etheridge 1995), moderate learning difficulties (Pinsent 1990), severe learning difficulties (Abbott 2000), PMLD (Lawton 1999) and generally throughout the population of children with SEN (Glenny 2000; Robinson 2000).

A model of communication

A model of communication proposed by Light (1989) has influenced models of service provision and classroom practice where augmentative and alternative communication (AAC) approaches are being developed. In turn, these models have sparked the creativity of practitioners in developing IEPs that are underpinned by appropriate augmentative communication approaches. Light has categorised core skills essential for the development of communicative competence using AAC systems, as follows:

- linguistic skills: e.g. learning the meanings of pictures and symbols, and combining symbols to produce sentences;
- operational skills: technical skills required to operate the communication system, e.g. learning the layout of symbols;
- social skills: knowledge and skills in social rules of interaction;
- strategic skills: developing skills to communicate effectively beyond the limits of AAC competence.

In the classroom situation, teachers recognise the need to work in all four areas. They all support, interact and develop skills across the main attainment target areas of the National Curriculum for English. Developing the use of Light's core skill areas to facilitate whichever AAC method, or combination of methods (e.g. objects of reference, symbols, signs, photographs, etc.), is preferred by the child will ensure access to the English curriculum in a meaningful, child-centred way.

A communication system can often be the key to many activities, environments and relationships for children with learning difficulties. This is why effective teaching of English, literacy and communication is critical to these pupils. There is an advocacy role for English, namely that of liberating pupils with learning difficulties and empowering them as active and interactive communicators. Michael Williams, an AAC user with cerebral palsy, writes how he has been empowered through an effective communication system that has enabled him to express himself as a literate human being: 'I am with you today empowered by the written word ... through high octane literacy' (Williams 1995). Moreover, Pat Pinsent (1990, p.10) argues that: 'In our society then it is particularly important to emphasise that literacy is not only the right of every individual, but also a means of enabling people to exercise their rights.' This is a message that is reiterated in later chapters in this book (see Chapters 22 and 23).

Towards augmented literacy

While there are many communication systems available, each must be tailored to the needs of the user. Part of this 'tailoring' involves an understanding of the skills that are relevant to communicative functioning for a child with learning difficulties (Baumgart *et al.* 1990). So, in selecting an appropriate augmentative communication system for a child with learning difficulties, what do we currently know about the effectiveness of various approaches?

Juliet Goldbart (1994) has provided an excellent working model of communication at the earliest stages of development. Helen Bradley (1998) provides a model designed to guide assessment and intervention by highlighting key stages and their implications in terms of broad communication needs. Her analysis of communication skills and communication needs clearly demonstrates how the earliest responses of crying, pushing, pulling, etc., form idiosyncratic communication systems. From these clear messages (communicative intent), more formalised modes of AAC can be developed for the child with profound and multiple learning difficulties. These may involve low technology such as symbol overlays or high technology such as speech synthesisers.

Objects of reference have gained increasing relevance in the foundation stages of communication programmes for children with learning difficulties. The theoretical basis for the use is well articulated in the work of Keith Park (1998b). Theo Peeters (2000) discusses, through case studies, the 'language of objects'. He stresses how children with autism can learn language most successfully when supported by concrete and visible forms of communication. For students with profound autistic spectrum disorder, objects have been used to devise daily schedules from which such children can predict their next activity and gain some control over their daily routines (Carpenter *et al.* 2001; Watson 1985).

Marion McClarty (1995) demonstrates how the use of objects of reference in the classroom to support relationship developments offers structure and choice. She builds on van Dijk's concept of a 'day rhythm', through her calendar boxes. These are made up of a number of small boxes (say shoe boxes) taped together. They may cover the five or so activities in a child's morning routine, ending with lunch. The objects are arranged (one per box) to correspond with, and cue, each morning activity. The child then feels the contents of each box, probably co-actively at first, and then sets off to his or her desk, workstation, gym, music room or wherever. This tactile clueing has been particularly successful with children with dual sensory impairment, but it reflects the schedule approach used with children with ASD in programmes such as TEACCH (Watson 1985).

The use of symbols as a manual (exchange) communication system is well documented (Van Oosterom and Devereux 1984; Walker *et al.* 1985). The advent of information technology saw the application of symbols to assistive technologies (Cook and Hussey 1995), and the development of computer programs such as WRITING WITH SYMBOLS 2000 (Widgit Software) has enriched considerably the participation of students with learning difficulties in a whole range of curriculum experiences previously denied them (see further Chapters 6 and 7 in this book). Symbols can act as a mediating strategy for activities related to language sequencing skills. This enables children to select and sequence symbolised word concepts, and to use hypothesis–test strategies to form a sentence of varying information-carrying word length. Children with learning difficulties have been given active learning opportunities through the problem-solving and decision-making required in these activities. The use of symbols to support emergent literacy (King-De Baum 1990), particularly writing (Carpenter and Detheridge 1994) and reading (Musselwhite 1993), is a most exciting prospect.

The literacy hour has been made more accessible to children with learning difficulties by using symbols to give meaning to text and to aid comprehension of the text (Abbot 2000). Symbols supporting the text help pupils to work with complex issues and demonstrate that these issues are within their grasp. This is a theme that Nicola Grove and Keith Park have promoted through their adaptations of classical texts for children with complex learning difficulties (Grove and Park 1996).

Abbott asserts that the use of symbols means that pupils with learning difficulties are not excluded from such experiences by reason of text. He gives an example from George Hastwell School in Barrow-in-Furness, Cumbria, which ran a literacy summer school for pupils with learning difficulties on the theme of 'Lakeland Writers'. The range of activities was designed to be wide, engaging and fully supported by symbols. This provided the pupils with opportunities to read from, and learn more about, writers who had lived in Cumbria – such as Beatrix Potter, Arthur Ransome and William Wordsworth. Information and communications technologies were used to the full, as were digital cameras for rewarding events. Strategies such as shared reading, group writing (on a whiteboard) and drama enhanced the experience. The staff leading this project concluded that it would not have been possible without the ready and reliable access to the support of symbols.

Attainable targets

Gains in provision result almost always in gains in learning. However, there used to be few ways to evaluate the success of the many different approaches, techniques and resources and to find out how much progress pupils were making. For example, pupils might have learned, through multisensory approaches, to push a switch in order to receive a reward such as a piece of music or a moving picture; but teachers were often left not knowing how to record this attainment or plan for progression. The success of the 'small steps to success' approaches, however, began to ensure that pupils' progress could be more effectively measured and that teachers had a clear idea of what to teach next.

The introduction of the 'P' scales in *Supporting the Target Setting Process* (DfEE/QCA 1998), and the subsequent guidance recently published by QCA (2001), have been an enormous step forward for teachers of children with learning difficulties. At last they have a clear focus for school improvement as well as for assessing pupils' development against that of similar pupils across the country. The implementation of the original 'P' scales has meant that a systematic evaluation process is now in place, and the new 'P' scales should offer an even more sharply focused framework for monitoring pupils' attainment. A common basis for measuring the progress of pupils with severe, profound and complex needs has been established, and schools can begin to look at how the progress of such pupils could be further improved. Targets can now be more closely

Figure 2.1 Symbolised training sheets used by George Hastwell School, Cumbria as part of their 'Lakeland Writers' Summer School (Abbott 2000)

linked to pupils' prior attainment, and a way forward established so as to ensure progression.

The 'small steps' approach and the Bristol Literacy Project

With the advent of the National Literacy Strategy in 1998, schools for pupils with very special needs began to try to find ways of accessing the objectives. The framework for literacy states that it 'covers the statutory requirements for reading and writing in the National Curriculum for English and contributes substantially to the development of speaking and listening' (DfEE 1998, p. 3). The challenge for teachers was to find ways of making the framework accessible for pupils functioning below Level 1. It is important that these pupils have the same access and rights as all other pupils. Thus they need to have opportunities that enable them to interact, communicate, make choices and affect the learning that takes place. Often, it is only by working with adults in a one-to-one or very small group situation that this becomes possible. Pupils can then be given the amount of time – sometimes a very long time – to respond to questions and to initiate their own answer. It is up to us as practitioners to create the right conditions for every individual child.

With the advent of the revised 'P' scales for English, it would appear that almost all the ingredients are available to enable pupils with even the most complex difficulties to make some progress in learning to develop literacy, particularly if by 'literacy' we also mean 'communication'. It was with this background that the Bristol Literacy Project began. The work of the Bristol Literacy Project identified ways in which the National Literacy Strategy could be developed to enable pupils with severe and complex learning difficulties, including those with sensory impairments, to improve their communication and literacy skills. Each objective in the National Literacy Strategy for pupils in Reception year was broken down into small steps so that pupils functioning below, and even well below, Level 1 of the National Curriculum could access the objectives at their own level. The work of the Bristol Project focused on the different activities and approaches that 'worked best' and that enabled pupils to develop, in whatever way possible, some autonomy in learning.

Within the work of the Bristol Literacy Project for pupils with learning difficulties, many of the ideas about developmental language acquisition (discussed above) have been incorporated. As a result of this, for example, the link between attainment targets AT1, AT2 and AT3 is much more securely established than it is in the National Literacy Strategy. This is because the Bristol Literacy Project believes that the acquisition of language – indeed, communication in whatever possible form – is the primary need for children functioning below Level 1.

In recent years, the work of many researchers has highlighted a common theme, namely that of the importance of developing interactions through whatever channel is available. Hence, in the Bristol Literacy Project, the use of multisensory approaches and a focus on interaction have been the major thrust of the work undertaken so far. The work undertaken in the dark room, for example, has an important role in literacy development. Until children can focus on objects, and learn to follow movements, they cannot take part in shared text. Where children have a severe visual loss, the work that they undertake in a tactile environment is crucial to the development of early Braille skills. At a more advanced level, the use of signs and symbols are considered to be crucial in the development of communication and literacy. The activities that the Bristol Literacy Project recommend are closely linked to a multisensory approach to learning (see Figures 2.2 and 2.3).

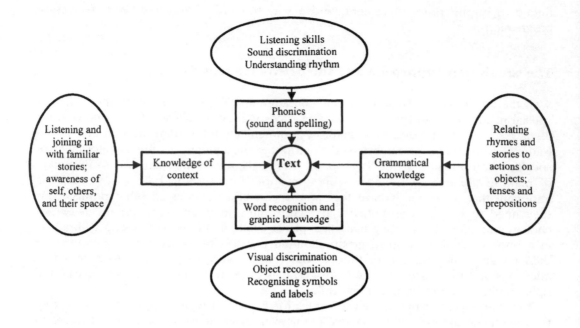

Figure 2.2 Access to reading

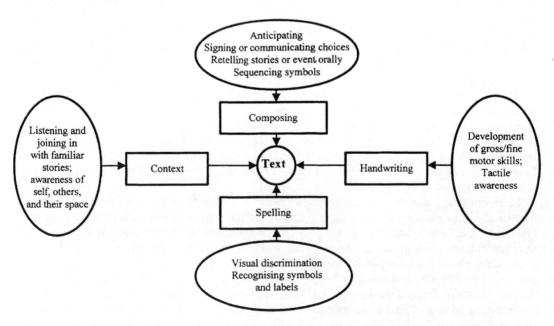

Figure 2.3 Access to writing

Figure 2.2 shows how pupils can access reading through multisensory channels. For example, they cannot distinguish word patterns unless they can hear and discriminate sounds; and they will not learn about the context of a story unless they have first listened to many different stories and become familiar with them. In order to recognise words, pupils need to first identify objects, symbols, labels, familiar people, and things. To learn about grammatical knowledge, they need to be physically involved in early play activities. (If they cannot play themselves, we as adults must play with them.)

Figure 2.3 shows how pupils can access the writing objectives at the earliest stages. Pupils cannot compose until they have experience of building up stories with adults. Day-to-day experiences are important here because these are what pupils know about. They can learn to remember what happened earlier, or this morning, or yesterday, and begin to sequence these simple events by using words, symbols, signs, pictures or technology. This is the early forerunner of writing from their own experiences. Writing itself may not be possible. But we must give them the opportunity. We must help them to develop their gross and fine motor skills through the multisensory channels. How many of us like to see children playing with dough, clay, sand, water, pasta, jelly, etc? These are the early stages of developing hand control. The work of the sensory room is vital where pupils need to develop their visual and auditory skills so that they can listen and look on request.

All of these are vital ingredients to early communication and literacy. The Bristol Project incorporated all of these into the 'small steps' approach. As Table 2.1 shows, activities that can be undertaken with an adult to promote the development of these skills are the main thrust of the work.

The Bristol Literacy Project pilot study

Originally, seven schools took part in the pilot study. During the Autumn Term of 1999, they began to assess their pupils against the 'P' level statements to set a baseline. They then began to use the 'small steps' approach to teach the objectives, and gradually up to eight steps were identified for each literacy objective, linked to the 'P' levels. The main approaches used were based on the language development and acquisition research previously mentioned. For example, teachers and pupils worked closely together to establish interaction. Each step was taught through multimodal communication channels, encouraging pupils to 'look', 'listen', 'follow' and 'respond' as they shared stories, games, rhymes, and even technology with adults. Because the steps were small, it was possible to see progress quite quickly and move pupils on to the next level.

Table 2.1 shows an example of an objective from the Reception year, which has been broken down into small steps. The activities that have been identified aim to promote learning in an interactive way. Pupils move through the small steps, and progress can be measured. It is recommended that teachers assess whichever level pupils are functioning at before they begin to use this small-steps approach. Hence, after an initial period of working with the activities, they can then identify how much progress has been made.

Communication games were implicit within each step on the way to making progress. For example, as Figures 2.2 and 2.3 show, in order to access text, pupils need to learn about sequencing, grammatical knowledge, word recognition and context. For many of the Bristol pupils there were steps before this that needed to be addressed. Children will not recognise a word, or read that word, unless they first know what that object represents. Sometimes children with very severe difficulties may have missed the early

Table 2.1 Word recognition, graphic knowledge and spelling

W.L. YR: LO 5
To read on sight a range of familiar words, e.g. children's names, captions, labels and words from favourite books.
See also: W.L. YR: LO 6; T.L. YR: LO 8; W.L. YR1 Term 1: LO 7, 8, 9; T.L. YR1 Term 1: LO 12, 13

STEPS LEARNING OBJECTIVES/ TARGETS	ACTIVITIES/STRATEGIES	
P1 Experiences being part of a group in which they hear names daily, and in which they regularly hear names of familiar objects.	Daily activities to encourage pupils to recognise own belongings, e.g. 'Whose coat is this?' Register symbols/names. Daily routines.	
P2 Responds in some way to hearing own name or to seeing own symbol. Responds to everyday objects, e.g. cup or biscuit, by body/eye movements.	Use a range of everyday objects in whole-class situations/group or 1:1 encounter to elicit recognition. Constant use of pupils' names.	
P3 Anticipates what comes next in registration, lunch-time and home time. Looks towards own objects when named.	Use a range of everyday familiar objects. Encourage anticipation by saying, 'Who's next?' in registration.	
P4 Shows interest in finding own familiar objects. Makes choices of own coat, cup, symbol, picture, and shows recognition by vocalising or body movement.	Use of pupils' own objects, names, name symbols and cards in groups, labels in classroom, daily tasks, classroom objects.	
P5 Begins to recognise simple pictures in a picture or photograph book.	Make own books of familiar objects or pupil's family. Make simple captions.	
P6 Recognises photos/pictures/ symbols/ word card of self and familiar peers. Recognises photos of own familiar objects.	In 1:1 encounter, add one word caption to pictures or photographs, e.g. mummy, car, dog.	
P7 Joins in with 'reading' simple photo books, class story books and class topic books, joins in with reading daily 'news', shows understanding that the words mean something.	Matching activities of pupil's name to photograph, or simple words or symbols to names of objects round the classroom to other pupils, classroom furniture, labels, and simple topic books.	
P.8 Reads simple text and 'news' in whole class times. Reads some labels and words independently and knows that they have meaning.	As above with extended opportunities to share text and written words e.g. adult modeling writing on board.	

stages of development. The challenge for us, as teachers and practitioners, is to provide activities, games and rhymes that will help them to learn about their world, understand the permanence of objects, and begin to interact to cause and effect.

A recent evaluation of the work undertaken in Bristol found that, without exception, pupils had made progress. Also – the most important feature – their progress was measurable. Teachers continue to use the wide range of multisensory approaches that grew up throughout the 1980s and 1990s, but now they can structure their approach so that each pupil receives a curriculum appropriate to his or her needs. For a child who finds instruction difficult, any means of gaining contact will be sought.

The impact of visual languages

Once we have established these concepts, we can lead children through the gradual steps to becoming early readers, and certainly towards interacting with others and enjoyment of literature. There are countless systems available to help pupils communicate. It is essential that practitioners identify the appropriate one for each pupil with learning difficulties; for them, it is as vital as pens and paper are to other children.

To do this, we need to marshal all that we know about how children with learning difficulties acquire literacy skills. The existing literature is in agreement on the need to provide consistent models of literacy use. Many writers assert that print (in all of its forms) must have a high profile in a learner's environment and must be granted high status through frequent use in a variety of purposeful activities (Koppenhaver and Yoder 1991). We have learnt much in the last two decades about the acquisition of literacy skills through a variety of alternative approaches (Bishop *et al.* 1994). Indeed, there are now conclusive studies demonstrating that some children with SLD will not acquire language and literacy skills through conventional means; their brain functioning may require alternative methods (Buckley 1985).

Visual clueing methods (e.g. objects of reference, photographs or pictures) have contributed much to the development of literacy skills in, for example, children with SLD. Buckley (1985) has written extensively on the use of whole-word approaches in reading to stimulate language in children with Down's Syndrome. Other studies have clearly indicated how signing can not only form a viable communication mode for children with SLD but can also provide a route to literacy (Carpenter 1991). Symbols have made a considerable contribution to literacy and the wider curriculum (Detheridge and Detheridge 1997; Carpenter *et al.* 1996). Objects of reference offer an excellent means of establishing not only a communication system for children at a very early developmental level but also of securely rooting the conceptual foundation of each linguistic concept (Park 1998b).

Sunfield School: finding a framework

Sunfield is a residential school that offers education and 52–week care to children from ages 6 to 19 with severe and complex learning difficulties. In seeking to implement the National Literacy Strategy in a meaningful way for pupils, the school staff asked themselves the question: 'What, within the context of literacy, do we want our children to learn?'

They sought answers to this question by taking one common concept that they could present to the children (e.g. 'house'). They considered a variety of ways in which this concept could be presented in all of its forms, through differentiated teaching. Not only were they seeking ways of input to the children, but also all of the ways in which the children could indicate emerging knowledge and understanding of the concept.

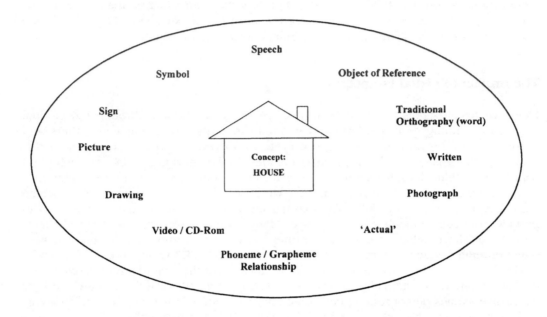

Figure 2.4 An example of a multi-tiered approach to literacy (outcome of staff training workshop, Sunfield School, April 1998)

What emerged was that literacy in the SLD setting necessitates a multi-tiered approach: there can be no single way of presenting a concept. A variety of strategies using sign, symbol, objects of reference and sensory channels must run alongside the presentation in all of its spoken, graphical and real dimensions. Presenting a multimodal definition for the concept of 'house' to a pupil (see Figure 2.4) involved introducing not just one form (e.g. sign or speech) but associated forms in a variety of media. This approach embraced learning in the areas of picture recognition, object matching, word building, and spelling, to name but a few.

The rigorous assessment of presentation opportunities in respect of each child's abilities enabled every child to access that concept at an appropriate level. Such an approach to concept presentation also allowed for progression to be made, e.g. moving on from understanding the representational value of a photograph to that of the corresponding symbol. It also ensured that each child received a relevant, needs-based approach and remained an active participant within the literacy learning experience.

With all of these teaching and learning variants, classroom management becomes a key issue. A framework that offers guidance, structure and focus for the teacher and learner becomes crucial. The 'literacy clock' (DfEE 1998) is a visually helpful framework

– the short bursts of teaching are wholly appropriate, but require modification if the literacy hour is to remain relevant for children with SLD. The content of each session (e.g. reading, writing or word work) needs a broader definition than that provided in the literacy hour guidance. There needs to be a clear acknowledgement that many of our children learn and communicate through augmentative modes, even a multiplicity of modes.

Taking the structure of the literacy hour, Sunfield School 'retimed' the clock to a pattern more appropriate to children with SLD. To ensure that their model remained child-centred, the model was set within a 'plan-do-review' cycle. Whole-class, small-group and individual teaching, as well as independent learning, are embodied within the adapted model (see Figure 2.5). This approach gave the Sunfield teachers the opportunity to identify skills fundamental to the learning growth of children with SLD. Skills such as visual discrimination, visual closure, auditory memory and auditory recall were set within the context of a curriculum initiative that was being presented for all children. As ever, the challenge to teachers was access to that curriculum domain. The essential skill areas afforded relevant routes into literacy for children with learning difficulties.

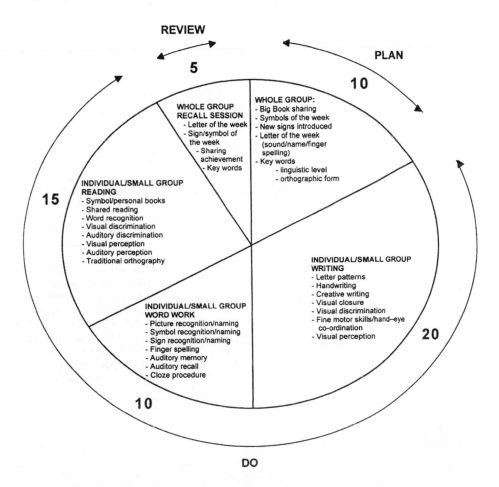

Figure 2.5 Managing the literacy hour: a multimodal approach

Implementing the model

Once the model was established, there was a need to identify the activities that would support its implementation. The curriculum manager, in conjunction with the literacy coordinators, prepared guidance sheets that took the model section by section and suggested a range of activities that would be appropriate to individual children in each class group. These activities were linked with the school's programme of study for English. An example of an activity for each section of the multimodal literacy hour is given in Table 2.2 below.

Table 2.2 Activity examples

SECTION	ACTIVITY	LEARNING GOAL	MATERIAL DEVELOPMENT
Whole group	Big Book sharing	To identify key words/ symbols in a story	Books from our Library Resources have been colour photocopied and enlarged. Symbols have been inserted to supplement the text. Each page has been mounted on to A4 card and laminated. Tactile stories, commercially produced by Chris Fuller (1990) have also been used.
Small groups/ individuals (Writing)	Creative writing	To compose a short story	During National Children's Book Week in 1998, children were introduced to a storyteller. They were then encouraged to 'tell' someone their story. This was either recorded for them or the student wrote their story in symbols using Widgit Software's WRITING WITH SYMBOLS computer program. These books were bound, catalogued and placed in the school library.

SECTION	ACTIVITY	LEARNING GOAL	MATERIAL DEVELOPMENT
Small groups/ individuals (Word Work)	Word/symbol recognition / naming	To identify key words	A dictionary box was developed as a class resource. Students who had grasped the initial letter of a word could locate this in the box. To 'cue' them into the whole word, each word card contained a symbol clue and the graphic version.
Small groups/ individuals (Reading)	Sentence construction	To construct a sentence in its spoken, symbolised, signed or written forms	Children selected words/symbols from a word bank hung on the wall to use on a large wooden sentence-maker. They would compose a sentence, which was then spoken and/or signed and then represented in a graphic form (symbol/word)
Whole group (Recall Session)	Sign/symbol word of the week	To acquire a new language concept in its oral, visual or graphic form	To reflect the range of ability within any class group, it was possible to differentiate the teaching of a single language concept by presenting it as an object (tactile) form, photograph, symbol, sign or written word.

To facilitate many activities within the literacy hour, further resource identification was necessary. For example, the tactile stories (Fuller 1990) have become invaluable for Big Book work for those children with more profound learning difficulties. Writing with symbols, either computer-aided (Widgit Software 2000) or freehand, has developed not only creative writing skills but also fine motor skills (Carpenter and Detheridge 1994). The acquisition of traditional orthography is a well-documented challenge for students with severe learning difficulties. Symbols can offer a 'perceptual bridge' (Carpenter 1991) that can aid the transition from picture through symbol to word.

The activities were tested through lesson planning for each section of the literacy hour. These lesson plans stated learning intentions, teaching activity, resources, learning outcomes and class organisation. Links were made with the IEPs for each child, which always contained literacy priority targets for each term. Records were kept to assess students' learning over time. These lesson plans enabled a full evaluation of the effectiveness of the literacy hour to take place later in the academic year.

The concluding part of any lesson always focused on the achievements of individual children, when they were able to review the cycle of literacy learning they had engaged in during the previous hour. Many students enjoyed having a new language concept to acquire each week, in any of its forms. These might be object or picture recognition, the signed form, or through symbol/word recognition. This simple focus meant that many students could measure their own progress in the course of the five days, which was a great source of stimulus.

The focus on literacy has encouraged teachers to participate in events such as National Children's Book Week. This has been a relevant experience for children of all abilities at Sunfield School through use of a range of artefacts, sensory materials, assistive technologies, as well as books in various media (Carpenter, 1999).

The correct style of literacy hour enables pupils' true learning goals to be met. For the literacy hour to have relevance for children with severe learning difficulties, we have to acknowledge that literacy has to be multimodal and that its delivery comes through a variety of augmented strategies. At Sunfield, this multimodal approach has led the school to evolve 'augmented literacy' as the means by which all pupils can engage in the National Literacy Strategy. Initiatives such as this can ensure that the National Literacy Strategy has something truly meaningful to offer children with severe and complex learning needs.

Conclusion: literacy for all

The extension of quality literacy experiences to include all children, including those with PMLD, has been a significant innovation in recent years. Pioneered by Chris Fuller (1999) through the Tactile Stories (subsequently termed Bag Books), there has been much creative interpretation of storytelling and story access for this pupil group (Grove and Park 2001).

The 'Reading for All' materials produced by Mencap (Lawton 1999) resulted from a National Year of Reading grant, which ensured that children with PMLD were included in a range of National Literacy Strategy-focused initiatives. The broad view adopted in these materials is that books should no longer be a barrier to literacy for those who cannot read traditional print; nor is the content of those books a barrier for those who cannot fully understand them. Building on the principles of communication discussed in this chapter the 'Reading for All' materials suggest access to the story experience through three major paths:

- communication systems (signs, symbols, moon, objects of reference, pictures of reference);
- technology to support the systems (switches, concept keyboard, electronic voice box);
- improving parents' and staff's interactions with children with PMLD (learning to listen, observe, giving choices, waiting for responses).

There are many recent publications advocating practical approaches to English. For example, Nicola Grove and Keith Park (2001), in their work *Social Cognition through Drama and Literature for People with Learning Difficulties,* provide advice and guidance on access for older people and develop a framework for linking skills of social cognition to drama. Nicola Grove, in *Literature for All* (1997), provides guidance on the challenges meeting teachers of pupils at Key Stage 3. She gives valuable insights into how the world of literature can be opened up to older pupils working at lower levels of attainment.

Materials such as these contain guidelines on designing books, construction, illustration and story themes; they promote access to literacy through individualised communication approaches, which ensure that literacy is for all.

There are ongoing in-service training (INSET) implications from such approaches, for not all teachers automatically appreciate, or have knowledge of, the various communication strategies that can be effective with this pupil population. Signing, symbol and assistive technology training needs to be linked with sessions on Big Books, shared reading, and family-based literacy. These are fundamental if we are to sustain the right style of literacy hour for pupils with learning difficulties. This needs to be a series of literacy-based learning experiences that enable pupils' true learning goals to be met and teachers to achieve the successful teaching indicators – 'interactive, well-paced, confident and ambitious Literacy Hours' (DfEE, 1998) – as outlined in the National Literacy Strategy.

It is evident that practitioners will continue to seek new ways to improve access to English. But we at least have a way forward: there is evidence now of access to literacy, through a small-steps approach, based initially on multimodal communication channels. These approaches enable pupils to benefit from a rich and exciting world of literature hitherto denied to them.

References

Abbott, C. (ed.) (2000) *Symbols Now*. Leamington Spa: Widgit Software.

Aird, R. (2001) *The Education and Care of Children with Severe, Profound and Mutiple Learning Difficulties*. London: David Fulton Publishers.

Alton, S. (2001) 'Children with Down's Syndrome and short-term auditory memory', *Down's Syndrome Association Journal* **95** (Winter), 4–9.

Barkley, R. A. (1990) *Attention Deficit Hyperactivity Disorder: A handbook for diagnosis and treatment*. New York: Guilford Press.

Baumgart, D. *et al.* (1990) *Augmentative and Alternative Communication Systems for Persons with Moderate and Severe Disabilities*. Baltimore: Paul H. Brookes.

Bishop, K. *et al.* (1994) 'Impact of graphic symbol use on reading acquisition', *Augmentative and Alternative Communication* **10**, 113–25.

Blunkett, D. (1999) 'Foreword', in DfEE/QCA *The National Curriculum for English*. London: DfEE/QCA.

Bozic, N. and Murdoch, H. (eds) (1995) *Learning through Interaction*. London: David Fulton Publishers.

Bozic, N. *et al.* (1995) 'Micro-computer based joint activities in communication intervention with visually impaired children', *Child Language and Teaching Therapy* **11**(1), 91–105.

Bradley, H. (1998) 'Assessing and developing successful communication', in Lacey, P. and Ouvry (eds) *People with Profound and Multiple Learning Disabilities*. London: David Fulton Publishers.

Bristow, J. *et al.* (1999) *Memory and Learning: A practical guide for teachers*. London: David Fulton Publishers.

Bruner, J. S. (1978) 'From communication to language', in Markova, I. (ed.) *The Social Context of Language*. New York: Wiley.

Buckley, S. (1985) 'Attaining basic education skills: reading, writing and number', in Lane, D. and Stratford, B. (eds) *Current Approaches to Down's Syndrome*. East Sussex: Holt, Reinhart and Winston.

Buckley, S. and Bird, G. (1994) *The Educational Implications of Down's Syndrome*. Portsmouth: Down's Syndrome Trust.

Carpenter, B. (1991) 'Unlocking the door: Access to English in the National Curriculum for children with severe learning difficulties', in Smith, B. (ed.) *Interactive Approaches to Teaching the Core Subjects.* Birmingham: Lame Duck Publishing.

Carpenter, B. (1999) 'A multi-modal approach to literacy', *The SLD Experience* **23** (Spring), 10–13.

Carpenter, B. (2001) 'Inclusive societies; inclusive families'. Inaugural lecture at the launch of the Irish National Institute for Learning Difficulties, Trinity College, Dublin (April).

Carpenter, B. and Detheridge, T. (1994) 'Writing with Symbols', *Support for Learning* **9**(1), 27–33.

Carpenter, B. *et al.* (eds) (1996) *Enabling Access: Effective teaching and learning for pupils with learning difficulties.* London: David Fulton Publishers.

Carpenter, B. *et al.* (2001) 'An evaluation of SIECCA: an intensive programme of education and care for students with profound autistic spectrum disorder', *Good Autism Practice.* **2**(1), 52–66

Clarke, M. *et al.* (2001) 'Speech and language therapy provision for children using augmentative and alternative communication systems', *European Journal of Special Needs Education* **16**(1), 41–54.

Clay, M. M. (1985) *The Early Detection of Reading Difficulties: A diagnostic survey with reading procedures* 3rd edn. Auckland, NZ: Heinemann.

Cook, A. M. and Hussey, S. M. (1995) *Assistive Technologies: principles and practice.* Missouri: Mosby.

DfEE (1998) *The National Literacy Strategy: Framework for teaching.* London: DfEE.

DfEE/QCA (1998) *Supporting the Target Setting Process.* London: DfEE/QCA.

Detheridge, T. and Detheridge, M. (1997) *Literacy through Symbols.* London: David Fulton Publishers.

Etheridge, D. (1995) *The Education of Dual Sensory Impaired Children.* London: David Fulton Publishers.

Fuller, C. (1999) *Tactile Stories.* London: The Consortium.

Fuller, C. (1999) 'Bag books tactile stories', *The SLD Experience* 23, 20–1.

Glenn, S. *et al.* (1995) 'Social interaction in multi-sensory environments', in Bozic, N. and Murdoch, H. (eds) *Learning through Interaction.* London: David Fulton Publishers.

Glenny, G. (2000) 'Approaches to reading difficulties', in Benton, P. and O'Brien, T. (eds) *Special Needs and the Beginning Teacher.* London: Continuum.

Goldbart, J. (1994) 'Pre-intentional communication: opening the communication curriculum to students with profound and multiple learning difficulties', in Ware, J. (ed.) *Educating Children with Profound and Multiple Learning Difficulties.* London: David Fulton Publishers.

Goodman (1984) 'The development of initial literacy', in Goelman, H. *et al.* (eds) *Awakening to Literacy.* Oxford: Heinemann.

Grove, N. (1997) *Literature for All.* London: David Fulton Publishers.

Grove, N. and Park, K. (1996) *Odyssey Now.* London: Jessica Kingsley.

Grove, N. and Park, K. (2001) *Social Cognition through Drama and Literacy for People with Learning Difficulties.* London: Jessica Kingsley.

Hinchcliffe, V. (1996) 'English', in Carpenter, B. *et al.* (eds) (1996) *Enabling Access: Effective teaching and learning for pupils with learning difficulties.* London: David Fulton Publishers.

Jarrold, C.*et al.* (1999) 'Down syndrome and the phonological loop: the evidence for, and the importance of, a specific verbal short-term memory deficit', *Down Syndrome Research and Practice* **6**(2), 61–75.

Jordan, R. and Powell S. D. (1995) *Understanding and Teaching Children with Autism.* Chichester: John Wiley.

King-De Baum, P. (1990) *Storytime: Stories, symbols and emergent literacy activities for young special needs children.* Georgia, USA: Meyer-Johnson.

Koppenhaver, D. A. and Yoder, D. E. (1991) 'Literacy issues in persons with severe speech and physical impairments', in Gaylord-Ross, R. (ed.) *Issues and Research in Special Education (Vol. 2).* New York: Columbia University Teachers College Press.

Kumin, L. (1994) *Communication Skills in Children with Down's Syndrome.* Bethesda: Woodbine House.

Laws, G. *et al.* (1996) 'The effects of a short training in the use of a rehearsal strategy on memory for words and pictures in children with Down's Syndrome', *Down's Syndrome Research and Practice* **4**(2), 70–8.

Lawton, J. (ed.) (1999) *Reading for All: Ideas for stories and reading for children and young adults with severe and profound learning disabilities.* London: Mencap.

Light, J. (1989) 'Towards a definition of communicative competence for individuals using augumentative and alternative communications systems', *Augumentative and Alternative Communication* 5, 137–4.

Longhorn, F. (1988) *A Sensory Curriculum for Very Special People: A practical approach to curriculum planning.* London: Souvenir Press.

Longhorn, F. (1991) 'A sensory science curriculum', in Ashdown, R. *et al.* (eds) *The Curriculum Challenge.* London: Falmer.

McClarty, M. (1995) '*Objects of reference*', in Etheridge, D. (ed.) *The Education of Dual Sensory Impaired Children.* London: David Fulton Publishers.

Mercer, N. (1988) *Language and Literacy from an Educational Perspective (Vol. 1).* Oxford: Oxford University Press.

Musselwhite, C. (1993) *RAPS: reading activities project for older students.* New York: Chapel Hill.

Park, K. (1998a) 'Form and function in early communication', *The SLD Experience* 21, 2–5.

Park, K. (1998b) 'Using objects of reference: a review of literature', *European Journal of Special Needs Education* **10**(1), 40–6.

Peeters, T. (2000) 'The language of objects', in Powell, S. (ed.) *Helping Children with Autism to Learn.* London: David Fulton Publishers.

Pinsent, P. (1990) *Children with Literary Difficulties.* London: David Fulton Publishers.

Portwood, M. (2000) *Understanding Developmental Dyspraxia.* London: David Fulton Publishers.

QCA (2001) *Planning, Teaching and Assessing the Curriculum for Pupils with Learning Difficulties: English.* London: DfEE/QCA.

Robinson, O. (2000) 'Approaches to spelling', in Benton, P. and O'Brien, T. (eds) *Special Needs and the Beginning Teacher.* London: Continuum.

Slinger, L. *et al.* (1999) 'Literacy: managing change and making it work at Forest Way School', *SLD Experience* **23** (Spring), 13–15.

Smith, D. (ed.) (2000) *Success in the Literacy Hour.* Tamworth: National Association for Special Educational Needs.

Snow, C. E. (1989) 'Understanding social interactions and language acquisition: sentences are not enough', in Bornstein, M. and Bruner, J. S. (eds) *Interaction in Human Development.* New York: Lawrence Erlbaum.

Sylva, K. and Hurry, J. (1995) *Early Intervention in Children with Reading Difficulties (Discussion Paper 2).* London: Schools Curriculum and Assessment Authority.

Van Oosterom, J. and Devereux, K. (1984) *Learning with Rebuses.* Stafford: NCSE.

Walker, M. *et al.* (1985) *Symbols for Makaton.* Camberley: MVDP.

Watson, L. R. (1985) 'The TEACCH communication curriculum', in Schopler, E. and Mesibov, G. (eds) *Communication Problems in Autism.* New York: Plenum Press.

Watson, A. J. and Giorcelli, L. R. (eds) (1999) *Accepting the Literacy Challenge.* Gosford, Australia: Scholastic.

Widgit Software (2000) WRITING WITH SYMBOLS 2000. Leamington Spa: Widgit.

Williams, M. (1995) Outcomes of AAC, *Augumentative Communication News* 8, 5.

Chapter 3

Mathematics

Sue Panter

Understanding and learning

This chapter raises issues for consideration and explores ways of achieving and enabling access to the entitlement (mathematics) curriculum. In doing so, it will be stressed that it is important for both the pupils and their parents that teachers re-signify all pupils with special educational needs as learners capable of demonstrating significant progress and achievement when taught well (see Chapter 10 for further discussion of this).

In the first edition of *Enabling Access*, Brian Robbins asked readers to consider the question: 'Do we view Mathematics as a subject, as a means of accessing other areas of the curriculum or as an essential skill for life?' (Robbins 1996a). He continued by acknowledging that, in fact, it was all three and that it was the *balance* among the three that needed to be struck in the teaching of mathematics.

Concepts, knowledge and skills are elements within the mathematics curriculum. Understanding the concepts, having the knowledge of the facts, having the skills and knowing when and how to use the skills may be seen as essential to the learning of mathematics. Skemp (1971), cited by Robbins (1996a), distinguishes between 'understanding' and 'learning without understanding'. If the balance between mathematics as a subject, as a means of accessing other areas of the curriculum and as an essential life skill is to be achieved, Skemp's argument must influence our own perspectives. For example, there is no point in learning to read unless we understand the content of what we are reading and it has meaning for us. Similarly, there is no point in learning the skill of map reading unless we can apply it. In both examples, there must be an understanding of the knowledge and skills that we are gaining.

However, does this negate the joy of actually learning to do something for the sake of learning to do it? Consider the pupils who have learned to read (i.e. to decode), understanding little of what they are reading, but who read voraciously because they take great pride in being able to read. We should recognise and celebrate that they learned important skills, but the comprehension of the text should be addressed. Also, consider the pupils who have learned to identify places and symbols on a map but have no conceptual understanding of where these are in relation to where they are. Their pleasure at being able to do this and relay it to others should not be dismissed, since the relationship of places to where they are can be addressed at a later stage. The skills learned by the children in these instances need to be given relevance by their teachers, but this does not have to be immediate as long as it is made apparent in a meaningful way to the pupils at some point. In the current educational climate, which emphasises achievement and reaching targets, the achievement of even a limited, situation-specific skill, and the celebration of this, can go some way to providing the relevance for the pupils.

Can the same be said for mathematical skills? The pupils who learn to add single digit numbers together may gain a feeling of achievement from the red ticks and other rewards. A conceptual understanding of the future relevance of the skill, of being able to apply it across the curriculum and use it as a life skill, will provide meaning to the learning. This link should be taught, not assumed. This is not to say that understanding of mathematical concepts, or why particular processes exist and how they might be used, is not important; but there needs to be a perspective on the pupils' achievements that gives balance. What is involved in the understanding of any concept needs to be seen as broken down into small steps – as the teaching of the particular knowledge and skills will be – so that pupils may readily achieve and recognise the small progressions that build into a whole.

The mathematics curriculum

The mathematics curriculum is clearly arranged in key stages of learning, with their associated programmes of study. National Curriculum Levels 1–8, plus a level for exceptional performance, are used to measure pupils' progress; they are like the rungs on a ladder, and the expectation is that the children will move up through the levels during their school career. The revised National Curriculum for mathematics provides teachers with greater flexibility to respond to the need of pupils with SEN by allowing material to be selected from earlier or later key stages to enable pupils to make progress and achieve (DfEE/QCA 1999a, 1999b). Table 3.1 shows the range of levels within which most children will work for each key stage and the target levels that most children are expected to achieve by the end of each key stage.

Table 3.1 Key stages and National Curriculum levels

Key stage	Year groups	Range of levels for average learners	target levels
KS1	1 and 2 Levels 1–3	Level 2	
KS2	3–6 Levels 2–6	Level 4	
KS3	7–9 Levels 3–7	Level 5/6	

Some children will not achieve, and some will exceed the targets for their key stage. The Cockroft Report on the teaching of mathematics (Department of Education and Science (DES) 1982) identified a wide range of achievement in a typical class of seven-year-olds that related, in chronological terms, to seven years of learning mathematics. Many pupils with SEN do not achieve the target levels, or even the lower levels in the typical range, for their key stage. For example, the majority of seven-year-olds with SLD will be unlikely to be able to achieve Level 1 in any aspect of mathematics (O'Toole and O'Toole 1989). It would not be appropriate, therefore, for them to be experiencing the same mathematical activities as seven-year-olds without SEN. The ranges expressed in Table 3.1 will therefore need to be extended and, if necessary, pupils can be allowed to work outside the PoS for their key stage if this enables them to make progress and demonstrate achievement.

As mathematical skills are hierarchical and related to application, it is possible to differentiate the curriculum for a typical class (in mainstream or special schools) of pupils with varying abilities and needs, as long as this range is not too great. In doing so, teachers need to bear in mind that Key Stage 1 is not the beginning for mathematical learning (Hughes 1986) and a wealth of learning happens before the age of five at home and through early-years provision, as indicated by the curriculum guidance for the Foundation Stage (QCA 2000) and research on the development of mathematics in young children. Consequently, teachers must, through carefully set targets, incorporate these fundamental experiences into their teaching for pupils with SEN to enable needs to be met and progress to be achieved.

Table 3.2 shows how mathematics in the National Curriculum is divided into four main attainment targets (ATs) which apply at different key stages.

Table 3.2 Areas of learning in mathematics

Using and applying mathematics	AT1 Key Stages 1, 2, 3, 4
Number and algebra	AT2 Key Stages 1 and 2 (number only)
	Key Stages 3 and 4 (number and algebra)
Shape, space and measures	AT3 Key Stages 1, 2, 3, 4
Handling data	AT4 Key Stages 2, 3, 4

The National Curriculum handbooks (DfEE/QCA 1999a, 1999b) do not include a separate section for AT1, 'Using and applying mathematics'. Although it remains an attainment target, it is delivered through the other three ATs of the curriculum. The subject-specific skills, the cross-curricular skills and the life skills referred to by Robbins (1996a) can all be seen within these ATs. However, for many pupils, particularly those with SEN, the relevance to life and other areas of the curriculum of the mathematics skills and concepts must be pointed out and, if possible, practically and materially linked within the teaching process.

This requirement has ramifications for the mathematics policy for a school, the schemes of work and the lesson plans of teachers. Because of the cross-curricular nature of some skills, they must also be seen within schemes of work and lesson plans of other relevant and related subjects. Number, for example, should not be seen in the isolation of manipulation of numbers but in relation to its use. Learning when to use the basic strategies of addition, subtraction, multiplication and division, and use of measures, for example, could be seen in relation to knowing how far it is from one point to another, or the distance around the outside of a garden in relation to fencing requirements. Handling data could relate to finding information that will then be useful to the learner, such as finding out from a table what time the bus leaves and arrives, and how long the journey will take.

This underlines the need for teachers to ensure that problem-solving is addressed while concentrating on access and achievement in the various aspects of mathematics. At the very least, mathematics lessons need to relate the skills being taught to other subjects and to life situations, where maths will be needed. In this sense, the application of number is properly viewed as a key skill and is recognised as such in the National Curriculum handbooks.

Examples of the use and application of number, shape, space and measures, and of handling the data

- Measure the area of a room, in order to work out how many floor tiles are needed – i.e. learning about area if life skill area relevant to geography.
- Measure the sides of a garden, to work out how much fencing is needed – i.e. learn about perimeter if life skill relevant to geography and technology.
- Work out the costs in each of the above – i.e. learn to use money and that multiplication is the process to use; this could also involve learning to estimate if life skill.
- Present the above in graphic or pictorial form – i.e. handling data if relevant to science.

The use of projects within the delivery of the mathematics curriculum is a good way – but not the only way – of ensuring relevance and motivation and achieving the balance. If projects are used, it is necessary to identify the skills that will be used to fulfil the project, teach the new skills, recognise that for some pupils the skills will need to be taught again, make the connection with previous teaching and experiences, and clarify the relevance to other areas. There is a direct link between the use of projects at Key Stages 1, 2 and 3 and that of the course requirements for GCSE at Key Stage 4.

The National Numeracy Strategy

The framework for teaching mathematics in the National Numeracy Strategy (DfEE 1999a) seeks to introduce a welcome rigour into the process of teaching children to recall and use rules, techniques and procedures and to develop ways of thinking about the concepts and ideas encountered in lessons and texts. The required local education authority (LEA) and school-based in-service education and training has no doubt led to a consideration and revision of how mathematics is taught in all primary schools and many special schools, as indicated by the annual report of Her Majesty's Chief Inspector of Schools for 1999/2000 (OFSTED 2001).

HMCI's report suggests that the Numeracy Strategy is having a positive impact. Tests taken by pupils in Years 3, 4 and 5 as part of an evaluation of the impact of the strategy in primary school by Her Majesty's Inspectorate show improvement by pupils across the full range of attainment. Pupils' oral and mental skills, particularly in number, show the greatest improvement; for instance, they recall number facts more quickly and more accurately. Problem-solving skills are improving too, but too many pupils do not make use of the knowledge and skills that they have acquired in other contexts. Teachers need to make this cross-curricular link and teach this skill to their pupils.

The National Numeracy Strategy gives much emphasis to the appropriate use of mathematical language (DfEE 1999b), and HMCI says that pupils in primary schools generally use mathematical vocabulary correctly and show increasing confidence in explaining how they perform calculations. With regard to special schools, rising standards are perceived by HMCI, in terms of more structured planning, the direct teaching of basic skills and a more consistent recording of pupil progress. The introduction of numeracy across the curriculum that will follow should encourage teachers to do exactly this.

The endorsement of the National Numeracy Strategy by HMCI does not mean that the techniques or the structure of the numeracy hour are necessarily suitable for *all* pupils. As with most other central initiatives, teachers of pupils with SEN have had to struggle to modify and adapt the developmental sequences of targets and teaching methods to suit their pupils, particularly those with poor language and memory skills. In this process, they have been aided by a number of publications, such as a series of pull-out supplements on the National Numeracy Strategy in the journal *Special Children*, and books on the National Numeracy Strategy for pupils with learning difficulties by Banes (2000) and Berger *et al.* (2000). The INSET materials for the National Numeracy Strategy included convincing video and workbook examples of teachers using the Numeracy Framework with pupils with SLD to MLD. Nevertheless, the struggle for many schools lies more in finding time for daily 45–60–minute sessions on mathematics in a crowded school day, and there are people who question aspects of the new orthodoxy (Watson 2001). In schools for pupils with SLD, particular problems lie in developing appropriate methods and structures for delivery of the mathematics curriculum to pupils with PMLD. The secondary phase, in whatever settings, has the opportunity to learn much from the primary phase with regard to delivery and the prevention of 'slippage' in the transition between the two phases.

The language of mathematics and teacher talk

It is important to ensure that the language ordinarily used by teachers is not a barrier to learning (Locke 1996). If a pupil has language and communication difficulties, these must be addressed. For many pupils, Makaton or other pictorial symbols may be used to assist understanding and language development (Abbott 2000; Detheridge and Detheridge 1998). Other visual clues and structures and concrete teaching apparatus will need to be used, along with the spoken word, in order to enrich pupils' vocabulary and their understanding of language. Making relationships with their ordinary knowledge about familiar things and situations ensures relevance, familiarity and a context that prevents skills being seen in isolation (Hughes 1986).

Normally, young children learn some of the vocabulary associated with mathematics before they enter their first school, and some mathematical concepts are learned long before they get any real grasp of formal numbers. The ideas seem so simple that most adults might not even consider it necessary to teach them explicitly. But pupils with learning difficulties cannot be expected to learn these simply by listening to adults, even though, paradoxically, these are words which are used frequently by adults without any realisation of the problems they may cause for pupils. Even basic counting has its pitfalls: for instance, there may be confusion between the pronoun 'one' and the number word 'one' as when someone points to a figure and says 'This one's three'. Then, there are homophones such as 'two', 'to' and 'too' as in 'Give one to Luke too'. For further examples, see Ashdown and Devereux (1990). Locke (1985) has developed a scope and sequence for teaching the vocabulary associated with various concepts – particularly words relating to space, size, time, quantity and simple number – that might be helpful for many teachers of pupils with SEN. Similar programmes have been developed by Boehm (1976) and Bracken and Myers (1986).

The 'technical' language of mathematics will need to be taught, reinforced, revised and used in all sorts of settings in order to embed it into the pupils' understanding, memory and use. A decision has to be made about what vocabulary and phrases to use, and staff must use these consistently. It will, therefore, be essential for teachers of other subjects to know when and how this is being taught, so that they may provide reinforcement and allow cross-curricular links to be made. Guidance has been published on the language of mathematics (DfEE 1999b), which lists the technical words of mathematics (such as 'angles') and other mathematics-related words (such as 'estimate'). This categorisation clearly indicates to teachers what their expectations should be of pupils. However, it assumes that there is no difficulty with the learning of language, and many pupils with SEN have difficulties both in understanding, acquiring, remembering and using language.

It is most important that teachers should have a good understanding of the linguistic problems involved in teaching mathematics. Mathematics is after all a very formal type of language. It has none of the redundancy of literary or everyday language. For instance, as Ashdown and Devereux (1990) point out, the simple utterance 'Here is a girl and her dog' contains several clues about the gender of the subject ('girl' and 'her') and the number ('girl', 'is', 'a' and 'her'); if one word is not understood, there are other clues to the meaning of the utterance. In contrast, mathematics economises on words. In the case of a statement such as 'One plus one equals two', the whole meaning is lost if a pupil misses or does not understand just one word. As a result, there is a need to expand mathematical statements and repeat them until understanding is established, and to explore with the pupils alternative words (as in 'plus' is also 'add' or 'and', and 'equals' can be 'makes') that relate to the mathematical symbols.

Number operations present a variety of linguistic and cognitive problems in terms of the vocabulary to be used and the lack of redundancy in mathematical language. Therefore, it is easier to teach addition using concrete, real-life situations and constructing sentences carefully, e.g. 'Here are two apples. Here are two more apples. There are four apples altogether.' Careful consideration must also be given to how desirable it is to introduce formal notation of number operations through workbook and paper exercises that involve a different style of language.

A variety of words with the similar and linked meanings with which pupils are familiar is needed alongside the technical mathematical words. Words that are within the pupils' experience extend their understanding and language and will enable them to talk about mathematical processes. For example, 'big', 'bigger than' and 'biggest' may be the relatively non-technical language needed by some for work on measurement, e.g. '1 metre is bigger than 50 cm', '2 metres is bigger than 1 metre', '2 metres is the biggest.' Use of other more technical words meaning 'big' may be introduced later. As another example, consider how often you would use the technically correct term 'fewer' when the lay person's terms 'less' or 'not as many as' will do.

Teachers of mathematics must remember that the mathematical language and the relationship to their world will need to be taught actively to some pupils, and constantly reinforced. Providing concrete, visual and tactile apparatus will enhance the learning process by making it easier to:

- be able to see 'long', 'longer', 'longest';
- be able to see that a 'square' has four 'sides' which are the 'same length' or 'equal length';
- be able to recognise and name a 'cone' by feeling the 'point' and 'flat, circular bottom' or 'base'.

Teachers will also need to consider the content and structure of written words and sentences. Published mathematics schemes and textbooks, even though they break down the process into small steps, can be profuse in their use of words in their effort to make explanations clear. To a pupil with a reading difficulty, this can be off-putting to say the least; an analogy would be for the teacher to be trying to learn an unfamiliar process in an unfamiliar language. The language used must be at the level of the pupil's understanding. It should be remembered that, although pupils may be able to read, hear and understand individual words, the sentence length or complexity may block the learning process. Concrete apparatus and visual diagrams need to be available and used in order to avoid any pupil experiencing a sense of frustration or failure.

Take, for example, learning to divide. This is a concept often more easily understood by using the word 'share'. Using counters, blocks, sticks, straws or any sort of concrete apparatus, counting out the 'big' number and then sharing them into the small number, making piles, and then counting the number in the piles not only allows the pupils to do the exercise practically and get the right answer, but it also brings some understanding to the concept of 'divide'. For this process, very simple language is needed and it can be presented on a worksheet or instruction sheet in visual form, either with pictorial symbols, or with simple, written language, or both, thereby providing another learning opportunity.

It is important for pupils to know what they are learning and what they should have learned by the end of the lesson or topic. If progress is to be seen by the pupils as well as the adults, there should be clear targets for learning that may be seen as relevant for the pupils. Ideally, the statements of targets need to be interpreted by the teacher into 'pupil-speak', and a visual, individual record should be seen by the pupil. Charts that can be coloured in by the pupil, which use symbols and language related to the mathematics curriculum and which can be understood by the pupil, are useful ways of recording progress, raising confidence and increasing self-esteem. These might show how many times a pupil completed an operation with or without help and would lead to identification of a next target.

Mathematics across the curriculum

Mathematics skills appear in, and are essential to, many other subjects – significantly science, geography, history, music, modern foreign languages, and design and technology. In particular:

- the skill of counting will be required in all subjects;
- the skill of measuring and reading scales – needed in science, geography, technology;
- the skill of constructing and reading graphs – needed in science, geography.

The list could go on; it is not intended to be exhaustive but rather to provoke thought within the reader.

The points to be made for teachers other than mathematics teachers are as follows:

- find out if the skill needed has been taught in mathematics;
- find out about the level of learning;
- do not assume that the skill has been learned/acquired;
- the skill may need to be re taught;
- do not assume that the skill will be transferred or generalised;
- the connection may need to be made for the pupil.

Shared knowledge about when and how skills are taught and learned is, therefore, necessary. Take the example of learning to count in French. Activities using addition and subtraction may be used to practise the skill. Calculators may be needed to allow the pupil to participate, if this mathematical skill has not been achieved and consolidated enough to think about two things at once, i.e. numbers and French. On the other hand, if the skill of adding is to be consolidated within the French lesson, time must be given to allow pupils to achieve the mathematical task and then translate. Information about the pupils from the mathematics teacher will allow this activity to be approached in a manner likely to bring success and consolidation in both subjects.

Accreditation at Key Stage 4

GCSE at Foundation Level now puts mathematics into real-life contexts, which is helpful for both those finding difficulty and those who are disaffected. Diet sheets, discounts, maps, scale drawings, VAT and the like feature in order to bring meaning and relevance, thus creating the opportunities for balance between mathematical skills in other areas of the curriculum, life skills and, thereby, mathematics as a subject in which to learn those skills. Teachers should capitalise on this, taking the opportunity for reinforcement, connection and most of all relevance. Examination boards vary regarding coursework requirements, and schools would be advised to examine the options available. Two pieces, one in Year 10 and one in Year 11 are usually required. It is possible to choose the coursework option to suit pupils' strengths, which can then be supported by the teacher at Foundation Level. The coursework is marked in-house and moderated by the examination board. The teacher can ensure that the criteria are met, at least at baseline level, and can ensure that it is presented to the pupils in an accessible, attractive and motivational way.

For those pupils who are unlikely to achieve Grade G at GCSE, Certificate of Achievement features as a method of accreditation. The latter is intended for those pupils who are at Level 3 or below. Considerable consultation and discussion is taking place at the time of writing on entry levels, which will provide access. Unlike 'Number Power' (from the Associated Examining Board), which is also a useful form of accreditation, these schemes follow National Curriculum mathematics at Foundation Level in all aspects of mathematics. This is an important feature to build and support self-esteem – doing the same as others without disapplication.

Pupils with severe to profound learning difficulties

Ashdown and Devereux (1990) and Ashdown (1990) are good sources of information about teaching mathematics to pupils with SLD and available resources. Of course, in the intervening years, other useful books have been produced, notably by Banes (2000), Berger *et al.* (2000) and Robbins (1996b). The organisation called EQUALS has produced schemes of work for pupils with MLD, SLD and PMLD (EQUALS 1999a, 1999b, 2000). And there is non-statutory guidance on the mathematics curriculum for pupils with learning difficulties that suggests aims for mathematics and appropriate activities at each key stage (QCA 2001). Added to this is a host of relevant material on teaching language and/or mathematics to other groups of pupils with SEN, or young children, such as the language programmes of Boehm (1976), Bracken and Myers (1986) and Locke (1985) and publications cited by Reynolds and Musij (2000) in an annotated bibliography for the National Numeracy Strategy.

Teachers should thus have few problems in finding materials on relevant and differentiated teaching methods to match the needs of pupils with SLD. However, mathematics teaching will continue to focus on simple skills throughout the entire school career of each pupil with SLD. Many will still be learning simple vocabulary and counting when they are well into their teenage years. Therefore, teachers are faced by the twin problems of having to teach very basic mathematics skills for some 10–15 years and, at the same time, making this an interesting experience for their pupils. They have to be imaginative in the teaching activities they design. It must be appreciated that good teaching of mathematics under such conditions is an immense challenge and poses great demands upon teachers. Even more difficulties may be experienced with regard to determining an appropriate mathematics curriculum for pupils with PMLD. These are pupils for whom the priority objectives are related to very basic communication and cognitive skills. They need to learn to:

- perceive patterns in their environment;
- be aware of things in their environment;
- inspect and explore objects;
- develop a concept of object permanence;
- be aware of the attributes of objects;
- be aware of similarities and differences of objects;
- learning names for objects and their attributes.

Specific activities may be aimed at teaching pupils with PMLD to:

- respond consistently to objects which are presented in view;
- grasp objects placed in a hand;
- manipulate and explore objects;
- visually examine parts of objects;
- use objects consistently in similar and appropriate ways;
- communicate preferences about objects used in activities;
- show awareness of the relative sizes of objects when choosing between items;
- retrieve objects hidden under covers while watching;
- show awareness of cause–effect relationships in familiar settings;
- imitate simple single actions;
- respond to instructions involving names of things;

- indicate preferences for items through gaze and/or body movements;
- imitate a sequence of two simple actions;
- use objects functionally;
- manipulate objects in ways which their attributes dictate;
- indicate 'more' and 'again'.

Learning the significance of numbers does not come easily for pupils with SLD (Ashdown 1990; Ashdown and Devereux 1990). Typical errors made when counting objects include missing out number names from the sequence, counting objects more than once, or missing objects out of the count altogether. Pupils may even say a different number from the final number in a correct count. When told to hand over a specific number of items, they often count beyond the number asked for because they fail to check mentally the number counted against the number asked for. On the whole, they make mistakes more often when giving a specified number of objects than when counting the same number of items. Thus, it is very important to have good diagnostic techniques to check for errors. Rigorous teaching techniques are needed for teaching counting skills, and counting in a variety of settings should always be encouraged. It is easy to make or buy a variety of simple number games that give plenty of opportunities for practice and that make the task of learning to count meaningful and fun (McConkey and McEvoy 1986). As well as being fun, these number games can provide repeated practice of counting and number operations. Adults or older more able children may participate in the games so that they can act as a model for following the rules of the game and give clear examples of counting. They must demonstrate and teach methods of self-checking and self-correction. If a pupil makes a mistake, they should not be told the right answer but made to check their counting.

The non-statutory guidance on mathematics for pupils with learning difficulties includes performance descriptions that may be used to demonstrate the attainments of pupils who are working towards Level 1 of the National Curriculum (QCA 2001). There are descriptions of eight levels, which show progression and which are quite specific as regards particular concepts, knowledge and skills. They enable teachers to recognise and record achievement and, to a certain extent, plan the next teaching point or learning objective. They are provided in relation to 'Using and applying number' and 'Shape, space and measure'. It remains to be seen whether they are fine-grained enough to show pupils' progress year on year; indeed, it is essential that schools develop their own methods of recording progress in relation to sequences of learning targets, but when they are, they should be cross-referenced to these progression indicators.

Teaching mathematics to pupils with MLD

The keywords at all key stages, at all ability levels, are 'access' and 'challenge'. Issues of equal opportunity include:

- enabling access to the age-appropriate mathematics PoS (wherever possible), so that the pupils can learn and be able to demonstrate the knowledge, understanding and skills;
- enabling access to knowledge, understanding and skills so that they can access aspects of other areas of the curriculum;
- enabling access to acquire knowledge, understanding and skills that will provide independent and competent living.

In order to do this, teachers of mathematics must:

- know and understand how children learn;
- know the preferred and most effective learning style of their pupils;
- be able to match these with their teaching methods/styles/strategies;
- have a variety of teaching strategies;
- be able to break down processes into small steps;
- have a scheme of work, into which these small steps are built;
- understand the value and necessity of repetition and re-enforcement;
- use concrete and visual apparatus;
- understand and use multisensory teaching;
- provide opportunities for over learning;
- differentiate;
- be aware of the pace of learning;
- provide opportunities for pupils to record what they are learning in different ways;
- provide opportunities for different methods of assessment;
- know the reading capabilities of pupils;
- know the language levels of pupils;
- make connections for the pupils to other subjects and life-relevant situations in more than words;
- provide opportunities for exploratory learning and investigation;
- know the key concepts and skills that are to be taught;
- ensure that the pupils know what they are going to learn and what their target is in relation to the National Curriculum.

The foregoing list might seem a lot to take into consideration when there is a prescribed curriculum and a set amount of time to complete it – but doing so is essential. Moreover, each class will have a variation in previous experience, knowledge, understanding and skills, which also must be taken into account. Within each class, pupils will have different needs, different targets, but are taught as a group. This is true of any class at any ability level, and in order to experience success in teaching and for the pupils to experience success in learning, the teacher must differentiate the lesson. The differentiated performance criteria for summative measurement of the attainments of pupils with SEN (DfEE/QCA 1998) are a relevant and useful tool at any key stage and in any setting for pupils with MLD, both as a way of establishing baselines and as a way of determining next teaching objectives.

Mathematics teachers in mainstream schools should try to work with their learning support teachers and/or teachers from special schools to enhance their knowledge and understanding of pupils' learning difficulties and needs for the planning and delivery of the mathematics curriculum. Sharing expertise in both the subject and the teaching of pupils with learning difficulties provides professional development opportunities that benefit both pupils and teachers, and such an approach will have positive effects for schools in terms of the levels of achievement of all their pupils and, hence, on the so-called league tables for schools. In the climate of inclusion, this element cannot be disregarded. In initial stages, the collaborative work with a teacher of SEN can be of great benefit to the mathematics teacher; but without the mathematics teacher, key elements of the mathematics curriculum may be lost. Creativity through concrete and visual materials and in the use of language, referred to earlier in this chapter, is of especial relevance here.

Table 3.3 shows a format that can be an aid to differentiation, guiding the teacher through what needs to be taken into account and enabling the teaching style to meet both the pupils' needs and the curriculum needs. The chart can be used for a class or group, or individual pupils, to plan a lesson. In the column headed 'Must be able to:' is noted the absolute core of the teaching objective for knowledge and concept. Other extension objectives are recorded in the columns headed 'Should be able to:' and 'Could be able to:'. The row headed 'Skills' is intended to identify the skills that are needed and that will need to be taught or reinforced in each of the sections. 'Teaching strategies' should include how it will be done, and the materials and apparatus used in each of the sections. 'Recording' will show how and where the pupils will record information, taking into account difficulties and the amount to be recorded. 'Assessment of learning' will include how assessment will take place and the criteria to be adopted (e.g. how many right answers? can the pupil measure? etc.).

Preventing failure

Preventing failure starts for all pupils at the beginning. Building upon previous experience and allowing for a lack of previous experience at the nursery and reception stages is the key to preventing 'mathematics phobia' and to creating a positive attitude towards mathematics, dispelling feelings of anxiety (often evident, particularly in pupils with SEN). Failure to address these issues might bring difficulties with the learning process for any pupil in mathematics.

When teaching mathematics to pupils with SEN, consideration must be given to:

- establishing a baseline of previous attainment and using it;
- teaching a concept or skill in more than one way;
- teaching styles;
- pupils' learning styles;
- experiencing different aspects in different ways;
- pace;
- the use of concrete and visual materials;
- making clear the relevance of a mathematics element to life and other subjects;
- the oral and written language;
- the pupils' language knowledge;
- the link to previous learning and experience;
- consolidation;
- practice;
- pupils' understanding of symbols;
- assessment;
- access;
- achievement marked in small steps;
- challenge;
- targets;
- enjoyment;
- progression;
- continuity.

Table 3.3 Lesson: Area of 4–sided regular shapes

	Must be able to:	**Should be able to:**	**Could be able to:**
Knowledge	Use cm on squared paper and on a ruler Recognise a new measure (cm^2) Name regular shapes: square, rectangle, etc.	Use other units of measure Recognise a new measure (m^2) Recognise, find and use terms: length and width/breadth	Make representative drawings of greater distances Make irregular shapes from regular shapes Use length and width to work out each area and total
Concept	Understand that area is the measurement of the space inside shapes Understand what is meant by 'regular shape'	Understand that all regular shapes have length and width	Make representative figures (not scale) Understand relationship between regular and irregular shapes
Skills	Count (squares inside shape) Recognise and name shapes (square, rectangle) Draw shapes with ruler	Multiply Understand length and width Use different units on ruler: mm, cm Draw from given measurements	Multiply, divide and add Divide irregular shapes into regular shapes Understand that 100 mm = 10 cm, etc.
Teaching strategies	Recognise and name shapes on the board together Recognise and name shapes on squared paper Count squares along shape sides and copy shapes Count squares to get area of a shape representing room Pattern for working out and recording	Introduce terms: length and width Area = length x width; link with 'long' and 'wide' Simple 1 x 1, 2 x 1, etc. Move into more difficult sums (could use calculator) Use different units of measure to measure different regular objects Use prepared sheets, moving on to drawing	Represent a room on paper Represent on paper other regular shapes that are familiar Place squares together to work out number of tiles needed to cover floor Find familiar shape that is not regular Divide up an L-shape on the board into regular shapes Process on paper to copy later; go through Use dominoes fixed together, separate, etc.
Recording	Produce definition that is written; cut and paste if necessary Provide sheet with shapes on to write on Use as model for writing on paper – templates	Copy in books – definition Provide sheets with shapes on – set out length and width to fill in answer Make own drawing in books, with support as needed (e.g. templates)	Write own definition Use sheets with larger shapes Use sheets with irregular shapes divided, then own divisions – templates

Table 3.3 Lesson: Area of 4–sided regular shapes (continued)

Assessment of learning	Must be able to:	Should be able to:	Could be able to:
	Count squares correctly every time Use correct term every time Draw from copy: 80% accuracy Draw from numbers – 70% accuracy Work out floor covering in cm2	Work out area from length x width using calculator: 100% accuracy Draw accurately from measures: 90% accuracy Name units: 100% accuracy Give correct answer without calculator: 80% accuracy	Draw representative drawings: 100% accuracy Divide irregular shapes: 90% accuracy Work out areas and add using calculator: 100% accuracy Work out areas and add without calculator: 80% accuracy Work out floor covering in units and number of tiles per m²: 90% accuracy

The need for pupils to be able to see their progress in relation to themselves is essential to their continued interest and motivation. The development of interest, motivation and enjoyment in mathematics, as well as of an awareness of its use and relevance, is paramount in achieving success within the mathematics curriculum. All teachers – and parents – have a part to play in this.

Parents

Learning takes place not only in the classroom. There are endless opportunities to talk about mathematics and to practise skills in the home and at other times with parents. Many parents recognise this and, in fact, take all opportunities open to them.

It is understandable, however, if this does not occur sufficiently often; there may be other issues to consider. In particular, parents of pupils with SEN may feel:

- that there is no point;
- that their children are not capable of doing it;
- that they don't know how to do it themselves;
- that they cannot help;
- that they are no good at mathematics themselves;
- negative toward school generally, or mathematics in particular, because of their own experiences of failure.

Some parents may have expectations that are too high and that cause them to pressurise their children too much, bringing negative reactions. Some parents may have expectations that are too low, and under-challenge and over-reward their children, with the result that the children feel patronised and negative. And some parents themselves have had poor experiences with mathematics and transmit negative attitudes to their children. It is, therefore, important that the school works with the parents to change attitudes, gives them information and realistic expectations, as well as the confidence and skills to provide relevant and valuable experiences to their children.

The opportunities are endless: just a few examples of the mathematical thinking that parents might foster at home include:

- 'Lets count the number of cars, spoonfuls, etc.'
- 'Is it full or empty? Half or quarter?'
- 'What shape is that garden, spire, building?'
- 'What is the time now? How long until 5'o clock?'
- 'Find me the longest piece of string. How long is it?'

Carpenter (in this book) and Hornby (1995, 2000) each suggest a number of ways of involving parents in their children's education. For all sorts of reasons and in all sorts of ways, parents may need enabling. Schools might give thought to the strategies set out in the rest of this section, among others that they advocate. And if parents are enabled, the promotion of a positive approach will have a beneficial effect upon learning, achievement and pupil-and-parent self-esteem – not to mention that of the teacher! Thereby, both parents and teachers may go quite some way towards the process of re-signification of pupils with SEN as learners.

Parent workshops

Parent workshops can:

- help parents understand mathematics and do it themselves;
- help parents understand how to help their children;
- help parents understand and see what their children *can* do.

Joint parent and pupil workshops

Joint workshops can help by:

- allowing parents to actually see what their children can do;
- giving scope for learning something new together;
- giving access to a computer in a variety of ways;
- enabling the sharing of the language of mathematics;
- providing a starting point for doing mathematics-related activities at home.

Other means

Two other means worthy of mention are as follows:

- numeracy or mathematics days in the holidays, where parents can join in for part of the time;
- creating mathematics trails with parents, which they can do with their children.

References

Abbott, C. (2000) *Symbols Now.* Leamington Spa: Widgit Software.
Ashdown (1990) 'Teaching the core subjects through interactive approaches: mathematics', in Smith, B. (ed.) *Interactive Approaches to Teaching the Core Subjects: The National Curriculum*

for pupils with severe and moderate learning difficulties. Portishead, Bristol, UK: Lame Duck Publishing.

Ashdown, R. and Devereux. K. (1990) 'Teaching mathematics to pupils with severe learning difficulties', in Baker, D. and Bovair, K. (eds) *Making the Special Schools Ordinary? (Vol. 2): Practitioners changing special education.* Basingstoke: Falmer Press.

Banes, D. (2000) *Spiral Mathematics.* Tamworth: NASEN Publications.

Berger, A. *et al.* (2000) *Implementing the National Numeracy Strategy for Pupils with Learning Difficulties: Access to the daily mathematics lesson.* London: David Fulton Publishers.

Boehm, A. E. (1976) *The Boehm Resource Guide for Basic Concept Teaching.* New York: The Psychological Corporation.

Bracken, B.A. and Myers, D. K. (1986) *Bracken Concept Development Program.* New York: The Psychological Corporation.

DES (1982) *Mathematics Counts* (The Cockroft Report). London: HMSO.

Detheridge, T. and Detheridge, M. (1998) *Literacy Through Symbols: Improving access for children and adults.* London: David Fulton Publishers.

DfEE (1999a) *The National Numeracy Strategy: Framework for teaching mathematics from Reception to Year 6.* London: DfEE.

DfEE (1999b) *Mathematical Vocabulary.* London: DfEE.

DfEE/QCA (1998) *Supporting the Target Setting Process: Effective target setting for pupils with special educational needs.* London: DfEE /QCA.

DfEE/QCA (1999a) *The National Curriculum: Handbook for primary teachers in England.* London: DfEE/QCA.

DfEE/QCA (1999b) *The National Curriculum: Handbook for secondary teachers in England.* London: DfEE/QCA.

EQUALS (1999a) *Schemes of Work: Mathematics for pupils with PMLD.* North Shields, Tyne and Wear: EQUALS.

EQUALS (1999b) *Schemes of Work: Mathematics for pupils with SLD.* North Shields, Tyne and Wear: EQUALS.

EQUALS (2000) *Schemes of Work: Mathematics for pupils with MLD.* North Shields, Tyne and Wear: EQUALS.

Hornby, G. (1995) *Working with Parents of Children with Special Needs.* London: Cassell.

Hornby, G. (2000) *Improving Parental Involvement.* London: Cassell.

Hughes, M. (1986) *Children and Number: Difficulties in learning mathematics.* Oxford: Basil Blackwell.

Locke, A. (1985) *Living Language.* Windsor: NFER–Nelson.

Locke, A. (1996) 'Speech and language impairments', in Upton, G. and Varma, V. (eds) *Stresses in Special Educational Needs Teachers.* Aldershot: Arena.

McConkey, R. and McEvoy, J. (1986) *Count Me In* (video and workbook). Dublin: St. Michael's House.

OFSTED (2001) *The Annual Report of Her Majesty's Chief Inspector for Education: Standards and quality in education 1999/2000.* London: The Stationery Office.

O'Toole, B. and O'Toole, P. (1989) 'How accessible is Level 1 Maths?', *British Journal of Special Education* **16**(3),115–18.

QCA (2000) *Curriculum Guidance on the Foundation Stage.* London: DfEE/QCA.

QCA (2001) *Planning, Teaching and Assessing the Curriculum for Pupils with learning difficulties: Mathematics.* London: DfEE/QCA.

Reynolds, D. and Mujis, D. (2000) *The National Numeracy Strategy: Annotated bibliography.* London: DfEE.

Robbins, B. (1996a) 'Mathematics', in Carpenter, B., *et al.* (eds) *Enabling Access: Effective teaching and learning for pupils with learning difficulties,* 1st edn. London: David Fulton Publishers.

Robbins, B. (1996b) *Mathsteps* (3rd edn.). Wisbech: LDA.

Skemp, R. (1971) *Psychology of Learning Mathematics.* Harmondsworth: Penguin.

Watson, A. (2001) 'Editorial', *Support for Learning* **16**(1), 2–3.

Chapter 4

Science

Ron Ritchie

Introduction

When the National Curriculum was first announced in 1986, the inclusion of science as a core subject came as a surprise to many teachers. At that time, science was effectively an 'optional extra' in the curricula of the majority of primary and special schools. However, now that we are in the new century, science can be regarded as one of the success stories of the National Curriculum. It has become generally accepted by teachers that all pupils have an entitlement to a high quality of science education, although there is still some way to go to make such an entitlement a practical reality.

The government had originally indicated its intention of introducing 'Science for all' in a policy document (DES 1985). This set an agenda covering breadth, balance, relevance, differentiation, equal opportunities, continuity, progression, links across the curriculum, teaching methods and assessment that led to the science National Curriculum. This chapter explores the implications of a science curriculum for all pupils aged from 5 to 16. It addresses the particular opportunities and challenges that this provides for teachers working in special schools in the context of the latest version of the science National Curriculum (DfEE/QCA 1999).

The development of science in the curricula of special schools has, in some respects, been slower than in mainstream schools. However, it has always had its advocates, who saw it as a means of enriching the curriculum as well as adding breadth, and who recognised the enthusiasm that pupils with special educational needs often had for science (Carter 1994). Indeed, science was argued to have particular benefits for such pupils.

When the National Curriculum was first introduced, guidance material from the National Curriculum Council (NCC) stated that 'activities in science have characteristics which will help pupils with SEN achieve success' (NCC 1992). The following reasons are often cited: science activities are based on direct first-hand experiences; science provides opportunities for children to make sense of the natural world, the made world and themselves; skills, knowledge and understanding can be developed in small steps through practical activity, so helping concentration; science activities can capture the imagination and may reduce behavioural problems; working in groups can encourage participation and interpersonal communication. The current curriculum guidelines for pupils with learning difficulties (DfEE/QCA 2001) emphasise several of these features.

Teaching science poses considerable challenges for many teachers, including those working in special schools. Perhaps of most significance is some teachers' lack of confidence to teach science. This results from a number of factors, but especially lack of subject knowledge (OFSTED 1998). The perceived problems of organising science in a practical way also inhibits its development. Teachers may recognise the importance of their pupils learning through doing, but they often find such activities difficult to manage.

The reasons for the somewhat uncertain development of science in some special schools becomes apparent when one considers the lack of resources in some schools, lack of suitable accommodation and technician support for older pupils, concerns about health and safety, lack of in-service education and training opportunities for teachers, and lack of guidance in the literature. Indeed, on this last point, two recent general handbooks on primary science – Cross and Peet (1997) and Sherrington (1998) – make no more than passing reference to working with pupils with SEN. The introduction of science as a core subject has not guaranteed opportunities for high-quality learning in science for all pupils.

The nature of science and science education

The importance of science is well articulated in the introduction to the latest version of the National Curriculum (DfEE/QCA 1999):

> Science stimulates and excites pupils' curiosity about phenomena and events in the world around them. It also satisfies this curiosity with knowledge. Because science links direct practical experience with ideas, it can engage learners at many levels.

The key purpose of science is to enable humankind to understand the physical and biological world. In this sense it could be argued that science is clearly of relevance to everyone. Science provides a particular means, or method, of gaining knowledge and understanding through a process of enquiry or investigation. This usually involves the collection of empirical evidence to test out ideas, or hypotheses, in order to falsify or support them, drawing on a range of skills such as predicting, estimating and measuring, fair testing, recording, and pattern seeking. Such skills are used by scientists working on new explanations for the behaviour of materials in a laboratory, or by pupils learning about the properties of materials in the classroom.

Scientists spend much of their time on routine laboratory work, perhaps of an observational nature. This can also be reflected in the way that science is taught. Regardless of the nature of pupils' particular difficulties, it is important for them to use their senses effectively – indeed, the 'sensory curriculum' is commonplace in special schools as a means of facilitating this aim. For example, much work associated with the early sensory cognitive areas of the curriculum for pupils with PMLD have direct links with science (Gibson 1991; Hemmens 1999). Science provides a context for pupils' observations to be carried out with purpose.

Scientists, like children, are curious; their observations often lead to questions that can be answered by investigating. Fostering pupils' curiosity is a key aim of science education, as indicated above. It is, of course, more challenging with some pupils than others. However, most pupils have a natural interest in the world around them, which can be built on through science. Attitudes (such as curiosity, perseverance, independence and respect for evidence) are fundamental to learning. Fostering such attitudes can be a positive outcome of science work and can contribute to pupils' self-esteem and learning in other areas of the curriculum.

An understanding of 'science' as a process leading to provisional understanding, rather than as a fixed body of knowledge, is another potential benefit of science education. The way that pupils work scientifically is as important in terms of learning as the ideas about science that they develop. Supporting pupils to approach activities systematically, perhaps using a framework such as 'plan/do/review', can make an important metacognitive contribution to their learning, helping them understand *how* they learn as well as *what* they learn. Science provides opportunities for pupils to work at their own level, testing their ideas systematically alongside those of others. The way in which they work can, in many ways, mirror the work of real scientists.

Pupils' learning in science

Pupils learn best in science when they engage in a practical way with the world around them. However, experience alone is rarely enough; we need to recognise the part that communication and the social context play. The way in which learners interact with each other, and with their teacher or other adults, is an essential element of the learning equation. Over the last 15 years, a great deal of research has been conducted into pupils' learning in science (e.g. CLIS 1988–92; SPACE 1990–98). Bell (1999) reports on similar research with pupils with SEN, linked to the Accessing Science for Special Education Needs (ASSEN) Project. From all of this research, it is evident that learners (of all ages and all levels of capability) approach new experiences in science with existing ideas about the world, and that these ideas, however naive and undeveloped, will significantly affect their future learning.

Learning is an *active* process of structuring existing understanding prior to restructuring ideas as a result of new experiences or teacher intervention. Consequently, research would suggest that it is important for teachers to elicit pupils' existing ideas and to use these to inform decisions about appropriate interventions. 'Starting from where the learner is' is hardly a new idea. However, the insights offered by research concerning the nature of pupils' existing ideas and the prevalence of 'common alternative ideas' (again, according to Bell (1999), these are commonplace across all ability levels) can help teachers plan their science work.

For example, it is common for pupils to think: that their eyes actively send out light when they see; that plants get their food from the soil; that evaporation is caused by water soaking into a surface; that electricity comes from both terminals of a battery and 'clashes' in a bulb; that 'cold' is something that travels into the body when a cold object is touched. Each of these has implications for the way we teach. To focus on the evaporation example, research (SPACE 1991) indicates that another common explanation among young learners of why the level of water goes down when left to stand in a tank was that small creatures came out at night and drank the water. Their teachers asked them how this could be tested. One group's suggestion was to leave a lump of cheese by the tank because, according to the pupils, a small creature would be sure to eat it; if it did not get eaten, an alternative explanation for the fall in water level would be needed. An activity like this is unlikely to be found in a traditional science book but could be argued to be an appropriate one for these pupils.

Research like this has led to the development of 'constructivist' approaches to teaching science (Ollerenshaw and Ritchie 1997). Such approaches usually include the following phases:

- *orientation* – the teacher sets the scene and seeks to arouse learners' interest and curiosity;
- *elicitation* – the teacher helps learners find out, clarify and share what they already think (structuring their existing ideas);
- *intervention* – the teacher encourages learners to test their ideas, and to extend, develop and replace them (restructuring their understanding);
- *review* – the teacher helps learners recognise the significance of what they have found out/learnt and how they have learnt it (metacognitive dimension);
- *application* – the teacher helps learners to relate what they have learned to their everyday lives.

Each learner actively constructs a unique understanding of the world, therefore learning should, as far as possible, be differentiated. Each learner will have a unique starting point and will follow a unique route to understanding. Progression in science is not something that can be easily documented as a linear path. Take the following example related to dissolving a spoonful of sugar in a mug of tea: does the level go up or stay the same? Very young children will usually say the level remains the same because the sugar 'disappears'. Slightly older children often claim that the level goes up, based on an understanding of conservation of matter – the sugar 'must go somewhere'. Pupils who have met and understood ideas concerning the particulate nature of materials through school science will, like the first group, recognise that the level stays the same, but have a more sophisticated explanation. In other words, as children learn, they may go 'backwards' before they progress. Ensuring progression in science requires a teacher to make an appropriate intervention based on evidence of a pupil's existing skills, knowledge and understanding. Eliciting pupils' existing understanding and skill level in order to plan appropriate next steps is ongoing formative assessment that is integral to teaching. An effective teacher has to be a good assessor; the two go hand in hand (Ritchie 1997 and 1998).

The approach discussed above has important implications when working with some pupils with SEN. They may need particular support in tackling investigations, especially if they have experienced failure in mainstream classes or been banned from practical work in laboratories, and have thereby established negative attitudes. Initially, such pupils may react more positively to learning basic scientific ideas – taking pride in being able to remember them when tested. Another problem arises from asking some pupils to express their own, perhaps naive, ideas in front of their peers. A fear of failure is common, and strategies for more private elicitation of existing ideas may be needed. However, the ASSEN Project (Bell 1999) found that teachers were often surprised by the level of understanding expressed by children with SEN during the elicitation phase. Bell warns that elicitation needs to be approached cautiously – closed questions may be a preferable starting point to more open ones; care needs to be given to the choice of language and the pupils' familiarity with that language; thought needs to be given to the nature of activities used to elicit existing ideas.

Pupils' fear of failure is also a reason why too much emphasis on pupils devising investigations to test their own ideas, before their confidence in science is established, could be detrimental. A more appropriate starting point will often be an investigation to test the teacher's idea or a teacher-directed illustrative activity. Some pupils may well hold unexpected and unusual ideas that are difficult to discover and even harder to modify. Pupils determinedly hold on to their own ideas unless they have good reasons for changing them. Those with SEN often exhibit a more irregular profile of achievement than others. They may find it harder to understand the links between ideas – for example, the common process of melting in the context of snow, butter and chocolate. Their learning can be more of a patchwork of concepts that may never link up. The challenge for a 'constructivist' teacher is to support the learner as she or he builds up a cognitive map of 'scientific' ideas that progressively gets closer to accepted scientific ideas.

Another important aspect to children's learning in science relates to learning styles (Smith 1996), multiple intelligences (Gardner 1993) and the emotional dimension (Goleman 1996). There is increasing evidence about the significance of children having different preferred styles and the need for teachers to identify these and work with them. In classrooms, according to Smith (1996, p. 34) it is likely that about one-third of learners will have preferences for using one of the senses, such as sound (34% of learners), sight (29%) and feeling (37%) (audible, visual and kinaesthetic learning). The first two are usually catered for reasonably regularly but the latter is usually less common.

An effective teacher will identify and work with a range of learning styles in any one topic. Pickard (1998) provides some good examples of supporting different preferred learning styles through multisensory approaches to science. She offers particularly good examples of ways of linking music to children's learning in science – for example, children writing a simple piece of music to illustrate the life-cycle of a butterfly whereby they contrast the energetic caterpillar phase with the silent chrysalis phase. She provides evidence of pupils having fun as they learn science; the emotions involved are strong and therefore the learning is more likely to be retained longer – memory and emotions are linked to the same part of the brain. Other senses (e.g. taste and smell) can also be used effectively in classrooms.

Hemmens (1999) describes her work with children with severe and profound learning difficulties and outlines the multisensory journeys she set up for her children linked to science. Her analysis of individual children's responses to these environments (for example, one representing 'a desert' with suitable smells, tastes, sounds and sights) makes fascinating reading and illustrates dramatically how children can benefit from opportunities to use all of their senses as well as showing practical ways in which this can be managed in the classroom.

Science in the National Curriculum

The history of the National Curriculum for science is a complicated one (Ritchie 1996), with eleven versions prior to the current requirements (DfEE/QCA 1999). All versions have sought to provide a balanced science curriculum that included two main aspects, one concerned with 'behaving scientifically' (the process dimension) and the other related to the knowledge and understanding that pupils should obtain (the content dimension). In the latest version, we are informed (DfEE/QCA 1999, p. 16) that:

> During key stage 1 pupils observe, explore and ask questions about living things, materials and phenomena. They begin to work together to collect evidence to help them answer questions and to link them to simple scientific ideas. They evaluate evidence and consider whether tests

and comparisons are fair. They use reference materials to find out more about scientific ideas. They share their ideas and communicate them using scientific language, drawings, charts and tables.

Furthermore, the same publication states (DfEE/QCA 1999, p. 21) that in Key Stage 2:

[The pupils] begin to make links between ideas and explain things using simple models and theories. They apply their knowledge and understanding of scientific ideas to familiar phenomena, everyday things and their personal health. They begin to think about the positive and negative effects of scientific and technological developments on the environment and in other contexts. They carry out more systematic investigations, working on their own and with others.

The programmes of study for each key stage are divided into four areas (with reference below to Key Stages 1 and 2 only):

- Sc1 Scientific Enquiry – what pupils should be taught about ideas and evidence in science; for example, the importance of collecting evidence from observations and measurements at Key Stage 1, and the investigative skills that they need for planning, obtaining and presenting evidence; considering evidence and evaluating within their scientific enquiries;
- Sc2 Life Processes and Living Things – what pupils should be taught about life processes, humans and other animals, green plants, variation and classification, and living things in their environment;
- Sc3 Materials and their Properties – what pupils should be taught about grouping and classifying materials, changing materials, separating mixtures of materials (Key Stage 2 only);
- Sc4 Physical Processes – what pupils should be taught about electricity (and magnetism at Key Stage 3), forces and motion, light and sound, the Earth and beyond (Key Stage 2).

There is also a section in the PoS (common to all subjects) labelled 'Breadth of Study'. This stresses that knowledge, skills and understanding (in this context, about science) should be taught through a range of domestic and environmental contexts that are familiar and of interest to pupils. It also refers to links with ICT (which is much more evident in the PoS for Sc1–4 of this version of the National Curriculum than any previous) and reminds teachers that first-hand and secondary data sources are relevant for scientific investigations. Finally, it addresses aspects of communication and of health and safety in science.

The first four areas (Sc1–4) are designated as attainment targets (ATs) in terms of the assessment requirements and, for each, level descriptions are provided that are to be used by teachers to make summative end-of-key-stage assessments on a 'best fit' basis, although they can also serve a formative function. The guidance on science for pupils with learning difficulties (QCA 2001) includes additional descriptors, which teachers of pupils with learning difficulties will find more useful. These provide detailed statements describing the achievements of these pupils at eight levels (designated P1–P8) leading to National Curriculum level 1. For example, Level P1 includes reference to 'encountering activities' and 'reflex responses'.

Additionally, as referred to in other chapters, there is a section at the back of the new orders entitled 'Inclusion: providing effective learning opportunities for all pupils'. This mainly generic advice includes two specific references to science – for example, how to address problems that pupils with hearing deficiency will have with PoS related to sound and, similarly, how the PoS for light may need special attention for those with limited vision. There is further advice in the non-statutory guidance, emphasising how science for pupils with learning difficulties can be promoted through: the use of resources (including ICT) to increase pupils' knowledge of their surroundings; the use of specialist aids and equipment; support from adults and peers; adaptation of tasks and environments; awareness of pace at which pupils work; and achieving a balance of consistency and challenge to meet individual needs (QCA 2001).

It is likely that many pupils with SLD/MLD will spend much of their time in science working within Levels 1 and 2, and therefore this is the focus of the next few subsections. Finally, it is important to remember that the National Curriculum is not the *whole* curriculum, nor should it restrict pupils' learning opportunities. There are aspects of science that teachers may wish to cover even though they are not statutory requirements. The National Curriculum offers a framework for science that seeks to ensure continuity between classes and schools and to support teachers in planning for progression. It is not a 'right answer', nor does it prescribe the only opportunities pupils should be offered.

Scientific enquiry (Sc1)

One of the battles that the profession won during the evolution of the National Curriculum was the retention of a 'process' strand, despite political pressure to restrict the science curriculum to its content. The importance of pupils behaving scientifically has already been stressed; however, the inextricable links between the two aspects of science must not be lost. The key purpose of behaving scientifically is to gain knowledge and understanding. The development of process skills is best (although not always) in the context of activities that are also intended to improve pupils' knowledge and understanding.

Pupils' learning in Sc1 will result from a variety of different types of practical work:

- observation activities;
- exploratory activities (structured or unstructured);
- collecting data (plants on a field) or doing surveys (favourite foods);
- teacher-devised and teacher-directed investigations;
- illustrative activities, planned by a teacher and carried out by pupils;
- focused practical tasks to develop and practise particular skills;
- teacher demonstrations;
- research using first-hand and/or secondary sources, including TV and video, books, ICT and other people's/pupils' earlier investigations;
- pupil-devised investigations.

All these have their place and can support and lead into each other (Ritchie 1995). For pupils with SEN, some of these approaches will be more appropriate than others. Often, exploratory activities will be of most value to pupils with SEN. Pupil-devised investigations offer potential, but only if the pupils are ready to deal with the demands involved. If these investigations become too complex, any development of new knowledge and understanding may get lost in pupils' attempts to deal with the sophistication of the skills and processes involved. Therefore, at times, teacher-directed activities may be more successful in developing specific knowledge and understanding (linked to Sc2–4). Similarly, a task focused on learning Sc1 skills and processes should be planned to ensure that the demands on pupils for knowledge and understanding are not too demanding, so that they can concentrate their effort on understanding the factors involved and the fairness of their test. The use of secondary sources should not be seen, necessarily, as a compromise and less valuable than first-hand experiences. For example, video or ICT may allow 'investigations' of the natural world or hazardous phenomena that are simply not possible for pupils through practical work.

As has already been noted, the 'sensory curriculum' (Longhorn 1991) provides a good starting point for science work in special schools. It encourages the development of all the senses and can be implemented through science activities. Such work can have the added advantage of drawing attention to enhanced skills of certain pupils; for example, the hearing of a pupil who is partially sighted. In order to provide a variety of opportunities for pupils to use their senses, many schools build up resource banks of suitable collections, such as shiny things, strong-smelling items, scratchy objects, squashy objects, smooth objects, things that make sounds, containers, wooden objects, metal objects, toys, elastic items, bottles, fasteners, markers, strings and threads, gloves, footwear, sugars, powders and breakfast cereals. Each of these can be used to practise and develop observation using particular senses, or mixed for more open-ended activities. Pupils should be encouraged to share their experiences in whatever way they can, and be supported in using appropriate vocabulary (when possible). Activities linked to these collections should be systematically built into pupils' programmes, ensuring that there is adequate time, space and adult support available. (For more detailed guidance on developing auditory, visual, kinaesthetic and olfactory awareness within Sc1, see Jones *et al.* 1993.) The school environment – inside and out – offers opportunities for extending observational activities such as these, or as a starting point for such work.

After basic experiences, with a focus on observation skills, some pupils will be ready to use collections of objects in other ways. They can be supported in a range of exploratory activities, using skills such as sorting, classifying, trying things out and, ideally, raising questions and talking about their ideas. Such work has considerable potential for pupils working within Levels 1 and 2. As an example, consider the following sequence of work with a collection of fruits (developed from a case study in Ollerenshaw and Ritchie 1997) for a small group of pupils working with their teacher or another adult. It can be adapted for the particular needs of the pupils involved and spread over more than one session. Provide the pupils with a collection of about six to eight different fruits, including some uncommon ones. Invite the pupils to handle the collection and talk about each item: *What are they called? What do you notice about each? How does it feel? What smell (or taste) does it have?* Use a 'feely bag' to focus on the feel of each. Give them plenty of time, and allow them to follow their own lines of discussion or activity. Encourage them to share what they already think or know about fruit. When they need more guidance, ask them to choose two examples that are different and say why. Ask them to choose two that have something in common. Devise other 'games' linked to similarities and differences. Introduce activities to encourage the pupils to order the collection: biggest to smallest, lightest to heaviest, thickest to thinnest, etc. Their work could be recorded in a variety of ways – drawing around, sticking on pictures, etc. Devise memory games (e.g. 'Kim's game'), perhaps played blindfold. *Which examples can be identified by their touch or smell?* Sort the collection yourself using an obvious criterion (shape) and ask them to decide why you have put them in the groups that you have. Now ask the pupils to think of ways to sort the collection into two or more groups. Suggestions might be colour, those eaten peeled or unpeeled, smoothness of surface or whether the pupils predict there are seeds or stones inside (later tested by cutting each in half). The pupils could be asked to record their method of sorting in some way (for example, drawing them in two shopping-basket outlines). The next stage might be to play '20 questions': tell the pupils you have chosen one fruit, in your head, and they have to find out which, but you will only answer their questions with 'yes' or 'no'. If this is successful, one of the pupils can choose an item for others to guess. More capable pupils could develop this work into simple identification trees, perhaps using a computer program (see Ollerenshaw and Ritchie 1997, p. 110).

Raising questions of a more open-ended type than those involved above would be the next stage of development. Brainstorm questions that the pupils have about the collection. Encourage *How?*, *Why?*, *What will happen if ...?* questions. The pupils' questions could be written down and discussed. How can they be answered? For example, some by looking (*Can you see where it was attached to a tree?*), some by observing over a period of time (*Does the apple stay shiny?*), some by looking in books or asking someone (*Which countries do oranges come from?*) – and some may not have an answer (*Where did the first apple come from?*). The 'best' questions from a scientific point of view are those that can be answered by carrying out some kind of investigation or test (*Does it contain seeds? Does it float? Does it bruise if dropped? Why do some fruits go rotten before others?*). It may require considerable help before pupils can raise such questions and devise ways of answering them – but it is an important goal.

Another approach to planning Sc1 activities for pupils with SEN is to break down the statements in the PoS into component parts and think of a range of activities that will support learning in each part. For example, at Key Stage 2, pupils should be taught 'to ask questions that can be investigated scientifically and decide how to find answers to them' (DfEE/QCA 1999, p. 21). This leads to components such as the following that can assist planning:

- What kinds of questions and what help do pupils need in 'framing' or 'building' questions? (How? Why? What will happen if?)
- What will stimulate questions? (First-hand experience or secondary sources.)
- Who will support the pupil in asking questions (teacher, other adult helpers, peers)?
- How might the questions be communicated? (Talk, draw, make, write, act, sing, sign.)
- How can questions be analysed? (Scientifically or non-scientifically – those that can be answered by observing, watching, testing, asking others, looking in books or can't be answered.)
- How might questions or ideas be turned into ones that can be investigated? (Turn into 'action' questions, simplify, limit the options or items, think of analogies, select more appropriate equipment.)
- What support do pupils need in carrying out an investigation? (Peer group discussion, adult prompts, adult guidance, adult demonstration.)
- What kinds of investigations might be involved? (Simple tests, repeated tests, one-off tests, observations over a period, collaborative or individual tests.)

In the context of the work with fruit, a pupil may have said, 'I like bananas best'. The teacher could facilitate learning in this aspect of the PoS by asking the pupil whether she or he thought others did as well. The question, *How could we find out?* could lead to a simple investigation into other pupils' preferences, recorded on a tick chart.

Jones *et al.* (1993) provide a thorough treatment of the previous National Curriculum orders using this method (described as 'milestones' to each statement at Levels 1 and 2), and their analysis and useful examples remain highly relevant to the new orders. A similar approach to amplifying statements in this way can be taken to the level descriptions (Russell 1995). The scheme of work for science (QCA 1998) also provides some valuable guidance to support planning, with clear outcomes identified for a range of activities linked to specific aspects of the PoS. As mentioned above, for teachers of pupils with learning difficulties, guidance has been produced to support teachers in using the National Curriculum orders (QCA 2001). However, this guidance is somewhat limited, although sound, in its treatment of Sc1.

The emphasis of this section has been on pupils working within Levels 1 and 2 of Sc1. For further guidance on devising more complex investigations by pupils, see the guidance by the Association of Science Education (ASE 1994).

Knowledge and understanding (Sc2–4)

The links between the process and content of science have already been stressed. It is evident that pupils will, potentially, be developing new knowledge and understanding in the context of any of the practical activities discussed above. This section addresses other content areas of science.

Life skills is a common and important aspect of special schools' curricula. Much of the work related to this theme has direct links with science. For example, the following areas are included in the PoS for Sc2 (Key Stages 1 and 2):

- that humans need food and water to stay alive (1:2b);
- that taking exercise and eating the right types and amount of food help humans to keep healthy (1:2c);
- the role of therapeutic drugs and medicine (1:2d);
- that humans can produce offspring and that these offspring grow into adults (1:2f);
- the function and care of teeth (2:2a);
- that tobacco, alcohol and other drugs can have harmful effects (2:2g).

The 'Breadth of Study' section of the PoS (at Key Stage 2) refers to pupils being taught to 'recognise that there are hazards in living things, materials and physical processes' and that they should 'assess risks and take action to reduce risks to themselves and others'.

Such an agenda is clearly appropriate to all pupils regardless of their specific difficulties. Each of the above statements can be amplified as a set of intermediate goals, or targets, for pupils. As an example (drawing on the work of Jones *et al.* 1993), consider the following intermediate targets for the statement 'humans need food and water to stay alive':

- communicate about sources of food or drink (eye contact, vocalisation, gesture, speech, or pulling at an adult);
- know that a person needs to eat or drink (communicates when thirsty/hungry or takes direct action to get a drink or eat);
- know that not eating causes hunger, and lack of fluids causes thirst (asks for a drink on a hot day and gives reasons);
- know that humans die if they get no food or drink (understands starvation in the context of a story, through pictures or video).

Analyses of statements in this way enable a teacher to plan work for individual pupils to progressively build on their existing understanding, ensuring repetition of experiences when necessary. Clearly, with some pupils who lack sophisticated language skills there will be problems of assessing and developing their knowledge and understanding. There is considerable scope for oral work in science and, of course, there are other means of communicating. Pupils with SEN may be capable scientific thinkers who lack the means to communicate their ideas – they need support in doing this.

Other areas of experience that are common in special schools, and relate directly to the science curriculum include:

Sc2:   keeping animals and plants in the classroom;
        maintaining a school garden or pond;
        visits to a local farm, park or woods;
        visits of doctor or nurse.

Sc3:   sand and water play;
        clay and Plasticine modelling;
        collecting and sorting rubbish;
        cooking;
        choosing clothes.

Sc4:   using toys, construction kits and large play equipment;
        making things move by applying a force;
        using mains electrical appliances;
        using kitchen tools and equipment;
        working with construction kits;
        dancing, swimming and sports;
        listening to sounds/singing/playing instruments.

For more information concerning activities such as these, see Jones *et al.* (1993), Ginn Science (1996), Nuffield Science (1996) and QCA (1998; 2001).

The roles of the teacher

The varied roles that an effective teacher of science should adopt include (based on NCC 1989):

- enabler (facilitates and plans learning opportunities);
- manager (coordinates activities and organises the pupils individually, in groups and as a whole class);
- presenter (sets the scene, clarifies ways of working, and gives information);
- adviser (actively listens, and offers ideas and alternatives);
- observer/assessor (elicits current understanding, gathers evidence of progress against learning objectives);
- challenger (comments critically on procedures and outcomes, asks appropriate questions);
- respondent (answers questions);
- negotiator (enables pupils to set appropriate learning targets and have some control of their own learning).

The earlier discussion about a constructivist approach indicates all of these roles are likely to be used by a teacher working in that way. Teachers need to be effective questioners: nothing facilitates learning more effectively than asking the right question at the right time. This is not always easy and will not necessarily be an 'open' question; 'closed' questions can be just as valuable, especially with pupils who may initially find open-ended questions too threatening. Feasey (1998) provides useful guidance on the types of questions a teacher should be asking (attention-focusing, open and closed, measurement, comparison, action, problem-posing), as well as exploring the way in which teachers can turn pupils' questions from being non-scientific or non-productive into action or productive ones.

Teachers have to ensure that all pupils have access to a science curriculum. Access can be facilitated through differentiation. In science, differentiation by task requires a teacher to consider aspects that will affect its difficulty: how familiar the pupils are with the materials and equipment used, and how appropriate they are; how familiar the pupils are with the concepts and vocabulary involved; the required accuracy of measurements; the number and type of factors involved; the extent to which the teacher leads or prompts. The alternative is to plan a task suitable for learners with a range of competences, to recognise that outcomes will be differential, and to interact with the pupils to support their individual learning. This chapter has already stressed the need for precisely-defined learning objectives to encourage small and manageable steps forward; this can also encourage pupil autonomy if pupils are made aware of the targets and take responsibility for aspects of their own learning.

Access is also helped by ensuring science is made meaningful for all learners: that activities are introduced in relevant contexts, possibly through an integrated topic approach (see Coulby and Ward 1996). This reinforces cross-curricular links and can increase pupils' motivation and interest in science. The National Curriculum, with its subject labels, should not deflect us from implementing science in a manner that allows all pupils to appreciate its relevance to their everyday lives. The manner in which work is presented to pupils can raise issues of access. This is clearly the case if written material is used, and guidance on presenting work, found elsewhere in this volume, should be applied to science as much as to any other subject. For older pupils who are working at lower levels, it is essential to set activities in contexts suitable for their ages and to ensure that the materials provided do not contain inappropriate language and images.

Bianchi (1999) stresses the need for structure in intervention, administration and undertaking of activities as of utmost significance when dealing with children who are having learning difficulties in science. Her small-scale study of pupils over a six-week period demonstrated the need for the science curriculum to be adapted to meet the pupils' needs. She also found that the pupils needed more opportunities than others to develop their scientific literacy skills, in order to avoid potential frustrations in pupils with regard to their own learning.

The final consideration when thinking about access is deciding how to cope with pupils' particular difficulties: physical disabilities may require the use of technical aids, for instance, when observing or measuring; hearing-impaired pupils will need to be offered more pictorial clues and simple language; visual impairment will need enhanced aural and tactile information, and adapted equipment; those with emotional and behavioural difficulties will need activities planned to build on a particular interest. For further guidance on improving access to the curriculum, see ACCAC (1998), Bell (1999), Gibson (1991) and DfEE/QCA (2001). Information technology, as discussed elsewhere in this book, can provide important tools to facilitate access. It can also enhance and enrich science work (Cross and Peet 1997, pp. 135–51; Frost 1995; Sherrington 1998, pp. 168–75).

The implementation of science activities in a special school is never going to be easy. However, there are ways of alleviating the problems – for example, by making use of other adults in the classroom (support teachers, parents or helpers). The key to making this strategy work is ensuring that the individual is well briefed and has a clear understanding of your objectives for the activity. A good way of using other adults is to get them to ask questions you have formulated and to scribe the pupil's responses in a large-format book (see Ollerenshaw and Ritchie 1997, p. 50) during the elicitation phase of work. There are many advantages to organising practical science as a small-group or paired activity in this way. Some pupils will, however, need a great deal of support in working with others during practical tasks and another adult enabler can be essential. If school policy allows for parental help in the classroom, an additional benefit can result from encouraging parents to support their children's learning in science at home, building on experiences in school (ASE 1995; Cross and Peet 1997, pp.169–84).

Conclusion

To conclude, let me revisit what pupils will learn through science and why it should be regarded as a fundamental and enjoyable facet of pupils' education. It brings:

- an appreciation and understanding of the natural and made world through first-hand experience wherever possible or second-hand experience where appropriate;
- skills, processes and ways of working that will help pupils cope with everyday living and that may be useful for future work and leisure activities;
- positive attitudes towards science and the development of attitudes such as curiosity, perseverance, independence and respect for evidence, all of which can be applied in other situations.

'Science for all' should mean exactly that, and it should not be allowed to become a meaningless slogan: it is for us, as teachers, to make it a reality.

References

ACCAC (1998) *Design and Technology – One in five: D&T and pupils with SEN.* Birmingham: ACCAC.

ASE (Association of Science Education) (1994) *Making Sense of Primary Science Investigations,* Hatfield: ASE.

ASE (1995) *Primary Science: a Shared Experience,* revised edn. Hatfield: ASE.

Bell, D. (1999) 'Accessing science for children with learning difficulties', *Primary Science Review* 56 (January/February), 27–30.

Bianchi, L. (1999) 'Less-able children's learning in science'. *Primary Science Review* 60 (November/December), 20–22.

Carter, P. (1994) 'Getting special needs in science', *Primary Science Review* 33 (June), 21–4.

CLIS (Children's Learning in Science) (1988–92) *Various Project Reports.* Leeds: University of Leeds.

Coulby, D. and Ward, S. (eds) (1996) *The Primary Core National Curriculum,* 2nd edn. London: Cassell.

Cross, A. and Peet, G. (eds) (1997) *Teaching Science in the Primary School: Book 1.* Plymouth: Northcote House.

DES (1985) *Science 5–16: A Statement of Policy.* London: HMSO.

DfEE/QCA (1999) *National Curriculum: Science.* London: DfEE

DfEE/QCA (2001) *Planning, Teaching and Assessing the Curriculum for Pupils with Learning Difficulties.* London: DfEE/QCA.

Feasey, R. (1998) 'Effective questioning in science', in Sherrington, R. (ed.) *A ASE Guide to Primary Science Education.* Hatfield: ASE.

Frost, R. (1995) *IT in Primary Science.* Hatfield: ASE.

Gardner, H. (1993) *Multiple Intelligences; the Theory in Practice.* New York: Basic Books,

Gibson, P. (1991) 'Science for all', *Primary Science Review* 17, 20–21.

Ginn Science (1996) *Primary Science.* London: Ginn.

Goleman, D. (1996) *Emotional Intelligence – Why it Matters More than IQ.* London: Bloomsbury.

Hemmens, A. (1999) 'Learning through the senses', *Primary Science Review* 59, 20–23.

Jones, L. *et al.* (1993) *Science for All*, 2nd edn. London: David Fulton Publishers.

Longhorn, F. (1991) 'A sensory science curriculum', in Ashdown, R. *et al.* (eds) *The Curriculum Challenge: Access to the National Curriculum for pupils with learning difficulties.* London: Falmer Press.

NCC (1989) *Science: Non-statutory guidance.* York: NCC.

NCC (1992) *Teaching Science to Pupils with Special Educational Needs: Curriculum guidance 10.* York: NCC.

Nuffield Science (1996) *Nuffield Primary Science*, 2nd edn. London: Collins Educational.

OFSTED (1998) *Standards in the Primary Curriculum 1996–97.* London: OFSTED.

Ollerenshaw, C. and Ritchie, R. (1997) *Primary Science: Making it Work*, 2nd edn. London: David Fulton Publishers.

Pickard, C. (1998) 'Multisensory science', *Primary Science Review* 55, 12–14.

QCA (1998) *Science: A Scheme of Work for Key Stages 1 and 2.* London: QCA.

QCA (2001) *Planning, Teaching and Assessing the Curriculum for Pupils with Learning Difficulties: Science.* London: DfEE/QCA.

Ritchie, R. (ed.) (1995) *Primary Science in Avon: A handbook for teachers by teachers.* Bath: Bath College of Higher Education Press.

Ritchie, R. (1996) 'Science in the National Curriculum', in Coulby, D. and Ward, S. (eds) *The Primary Core National Curriculum*, 2nd edn. London: Cassell.

Ritchie, R. (1997) 'Assessment and recording as a constructive process', in Cross, A. and Peet, G. (eds) *Teaching Science in the Primary School: Book 2*, Plymouth: Northcote House.

Ritchie, R. (1998) 'Implementing Assessment and Recording as a Constructive Process, in: Cross, A. and Peet, G. (eds.) *Teaching Science in the Primary School: Book 2.* Plybridge: Northcote House Publishers.

Russell, T. (1995) 'Progression in the post-Dearing curriculum: getting a feel for levels', *Primary Science Review* 37, 8–11.

Sherrington, R. (ed.) (1998) *ASE Guide to Primary Science.* Cheltenham: Stanley Thornes Publishers.

Smith, A. (1996) *Accelerated Learning in the Classroom.* Stafford: Network Educational Press.

SPACE (Science Processes and Concept Exploration) (1990–98) *Primary SPACE Project Reports.* Liverpool: University of Liverpool Press.

Chapter 5

Physical Education

David Sugden and Helen Wright

Inclusion and revision: the challenges and opportunities

What inclusion means

The almost worldwide move towards inclusive policies and practices has continued as we have moved into the new millennium. Although different definitions of inclusion abound, the foreword to the National Curriculum documents by David Blunkett, Secretary of State for Education and Employment, and Sir William Stubbs, Chairman of the Qualifications and Curriculum Authority, note (DfEE/QCA 1999, p. 3):

> An entitlement to learning must be an entitlement for all pupils. This National Curriculum includes for the first time a detailed, overarching statement on inclusion which makes clear the principles schools must follow in their teaching right across the curriculum, to ensure that all pupils have the chance to succeed, whatever their individual needs and the potential barriers to their learning may be.

This is supportive of the Salamanca Statement (1994), which identified a set of beliefs that every child has a fundamental right to education, identifying core principles of providing children with an opportunity to learn, catering for diversity and the acceptance of an inclusive orientation, and moving towards an inclusive society.

In November 1999, the revised National Curriculum was circulated to schools, with implementation due in September 2000 for Key Stages 1–3 and 2001 for Key Stage 4. The brief for many subjects, including physical education (PE), was to keep the changes to a minimum, where possible to make reductions in content, to increase flexibility for schools, to simplify and clarify the requirements, and to ensure that there was better progression in and between key stages. In addition, many parts of the revised curriculum took notice of DfEE publication *Excellence for All Children* (1997), which presented an inclusive vision for education.

Physical education curriculum

The revised PE programmes of study have been constructed around the following key requirements of *knowledge, skills* and *understanding*, and they involve the four strands of:

- acquiring and developing skills;
- selecting and applying skills, tactics and compositional ideas;
- evaluating and improving;
- knowledge and understanding of fitness and health.

These aspects should be seen as connecting, interrelating and impacting on each other, so that, for example, evaluating and improving connects to skills acquisition, composing, and fitness and health. The UK government believes that two hours of physical activity per week that encompasses the National Curriculum, plus extra-curricular activities, should be an aim for all schools.

Key stages

During Key Stage 1, pupils are taught knowledge, skills and understanding through dance, games and gymnastic activities. In Key Stage 2, five areas of activities are included, with dance, games and gymnastics as compulsory and two others to be chosen from swimming and water activities, athletics and outdoor and adventurous activities. In Key Stage 3, four areas of activity are required, with games and three others from dance, gymnastics, swimming and water safety, athletics, and outdoor adventurous activities, one of which must be dance or gymnastic activities. In Key Stage 4, pupils must be taught knowledge, skills and understanding through two of the six areas of activity.

Competitive games are compulsory in Key Stages 1–3 while, in Key Stage 4, pupils can choose other activities than those of a competitive nature. The attainment of pupils is then assessed through the use of an eight-level scale, which replaces the end-of-key-stage descriptions and which brings PE – along with art and music – into line with all other National Curriculum subjects. The reaction among the various bodies in the physical education world, such as the Physical Education Association (PEA), is one of satisfaction – with particular pleasure at the increased flexibility, minimisation of change, and reduction in content (PEA 1999).

Pupils with special educational needs

Of crucial significance to pupils with special educational needs is the section in the PE National Curriculum document entitled 'Inclusion: providing effective learning opportunities for all pupils' (DfEE/QCA 1999, p. 28), which sets out three principles that are essential for developing a more inclusive curriculum:

- *Setting suitable learning challenges.* This first principle stresses that teachers should provide experiences of success for children in an effort to achieve high standards. This may include choosing knowledge, skills and understanding from earlier or later key stages in an effort to enable pupils to progress. A greater emphasis on differentiation is given, with the inference that inclusion may be about focusing on earlier developmental expectations rather than on how existing units of work can be modified or made more flexible. In PE, the use of task analysis to break down complex actions to simpler ones often provides the basis for differentiation.
- *Responding to pupils' diverse learning needs.* This second principle involves teachers setting high expectations, and providing opportunities for all pupils to achieve. It is suggested that this can be done through creating effective learning environments, securing motivation and concentration, providing equality of opportunity through teaching approaches, using appropriate assessment approaches, and setting targets for

learning. Generic examples are provided, together with how these can be achieved in PE through creative grouping, choosing targets with integrity, and a shared understanding by all of the children in the class.

- *Overcoming potential barriers to learning and assessment for individuals and groups of pupils*. This principle in particular targets children with special educational needs or disabilities. For many cases, greater differentiation will be required, while for others special equipment, adapted programmes and/or external help may be necessary. Adapted activities and games are another cornerstone in the repertoire of approaches in physical education that promote inclusion.

Furthermore, in the additional information for PE in the National Curriculum (DfEE/QCA 1999, p. 36), it is noted that some pupils may require 'adapted, modified or alternative activities that have integrity and equivalence to the activities in the programmes of study and that enable the pupils to make progress' and 'specific support to enable [pupils] to participate in certain activities or types of movement'.

The curriculum guidelines for teachers of pupils with learning difficulties have elaborated on the subject of PE in the National Curriculum and made laudable efforts when considering its implementation (QCA 2001). The guidelines detail each key stage, illustrating how all pupils can achieve knowledge, skills and understanding. In particular, there are useful examples of modification, such as the use of signs and symbols to physically describe movement activity when evaluating and improving performance. Modifications to the activities themselves are provided with the encouragement of 'Sherborne' activities (see 'Further reading' at the end of the chapter), and examples of how differentiation can take place. With the later key stages, it is important to ensure that the activities are age-appropriate as well as within the range of ability of the pupil. In Key Stage 3 for example, the document places great emphasis on working with others, cooperating, helping or being assisted.

An important part of the QCA document deals with performance descriptions of attainments of pupils working towards Level 1 of the National Curriculum. It is recognised that many pupils with severe, or especially profound and multiple learning difficulties, may not achieve Level 1, and the suggested activities for pupils at the levels leading up to Level 1 are particularly welcome. The levels are labelled P1–P8, with some levels involving more than one component. For example, P1(i) involves responses to various stimuli, while P1(b) involves a focus on a particular event and P2(ii) includes pupils responding consistently to novelty and familiarity. As the pupils move through level P3, they start to use conventional communication, greet people, and start to anticipate known events; they also actively start to explore objects and share objects. By level P7, pupils are expressing themselves through repetitive and simple sequences and movement patterns, as well as rolling or throwing a ball. The recommendations for appropriate activities appear to be worthwhile and are based upon real-world knowledge of progressions that children make. A cautionary note would be to not accept the sequence P1 through P8 as immutable and unbending, because we are aware that individual differences will require some flexibility in applying the various levels. However, the QCA document and any future modifications will provide help to those looking for ideas to include pupils with more severe needs.

Outcomes in PE: what do we want?

The attainment target for PE sets out the knowledge, skills and understanding that pupils of different abilities are expected to show by the end of each key stage. The attainment target consists of the descriptions of eight levels of increasing difficulty, and these descriptions indicate progression in the aspects of knowledge, skills and understanding set out in the programmes of study.

The importance of physical education goes beyond the level descriptions of the attainment target by also developing physical competence and confidence, skilfulness, and a knowledge of the body in action. PE provides opportunities for competition, challenge and creativity while at the same time promoting positive attitudes to active and healthy lifestyles. Planning, discovering attitudes, abilities and preferences are all part of the contribution that PE can make (DfEE/QCA 1999).

In addition, the National Curriculum handbook provides guidance on how PE can make contributions across the curriculum. For example *social development* can be achieved through activities involving cooperation, collaboration, personal commitment and teamwork; *moral development* can be attained through activities stressing rules, fair play and the acceptance of decisions and authority; *pupils' cultural development* can be encouraged through the understanding and participation in activities from their own and other people's cultures; and *spiritual development* can be attained through a sense of achievement and the development of positive attitudes to themselves and others.

There are also more specific key skills that can be promoted through physical education. Communication is one that is involved in every lesson through the giving and receiving of instructions, feedback and explanation, and planning and organising. Both ICT and number are involved in many lessons – measuring, counting, collecting, analysing and interpreting data by means of a variety of measuring and recording equipment, together with spreadsheets and databases. Working with others is a common and essential part of a PE lesson and pupils take on a variety of roles in which this occurs. Problem-solving and thinking skills are promoted through composition and creative works as well as via tactics and strategies.

In very basic terms, we can say that PE provides an opportunity for both *learning to move* and *moving to learn*. These are very simple notions, with knowledge, skills and understanding being part of the core learning to move – and in moving, children learn other skills related to the movement context. These interrelated concepts are particularly important when teaching children with SEN, where priorities are crucial and targeted teaching essential.

A changing emphasis

In any PE lesson, or part of a lesson, where does the emphasis lie? With the foregoing paragraph in mind, does the emphasis lie in the pupils learning how to move or is the emphasis more on pupils moving in order to learn? Naturally, any answer would have to include both of these as desirable outcomes, and this is confirmed by looking at PE attainment targets, but a closer examination may reveal that the emphasis of one or the other may change according to the needs of the pupils.

A class teacher may be using an activity circuit with pupils showing severe learning difficulties, so as to start a lesson by trying to involve all the pupils. A number of outcomes are desirable from this activity. If there is a range of tasks such as jumping, crawling, balancing and climbing, the teacher may be reinforcing these by simple repetition in the activity circuit. It may be that part of the circuit is quite difficult or involves the pupils performing an activity that they have not perfected. In this case, it may be desirable to provide support and help at this point. Even so, the pupils will be learning how to move, perfecting a behaviour they have done many times before or acquiring a previously partially learned skill. The pupils are learning how to move.

Using the same activity, the teacher can change the emphasis according to the needs of the group. She or he may have pupils who show inappropriate behaviours, such as pushing and poking other pupils, not being able to take turns, and/or being inattentive and distractible. The objectives of the circuit could then change, with simple rules being introduced about not touching other pupils, and only one person being on the apparatus at any one time. A range of rewards (i.e. choice of activity) could be available for the appropriate behaviour, and the withdrawal of privileges for inappropriate behaviour.

A second example concerns decision-making and choice. Pupils may evidence appropriate behaviour as well as perform on the circuit quite competently, but a teacher might wish to stretch their learning capacity. At various points of the circuit, decisions can be inserted, such as jumping into the 'red hoop', 'small square', crawl 'under' the mat. This can be made more demanding by asking the pupils to set the tasks for each other.

A final example involves pupils cooperating with each other on the circuit to achieve a joint objective. Two pupils could start at the beginning and end of the circuit and move toward each other, but might only be able to pass one another by giving each other physical support.

Some interesting recent work by Penny and Chandler (2000) impacts upon these ideas, with proposals about how the curriculum can be changed to encompass learning that connects to other areas of education, and to children's lives and learning beyond school. Their work addresses Young's (1998) 'connective specialisms' by outlining what is realistic to attempt to develop *in and through* PE and the importance of clarity of focus in these methods. In every PE lesson, the twin outcomes of learning to move and moving to learn are being set and achieved, but with pupils showing learning difficulties it is more important that these outcomes are clear and planned for, and that the balance between them is geared to the needs of each child.

Learning and teaching for children with special educational needs

As mentioned above, a document that is of considerable current assistance is the curriculum guidance published on PE for pupils with learning difficulties (QCA 2001). This provides useful guidelines for the four strands of acquiring and developing skills, of selecting and applying skills, tactics and compositional ideas, of evaluating and improving, and of knowledge and understanding of fitness and health. In addition, it gives examples of how PE practitioners may support learning and how promoting access and full participation can be achieved by a range of modes (such as ICT, specialist aids, and peer and adult support) and by the use of alternative and augmentative communication (such as body movements, eye gaze, facial expression, gestures, symbols and pictures, and electronic communication modes). Examples are given for the four strands through all key stages.

The PE curriculum involves pupils acquiring skills in a movement context, and in order to establish what we know about how pupils acquire, retain and generalise motor skills it is appropriate to examine the learning process to determine what is involved in the acquisition of those skills. A simple model of motor-skill acquisition involves three phases: understanding, acquiring and refining, and automating. This old but classic model has stood the test of time, and it has been refined and elaborated to involve instructional variables (Henderson and Sugden 1992).

The early part of any motor skill is cognitive in nature; the pupils need to understand what is required of them and how this requirement is linked to their ability and their previous knowledge and experience. This in turn has enormous implications for how the skill is presented, introduced and demonstrated. The situation has to be meaningful to the pupil, or the pupil has to abstract meaning him or herself, and in many pupils with learning difficulties this ability may be at a lower level than their peers. The more complex the situation, demanding choices, memory and selection, the more cues the teacher will need to provide. This early part of the learning process is crucial to pupils with special educational needs, for research has shown that very often such pupils fail to acquire a skill because of a lack of understanding rather than because of poor motor ability.

The 'associative' stage of learning is when a pupil is acquiring and refining a skill, and it traditionally involves the presentation of appropriate tasks, structured in such a way as to lead the pupil through progressively more complex practices. Careful observation and matching the task to the resources of the pupil is a fundamental principle during this stage.

Finally, a pupil may reach the automatic stage of acquisition, where a task is performed almost without thought and with few errors. Even when a pupil reaches this stage, it is still possible to facilitate more complex and advanced skills. For example, a pupil with severe learning difficulties may have a balance difficulty, and she or he may have been working toward walking on a wide bench. Once this has been accomplished, the pupil can be asked to modify the walk by placing targets to walk into (or avoid), by walking backwards or sideways, by counting steps during walking, by carrying or throwing a beanbag while walking, etc. Most skills can be modified, made simpler or more complex by changing the demand, or adding or taking away a subcomponent, and this will facilitate creativity as the pupil has to provide alternatives.

Planning a programme

To ensure that the curriculum is coherent, a breakdown of the total time allocation for each area is a useful exercise. It enables the teacher to see how activities are distributed across the year and to determine how continuity and progression is achieved. It is not simply a matter of allocating a half-term block to an activity; it involves determining how much time is required for a particular programme of study and allocating accordingly. For example, double lessons raise a number of issues. First there is considerable variability in the length of such lessons – perhaps 60 to 100 minutes. Effective working time is also dependent upon changing times, which again vary considerably. In such lessons, it may be more appropriate to present two activities rather than spread out one activity over the whole session. Maximising the available time is the key issue, because time spent learning a skill is an important variable that affects the outcome.

Attainment targets in PE

The revised National Curriculum does not require statutory teacher assessment at the end of a key stage but, instead, level descriptions set the standards against which pupils' achievement can be measured; they also provide the basis for reporting on pupil progress. Pupil achievement and progress should be monitored throughout a unit of work, helping to plan lessons and inform individual programmes. The school-based stages of the *Code of Practice for the Identification and Assessment of Special Educational Needs* (Department for Education (DFE) 1994), particularly the IEPs, require that teachers have an assessment and recording system in place such that information about a pupil's progress can be communicated to other appropriate professionals.

An attainment target sets out the knowledge, skills and understanding that pupils of different abilities are expected to have by the end of each key stage. There are eight levels of description of increasing difficulty, and the majority of pupils would be expected to attain Level 2 at age 7 (end of Key Stage 1), Level 4 at age 11 (end of Key Stage 2) and Level 5/6 at age 14 (end of Key Stage 3). In the revised curriculum for PE these descriptions for the end of the three key stages are as follows:

- Level 2 involves pupils copying, repeating and exploring basic actions while showing control, and then linking these actions, together with some comment and description.
- Level 4 involves pupils linking skills, techniques and ideas with performance that shows fluency, precision and control. They should be able to demonstrate understanding of tactics and composition, and learn both from their own observations and from the comments of other pupils. Specific knowledge about the benefits of activity and actions such as warm-ups would also be expected.
- Level 6 involves pupils selecting, combining, and applying skills, techniques and ideas with precision, control and fluency. They should be able to use tactics, strategy and composition in changing circumstances, and be able to analyse and comment how these have been used in their own and others' performance. They should also be able to explain how to prepare and recover from activities, and how different activities contribute to fitness.

In the recent curriculum guidelines for PE for pupils with learning difficulties (QCA 2001), performance descriptions of attainment of pupils working towards Level 1 of the National Curriculum are provided. Examples are provided that move from simple reflex responses, through communicating consistent preferences and actively exploring, to such actions as showing awareness of cause and effect, and recognising and requesting familiar pieces of equipment.

Grouping and support issues in the PE lesson

When planning and organising a lesson or programme of work, the starting points are the needs of the pupil and the situation that already exists. More often than not, it is minor changes in this area that can lead to a substantial change in the accessibility of the curriculum for the pupil with learning difficulties. Grouping and support are interrelated, in that the type of grouping often dictates the support required and vice versa.

The grouping of pupils is an important issue within any PE lesson. A PE lesson can be divided into a number of sections that require pupils to work on their own, in pairs, in large or small groups, and with or without support. Accessibility to the PE curriculum for pupils with learning difficulties can be helped or hindered by a teacher's ability to group the pupils. Both the demands of the situation and the resources of the pupil must be considered, and our experience in this area leads us to recommend flexible grouping.

A class of 30 primary school pupils may contain, say, 2 pupils with learning difficulties, who are having difficulty in understanding, acquiring and performing the motor skills that will allow them to successfully participate in some activities in the PE lesson. When the pupils are working individually, grouping is not a problem as the pupils will be choosing their own level of performance. However, when these pupils are required to work in pairs for skills learning or sequence building, then the teacher must decide how best to group the pupils. For activities such as sending and receiving objects, it may be advisable to pair a pupil with learning difficulties with a pupil who is competent in the activities being undertaken. In this way, the partner will be a good enough 'sender' to provide the pupil with learning difficulties with accurate feeds, thus facilitating practice in receiving. In addition, the capable pupil is competent enough to deal with any awkward throws or kicks that may come from the pupil with learning difficulties. Schmidt (1991) has suggested that more varied experiences during skill acquisition can have beneficial learning effects through the transfer of skills to novel situations. If this is the case, not only is the pupil with learning difficulties benefiting from a stable, predictable environment that has been constructed by the capable pupil, but the pupil with difficulties provides the variable practice for the able pupil to develop his or her own skills. In this case, both pupils are served from the pairing.

On other occasions, it may be more beneficial to place the pupil with learning difficulties in pairs or in groups of pupils with similar ability. For example, the pupils may be asked to perform a joint sequence involving a roll, a jump and a balance in a gymnastic lesson. Two pupils of similar ability will complement each other, and will not feel that one is exemplifying the other's difficulties or holding back the other. The pupils can perform to the best of their ability level, and this should be remarked upon by the teacher.

When pupils are expected to work in larger groups, the nature of the activity and desired outcome will influence the make-up of the group. For competitive activities, random selection of the groups will usually bring parity. If, however, the pupils are involved in skills-acquisition practices, it is important to have pupils in the group who are physically and emotionally supportive of pupils with learning difficulties. The physical support is seen by their skilled feeding in ball situations, for example; their emotional support is shown by their constant encouragement and praise of the pupil with learning difficulties. This provides an atmosphere that motivates the pupil with learning difficulties to strive to gain skills and makes the pupil feel welcome.

The needs of such a pupil, linked to the desired outcome for the activities, give the lead to the teacher with respect to grouping. The needs of pupils with learning difficulties are both emotional and physical, and as such demand that the teacher examines the grouping and support issues thoughtfully. Flexibility in this dimension of lesson planning, rather than a response to each situation with a rigid doctrine, can bring great rewards for pupils with learning difficulties.

Adapting and analysing the learning context

Teaching is an interactive process, involving the resources of the pupil, the activities to be learned, and the context in which these are learned. Of these three variables, the teacher is able to control the last two. The context can be arranged in terms of grouping, as previously described, and activities can also be manipulated. In order to do this, two related concepts are focused on, which are explained separately for practical purposes but in reality merge into each other. These concepts are task adaptation and task analysis. The terms 'learning-context adaptation and analysis' are preferred as they help focus the attention on all the players in the situation, not just the task (Sugden and Wright 1996). However, adapting and analysing tasks has come to be a recognised role for teachers when working with pupils with learning difficulties. Entitlement to participation is a fundamental right for all pupils, and this often requires modifying activities to meet the resources of the pupils.

Task adaptation involves changing a task, the rules of a game, or the requirements of an activity, and modifying equipment and apparatus such that all pupils can take part in the activity. These changes need not be massive. A ball that moves more slowly through the air, such as a sponge ball, makes catching or trapping easier; hitting a ball off a cone rather than from a thrown ball gives the pupil more control over contact with the ball, as well as placement; altering rules so that all pupils in a game have to pass the ball before a score can be registered; adjusting the height of equipment for pupils; offering a choice of difficulty in an activity circuit – all these facilitate the participation of pupils. Increased participation in this way leads to increased learning (Brown 1987). Good guides are available for adapting game skills and activities (Sleap 1983; Smith and Williamson 1993; Williamson 2000).

Task analysis is a direct way of facilitating skills learning. The task to be learned is analysed into its component parts so that it is easier to approach. The parts can be considered wholes in themselves, but they can also be reassembled to make the original whole again. This offers the opportunity for the pupil to be successful throughout the learning experience. The guiding principle behind task analysis is that the teacher orders the components of a task from simple to more complex. This not only includes the task itself but should also include the environment in which the task occurs. Gentile *et al.* (1975), Spaeth-Arnold (1981) and Henderson and Sugden (1992) all consider the mover–environment interplay to be crucial to task analysis. A stationary pupil in a stable environment is dealing with a less complex situation than when the pupil is moving and the environment is changing.

The demands of the environment should not be overlooked when trying to simplify a task. Physical activities are made up of perceptual, cognitive and motor components, and therefore any simplification of activities or tasks involves reducing the demands in one or more of these three facets. For example, in receiving a moving ball the perceptual demands can be reduced by having a brightly coloured ball or one with a bell in it for pupils with visual impairment; cognitive components can be reduced by taking out the parabola, for instance by rolling a ball along the ground to intercept; motor demands can be reduced by slowing the ball down, by using a bigger ball, or one that is easier to catch. All of these practices are progressive in that the initial step is to find the level where the pupil can be successful. Incorporated in this approach is encouragement and praise for successful completion, followed by a progressive increase of the task's demands. This moves the pupil onwards in small successful stages (Brown 1987; Henderson and Sugden 1992; Sugden and Wright 1996).

From principles and guidelines to practice

In the first example in this section, we highlight a gymnastic-cum-movement lesson for 7–8-year-olds that includes two pupils who have learning difficulties and shows how the lesson can be planned and organised to ensure that these two pupils are involved and profit from the lesson. Pupils with learning difficulties can and do have difficulties understanding the requirements of set tasks. Before a teacher is in a position to deal with the practical situation, it must be established that a pupil with learning difficulties has understood what is being asked of her or him. The teacher needs to simplify instructions, offering a visual representation via demonstrations. It may be necessary to reduce the requirements of the task for the pupil with learning difficulties such that the number of components within a task are less for the learning-difficulties pupil than for the other pupils in the class.

Pupils with learning difficulties are often lacking in confidence through a perceived reduced ability when they compare themselves with their peers. This can be because their shyness, for instance, has limited their experiences or that their poor motor skills have led to failure and a subsequent lack of belief in themselves. Either way, it is the case that the self-concept of pupils with learning difficulties has to be improved and nurtured in a positive way through their PE experiences, before the more specific motor skills that cause them difficulties can be tackled. Improving the pupil's confidence through adapted movements can be achieved. Curriculum gymnastics offers an ideal opportunity for individualised learning to take place, where pupils can visibly take part and progress despite not performing exactly the same skills as peers. The opportunities abound for task adaptation and task simplification so as to meet the needs of pupils with learning difficulties.

The two pupils with learning difficulties in our example are different from each other despite both finding certain movements difficult to execute and control. For pupil A, there is an overall impaired ability across the movement spectrum, which has in turn led to a desire to withdraw from PE activities where possible. For pupil B, the problems arise more specifically when the environment is changing and is not directly under the pupil's control – e.g. when asked to move in sequence with others or change direction suddenly in a crowded gym with all the class on the move. When left to his or her own devices from a stationary position and in his or her own timing, pupil B has a lot more success. Pupil A needs to be encouraged to participate and become more involved, while pupil B needs to have the opportunity to develop control in his or her own time before tackling the complexities of a changing environment not under his or her control.

Working on a thematic approach to curriculum gymnastics allows the material within the lesson to be challenging and different for each and every pupil as necessary. In our example, the main theme is 'travelling', with a sub-theme for the lesson being stretching and curling. Each lesson taught, based on this overall theme, is expected to include a warm-up session containing expansive body movements, flexibility work that is specific to the sub-theme of the lesson, skills development, strength work, and a cool down. The aim of this example gymnastics lesson is to develop a sequence of different movements on the floor that transport the pupil from point X to point Y using alternate stretching and curling movements.

The warm up will begin with a game that the pupils work on alone, called 'body parts', where they start slowly jogging around the gym avoiding each other; when the teacher calls out a certain body part they must put that body part on the floor and then get up and jog around again. The game is simple enough for pupil A to take part in successfully so long as the teacher starts with easy-to-place body parts such as the hands, bottom or back, and keeps the game at an orderly pace. Even though the teacher would want the game to speed up from its initially slow pace, in order to allow pupil B to remain in control and to participate, the teacher should ensure that pupil B has enough time to start jogging again before the next body part is called. Manipulating the warm up in this manner will mean that, while all the pupils participate, both pupil A and pupil B have not encountered a threatening environment at the start of the lesson.

For the flexibility work, again the pupils are working individually so that as long as pupil A can follow the teacher's lead, and pupil B has enough room to operate within, neither of them should experience difficulties. It is important for both pupils that they are encouraged by being successful right from the start of the lesson, and that they enter the major part of the lesson, namely the development of the theme, with a positive experience from the warm up.

Moving on to the next part of the lesson, the teacher must ensure that the pupils have a practical as well as theoretical concept of the task requirements and the notion that these tasks, whilst challenging, are within their capabilities. In this case the pupils must be sure what constitutes stretching and curling movements. The teacher can introduce simple stretched and curled shapes for the pupils to try, followed by the opportunity to use some of those shapes to move from one place to another, with the pupils' own ideas added too. Pupil A should be physically close to the teacher so that the teacher is in a position to encourage, reinforce and help correct or develop the pupil's attempts. Pupil B should be given plenty of space within which to work so that he or she can have the chance to learn to control the movements in the first place without being encumbered by the close presence of others. All the pupils should be encouraged to identify the movements that they enjoy best and practise them so as to improve upon their quality – tighter curl, longer stretch, or more fluid transition from one movement to the other. All the pupils can be congratulated on their level of control and persistence to 'smooth' their attempts.

From individual work, the pupils can further be grouped in pairs to learn from each other their favourite sequence. The teacher should organise the grouping: for pupil A the partner should be someone who is working at a similar level and is not seen as a threat; for pupil B the partner should be one who has a good level of control and can act as a role model. As the pupils work in pairs, the teacher can privately set differing tasks for the respective pairs according to their abilities. For instance, the pair that includes pupil A can continue simply to teach each other their sequences, while the pair that includes pupil B can be asked to do their respective sequences in unison, mirroring each other and by so doing giving pupil B the opportunity to work to someone else's timing. Provided that the teacher feels that either or both pupil A or pupil B has mastered the sequence sufficiently well, and can cope with the publicity, the pupil's efforts can be reinforced and rewarded by showing the other pupils their efforts.

For the closing part of the lesson the strength work can also be done in pairs, with the pupils partnered in the same manner but this time with pupils that complement them in a non-threatening way yet are different from their earlier partners. The cool down should be done individually, using the stretches and curls from the sequence. In this manner the teacher has managed to cover the aim of the lesson in such a way that the two pupils with learning difficulties are included with integrity, while at the same time the others in the class have been sufficiently challenged.

The second example lesson offers guidelines and suggestions for the inclusion of two pupils with learning difficulties in a mainstream basketball class for 12–year-olds. As previously stated, good practice must prevail and this lesson is organised to include a warm-up, revision of previous work, new work and a cool down.

The aim of this particular basketball lesson is to use dribbling and passing skills, previously taught, in a small-sided game of three versus three, in order to achieve a position on court where a high-percentage shot at the basket (i.e. a shot with a good chance of success) may occur. The basketball lesson begins with a dribbling tag-warm-up using the lines of the basketball court. At least five of the class will dribble the basketball and attempt to tag their classmates whilst remaining on the lines of the court. Once tagged, the basketball is passed to the next pupil. The game begins with walking and develops into running.

The idea of tag with a basketball is an easily understood concept for a pupil with learning difficulties to grasp quickly. Revision work in this lesson focuses on passing the ball forward and ahead of your team-mates in order to attack the basket area. The pupils work in threes across the court, passing the ball to a team-mate who is slightly ahead of them, trying to use a chest pass and timing the pass to reach the player's hands without them having to reach back for the ball. If the receiving player is not in a forward position, the passer of the ball will dribble forward until a team-mate has got slightly in front. A clear demonstration of the task will ensure that the pupil with learning difficulties understands.

The lesson will then develop into a conditioned game that through its design will highlight certain high-percentage areas of the court. The basketball court or teaching area will be divided into three separate sections for three games to be played simultaneously. Nine pupils will be assigned to each small court and three teams established; two teams will play while the third team watches. Alternatively, the third team of three could be split into one referee and one coach for each of the two playing teams. The pupils will be asked to use their forward-movement skills to attack the target – in this case two skittles inside a circle placed near but not on the baselines of the courts. If the pupils knock down one skittle with one shot, 10 points will be awarded; however, if the pupils manage to knock down both skittles from one attempt, 30 points will be given – so encouraging the pupils to get into a position for a high-percentage shot. At the same time this will encourage the defence to take up positions to defend high-percentage shots, which can be discussed with the class as a whole or in their small groups.

As the 'full' game of basketball includes time-outs for the discussion of tactics and this conditioned game encourages the pupils to think of tactics to achieve the best chance of a 30–point score, the teacher can schedule time-outs for the pupils too. To include pupils with learning difficulties in the discussion, the teacher can ask such a pupil to show the others the best place to stand for the best chance of a 30–point shot. A rotation of teams will allow the pupils to play against all the other teams.

After a discussion of the tactics required to be successful in the small-sided game, followed by the transferable use of the tactics to the 'full' game, the pupils will cool down by working in pairs doing ball-handling skills with the basketball. These skills should include those that demand control and stretching from a stationary position, and they should be easy to follow by demonstration for the inclusion of each learning-difficulties pupil – as the skills are done using the hands from a stationary position, a stable and simple environment, the demands placed on the pupil are reduced.

A problem often encountered for pupils with learning difficulties is that of acceptance from the other pupils. They must believe in themselves and, to help such pupils, a teacher's feedback and inclusion of pupils in discussions are vital. If pupils with learning difficulties can be with pupils who ask 'What do you think?' with regard to tactical discussions and solutions to problems, then the pupils' difficulties are much reduced. Thoughtful presentation of material in such a way that communication is not impeded for the pupil with learning difficulties will allow the same inclusion and access to the curriculum that other pupils experience.

Concluding comments

Whatever resources the pupil brings to the PE situation, the processes of providing access are the same: careful planning of outcomes linked to the particular activities; suitable grouping of pupils, including the provision of support; the adaptation of games and activities such that all children can participate; the analysis of individual tasks, facilitating learning; sensitive presentation of tasks with explanations, demonstrations, instructions and feedback, all geared to the individual needs of the pupils; and, finally, a commitment to inclusion, with an attitude that welcomes and celebrates differences.

References

Brown, A. (1987) *Active Games for Children with Movement Problems*. London: Harper and Row.

DFE (1994) *Code of Practice on the Identification and Assessment of Special Educational Needs*. London: DFE.

DfEE (1997) *Excellence for All Children: Meeting special educational needs*. London: HMSO

DfEE/QCA (1999) *Physical Education: The National Curriculum for England*. London: DfEE/QCA.

Gentile, A.M. *et al.* (1975) 'The structure of motor tasks'. *Movement*, 7, 11–28.

Henderson, S. E. and Sugden, D. A. (1992) *Movement Assessment Battery for Children*. London: The Psychological Corporation.

PEA (1999) 'National Curriculum 2000 – PEA UK's response to the Secretary of State's proposal', *British Journal Of Physical Education* **30**(3), 44.

Penny, D. and Chandler, T. (2000) 'A curriculum with connections?' *British Journal of Teaching Physical Education* **31**(2), 37–40.

QCA (2001) *Planning, Teaching And Assessing The Curriculum For Pupils With Learning Difficulties: Physical Education*. London: DfEE/QCA.

Schmidt, R. A. (1991) *Motor Learning and Performance: From principles to practice*. Champaign, Ill: Human Kinetics Publishers.

Sleap, M. (1983) *Mini Sports*. UK: Heinemann.

Smith, R. and Williamson, D. C. (1993) *Practical Innovations for Nine Adapted Activities, Games and Sports*. Nottingham: Nottingham Trent University.

Spaeth-Arnold, R. K. (1981) 'Developing sports skills', *Motor Skills: Theory into Practice*, monograph 2.

Sugden, D. A. and Wright, H. C. (1996) 'Curricular entitlement and implementation for all children', in Armstrong. N. (ed.) *New Directions in Physical Education Vol. 3: Change and innovation*. London: Cassell.

Williamson, D. C. (2000) 'Polybat and table cricket: from adaptations to sport status', *British Journal of Teaching in Physical Education*, 31(2),16–18.

Young, M.F.D. (1998) 'The Curriculum of the Future', from the *'New Sociology of Education' To A Critical Theory of Learning*. London: Falmer Press.

Further reading

Allen, A. and Coley, J. (1995) *Dance for all (2 and 3)*. London: David Fulton Publishers.

Gray, J. (1995) 'Physical education', in Ashcroft, K. and Palacio, D. (eds) *The Primary Teacher's Guide to the New National Curriculum*. London: Falmer Press.

Sherrill, C. (1998) *Adapted Physical Activity, Recreation and Sport* (5th edn.). Boston: McGraw-Hill.

Sherborne, V. (1990) *Developmental Movement for Children*. Cambridge, UK: Cambridge University Press.

Sugden, D. and Wright, H. (1999) *Physical Education For All: Developing Physical Education in the Curriculum for Pupils with Special Educational Needs*. London: David Fulton Publishers.

For further information about Sherborne movement activities and regular in-service sessions, contact Sherborne Foundation UK, The Sherborne Centre, Office No. 5, Old School House, Britannia Road, Kingswood, Bristol BS15 2DB, United Kingdom.

Chapter 6

History

Clare Martin and Bernard Gummett

We are not the first who have fried our sausages in Groenavika!
(e-mail message from Oystein, grade 9, Rovaer School, Norway)

Introduction

The UK's Education Reform Act 1988 gave all pupils of compulsory school age, including those with a wide range of special educational needs, a legal entitlement to the National Curriculum programmes of study for history. This chapter will look at the requirements of the statutory orders (revised in 1999 and effective from the beginning of the autumn term 2000), explore some of the issues concerned with relevance and access for pupils with learning difficulties, and give examples of activities in history with reference to the relevant PoS.

History within the National Curriculum

The introduction of the original statutory orders for National Curriculum history were marked with controversy, including what focus should be placed on British history and whether the subject should be more concerned with the processes involved with learning history or the acquisition of historical facts. There were also tensions about the relevance of history for pupils with SEN and about the ways in which it should be taught (Sebba and Clarke 1993; Ware and Peacey 1993) – tensions that continued, to some extent, into the new millennium. Subject-specific guidelines for teaching history, written for teachers working with pupils with learning difficulties (QCA 2001), may help to resolve the tensions that remain.

If history is defined as the study of the past in order to better understand the present, then clearly history is more than just learning lists of dates or studying the lives of former kings and queens. The study of history can 'give pupils a sense of identity' (DES 1990), and that in itself is central to the process of education. As Sebba and Clarke (1991) assert:

In all the strategies which teachers adopt to heighten their pupils' perceptions of their individual identities, they can remind themselves that not only are they attempting something which has always been a pre-eminent aim of the personal and social curriculum, but also that they are working within the framework of National Curriculum history.

If the study of history can help pupils with learning difficulties develop a greater awareness of their own existence, this provides a powerful justification for history having a place within their curriculum.

The PoS for Key Stage 1 within the statutory orders sets out the knowledge, skills and understanding that are expected to be developed within the key stage, and it then sets out areas to be considered under the title 'Breadth of study'. At this first key stage, the programmes do not refer to any specific periods of history but indicate that pupils should be taught about changes in their own lives and the way of life of their family and others around them. They should learn about the way of life of people in the more distant past both locally and elsewhere in Britain. There is also the requirement that pupils should be taught about the lives of a range of famous men and women and about different types of past events. While examples of these are given, the advice is not statutory. For Key Stages 2 and 3 under 'Breadth of study', the areas to be studied are set out, some of which refer to specific historical periods such as the Romans, Anglo-Saxons and Vikings in Britain (Key Stage 2) and Britain 1066–1500 (Key Stage 3), with schools having a choice between some of the options. These areas of study, which are to be taught in order to develop knowledge, skills and understanding, are described more fully under the titles of:

- chronological understanding;
- knowledge and understanding of events, people and changes in the past;
- historical interpretation;
- historical enquiry;
- organisation and communication.

The guidance from QCA (2001) looks at each of these areas and explores their significance for pupils with learning difficulties.

As the key stages advance, the content of what should be taught in relation to these areas becomes more demanding. For example, at Key Stage 1, within chronological understanding, pupils are to be taught 'to sequence events and objects, in order to develop a sense of chronology' and 'to use common words and phrases relating to the passing of time (for example, before, after, a long time ago, past)'. At Key Stage 3, the requirement for chronological understanding is for pupils 'to be taught to recognise and make appropriate use of dates, vocabulary and conventions that describe the historical periods and the passing of time'.

Until the guidelines for pupils with learning difficulties (QCA 2001) were issued, assessment of a pupil's progress in history relied on the use of the level descriptions listed under the heading of 'Attainment target for history' in the statutory orders. Teachers were required to judge which level best fitted each pupil's performance at the end of each key stage. Byers (1994) expressed some concern about assessment. For example, would teachers use the level descriptions to assess pupils in mid-key stage or would they use the PoS? There was a strong temptation for teachers to break down the level descriptions into individual elements, yet such an approach was against the spirit of the orders, which instead sought to continue the move away from checklists that took place with the 1995 revision of orders. However, the guidelines (QCA 2001) contain a breakdown of the skills into small steps, which precede Level 1 and which are usually referred to as P-scales, starting at an early developmental level.

Schools are legally required to report the progress of pupils in all subjects covered by the National Curriculum. Care needs to be taken to ensure that what is reported actually represents what pupils with learning difficulties have achieved and not merely what they have experienced. For pupils with learning difficulties who may make progress in small steps, achieving this aim presents staff with a major challenge that the history P-scales may help them to meet.

The executive summary following research by the National Foundation for Educational Research (NFER) into assessment, recording and accreditation, as commissioned by the School Curriculum and Assessment Authority (SCAA), made several recommendations that teachers should take into consideration (NFER 1995). These include the suggestion that 'Record keeping systems in school should be manageable yet provide sufficient information to enable teachers, parents and other professionals to maintain an overview of pupils' progress.' The summary also recognised the value of pupils being involved in their own learning and assessment.

It is important that each pupil's Record of Achievement should cover all areas of an individual curriculum, including history, and that these records should continue to be meaningful to the pupil even years after they have been compiled. The use of photographs and video can help to achieve this, as can the use of information technology in conjunction with symbol writing software (e.g. WRITING WITH SYMBOLS 2000 from Widgit Software). Indeed, as Sebba (1994) points out, Records of Achievement capture part of a pupil's own personal history. Of pupils with severe learning difficulties, Carpenter (1995) asks 'can symbols enable our pupils to participate in the assessment process, to gain some degree of control over this formative process and begin to make judgements about their own learning?' He demonstrates that they clearly can, and he concludes that

> Symbols enhance the participation of students with learning difficulties in a range of social and educational activities. They help to bring a sense of achievement, a precious tool in building self esteem, and as such can make a valuable contribution to the lives and education of those with learning difficulties.

Planning to teach history

The teaching of history requires careful planning in order to ensure coverage, continuity and progression. All schools should have developed policies for National Curriculum subjects, including history, and most will have recognised the value of identifying a history coordinator. Sebba (1994) suggests that the responsibilities of the coordinator might include:

- drafting of the school's policy statement, long-term plans (across key stages) and schemes of work for history;
- planning for progression and differentiation;
- auditing current curricular coverage;
- developing a good understanding of the curricular requirements;
- creating resource 'boxes';
- developing a range of appropriate activities for others to use;
- monitoring progress across the school;
- listing and acquiring resources for teachers;

- ensuring history is prioritised on the school development plan when appropriate;
- providing staff development through team teaching and staff meetings.

One of the major issues to be addressed when planning the teaching of history is whether pupils will follow PoS for the age-appropriate key stage – possibly covering the material identified for that key stage but at the earlier levels – or continue to work on material from earlier key stages. The advice from the SCAA was that the age-appropriate key stage PoS should be the starting point for teachers when they are planning pupils' work, and that material should only need to be selected from earlier key stages for a small number of pupils (SCAA 1996; Stevens 1995). To illustrate the opportunities that this presents, an area can be taken from Key Stage 3 and explored to discover how coverage is possible at Level 1. The PoS for Key Stage 3 specifies that pupils should complete a world study before 1900, specifying that this study ought to include the cultures, beliefs and achievements of an African, American, Asian or Australasian society in the past. It offers a list from which a suitable society can be selected, and for this example a study of the indigenous peoples of North America has been chosen. This area of study provides an appropriate framework within which pupils can be taught 'to use common words and phrases relating to the passing of time', a phrase taken from the knowledge, skills and understanding listed for Key Stage 1 in history. The study of Native Americans provides an ideal opportunity for pupils *'to use common words and phrases relating to the passing of time (for example, before, after, a long time ago, past)'* (my italics) within a new and interesting framework.

Many pupils with learning difficulties are placed within a mainstream school or within a teaching group that has a wide range of learning difficulties. This will increase the likelihood of material from the age-appropriate key stage being used, but it will also present teachers with the challenge of differentiating the teaching material so that it is accessible to all the pupils in the group and of ensuring that all the pupils are able to demonstrate achievement and progression.

It is also necessary to decide whether to teach history as a separate subject or as part of an integrated theme – or, indeed, as a combination of the two approaches. Much has been written about the use of 'themes', sometimes referred to as 'topics' or 'projects' (Byers 1990; Sebba *et al.* 1995). One of the strengths is that themes allow the cross-curricular links between subjects to be fully exploited, but the demands of the National Curriculum do not allow teachers and pupils to pursue themes guided solely by the way the theme evolves.

Themes can be used to ensure curriculum coverage for history. In order to do this, one school drew up a four-year cycle of themes. During a curriculum planning meeting, the staff identified elements and study units to be covered within history and copied them onto small cards. The cards were shuffled and distributed among staff, who were then responsible for placing their cards onto a large grid containing the four-year cycle of termly themes. It was quite easy to decide the place of some cards, but others were not so easy to position and for some the connection to the theme was tenuous. One of the chosen themes is 'Buildings' and, under this, at Key Stage 1, the card was placed that contained 'Pupils should be taught: how to find out about the past from a range of sources of information – including historic buildings.' The card containing the study of 'Britain since 1930', which could include the Blitz and Evacuation, was placed at Key Stage 2, and the card placed at Key Stage 3 referred to the study of '1066 to 1500' and specifically the study of secular art and architecture.

The session stimulated a very useful discussion about what might be covered within each area and how it might be possible to differentiate activities so that they were accessible to pupils of all abilities within each of the teaching groups. It was agreed that, at the end of each theme, the staff would meet to review whether or not it had been possible to cover the identified material and to share what had and what had not worked well. This theme grid allows teachers to ensure that pupils are covering the PoS for history because it contains all the areas required within the programmes of study.

Including pupils with profound and multiple learning difficulties

It has to be recognised that it may not be possible to cover all the areas required by the National Curriculum for pupils with profound and multiple learning difficulties, because of the competing demands made on their time in school. For example, some pupils may need daily physiotherapy sessions, or it may take them longer than usual to eat their midday meal. Guidance from SCAA (1996) indicates that for this group of pupils it may be necessary to cover material from later key stages in outline rather than in depth, or that teachers might plan work for pupils in Key Stages 2 and 3 using material from an earlier key stage but presented in an age-appropriate way.

The biggest question about relevance and access has been about whether or not history should have any place at all within the curriculum of pupils with PMLD. Ware (1994), talking about the National Curriculum in general, suggests that 'the imaginative use of the programmes of study can both provide a wider range of teaching contexts for essential skills and offer pupils the opportunity to develop these skills in meaningful contexts'. Ware outlines some of the arguments for and against the inclusion of pupils with PMLD within the National Curriculum and concludes that it serves 'as a useful reminder that knowing about science, history, geography, etc. can contribute to a full life'.

Some pupils with PMLD have a minimal ability to demonstrate their understanding of what is happening around them. However, these pupils should not be excluded from activities that might provide them with enrichment and enjoyment. The subject-specific guidelines (QCA 2001) refer to the possibility of using sensory modes to support the teaching of history – advice that may further help to include pupils with PMLD in history activities.

Many pupils with PMLD are placed within groups alongside pupils whose learning difficulties are less severe. The use of carefully planned group work can increase the access of all pupils, including those with PMLD, to activities within history. Sebba *et al.* (1995) explore the value of group work and, while recognising the need for all pupils with learning difficulties to have access to individual teaching, they argue that 'all pupils, regardless of need, have a right to participate in education alongside their peers'. They describe different methods of grouping pupils, such as 'jigsawing' and pairing: 'Often the teaming of a skilled pupil with one whose needs are greater and in some cases profound can have mutual benefits' (Sebba *et al.*, 1995).

Historical resources

When planning to teach history, the provision of, or access to, the necessary resources has to be considered. Once a school has decided what study units to cover, the resources for that period can be acquired. This will involve finding books that cover the chosen periods at the correct level of difficulty, a task that is becoming easier as publishers respond to the demand created by the National Curriculum. It is also extremely beneficial to give pupils access to objects and artefacts that stimulate thought and discussion about a particular period and encourage them to become more aware of change. Giving pupils the opportunity to look at and handle a flat iron, for example, can lead to them deducing that in the times when the iron was in use there was no electricity and to then contemplate what life was like without electricity. Being able to handle the large iron shoe from a cart horse can stimulate a discussion about how horses used to do the work that is now performed by tractors and other vehicles.

It is also important that schools make good use of the physical resources within their local environment. Not only are local museums rich sources of historical artefacts, but there are now many opportunities to experience living history – for example, at Jorvik, Stott Park Bobbin Mill, Beamish and the Ironbridge Gorge museums.

People are also resources for teaching history. During the 1995 commemorations surrounding the 50th anniversary of the ending of the Second World War, the period was brought alive, for some pupils, by the school caretaker, who was able to talk about a wartime childhood and tell tales of ration books and gas masks.

Other resources that can help to bring periods of history to life are computer programs, CD-ROMs and virtual reality. Mention has been made of the use of symbol-writing software to increase pupil access to written material and to increase the ability to write about history. Other computer programs follow an adventure-game format or allow the production of time lines. An increasing number of CD-ROMs permit pupils to explore a wide range of historical data. For example, the Dorling Kindersley CD-ROM entitled *Stowaway!* (see the resources list at the end of this chapter) enables pupils to examine an eighteenth-century warship. As the ship is explored, animation and sound augment the knowledge of what it must have been like to be aboard such a vessel, including having a limb amputated! The interactivity of these computer programs is both engaging and informative.

The Internet has been described as the world's biggest library of information. Pupils studying a particular subject may be able to go online in order to find out more about it. As the Net moves from containing mostly text-based data towards information illustrated with pictures, sound and animation, it will become more relevant to pupils with learning difficulties.

The technology of virtual reality, which is currently being developed, presents the exciting possibility of allowing pupils to visit historical sites and actually to experience involvement in historical events. Jonathan Grove, a student at Sheffield Hallam University, conducted research into whether or not virtual reality can work in the classroom. As part of this project he developed a virtual Greek villa. Pupils can move through the building, and pick up and examine artefacts. Another example is the 'virtual' reconstruction of Fountains Abbey. These developments will provide pupils with experiences that will increase their awareness of what it might have been like to have lived during a particular period.

Teaching history

The following examples of real activities concerned with the teaching of history to pupils with a range of learning difficulties, as undertaken in schools, are offered not as perfect examples but to illustrate ways in which the teaching of history has been approached and also to highlight some issues about relevance and access. A common thread running through the examples is that they are all, in some way, linked to the pupils' own experiences. The subject-specific guidance (QCA 2001) contains further examples of activities linked to the QCA Schemes of Work.

During a term when the theme was 'Work', a group of Key Stage 3 pupils studied the history of Barrow-in-Furness (Key Stage 3: 'Britain 1750–1900, a study of how... industrialisation and political changes affected the United Kingdom, including the local area'). The pupils were encouraged to think about the time before Barrow existed. They talked about how there were very few houses on the map and lots of fields. A series of maps of Barrow, showing its historical development, helped illustrate the changes. The pupils talked about how people needed iron to make things, how iron was found in the land around Barrow and why the ironworks was built. They talked about the iron being used to build ships – hence the development of (what was ultimately named) Vickers Shipbuilding and Engineering Limited (VSEL), now part of BAE Systems. The ironworks and VSEL each needed people to work in them, and so houses were required. The people needed shops and leisure facilities, and so the town continued to grow – and it is still growing, even though shipbuilding has declined.

This example was all a little too theoretical, and so to make the subject come alive the pupils reconstructed the growth of Barrow-in-Furness and they did it in a single afternoon. They started with a very large sheet of white card. On this was drawn the outline of Barrow. The group were equipped with smaller sheets of card, coloured pens, glue and scissors. The first thing to be added to the map was the ironworks, then some houses for the workers to live in. The pupils drew the buildings which were cut out and stuck onto the map. VSEL, the main employer in the town and closely associated with many of the pupils' families, was added to the map along with some cardboard ships and submarines.

The most important feature of the activity was that it made the pupils really think about how the town evolved. For example, as soon as the pupils had put some houses on the map, they were encouraged to think about where the people would buy their food; hence the need for shops. The group talked about what the people would do in the time when they were not working, so the park, the cinema, the pubs and the clubs were constructed and added to the map.

In response to questions about how people might travel out of Barrow, for example to go on holiday, the railway station was added to the map. Roads, schools, churches, the bus depot and the hospital were all added as the group considered how people lived and what they needed. The pupils were enthusiastic about the activity and were able to make good deductions. For example, one pupil spotted that a bridge was needed between Walney Island and mainland Barrow, a requirement quite overlooked by the staff. At the end of the afternoon, all the pupils had increased their awareness of the history of Barrow-in-Furness. The theme had relevance for this group of pupils because it was concerned with *their* town and involved places that were within their experience.

One of the areas listed under knowledge, skills and understanding at each key stage is 'historical interpretation', for which pupils need to develop the ability to identify different ways in which the past is represented. This includes being able to differentiate between fact and fiction. During a term when 'media' was the integrated theme, a group of pupils tackled this issue. Many of the pupils were keen television viewers, and it was apparent that many of them thought that the events on programmes like *Coronation Street* and *Neighbours* were true. For this reason the theme 'Soap operas are not real!' was introduced. In order to elucidate that these programmes are written and then acted, the group wrote a script, selected the cast and rehearsed their own soap opera. Script writers' meetings were convened. The pupils went on to complete a range of work sheets associated with the same theme. The activity illustrated a number of cross-curricular links. There were many strong links with English and also with religious education, as the pupils discussed which characters in the soap operas were 'good' or 'bad'. The pupils also considered what behaviours or characteristics were significant in making these deductions.

A study of Vikings, by a group of Key Stage 3 pupils with learning difficulties, was enhanced by an email link that the pupils had with Rovaer School, an all-age mainstream school situated on a small island off the coast of Norway. The pupils had already taken part in a simulated archaeological dig and had unearthed the foundations of a model Viking farmhouse, which they reconstructed using timber and small pieces of green cord carpet for turf. The group then considered what questions they would like to ask the pupils in Norway about the Vikings.

The questions included: What sort of animals did the Vikings have? What were their houses like? What sort of food did they eat? What were their clothes like? What did the Vikings do in their leisure time? Did the Vikings have shops and money? The response from Rovaer School exceeded the request, and a pupil called Oystein provided some magnificent material:

> Our forefathers called their country Norvegr, which we have shortened to Norge. It means simply 'the way to the North' – or Norway. The archaeologist Per Haavaldsen and his assistant Helge Viken from [the] Archaeological Museum in Stavanger visited Rovaer from 2/8–4/8 1988. The reason was that a new economic map was to be made. Relics of antiquity were to be included. The discoveries at Rovaer were very interesting indeed!
>
> In Groenavika (The Green Bay) which is the people of Rovaer's bathing place, 12 sites were found, and maybe there are more. The experts don't think that people have been living there the whole year. It may have been a site people were living at in seasons, during the fisheries. People living on Rovaer today think it's funny that there have been people here from a long time ago. We are not the first who have fried our sausages in Groenavika!

The reply from Norway seemed particularly vibrant because it was such a direct source of information. The whole group gathered around the computer, while the data was downloaded and printed out. The study was extended by the availability of a set of Viking symbols (Widgit Software). Pupils were able to use a computer, some with the support of an overlay keyboard, to produce their own written material to include in their booklets on the Vikings. The pupils enjoyed being able to read from their booklets in a group and, in order to include a pupil who had no speech, some phrases about the Vikings were programmed into a communication device. That pupil was then able to use a string switch to activate a phrase when it was his turn to speak. His response indicated that he was pleased to be able to join in with the other pupils in this history activity.

A theme on 'materials' provided the impetus for some pupils to study the Bayeux Tapestry and subsequently the Battle of Hastings (Key Stage 3: 'Britain 1066–1500'). It was noted that if the pupils could memorise the date of the Battle of Hastings they would know as many historical dates as a large proportion of the population. Scenes from the tapestry were enlarged and then coloured. The pupils were encouraged to think about the content of the picture they were working on and to comment on how the people were dressed, what weapons they used in the battle and why the Normans needed to take horses in the boats with them. The pupils made quite sophisticated observations during these sessions and then made their own tapestry about life at their school. They included all the pupils in the school, the minibuses, the classrooms and the sensory room. In this way they were able to make links between the past and the present.

A group of Year 10 pupils, with a wide range of abilities, followed programmes of studies from Key Stage 3 at different levels. Some pupils considered and understood why the Domesday Book was written, while for others the study presented a further opportunity to practise recalling their names and addresses within a different framework. Names and addresses also featured on each pupil's page in their updated version of the Domesday Book, which they produced using computer-based multimedia. They looked at how the book was originally written by hand and then were questioned about how a task of this magnitude would be tackled now. As the use of technology is an important element in their daily life, it was not long before computers were suggested.

During a theme on 'dwellings' (Key Stage 1: 'Pupils should be taught about ... the way of life of people in the more distant past ...'), a group of pupils with learning difficulties constructed a time line, arranging pictures of dwellings into chronological order. The first picture in the time line was a cave. The pupils were encouraged to think about what it was like to live in a cave, and what modern-day comfort they would most miss. The list included television, videos, washing machines and tea-bags! This activity not only encouraged the pupils to think about life in the Stone Age but also increased their awareness of their own environment and way of life.

Conclusion

History is a subject that is accessible and has relevance for all pupils, including those who have learning difficulties. It has the potential to enrich the curriculum and provide many interesting contexts in which learning can take place. It also provides a framework for other skills to be practised and developed. The teaching of history will be most effective where teachers have a positive attitude to the benefits of the subject for their pupils. The statutory orders for history provide a degree of flexibility that teachers can use to plan interesting and imaginative work in order to enable pupils to gain access to the programmes of study for history. Studying history will encourage all pupils to develop a sense of time and to be more aware of – and interested – in the world around them.

References

Byers, R. (1990) 'Topics: from myths to objectives', *British Journal of Special Education* **17**(3), 109–12.

Byers, R. (1994) 'The Dearing Review of the National Curriculum', *British Journal of Special Education* **21**(3), 92–6.

Carpenter, B. (1995) 'Self assessment using symbols', in *Extending Horizons*. Coventry: National Council for Educational Technology.

DES (1990) *History for Ages 5 to 16*. London: HMSO.

NFER (1995) *Small Steps of Progress in the National Curriculum: Executive summary*. Slough: NFER.

QCA (2001) *Planning, Teaching and Assessing the Curriculum for Pupils with Learning Difficulties: History*. London: DfEE/QCA.

Sebba, J. and Clarke, J. (1991) 'Meeting the needs of pupils within history and geography', in Ashdown, R. *et al.* (eds) *The Curriculum Challenge: Access to the National Curriculum for pupils with learning difficulties.* London: Falmer Press.

Sebba, J. (1994) *History for All.* London: David Fulton Publishers.

Sebba, J. and Clarke, J. (1993) 'A response to "We're doing history"'. *British Journal of Special Education* **20**(4), 141–2.

Sebba, J. *et al.* (1995) *Redefining the Whole Curriculum for Pupils with Learning Difficulties*, 2nd edn. London: David Fulton Publishers.

SCAA (1996) *Planning the Curriculum for Pupils with Profound and Multiple Learning Difficulties.* London: SCAA.

Stevens, C. (1995) 'News from SCAA', *British Journal of Special Education* **22**(1), 30–31.

Ware, J. and Peacey, N. (1993) '"We're doing history" – What does it mean?', *British Journal of Special Education* **20**(2), 65–9.

Ware, J. (1994) 'Implementing the 1988 Act with pupils with PMLDs', in Ware, J. (ed.) *Educating Children with Profound and Multiple Learning Difficulties.* London: David Fulton Publishers.

Other resources

Widgit Software, 26 Queen Street, Cubbington, Leamington Sp CV32 7NA (Tel.: 01926 885303).
Dorling Kindersley, 9 Henrietta Street, London WC2E 8PS (Tel.: 020 7836 5411).

Chapter 7

Geography

Bernard Gummett and Clare Martin

At 12.40pm Sulphur Mountain Doppler Radar showed the showers moving into the mountains. Four to seven inches of snow has fallen in the Big Bear area. New showers were blossoming over northern Ventura County and north-western Los Angeles County and these showers were likely producing snow above 2500 feet. Travel to the mountains and north-western desert areas is discouraged. If you absolutely must travel to these areas today ... Remember to take emergency supplies and tire chains in preparation for hazardous winter weather conditions.

(National Weather Service, Oxnard, California, USA).

Why study geography?

Geography can be defined as the 'science of the earth's surface, form, physical features, natural and political divisions, climate, productions, population, etc.' (*Concise Oxford Dictionary*) but in the introduction to *Geography for All*, Sebba (1995) defines geography more simply as being 'about the relationships between people and places'. Sebba goes on to state that geography 'aims to help pupils make sense of their surroundings and develop an understanding about the interaction of people with the environment'. The dictionary definition provides a more traditional view of geography but it does not conflict with Sebba's definition.

The HMI 'Curriculum Matters' document entitled *Geography from 5 to 16* (DES 1986) suggests (pp. 5–6) that the study of geography will enable pupils to:

- extend their awareness of, and develop their interest in, their surroundings;
- observe accurately and develop simple skills of enquiry;
- identify and explore features of the local environment;
- distinguish between the variety of ways in which land is used and the variety of purposes for which buildings are constructed;
- recognise and investigate changes taking place in the local area;
- relate different types of human activity to specific places within the area;
- develop concepts that enable pupils to recognise the relative position and spatial attributes of features within the environment;

- understand some of the ways in which the local environment affects people's lives;
- develop an awareness of seasonal changes of weather and of the effects that weather conditions have on the growth of plants, on the lives of animals and on their own and other people's activities;
- gain some understanding of the different contributions that a variety of individuals and services make to the life of the local community;
- begin to develop an interest in people and places beyond their immediate experience;
- develop an awareness of cultural and ethnic diversity within our society, while recognising the similarity of activities, interests and aspirations of different people;
- extend and refine pupils' vocabulary and develop their language skills;
- develop mathematical concepts and number skills;
- develop their competence to communicate in a variety of forms, including pictures, drawings. simple diagrams and maps.

This list has been reproduced elsewhere (Sebba 1995; Sebba and Clarke 1991) but it bears repetition because it removes geography from being the study of glaciers, volcanoes and peninsulas to being a subject that is accessible to, and has relevance for, all pupils, including those with learning difficulties.

Geography in the National Curriculum

Towards the end of 1999, new statutory orders for the subjects within the National Curriculum were published, with the requirement that pupils should follow the orders from the beginning of the autumn term 2000. Following the review of the curriculum in 1995, the content of what was to be taught was significantly reduced. The new orders have seen some further reduction in content, with an emphasis being placed on developing geographical knowledge, skills and understanding. The advice issued, following the publication of the 1995 statutory orders (DfE 1995), by SCAA (Stevens 1995) was that:

> For the small number of pupils who may need the provision, material may be selected from earlier or later Key Stages where this is necessary to enable individual pupils to progress and demonstrate achievement. Such material should be presented in contexts suitable to the pupil's age.

This advice remains sound when applied to the new orders, the spirit of which is indicated by a section on inclusion that offers guidance and support on how to provide effective learning opportunities for *all* pupils. The subject-specific guidance for teaching geography to pupils with learning difficulties (QCA 2001) further supports the inclusion of all pupils.

It is important that teachers – especially those working with pupils whose learning difficulties are severe – do not just use the PoS for Key Stage 1 when planning work for pupils who may be working within Level 1 for most if not all of their school career. Indeed, the advice from SCAA about pupils with profound and multiple learning difficulties (PMLD) is that 'teachers should familiarise themselves with the full range of programmes of study in all National Curriculum subjects before making decisions on which is the most appropriate content' (SCAA 1996). Within the same document, there is also advice that teachers of pupils with PMLD might wish to select material from the later PoS, 'for coverage in outline rather than depth'.

For each of the three key stages covered by the PoS for geography, the 'knowledge, skills and understanding' to be covered are divided into four sections:

- geographical enquiry and skills;
- knowledge and understanding of places;
- knowledge and understanding of patterns and processes;
- knowledge and understanding of environmental change and sustainable development.

The orders state that 'Teaching should ensure that *geographical enquiry and skills* are used when developing *knowledge and understanding of places, patterns and processes, and environmental change and sustainable development*.' The guidance for teaching geography (QCA 2001) looks at each of these areas and explores their relevance and means of access for pupils with learning difficulties.

In the statutory orders, the description of what is to be covered within each of these areas is followed by a section titled 'Breadth of study'. This part of the PoS outlines the areas of study that are to be pursued while developing the four sections listed above. As pupils progress through the key stages, the material being covered becomes more complex and the areas to be studied cover a wider selection of geographical topics. At Key Stage 1, the areas in the 'Breadth of study' are the locality of the school and a contrasting locality; at Key Stage 2, pupils are required to study two localities in addition to three themes; and at Key Stage 3 the 'Breadth of study' is extended to the study of two countries and ten themes.

When planning geography for pupils with learning difficulties, staff should recognise that, for example, for pupils in Key Stage 3, areas to be covered from the section 'Breadth of study' could be studied while developing *knowledge, skills and understanding* taken from Key Stage 1. A school might plan to cover the characteristics and distribution of tropical rainforest (an area taken from Key Stage 3) with some or all of the pupils in the group, continuing to develop their knowledge and understanding of places, and identifying and describing what places are like (a skill taken from Key Stage 1).

At Key Stage 3, the terms 'tectonic' and 'geomorphological' processes are used to describe two of the themes. These terms might make some teachers recoil in horror, yet a closer examination of the PoS reveals that tectonic processes actually involve studying earthquakes and volcanoes. Consequently these areas will provide stimulating contexts for learning, as well as opportunities for pupils to develop geographical skills that include those taken from Key Stage 1. Using a CD-ROM entitled *This Violent Earth* (Wayland Multimedia), pupils are able to use 'secondary sources of information', a skill taken from Key Stage 1, to extend their knowledge of volcanoes or earthquakes.

Another major change that took place in all subjects, including geography, following the Dearing Report (SCAA 1994) was the move away from the use of statements of attainment for assessing achievement, towards the use of level descriptions. This remains the case for the revised 2000 orders, with the subject-specific guidance for pupils with learning difficulties (QCA 2001) providing pre-Level 1 assessment scales.

SCAA commissioned the National Foundation for Educational Research (NFER) to carry out research into effective practice in assessment, recording and accreditation (NFER 1995). Their recommendations include the following:

- Assessment procedures and materials, incorporating a small-steps approach within the revised PoS, should be developed to take account of the needs of pupils with learning difficulties. Publishers could play an important role in this.

● Approaches to assessment should be developed through collaboration between specialists in learning difficulties and disabilities and specialists in subject areas, not only within schools but within clusters of schools. Such cooperative working could also be linked to the development of individual education plans (IEPs.)

The recommendation that teachers should collaborate in order to assist with the teaching of subjects such as geography is an important and potentially convincing one. However, the practical outworking of this may be constrained by the demands being made on teachers' time and by the inexorable contraction of the local advisory services as personnel have become absorbed within the inspection process.

The teaching of geography has been influenced by the round of school inspections by OFSTED. If the arrival of the National Curriculum did not stimulate the development of policies in curriculum areas, including geography, then the expectation of an OFSTED inspection is almost guaranteed to do so. Prior to an inspection, schools are required to provide 'curriculum plans, policies and guidelines or schemes of work, already in existence' (OFSTED 1999. Bines (1993) points out that 'the National Curriculum requires collaborative planning of the curriculum, to map and ensure coverage of National Curriculum requirements and promote progression and continuity'.

Planning in order to teach geography

The formulation of policies and the identification of subject coordinators for geography has resulted in a good deal of positive curriculum development. The role of the subject coordinator is an important one and should include playing a key role in drafting the school's policy statement on geography, monitoring the delivery of geography and pupil progress throughout the school, and maintaining the resources required for the successful teaching of the subject. Ideally, the coordinator will be a teacher who has a specialism in geography, but in many schools this is not possible and the school will rely on a teacher who has an interest in the subject and who is committed to developing personal expertise, possibly by pursuing in-service training opportunities.

Sebba (1995) lists seven principles that should assist in developing a coherent structure for planning, recording and assessing in geography:

1. Ensure the planning system in the school provides a broad and balanced curriculum that is planned sufficiently far ahead to ensure continuity and progression.
2. Include opportunities for assessment at the planning stage rather than bolting them on as an afterthought.
3. Ensure that the primary reason for assessing pupils is to identify what they have learnt so that the teacher knows what to do next.
4. Adopt a recording system that enables pupils' progress in geography to be noted in sufficient detail to inform assessment but that does not generate volumes of unused information.
5. Assess pupils through a variety of methods to ensure they can demonstrate what they have learned.
6. Involve pupils where possible in planning, recording and assessing.
7. Define a clear, realistic role for the subject coordinator and ensure adequate support is provided.

A school's policy for geography should contain the aims and objectives in geography and the curriculum plan for how the subject will be taught. It is important that the policy should reflect the actual practice in the school; this can only be achieved if all the staff are actively involved in preparing the policy. Another issue that has become increasingly significant, particularly in the light of OFSTED inspection reports, is the time allocation of each subject, including geography. The advice from SCAA (1996) with regard to pupils with PMLD is that planning needs to take account of the learning time available for each individual and that (p. 17):

> [i]t is important to avoid anxiety over allocation of specific hours and minutes to each subject: schools will wish to aim for balance and breadth in the time available over the year or Key Stage, utilising the time most profitably and ensuring a productive atmosphere is established.

Although there is a general consensus that geography has a place in the curriculum for pupils with learning difficulties, there remains some contention about its relevance for pupils with PMLD. The consultation exercise that took place after the publication of the draft proposals for the new orders for each subject indicated that many teachers were concerned about providing access for this group of pupils. Ware (1994) reviews the debate and concludes that the introduction of the National Curriculum has had a positive effect on the curriculum for pupils with PMLD. It should also be recognised that the PoS for geography can provide an interesting framework for the development of other skills. Ware also points out (p. 81) that the National Curriculum:

> has reminded us that that there is more to being a member of the human community than the acquisition of minimal independence skills. The National Curriculum has served as a useful reminder that knowing about science, history, geography, etc. can contribute to a full life.

The inclusion of pupils with PMLD in geography teaching is also supported by the guidance for teaching geography to pupils with learning difficulties (QCA 2001), which contains examples of relevant activities.

An important planning decision to be made by schools is what teaching style to use for geography. In some schools, geography is taught as part of an integrated theme, while in others it is a separate subject. A solution that has been reached by some schools, including some special schools, is that geography is taught as part of an integrated theme for pupils within Key Stage 1 and Key Stage 2, while for pupils at Key Stage 3 and Key Stage 4 it is taught as a discrete subject. This model has the added advantage that it also replicates the way that geography is often taught in mainstream schools (Halocha and Roberts 1995). The way in which pupils are grouped will also influence how geography is to be taught and the way in which the differentiation of learning will be managed. One of the strengths of using themes is that they allow the cross-curricular links between subjects to be fully exploited, but it has to be recognised that the demands of the National Curriculum do not allow teachers and pupils to pursue themes guided solely by the way a theme evolves.

The statutory orders for the revised National Curriculum, effective from the beginning of the autumn term 2000, make frequent reference to the use of information and communication technology (ICT.) Within the section of the orders on inclusion, specific reference is made to using ICT and alternative and augmentative communication, including signs and symbols. For many pupils with learning difficulties, the use of technology, symbols and signing has a tremendous relevance because these systems have the potential to increase dramatically the access of pupils to all curriculum areas, including geography. The subject-specific guidance for pupils with learning difficulties lists ways in which full participation in geography may be promoted, and this includes the use of ICT and the use of specialist aids and equipment.

It is possible to use symbols in conjunction with technology to accompany words, so that written material becomes accessible to pupils who have little or no 'reading' skills. Some pupils with learning difficulties may not be able to recall all the symbols but, nevertheless, will be able to understand sufficient symbols to gain an overall impression of what is 'written'. For example, a pupil completing a geographical study may be given a sheet to record the work that has been done and the areas that have been covered. This sheet may be filed away and after a short time have little meaning to the pupil. The addition of symbols will allow the pupil to recall the work that they did during that theme, even some years later. In this way, pupils can become actively involved in their own Records of Achievement.

Similarly, the use of symbols can allow pupils to construct their own written material. Carpenter and Detheridge (1994) have examined how the use of symbols, in conjunction with information technology, has enabled pupils who have learning problems to construct written material, and they describe the positive effect that this has on the pupils' cognitive skills.

One example of this is provided by a group of Key Stage 3 pupils with SLD who, as part of a theme on 'dwellings', set up their own estate agency in which they displayed their own houses for sale. They used an overlay keyboard to construct their house specifications, selecting from a bank of appropriate words/symbols (using, for instance, WRITING WITH SYMBOLS 2000 from Widgit Software). They were able to think and then write about not only what features their own houses had but also the geographical location of their homes. The overlay encouraged them to make decisions about whether their homes were near a park, near a hospital or close to town-centre shops. When they found it hard to make a decision, they were helped by studying a map of the town (see Key Stage 3, PoS 6g: During the key stage, pupils should be taught the *knowledge, skills and understanding* through the study of … reasons for the location, growth and nature of individual settlements).

Resources for geography

There is a growing range of geographical resources. Books, including children's stories that are not written for geographical purposes but that, for example, involve journeys, are available and can be very relevant to pupils with learning difficulties. There are maps, including three-dimensional maps, that will fulfil a variety of purposes. An increasing number of originally paper-based resources are becoming available on CD-ROM and other computer media, with the added facilities of sound and animation. There are simulation programs that allow the establishment of settlements with or without ensuing disaster. Videotapes of foreign countries and the coastline of the United Kingdom can enhance the geographical understanding of all pupils, and virtual reality promises the opportunity to explore a variety of areas.

A digital camera has the potential to greatly enhance geographical experiences and aid the acquisition of geographical skills. Such a camera allows 'photographs' to be recorded on trips out of school and then viewed immediately on return. The pictures can be transferred to a computer, accompanied by text, and then displayed or used as the basis of a multimedia presentation.

The Internet provides a vast resource of information about the weather (among many other topics). The quotation at the beginning of this chapter was gathered via the World Wide Web, and daily weather satellite images are also readily available. It is possible to gather real-time images from fixed cameras in different global locations, so it is possible to visually check the weather, for example, in Tromso. Video-conferencing facilities allow these cameras to be moved so as to take in the wider panoramic view and also to engage in conversations with people in different parts of the world.

Teaching geography

The following real-life examples of activities concerned with teaching geography to pupils with a range of learning difficulties are offered, not as perfect examples but in order to illustrate some ways in which geography has been approached and to highlight some issues about relevance and access. The subject-specific guidance for geography (QCA 2001) contains further examples of activities linked to the QCA Schemes of Work.

During an integrated theme on 'work', a group of pupils were driven around the local environment to identify places of work. The minibus stopped at each workplace and the pupils were encouraged to talk about the location. They completed a worksheet accompanied by symbols that asked questions requiring a 'yes' or 'no' answer, and a digital photograph was taken at each location. On return to school, the camera was connected to a monitor and, as they reviewed the pictures, the pupils were immediately able to discuss the journey and to recall facts about each of the workplaces they had visited. The pictures were transferred to a computer, and then the pupils inserted the pictures into a word-processing program and wrote about each site. The pictures were subsequently used to illustrate a map of the town on a display board, which allowed the pupils to see the workplaces in relation to each other and to make judgements about why some of them were located in particular positions. For example, one pupil with SLD deduced why the factory that built submarines had to be so close to the sea (see Key Stage 1, PoS 4a: Pupils should be taught to make observations about where things are located).

Another group of pupils were involved in making a computer-based multimedia presentation about the small town where they lived. The group gathered around the computer and were encouraged to think about what people might like to know about the town. One pupil suggested that it was important to say how many people live in the town. When questioned about how that information could be obtained, several suggestions were made, including standing outside a high-street store and counting people as they went past. When it was pointed out that not everyone would be visiting the town centre at the same time, another pupil suggested counting the names in the telephone directory. When the observation was made that not every individual would be listed in the directory, another pupil suggested that a telephone call to the Town Hall would provide the answer – and it did. (Key Stage 3, PoS 1c: In undertaking geographical enquiry, pupils should be taught to ... collect, record and present evidence.)

Email can be used to extend geographical knowledge. A group of pupils in a school for pupils with learning difficulties have access to email. Membership of the Apple Global Education (AGE) project has enabled them to link with schools in other countries, gradually developing a global awareness and increasing the understanding of other cultures by pupils and staff. The map of the world on the classroom wall became an important reference point, and pupils were encouraged to find the countries from which the messages had originated. The countries were marked and a discussion took place about comparative distances, how long it would take to travel to each of the countries and what kind of transport might be used. The project gave rise to several interesting exchanges. For instance, the following unsolicited request arrived:

Hello! My name is Corinne and I am in the Seventh Grade at the Upper Pittsgrove Middle School in Monroeville, New Jersey, United States of America. In our social studies class we are studying your country, Great Britain. We would like it if you would send us a flag of your country. It should be about 90 cm tall and 130 cm wide. If you send us a flag of Britain we will send you a flag of our country, the United States of America. Sincerely,

Corinne and your friends in the United States of America. Upper Pittsgrove Middle School.

This request caused a discussion about how every classroom in the United States usually has a flag. There were several electronic exchanges as the school in the United Kingdom explained, with some embarrassment, that very few schools in this country have even one flag. This particular school had to undertake some research to discover a suitable flag before the swap took place. What is particularly inspiring about the exchange is that Corrine and her friends did not know – nor did they need to know – that the pupils they were writing to had learning difficulties. Email can provide a cloak of anonymity, giving everyone an equal opportunity on a global scale (National Council for Educational Training (NCET) 1995).

Another electronic exchange was with pupils on the Norwegian island of Rovaer, which was the chosen contrasting location for a group of pupils who undertook a comparative study of two islands (Key Stage 1, PoS 6: During the key stage, pupils should be taught the *knowledge, skills and understanding* through the study of two localities). The exchange began with a series of questions, which in due course received the following reply:

Here come our answers to your questions! Sorry for the delay.
How big is your island? The island is 1,4 square kilometers. (!!!)
Do you have lots of boats? We have 2 big fishingboats on the island, about 15 other smaller fishingboats and our ferry.
How far away are you from the main land? About 10 kilometers.
How long does it take you to get to the main land? It takes 45 minutes by our ferry.
Does your island have some shops on it? Yes, the island has a small shop where you can buy the things you need.
Does your island have a swimming pool? No, we swim in the sea (in the summer, of course!).
Are your houses made out of wood or are they made out of
bricks? Most houses are made out of wood; but none are made out of bricks.
Do you have a golf course on your island? No, we don't have
any golf course. There is none in Haugesund, either.
Our weather has been very stormy lately. What is your weather like at the moment? At the moment we have a north-western storm with some rain and sleet.

Although the exchange began with email, it soon required the services of 'snail mail' to deal with the packages of maps, leaflets and photographs that were collected and swapped. An added dimension to this was that although the two schools had been corresponding for over two years, this produced the first Norwegian stamp!

During a study of 'weather', pupils were encouraged to make their own daily records of the weather. In order to add to the interest, the weekly long-term forecast, shown on the BBC each Sunday, was recorded and played back to the pupils on Monday morning. A record was made of the daily forecast for the subsequent week. Each day before the pupils went home, they referred to the weather predictions and decided whether or not it had been accurate. The pupils made their own weather maps, selecting the appropriate symbols for the weather that they predicted would occur in each of the countries in Britain. They were then recorded on video, reading their forecasts. Not only did this activity enhance their awareness of the weather and extend their knowledge of weather symbols, but it also helped to improve their knowledge of the relative positions and names of the countries in the British Isles (Key Stage 2, PoS 3a: Pupils should be taught: to identify and describe what places are like, for example, in terms of weather, jobs).

During a study of 'transport and travel' and in order to extend their knowledge of their own locality, some pupils in Barrow-in-Furness, Cumbria, studied the A590, a trunk road that plays an important role in the economy of the region in which they live. The pupils went to junction 36 of the M6 motorway (where the A590 starts) and they then tracked it for over 30 miles to where it ends on Walney Island, close to the pupils' school. They were required to make notes of the towns and villages through which the road passes and any other important features. On another occasion the pupils went to a lay-by midway along the road, where a mobile snack van was providing refreshment for commercial-vehicle drivers. Under careful supervision, the pupils questioned the drivers about where they had come from, where they were going and what, if anything, they were carrying in their vehicles. The pupils' level of motivation was greatly increased by being able to sample the bacon butties for which the snack van is renowned! (Key Stage 3, PoS 6g: During the key stage, pupils should be taught: the reasons for the location, growth and nature of individual settlements).

Conclusion

If geography is more 'about the relationships between people and places' (Sebba 1995) than the study of physical features, political boundaries and climatic processes, then it has relevance for all pupils – including those with learning difficulties. All have a right to be assisted to make sense of their surroundings and to develop an understanding about the interaction of people within their environment. When this is accomplished, all pupils can be recognised as the geographers they already are.

References

Bines, H. (1993) 'Whole school policies in the new era', *British Journal of Special Education* **20**(3), 91–4.

Byers, R. (1994) 'The Dearing Review of the National Curriculum', *British Journal of Special Education* **21**(3), 92–6.

Carpenter, B. and Detheridge, T. (1994) 'Writing with symbols', *Support for Learning* **9**(1), 27–32.

DES (1986) *Geography from 5 to 16*, Curriculum Matters 7. London: HMSO.

DFE (1995) *Geography in the National Curriculum*. London: HMSO.

Halocha, J. and Roberts, M. (1995) 'Geography', in Ashcroft, K. and Palacio, D. (eds) *The Primary Teacher's Guide to the New National Curriculum*. London: Falmer Press.

NCET (1995) 'A sense of the world', in *Extending Horizons*. Coventry, Warwickshire: National Council for Educational Technology (NCET).

NFER (1995). *Small Steps of Progress in the National Curriculum: An executive summary*. Slough: NFER.

OFSTED (1999) *Handbook for Inspecting Special Schools and Pupil Refural Units*. London: HMSO.

QCA (2001) *Planning, Teaching and Assessing the Curriculum for Pupils with Learning Difficulties: Geography*. London: DfEE/QCA.

SCAA (1994) *The National Curriculum and its Assessment: Final report*. (The Dearing Report), London: SCAA.

SCAA (1996) *Planning the Curriculum for Pupils with Profound and Multiple Learning Difficulties*. London: SCAA.

Sebba, J. (1995) *Geography for All*. London: David Fulton Publishers.

Sebba, J. and Clarke, J. (1991) 'Meeting the needs of pupils within history and geography', in Ashdown, R. *et al.* (eds) *The Curriculum Challenge: Access to the National Curriculum for pupils with learning difficulties*. London: Falmer Press.

Stevens, C. (1995) 'News from SCAA', *British Journal of Special Education* **22**(1), 30–31.

Ware, J. (1994) 'Implementing the 1988 Act with pupils with PMLDs', in Ware, J. (ed.) *Educating Children with Profound and Multiple Learning Difficulties*. London: David Fulton Publishers.

Other resources

Widgit Software, 26 Queen Street, Cubbington, Leamington Spa CV32 7NA (Tel. 01926 885303).
Wayland Multimedia, 61 Western Road, Hove, East Sussex, BN1 1NH.

Chapter 8

Art and Design

Melanie Peter

The state of the art

'Art and design stimulates creativity and imagination. It provides visual, tactile and sensory experiences and a unique way of understanding and responding to the world' (DfEE /QCA 1999a, p. 116). The National Curriculum has given status and recognition to art (including design and craft) as a foundation subject in its own right – 'art for art's sake'. No longer is it sufficient for art activity solely to service other areas of the curriculum, for example to illustrate topic work. OFSTED inspection teams are required to make judgements on the extent to which schools provide a broad and balanced curriculum for *all* their pupils. In principle at least, the National Curriculum is committed to the notion of one 'art for all', with teachers answerable for the progress of *all* their pupils in understanding and using art as a means of expression and communication. Besides, certain young people with learning difficulties may have exceptional ability in art; for example, the outstanding work of Stephen Wiltshire, the 'boy who draws buildings' – who is renowned also because he happens to have autism. Teachers have an obligation to ensure quality learning by pupils and that good standards are achieved in art, and to develop an inclusive curriculum framework that takes account of pupils' relative ability to record what they have seen, imagined or recalled.

Developing an inclusive art curriculum entails selecting appropriately challenging skills, knowledge and understanding from earlier – or later – key stages to enable individual pupils to participate fully, and to progress and demonstrate achievement in suitably differentiated and motivating programmes of study. Teachers will need to decide on which aspects their pupils will focus in depth and which aspects may receive more light-touch consideration. Pupils will need opportunities to maintain, reinforce, consolidate and generalise learning in art, as well as access to new knowledge, skills and understanding.

Curriculum guidance for the Foundation Stage (QCA 2000a), offers a framework for the holistic, creative development of children at early stages of learning, and the original 'Desirable Outcomes' framework for nursery education (SCAA, 1996) was the basis for the EQUALS guidance (1999a, 1999b) on curriculum development for pupils with severe and profound and multiple learning difficulties. Schemes of work compatible with the

National Curriculum (QCA 2000b) may further support planning to meet the needs of those pupils attaining significantly below expected 'norms', as well as the subject-specific art and design curriculum guidelines for planning, teaching and assessing the curriculum for pupils with learning difficulties (QCA 2001).

However, the starting point for planning should always be consideration of requirements for pupils' actual chronological age, and revisions to the National Curriculum order for art have been made deliberately broad and enabling, so as to embrace pupils of all abilities. The associated schemes of work for art and design at Key Stages 1 and 2 (QCA 2000b) provide some practical guidance for making an inclusive framework; expectations for the end of each of the 18 themed units (1 per term for Years 1–6) are differentiated on 3 levels, and certain inclusive approaches and principles are also established within the units. For example:

- The subject matter of early units (eg 'self-portrait' – unit 1A; 'investigating materials' – unit 1B) is intended to establish an inclusive philosophy from the outset.
- Children are encouraged to respond 'hands on' to natural and made objects and environments as stimuli, and so begin with concrete experiences, using a multisensory approach, before they are expected to develop their own work. (This may particularly support pupils unable to gain from incidental learning of the wider world.)
- Working directly with materials and processes for textiles and three-dimensional (3D) work provides access for children who need a sensory approach – for example, children who are visually impaired. (Multimedia contemporary works such as installations potentially offer access through a range of sensory modes, and therefore differing preferred learning styles to meet diverse needs within a group.)
- Investigating the work of artists, craftspeople and designers from different times and cultures helps children to understand and value different interpretations and viewpoints. (This might include first-hand experiences that extend into music, dance or drama, as well as visits to galleries, museums, sites and sensory environments.)

Art, craft and design can provide 'a distinctive way of learning, where seeing, feeling, thinking and making are combined in a powerful form of visual and tactile communication' (QCA 1999a, p. 156). In order for this to be meaningful, pupils will need to be *enabled* in order to engage with the experience. In addition to enabling access through a range of sensory modes as indicated above, teachers may promote full participation for their pupils with learning difficulties through employing other approaches. The curriculum guidelines for art and design for pupils with learning difficulties (QCA 2001) list a range of inclusive strategies to promote access to the subject; these include use of ICT and of specialist aids and equipment, additional support from staff or peers (including partnership with artists in residence) to allow pupils to work at their own pace, and alternative activities to overcome manipulative difficulties with equipment and to enable a pupil to work in a preferred learning style. Pupils of all abilities will need a balance not only of familiar art experiences in which they may express themselves with confidence and improve their proficiency with techniques, but also new experiences in which they will be challenged to discover different and/or more complex approaches to art-making.

Empowering pupils to 'read images', may offer them insight into different cultures and traditions and enjoyment of their artistic heritage, as well as inspire and inform their own art-making. It may also prepare them to discern meanings (explicit and implicit) from the bombardment of visual imagery that they are likely to experience during their lifetime, and help to develop their ability to engage critically with a rapidly changing visual culture, obtaining an awareness of the diverse roles and functions of art, craft and design in contemporary life.

Art and design makes a significant contribution towards developing self-advocacy in young people with special educational needs. This shows itself by a gaining of control over powers of expression other than in a written form, and a discovery of their own ability to have impact on – and influence the behaviour of – other people. Children's communication skills may be encouraged through collaboration and discussion of their own and others' work, with a growing awareness of and respect for the opinions and contributions of others.

Looking at art can foster pupils' spiritual, moral, social and cultural development, and also contribute to other foundation subjects across the curriculum. For example, aspects of social history may be revealed in the depiction of clothing, buildings, transport, occupations and landscape. Principles of 'breadth and balance' need to be applied rigorously: children may be very alert to 'pleasing teacher' and, as a result, care should be taken to present a range of works beyond one's personal taste! Pupils will need access to their cultural heritage: the work of other arts, craftspeople and designers – male and female, from different cultures, past and present – to inspire and inform their own work. This should be on different scales, and in a range of two-dimensional (2D) and three-dimensional (3D) media, including textiles and ICT. Visits should be made to see practising local artists, galleries, museums and sites. At the very least, pupils may then discover that original works of art are not all the same size as a postcard reproduction, and that sculpture is one medium that is crucially dependant on its location to create a full impact. Regrettably, the revised National Curriculum (DfEE/QCA 1999a; 1999b) rather missed the opportunity to give this important aspect due emphasis, although the schemes of work for art and design at Key Stages 1 and 2 redress this somewhat, for they include a generic unit on visits for Key Stage 2.

Art and design can offer important opportunities to young people of all abilities. It can help with:

- individual and collaborative working in response to a stimulus or brief;
- problem-solving – often with no predetermined action or outcome;
- divergent thinking – creative, imaginative, enquiring, questioning, making connections, synthesising ideas;
- active learning – manipulating materials, processes and technologies, responding, experimenting, adaptation of thinking, arriving at divergent solutions;
- celebrating achievement of named and unnamed artists from different cultures, past and present;
- visual literacy – exploring and critically evaluating meanings and interpretations in images in contemporary life;
- aesthetic sensitivity – making informed choices and practical decisions to shape the environment.

However, there would appear to be a conflicting tension between a commitment to value the role of the arts – for example through the work of the National Advisory Committee on Creative and Cultural Education (DfEE 1999) – and a continuing emphasis on the core subjects of English, mathematics and science as set out in the National Curriculum (Robinson 1998). With literacy and numeracy being a major preoccupation in many schools, teachers are under pressure to find sufficient opportunity for those subjects that are not compulsory within the National Curriculum framework – especially when they are inherently time-consuming, as in the case of art.

In order to present a meaningful, coherent programme of study to pupils, teachers are being encouraged to explore natural links between subjects; for example, pattern in art and mathematics (QCA 1998). A work of art may also provide a wonderful stimulus for pupils' creative writing, or be brought to life in drama or dance. The exemplar schemes of work for art and design (QCA 2000b) endeavour to provide examples of curricular links that are cross-referenced to the respective programmes of study in the subjects concerned. The challenge for teachers is how to work in more than one curriculum area at any one time, but *without compromising learning in the art form,* at the expense of servicing other subjects. Indeed, if art is to provide a means of accessing other areas of the curriculum, then activities must be appropriately pitched in order for pupils to participate fully in a way that is perceived as relevant and meaningful.

If teachers have a secure grasp of how children develop in art, then it should be possible to plan appropriate experiences to meet the creative needs of all their pupils – *and* to provide an imaginative and economic approach to curriculum planning and timetabling! Ultimately, the creating child should have 'ownership' over a piece of work and make the final executive decisions. However, it is the responsibility of the teacher to ensure that choices are made from an informed basis, and to encourage children to become as independent as possible in organising and executing a piece of work in a range of art practices. In this way, pupils may be enabled to select the most appropriate medium to achieve a desired intention.

This will not be achieved through offering a 'free for all' at the easel. In order to gain control over processes, children need to develop creative responses within clear parameters, through being offered carefully planned choices according to their stage of development. Materials and processes are no longer prescribed at each key stage of the National Curriculum; even so, teachers need to be aware that some procedures are inherently more challenging and complex than others. Teachers need a clear sense of direction in the different forms of art-making, in order to offer appropriate experiences and give shape to pupils' work in progress.

Developing 'art for art's sake'

At particular stages in children's development in art, certain characteristics tend to 'hang together'. Patterns of growth in art are similar across cultures, although rates of progress might be affected by environmental factors, children's direct experiences and materials available; particular disabling conditions and emotional stability may also be contributory factors. Teachers need to have an awareness of these patterns in order to plan and implement developmentally appropriate activities. In this way, work will then be truly differentiated, to meet the individual needs of pupils in all aspects of the subject of art and design.

A series of overlapping stages of artistic development may be identified and related to the characteristic attainments of average learners, both at the Foundation Stage and across the key stages. They are:

- the *scribbling* stage (Foundation Stage);
- the *pre-schematic/symbolic* stage (Key Stage 1);

- the *schematic/emerging analytic* stage (lower Key Stage 2);
- the Stage of *visual realism/analytic* stage (upper Key Stage 2 into Key Stage 3).

Children's artistic expression reflects the way they organise information and make sense of their world. Pupils with learning difficulties may pass through the same developmental stages as their peers, although the actual chronological timing will differ. Children at early stages of learning may engage in sensory exploration of materials and their environment, to which they may develop their responses and ideas, with awareness of cause and effect in certain art practices (especially drawing, painting, printing, collage and 3D sculpture). Initially, this is known as a stage of *random scribbling* (Foundation Stage), which gradually becomes more *controlled* in a range of marks, with children possibly *naming* them and thereby attaching representational significance (a huge conceptual leap). As their symbolic development becomes consolidated (*pre-schematic/symbolic* stage – equivalent to Key Stage 1), so they may commonly represent what they know and what has personal significance, not necessarily what they see; this growing ability to want to organise experience is paralleled in abstract work with a greater sense of arranging and rearranging marks or items and with greater control. During the *schematic/emerging analytic* stage (equivalent to lower Key Stage 2), children characteristically begin to attend to detail, and strive for a greater sense of order. Typically, they arrange images along baselines in representational work, and achieve more complex arrangements of items and marks in abstract work; children also generally become more able to develop their creativity. The fourth stage of *visual realism and analysis* (Key Stage 2 into Key Stage 3) reflects children's developing powers of observation and social awareness, and their growing understanding of the wider world. This manifests itself as a preoccupation with creating a sense of volume, depth and three-dimensionality in both representational and abstract work, and the potential for harnessing a range of artistic styles and techniques to express and communicate ideas, thoughts and feelings.

Development, however, should not just be considered as pupils' relative ability to recreate naturalistic images. As indicated above, children's progress in *abstract* work – exploration and use of the art elements (pattern, texture, colour, line, tone, shape, form and space) for their own sake – may become equally sophisticated and refined. Teachers need to be aware of features in their pupils' work that may be indicative of development towards a next stage, and be ready to point this out to the children involved. However, points of transition between stages of development are often fuzzy: children typically may take a long time to move into a new stage, and may appear to regress for a while, preferring to express themselves in a way characteristic of an earlier stage. Many pupils with learning difficulties may have irregular developmental profiles in different aspects of art. For example, a child who is blind may have particular ability for working with textiles or in three-dimensional sculpture, but be severely compromised over use of colour in painting; the National Curriculum requires appropriate provision to be made for those pupils who need emphasis on a tactile approach to art (DfEE/QCA 1999a, 1999b).

The National Curriculum also provides a broad overview of most children's likely development in the *process* of art-making. Requirements for art and design have been simplified, with a reduced number of strands for programmes of study, and one attainment target that integrates practical and theoretical aspects (DfEE/QCA, 1999a, 1999b). Strands are expressed as *processes*, aimed at promoting children's development in:

- exploring ideas (from observation, imagination and responses to a range of stimuli);
- investigating and making art, craft and design (possibly with tools, materials, techniques or processes);
- evaluating and developing their work (reviewing and adapting their work as it progresses);
- applying their growing knowledge and understanding (of the art elements, various art practices, and approaches of different artists across cultural and historical traditions).

During the Foundation Stage, it is assumed that children are encouraged to explore ways of expressing their response to their environment. Curriculum guidance (QCA 2000a) offers an inclusive, differentiated framework of stepping stones towards achieving early learning goals in the area of creative development, supported by clear examples and strategies for the practitioner. The guidance document highlights certain principles as being fundamental to all children at early stages of learning. These principles will have particular continuing relevance to pupils with severe and profound and multiple learning difficulties, in relation to:

- children having sufficient time to explore and experiment;
- children being supported in feeling secure and sufficiently confident to take risks;
- children learning through all of their senses.

The National Curriculum itself (DfEE/QCA 1999a, 1999b) is a more skeletal document altogether. Eight broad level descriptions of attainment are indicated (plus one for exceptional performance), and there is very limited subject-specific, practical guidance for teachers. Those overseeing pupils with learning difficulties in particular may experience the tension of translating essentially *process-based* open-ended programmes of study into teaching objectives with clearly observable, realistic outcomes by which they may assess pupils' progress in sufficiently small steps.

Statements relating to teaching methodology have been removed from the National Curriculum. While this is in one sense liberating, the generalist class teacher may find it problematical to know where to begin planning sufficiently challenging, developmentally appropriate activities for groups with diverse needs. The associated QCA schemes of work provide detailed guidance on aspects of progression in the strands of the programme of study (processes of exploring, investigating, evaluating and applying knowledge – see above). The subject-specific art and design guidelines for pupils with learning difficulties (QCA 2001) offer a *flexible* interpretation of the National Curriculum requirements, and propose a differentiated programme of study to cater for three levels of ability within each key stage. For each key stage, they also offer practical examples of opportunities and activities that explicitly reflect the strands (aspects) of the art-making process in the National Curriculum programmes of study, with clear links also to other areas of the curriculum.

Essentially, Key Stage 1 of the National Curriculum aims to build on the Foundation Stage, and to develop children's creativity and imagination in relation to familiar contexts. Pupils with learning difficulties may be taught and encouraged to engage in sensory exploration of materials and processes, and harness these to represent ideas and feelings using colour, shape, space, pattern and texture; also to respond to art, craft and design in the environment (QCA 2001). Key Stage 2 of the National Curriculum seeks to engage children in more complex activities, and to broaden their understanding of the roles and functions of art and design, not just in their locality but also in the wider world, with a growing awareness of the impact of art. At Key Stage 2, teachers may focus on their pupils with learning difficulties being encouraged to build on their developing control over materials and processes, and to use visual and tactile elements to communicate their responses – and also to review works from different times and cultures (QCA 2001). Into Key Stage 3, pupils with learning difficulties may focus on developing their independence in existing approaches, as well as extending their knowledge and experience of new processes; and they should also engage in the comparison of art from different traditions (QCA 2001).

The National Curriculum implicitly requires teachers to plan for pupils' progress in *art practices* (using a range of two- and three-dimensional media, including textiles and ICT), and in the visual and tactile *elements* (pattern and texture, colour, line and tone, shape, form and space). As noted in *Art for All 1 – The Framework* (Peter 1996a), this all begs the question as to what actually constitutes progress. Is it being able to do things that are increasingly more complex (*breadth* of content)? Or is it doing the same thing but better (*depth* of knowledge and understanding, and degree of independence in a range of contexts)? Or the same thing, but with greater awareness and understanding of the process involved (*quality* of response and outcome)? The level descriptions of attainment in the National Curriculum (DfEE/QCA 1999a, 1999b) refer to children's growing ability in the way that they set about their art-making – in other words, pupils' attainment in the *process* not the *product*.

The art and design guidelines for pupils with learning difficulties (QCA 2001) offer eight additional levels of performance descriptions leading to Level 1 of the National Curriculum. These, too, reflect pupils' progress in their *engagement* with art activity rather than the actual outcome: their growing awareness of art as a means to explore and develop their ideas; the increasing purposefulness with which they are able to follow established patterns of activity towards achieving an artistic intention; and their developing understanding that meaning may be conveyed through their own work and in that of others.

From all the Foundation Stage and National Curriculum documentation, and accompanying schemes of work and guidelines for pupils with learning difficulties, it is not clear what exactly should influence teachers' planning. In fact, planning art to give breadth and balance of experiences, and to enable pupils to progress, should be driven by each pupil's ability to understand and use the *art elements*: pattern, texture, colour, line, tone, shape, form and space. Children need to be enabled to develop their control over the visual and tactile art elements in a range of materials, in order ultimately to be able to express themselves in a medium of their choice. They also need to learn, however, that their artistic intention may be interpreted differently by the viewer, in ways that may be equally valid. Abstract art that explores the use of art elements for their own sake might be very liberating for all concerned, getting away from the notion that a piece of work only rates consideration if it offers a close approximation to a photograph! An emotional response may be just as valid as a naturalistic interpretation, even if not one's personal preference.

Coming to terms with art

At first glance, art terminology can seem very bewildering, if not de-skilling, to the non-specialist. For example, what is progress in the 'art elements'? How can teachers recognise it and plan for the artistic development of all their pupils? The development of

Table 8.1 Progression in the art elements

THE ART ELEMENTS	THE 'SCRIBBLING' STAGE (Foundation Stage) *Awareness and exploration of the art elements in increasingly controlled mark-making*	THE 'SYMBOLIC'/PRE-SCHEMATIC STAGE (Key Stage 1) *Basic understanding of the art elements with an emerging sense of order in abstract and representational work*	THE 'EMERGING ANALYTIC/SCHEMATIC STAGE (Lower Key Stage 2) *Refining subtlety and complexity of control over the art elements with greater attention to detail and placement of images*	THE 'ANALYTIC' STAGE OF 'VISUAL REALISM' (Upper Key Stage 2/Key Stage 3) *Integrating the art elements to express ideas, thoughts and feelings in a range of media and artistic styles*
Pattern and texture	• multisensory exploration of a range of materials • sorting materials for gross difference • making random, irregular arrangements	• sorting, choosing and placing materials in ordered arrangements • making a range of marks to create ordered arrangements	• making alternating and repeating patterns of increasing complexity in a range of textured materials • making increasingly detailed patterns using graphic materials	• using pattern and texture for a particular purpose (functional, decorative, etc.) • complex, intricate repeated designs with attention to spaces between motifs
Colour	• sorting fabrics and papers for increasingly finer difference • identifying and naming colours • discovering the behaviour of colours using fluid materials • lightening using white	• discovering and learning to mix secondary colours (green, orange, purple) by combining controlled amounts of primary colours (red, blue, yellow) • mixing tints and shades by combining controlled amounts of white or black	• mixing a range of secondary and tertiary colours (browns and greys) from a limited palette • lightening and darkening to create a range of tints and shades	• mixing desired colours to a required intensity • using colours for effect (e.g. muted, harmonising, discordant, complementary)
Line and tone	• discovering a range of possible marks of different lengths and thicknesses • enclosing lines to make shapes and images of different sizes • discovering tones by observing fluids on wet and dry surfaces	• combining lines to create abstract and/or representational images • exploring tones by adjusting pressure with sensitive drawing materials • creating shades and tints using white	• versatile use of marks to create outlines and detail • creating tones by shading patches using pressure-sensitive materials, wiping areas with an eraser, and diluting fluids	• using a range of lines to different densities and lengths for detail and decoration • creating illusions of texture, volume and depth by shading and cross-hatching in a range of densities and pressures
Shape, form and space	• manipulating and moulding malleable materials • applying items within a prescribed area • cause–effect mark-making	• making controlled marks with regard to space available and between images • sorting, arranging and rearranging items within a prescribed area • combining and reforming malleable and rigid materials to make abstract and/or representational forms	• ordering images within a composition (abstract and representational) • greater awareness of relative size and placement of items and images to one another	• integrating images within a composition with attention to detail, proportion and scale • creating a sense of depth, perspective and three-dimensionality in 2D and 3D abstract and representational work

even be the stimulus itself, with which the pupil may interact and where meanings might change in the process. Pupils at early stages of learning may be actively involved in collecting items 'in the field' in order to develop ideas of colour, shape, pattern, texture, line, tone, form and space. These may be incorporated in their art-making, with pupils encouraged to select starting points for their work by making simple choices, and retrieving pre-selected resources from where they are stored. Pupils may need to consolidate their symbolic understanding, that experiences may be (literally) re-presented in art-making.

The gap may be gradually widened between a direct experience and following it up in art, as pupils reach the *pre-schematic/symbolic* stage (equivalent to Key Stage 1). pupils may be encouraged to work freely from memory and recall aspects of greatest personal significance, through repeated opportunities to work on favourite topics, shapes and forms (abstract and representational) using a range of visual and tactile materials. Pupils may learn to be mindful of amassing resources for themselves to inspire and inform their art-making (Key Stage 1) – collecting souvenirs and 'found' sources, taking photographs as *aides-mémoire*, and beginning to develop the habit of using a sketchbook to record personal/private findings and collections.

By the time pupils have reached the *schematic/emerging analytic* stage (equivalent to lower Key Stage 2) in their art development, they may be encouraged to develop their own skills in working from direct observation: looking carefully at what they can actually see, not just what they know, and selecting ideas and experiences to use in their own work. This should be in a range of tactile and visual media, with children encouraged to have a growing awareness of the purpose and likely audience for their work. They may sketch 'in the field' and use reference material back in school, as well as returning to working directly from a stimulus in the classroom. This process may become increasingly selective (lower Key Stage 2): sketching features attention to detail, assembling a range of reference material to support art-making, using computers to generate options, and slowing down the art-making process to 'research' a piece of work. Pupils at the *analytic stage of visual realism* (equivalent to upper Key Stage 2 into Key Stage 3) may subsequently develop an ability to work from secondary reference material (photographs, reference books, computer graphics, etc.) in addition to using a sketchbook to stimulate and develop their ideas, including using reference sources in the community for a specific purpose (e.g. libraries). They may take time to select, assemble and rearrange materials and resources (e.g. a still-life set-up, appropriately lit). They may plan and research their work with growing independence for specific details, and take inspiration from a range of approaches of other artists in developing their own style, in order to communicate their experiences, ideas, feelings, moods and preferences, using a range of visual and tactile media.

Investigating and making art

Pupils need to become aware of a range of options for expressing themselves in art, through exploration of materials and visual and tactile qualities of their environment, and to become proficient in a range of techniques from which they may select, in order to record and represent their responses and interpret ideas and qualities through images and artefacts in different media. They need to learn to control and use a range of tools and materials, with the introduction of these paced to involve a suitable level of 'risk-taking'. They may become gradually more proficient in experimenting with and using media in two and three dimensions and on a variety of scales.

Pupils' confidence and pleasure in art-making will develop through learning to control and use a limited range of tools and materials at any one time, rather than superficially experimenting with a bewildering array. The introduction of new equipment needs to be sensitively paced, with the available range gradually being broadened to enable pupils to work in open-ended tasks. Instruction needs to be succinctly presented and clearly illustrated with visual aids – pictures and objects of reference. Teachers need to be aware of steps involved in art-making activities, in order to present pupils with procedures that are developmentally appropriate. Teachers should be aware, too, how an activity may be 'revisited', and challenges gradually broadened and/or increased to extend and improve pupils' perception and practical skill. *Art for All 2 – the Practice* (Peter 1996b) contains an example of a fabric collage activity, differentiated at four levels of ability.

Initially, pupils at early stages of learning (equivalent to the Foundation Stage) try out tools and techniques in two and three dimensions and on a range of scales, and apply these to art practices, in order to record their responses to a direct experience and to create a range of visual and tactile effects. They may learn to recognise tools and materials by name, and develop an understanding of which tools and materials are associated with particular art practices (e.g. a felt pen for drawing), and learn to control them purposefully, accurately and safely. Pupils may learn to follow and implement basic art and craft techniques, with respect for the care and use of materials and a widening range of suitable tools (Key Stage 1). As pupils progress through Key Stage 2, they may learn to combine different processes creatively (e.g. experimenting with wet and dry surfaces), with a growing awareness of the visual and tactile quality of appropriate materials for the desired purpose of the work, in order to record their response to a stimulus (e.g. exploring textures of an object and then making impressions in clay). Dry techniques tend to be inherently less complicated: pupils may become independent in organising themselves for drawing (lower Key Stage 2), while still requiring support to execute a more complex procedure such as print-making, using rollers, inks and stencils. They may refine their control over tools and techniques, and experiment with and combine methods to express and communicate ideas, thoughts and feelings for different purposes in 2D and 3D work. In time (upper Key Stage 2 and into Key Stage 3), pupils may become proficient in executing 'wet' procedures independently, as they consolidate and extend their control of tools and methods, and with a greater sense of preference and choice in designing and making; this may include complex 'joining' techniques such as gluing and knotting, with appropriate attention also to protecting themselves and the work space.

Evaluating and developing work

Communication and interaction skills (including appropriate vocabularies), and social skills of cooperation and negotiation, are intrinsic to evaluating and developing work. Pupils need to acquire an ability to review and modify work, both during the process and after its completion, with a view to future developments. They should be encouraged gradually to develop, change and reorder their ideas, accepting or rejecting the opinions of others, and to identify and negotiate their learning needs. While art-making may be a highly personal and private form of *expression*, art also makes *impression*, and children need to be made aware of the impact of their work on others. This requires time and sensitivity on the part of supporting staff, regarding timing of comments, probing questions and intervention. Supporting staff should develop flexibility in their questioning skills in order to draw out pupils' creative responses. Even if pupils cannot express themselves verbally but are capable of indicating 'yes' or 'no', they may be empowered to make creative decisions, at the very least regarding their choice of tools and materials (e.g. 'Would you like to use this colour paint – yes or no?'). Alternatively pupils may be able to eye-point or show an adult (possibly even taking their hand to place it directly on the required item). Staff may also use a range of other communication and literacy strategies, including ICT and other technological aids; visual, written and tactile materials in different formats (e.g. large print, pictures and objects of reference, symbols and symbol text); and alternative and augmentative communication. These should be combined with an encouragement to interaction with other pupils (QCA 2001).

Pupils at early stages of learning (equivalent to the Foundation Stage) may spend a matter of minutes on a piece of work, the satisfaction being in the immediacy of the process. They should be given maximum opportunity to make guided decisions regarding choice and placement of tools and materials. They should be encouraged to look at their work and develop an awareness of (for example) drawing, painting and printing, where they are engaged in direct cause–effect processes (e.g. printing with a part of the body), with opportunity to follow up straightaway with another piece of work. After completion, they may focus on and recall what they and others have done, recognising similarities and differences, and communicating likes and dislikes. As pupils spend longer on a piece of work (Key Stage 1), so they may be more receptive to considering their work in process, with supporting staff timing comments and offering suggestions when they pause momentarily. Children may be encouraged to reflect on their work afterwards, particularly regarding its content and distinctive features, being requested to explain what they think and feel about it (likes and dislikes). They may also consider what they might change in existing work or develop in a future piece, using signs, symbols or keywords as necessary.

As they become habituated to standing back from their work and being more concerned with detail, so pupils may learn to slow down the art-making process (lower Key Stage 2). They might then be able to reconsider their work in the light of an original intention, or to research or practise a required technique for further development. They might be encouraged to explain how their piece was created as they reflect on it afterwards, and compare their methods and approaches with those of others. As pupils' knowledge of artistic styles and traditions expands, so they might be encouraged to develop a greater flexibility and open-mindedness to future developments, both in process and with regard to returning to their work at a future point (upper Key Stage 2 into Key Stage 3). Pupils need to consider how others evaluate their piece, in order to contemplate possible revision to their intention. Equally, they should be encouraged to express their own opinions on the work of others, in a way that is positive, purposeful, and that offers constructive criticism towards improving a piece. This may need to be sensitively handled on the part of the teacher, to avoid negative group dynamics.

Knowledge and understanding

Knowledge and understanding informs the process of investigating and making, which itself begins with exploring and developing ideas and evaluating and expanding them (QCA 2001). As stated at the front of this main section, The National Curriculum (DfEE/QCA 1999a, 1999b) has endorsed and strengthened the close relationship between appraising the works of other artists, and pupils' own art-making – pupils' understanding and use of visual and tactile elements (pattern and texture, colour, line and tone, shape, form and space), and of different materials and processes. Across the key stages, pupils with learning difficulties will need direct experiences of natural and made materials and objects to inform their art-making, as well as opportunities to change visual and tactile elements in a range of art processes, and to observe similarities and differences in works from different artistic traditions (QCA 2001). Pupils' ability to relate to the work of other artists will reflect their own stage of development in art-making (their own mode of expression) and the way they perceive and organise information. Works of other artists should be presented in a way that will support and reinforce pupils' own art-making, but also with a view to broadening pupils' awareness of a range of cultural and historical artistic traditions. Choice of work should be dictated by pupils' learning need in art, and the opportunity presented by a particular piece to provide a starting point – a stimulus – either thematically or for developing an approach or technique that emphasises a particular art element. Alternatively, a work may be introduced *after* an art-making experience developed from a different kind of stimulus (e.g. a shell, a visit to the beach), by way of consolidating, reinforcing or extending pupils' own work. In this way, a work may be used to present an alternative interpretation, in order to validate and celebrate diversity in approaches.

Pupils should be allowed time to react spontaneously to a work as a whole that is presented to them, before they are engaged in more in-depth discussion that aims to focus them on features in the work, especially how the artist has made use of a particular art element.The teacher may also decide to feed in information relating to the context in which it was created, and to raise awareness of the artist's intentions. This may then be followed up with a related art-making experience, in which pupils make their own interpretations, suitably inspired and informed.

Follow-up art-making activities need to be pitched in a way that will challenge and extend pupils' own artistic expression while illuminating their understanding of the work of others. It is important that works are presented in a meaningful way that offers pupils an appropriate point of contact and that has relevance to their own experience. Teachers need to be mindful of the kinds of information that pupils may prioritise and wish to express (their interests and life experiences), and also of the pupils' ability to control media and realise their intentions through combining the art elements and harnessing particular materials and processes.

Young people at earlier stages of learning may be able to relate to concrete objects and events common to human experience and in their immediate locale (for example, themes such as animals, the home, food or the weather) and to certain uses of the art elements in more abstract work (for example, colour, shape), with a crude awareness of similarities and differences between works of art from different times and cultures. Older pupils may be able to cope with more abstract themes in the wider world (e.g. war) and the portrayal of feelings and emotions in naturalistic and abstract work, with an awareness of the social context in which a work of art is produced (roles and purposes of artists, craftspeople and designers working in different times and cultures). Units within the QCA schemes of work reflect pupils' growing worldliness and offer examples of thematic planning, rigorously infused with pupils' development in art-making processes, in their understanding and use of the art elements and in a range of art practices, and with reference also to illustrative works of art that may be used as stimuli for children's own work (QCA 2000b). The art guidelines for pupils with learning difficulties (QCA 2001) illustrate how some of these projects may be interpreted and accessed for those attaining below national expectations.

Teachers should encourage pupils to develop an enquiring attitude when looking at art. Pupils of all abilities may respond to and evaluate works of art, even though this may require imaginative presentation on the part of the teacher (e.g. projecting slides large, or 'hands on' for certain pupils). Teachers will need to question pupils skilfully and interpret pupils' reactions – positive or negative – sensitively and encourage them to substantiate their responses according to their ability. Pupils at the early stages of learning (equivalent to the Foundation Stage) might respond non-verbally (flinching, grimacing, smiling, gasping). They may be able to indicate 'yes' or 'no' in reply to a closed question ('Do you like it – yes or no?') and be able to notice certain features about the work ('Show me the cat!'), as well as recognise visual elements of colour, pattern, line and tone, and investigate tactile elements of texture, shape, form and space.

Pupils may be encouraged to bring their own personal experiences and associations to the content and subject matter of a work (Key Stage 1), to describe it in simple terms, and offer their thoughts and feelings. As pupils become more preoccupied with detail in their own work (lower Key Stage 2), and as their own experience of art-making broadens, so they may be able to comment more systematically on how a work was created, as well as its content or subject matter. Pupils may be encouraged to use appropriate art-and-design vocabulary and to draw on their knowledge (upper Key Stage 2 into Key Stage 3) to substantiate their ideas and opinions about a work and the context in which it was created (e.g. social, cultural and historical influences).

Understanding and applying knowledge of the work of other artists has to be grounded in pupils' own direct experience and knowledge of artistic methods, tools and materials. Through active investigation of the work of others, they may be led to develop insight into how – and why – a piece was created. Young people at early stages of learning (equivalent to the Foundation Stage) will need the opportunity to experience examples of work in the basic art practices (drawing, painting, collage, sculpture and print-making) in their immediate environment – a reproduction may not look like a real painting to such pupils! Ideally, they should have the opportunity to witness others involved in art-making, including artists-in-residence or in the community, in order to generalise their understanding of practices. They may experience art from different times and cultures through multisensory activities – especially linked to festivals, carnivals or celebrations. They may be encouraged to emulate certain processes, with direct experience of cause and effect with colour, pattern, texture, line, tone, shape, form and space: some techniques used by modern artists are accessible to children of all abilities (e.g. trailing paint in the abstract style of Jackson Pollock). As pupils' own symbolic development becomes consolidated in their own visual representations (Key Stage 1), so they might be able to consider similarities and differences between works. They might also emulate appealing or intriguing features in the work of others, and their visual, tactile and material qualities – for example, the way Modigliani used the elements of art to create distortions of the human figure.

As pupils' awareness of different approaches broadens, so they may be able to consider the way a range of artists have treated similar themes or combined, manipulated and used visual, tactile and material qualities for a particular purpose. They may make their own interpretations by harnessing a particular technique or preferred style (lower Key Stage 2). This may include sensory investigations of artistic processes used in Western Europe and the wider world – cultures from different historical times and traditions (e.g. medieval or aboriginal art). Pupils may be challenged to grasp something of the social, historical and cultural context of a work (upper Key Stage 2 into Key Stage 3), particular artists' respective philosophy, and how ideas and beliefs can be represented in art with an awareness of purpose and audience. Pupils may develop a growing awareness of how and why representations and views change or continue over time; they may be encouraged to select, explore, recognise and combine visual and tactile qualities from a range of styles and traditions, towards developing and consolidating their own preferred form of expression in a preferred medium.

Art in practice

So how does all this translate into quality teaching and learning in the classroom? The classroom environment needs to be structured and orderly so as to enable pupils of all abilities to negotiate their working space confidently and as independently as possible. Effective use should be made of designated areas. Pupils' imagination and inventiveness at all levels of ability may be promoted, enriched and challenged through displays of stimuli for art-making – both pupils' work and that of other artists. There should be access to a range of art equipment, with pupils encouraged to use tools and materials judiciously and economically, and with respect. Tools and materials should be sufficiently varied and challenging, and of a suitable quality, to foster pupils' art-making and to develop their skills in two- and three-dimensional work and in their use of information technology. There should be access to a range of resources also for teaching historical and critical aspects of art: collections of prints and reproductions, books and slides of Western and world art. An ethos should be encouraged where everyone is mindful of the safety of others and takes responsibility for keeping the environment clean and tidy, with items replaced after use.

Planning should begin with pupils' needs, not by the teacher arbitrarily plucking out of the air an 'idea for art'. As suggested in *Art for All 2 – The Practice* (Peter 1996b), art lends itself to mixed-ability group work although, in the teacher's mind, pupils may be organised according to their general stage of artistic development in order to give a broad indication of the kind of art experiences that will be appropriate. However, a teacher needs to be aware of how to *differentiate* aspects of art within the basic art practices (drawing, painting, collage, print-making, sculpture/3D, textiles, and computer-generated work) to meet individual needs, and also how to cater for *progression* (i.e. how the same activity may be revisited, but with new challenges, in order to build on previous experiences).

For instance, an art activity in every teacher's repertoire will invariably include print-making with a potato 'block', but individuals should be challenged and extended according to their ability to:

- engage in experimental cause-and-effect mark-making using a prepared potato 'block' (Foundation Stage);
- make ordered marks using a choice of 'blocks', with prints placed selectively in designated space available (Key Stage 1);
- make alternating or repeated patterns, including carving away the potato to make an original 'block' (lower Key Stage 2);
- make complex repeated patterns, including etching a design into the potato with a sharp tool (upper Key Stage 2 into Key Stage 3).

Practical consideration will need to be given to allocation of staffing, with appropriate briefing and training as necessary. Staff will need to be assigned to support individuals and groups of pupils, but must be sufficiently briefed to prevent them from dominating the activities. Pupils of all abilities should experience working on individual and collaborative pieces. The session will need to be paced to ensure that it runs smoothly, with sufficient time for reflection and clearing up (important parts of the whole learning process). Thought will need to be given to which materials will be prepared and how the room will be organised so that resources are readily available and retrievable by pupils. Choice of tools and materials will need to be carefully structured so that pupils are not bewildered by a dazzling array yet have sufficient scope to make informed selections.

A further consideration will be the amount of space required according to the scale on which pupils will be working, how many pupils will be engaged in art-making, and the nature of the art-making process(es) in which they will be engaged. 'Wet' activities tend to be more space- and time-consuming, and should involve the pupils in adequately protecting both themselves and their environment. Space will be required for pupils to handle visual and tactile resources and multisensory displays, to inspire and inform the art-making process – for example, natural objects, artefacts, walk-in environments and 'corners', and pictorial reference material – all well away from the sink or messy area. Furthermore, it might be viable to arrange the space to include a dry 'containing' activity at which pupils may work independently while staff are absorbed 'hands on' elsewhere.

With regard to supervising pupils at their art-making, teachers will need to be aware of the kind of developmental changes to expect from their pupils with learning difficulties. Pupils should be encouraged to engage in divergent thinking and develop a sense of resourcefulness and individuality in this regard. 'Ability' needs to be considered in a multidimensional way (Eyre 1997), not just in relation to aptitude in terms of pupils' developing skills, knowledge and understanding. Potential will only be truly unleashed if pupils feel a sense of *commitment to the task* (motivation), and are provided with appropriate opportunities in a supportive, encouraging atmosphere. For instance, potential sculptors will never emerge unless such pupils are presented with opportunities to carve in three-dimensional work! Relative neglect of the arts could leave whole areas of every child's intellectual capabilities untapped (Robinson 1995). Art can make children 'feel good' through awareness of their own developing personal powers of expression and communication and ability to influence others. Their confidence and self-esteem will be genuinely raised by their being enabled to make *real* choices, decisions, changes – and by their seeing these acted upon by others (Peter 1998a).

Art and design explicitly seeks to *empower* pupils in a way that may also support the release of tension or the containment of feelings (Prokofiev 1994). It is important that pupils feel secure through setting clear boundaries within which they are to create, in order not to transgress boundaries of physical or emotional control, or loss of control of ideas (Peter 1998b). It may be necessary to establish trust by keeping certain aspects of an activity consistent and predictable (for example, materials set out in a particular way). Also to respect pupils' tolerance of their physical proximity to others within a preferred working space. Good art and design practice exemplifies an *interactive teaching and learning style* (Collis and Lacey 1996). The position of the teacher shifts, so that responsibility is placed on pupils to devise and research their own solutions to problems, and to negotiate their own outcomes and learning needs. Staff will need to spend time observing and listening, as much as talking and intervening. Timing comments and intervention is a sensitive matter, as already indicated.

Art-making is inherently *playful* – the natural way that children learn, however transformed that becomes into adulthood. Play is a crucial aspect of the creative process, for it energises the individual, encouraging discovery of possibilities, exploration and experimentation, and practice time to enhance and consolidate skills, knowledge and understanding. Indeed, it is creativity that can make the crucial difference between an average outcome and an above-average outcome for a particular child.

Teachers of art and design should be able to promote creativity in a range of ways (George 1992). They can encourage:

- *fluency of thought* in their pupils – the generating of solutions, alternatives, or a number of ideas; for example, 'How many different kinds of marks can you make with this stick of charcoal?'
- *flexibility of thought* – shifting from one type of thinking to another; for example, 'How many ways can we think of to create the impression of snow by printing?'
- *originality of thought* – coming up with possibilities that to the individual student are unusual, novel or unique; for example, 'Can you show me a way to print using a different part of your hand?'
- *elaboration* – developing an idea, seeing new relationships between things to improve or change a situation; for example, 'Now see if you can make a sculpture of the cat in your painting.'

Teachers need to cater for breadth and balance in art experiences. Within a lesson, this should include a balance between structured and unstructured tasks, with opportunity for decision-making, experimentation and problem-solving. Pupils may require a range of intervention strategies at different stages of a lesson, for example:

- *looking and responding to a stimulus* – the opportunity to return to a stimulus and to consolidate the original response, through being asked probing questions that highlight salient features and learning points;
- *explaining and demonstrating approaches and techniques* – the opportunity to consider possible ways of responding to a stimulus by following a particular procedure;
- *exploring processes* – support in practising and experimenting with methods and procedures in structured exercises and tasks;
- *selecting and creating* – support in executing particular skills and techniques to rectify 'problems' emerging in the pupil's chosen approach in an open-ended piece of work;
- *evaluating work* – commenting critically on their own work and that of others in teacher-led discussion, to highlight aspects of learning.

Over the school year, medium-term planning should cover experiences in a range of art practices and on a range of scales, with a balance between the particular art elements to be given emphasis. Similarly, long-term planning should reflect a breadth and balance with consideration of how art practices will be revisited across the phases, to challenge and extend pupils at different stages of their artistic development. Mention has already been made of guidance on planning to meet the needs of pupils attaining below national expectations (QCA 2001), which is additional to the QCA schemes of work (QCA 2000b) and to the curriculum guidance for the Foundation Stage (QCA 2000a). Further suggestions for developing an art and design curriculum for pupils with SLD/PMLD are also provided within the EQUALS framework (EQUALS 1999a, 1999b), and specialist publications (Peter 1996a, 1996b). Drawing and painting should not be compromised for the sake of working in other art practices, as they most readily facilitate self-expression in many pupils. It may be appropriate to consider pupils spending as much as one-half of their time engaged in these practices, with the remaining time shared among a range of other practices, including more specialist ones (e.g. photography, jewellery making, or ceramics). Information technology is proving a liberating tool for art for many young people with learning difficulties, with the satisfaction of producing a professional looking outcome. However, one important caveat is to not be beguiled by the hypnotic quality of many art software programs, and the implication that anyone can 'press the button and become an artist'. The point is that ICT should be regarded as a valuable tool for exploring the art elements, and as a means for personal expression and communication of ideas, thoughts and feelings to others.

Art for all

Regardless of how 'artistically challenged' a teacher may feel personally, from the pupils' point of view it is more important that a conducive atmosphere is established: not where there may be a 'right' response, but where they may feel that they are collaborating in a shared venture, motivated and inspired by their teacher's commitment and enthusiasm.

Teachers should be aware of their own personal developmental needs regarding art in education. Pupils should perceive art as having status and importance as a means for personal and cultural expression. Attitudes to art will be revealed explicitly and implicitly – through the way it is taught, by how it is presented in the school environment, and as evidenced in the sensitivity of pupils' responses. Pupils' work should be displayed thoughtfully, with pride and esteem set on the achievements of all abilities, where responses should be regarded as valid statements in their own right, not as an inferior form of adult art.

There should be a vitality, vigour and excitement over art-making that permeates the school environment, where teachers and pupils of all abilities enjoy art and relish the challenges the subject presents. Art is essentially concerned with the *aesthetic*. Although this has come to imply notions of taste and beauty, *aesthetic* literally means a concern with *feeling* responses – knowing through the senses (Witkin 1974). Pupils should be moved by their art experiences in school, and it has to be our responsibility at the very least to prevent them from experiencing art as *anaesthetic!*

References

Collis, M. and Lacey, P. (1996) *Interactive Approaches to Teaching.* London: David Fulton Publishers.
DfEE/QCA (1999) *All Our Futures: Creativity, Culture and Education.* London: DfEE Publications.
DfEE/QCA (1999a) *The National Curriculum: Handbook for Primary Teachers in England.* London: DfEE/QCA.
DfEE/QCA (1999b) *The National Curriculum: Handbook for Secondary Teachers in England.* London: DfEE/QCA.
EQUALS (1999a) *Schemes of Work – Creative Development (Part One) for pupils with SLD – Art.* North Shields, Tyne and Wear: EQUALS.
EQUALS (1999b) *Schemes of Work – Creative Development (Part One) for pupils with PMLD – Art.* North Shields. Tyne and Wear: EQUALS.
Eyre, D. (1997) *Able Children in Ordinary Schools.* London: David Fulton Publishers.
George, D (1992) *The Challenge of the Able Child.* London: David Fulton Publishers.
Peter, M. (1996a) *Art for All 1 – the Framework.* London: David Fulton Publishers.

Peter, M. (1996b) *Art for All 2 – the Practice*. London: David Fulton Publishers.

Peter, M. (1998a) 'Accessing the curriculum through the arts for pupils with special educational needs', *Support for Learning* **13**(4), 153–6.

Peter, M. (1998b) 'Good for them, or what? The arts and pupils with SEN', *British Journal of Special Education* **25**(4), 168–72.

Prokofiev, F. (1994) 'The role of an art therapist, part 4: Different roles', *Art and Craft, Design and Technology*, October, 22–3.

QCA (1998) *Maintaining breadth and balance at Key Stages 1 and 2*. London: QCA

QCA (1999a) *The Review Of The National Curriculum In England: The Consultation Materials*. London: QCA.

QCA (2000a) *Curriculum Guidance for the Foundation Stage*. London: QCA.

QCA (2000b) *Art and Design: A Scheme of Work for Key Stages 1 and 2*. London: QCA.

QCA (2001) *Planning, Teaching And Assessing The Curriculum For Pupils With Learning Difficulties: Art And Design*. London: QCA.

Robinson, K. (1995) 'Features and arts: that vision thing', *Times Educational Supplement*, 25 March.

Robinson, K. (1998) 'Platform: Creativity knows no stereotypes', *Times Educational Supplement*, 13 March.

SCAA (1996) *Nursery Education: Desirable Outcomes for Children's Learning On Entering Compulsory Education*. London: SCAA.

Witkin, R. (1974) *The Intelligence of Feeling*. London: Heinemann.

Further reading

Barnes, R. (1987) *Teaching Art to Young Children, 4–9*. London: Allen and Unwin.

Barnes, R. (1989) *Art, Design and Topic Work, 8–13*. London: Routledge.

Gentle, K. (1993) *Teaching Painting in the Primary School*. London: Cassell.

Lancaster, J. (1990) *Art in the Primary School*. London: Routledge.

Morgan, M. (ed.) (1991) *Art 4–11*. Hemel Hempstead: Simon and Schuster Education.

Taylor, R. (1986) *Educating for Art*. London: Longman.

Chapter 9

Music

Penny Lacey

Introduction

In the first edition of this book, I began this chapter with great enthusiasm. I applauded the fact that music was one of the 11 subjects of the National Curriculum, which ensured that it would be taught in mainstream and special schools throughout the country. I suggested that it would take time to train sufficient teachers to ensure children's entitlement across the country, but that fact seemed to be a technicality.

Music is still one of the National Curriculum subjects but the rules around it have changed. No longer is there a requirement to teach music until the age of 16, nor do pupils have to be tested formally in it. Other imperatives have taken centre stage, and once again music appears to have been sidelined. The Literacy and Numeracy Strategies launched by the UK government at the end of the 1990s have forced teachers to concentrate on the basics of education, especially in the primary stage, at the expense of subjects seen as frills, such as art, drama and music.

So, because music has once again become a Cinderella subject, it is important to establish (or re-establish) a rationale for teaching music, especially to pupils who find learning the basics of literacy and numeracy so difficult. It could be argued that, because learning to read and write and calculate is such a struggle, extra time should be spent on these topics, leaving little time for anything else. In my opinion this is not only short-sighted but also erroneous. It is short-sighted because it presupposes that a diet composed mainly of literacy and numeracy will equip children for adult life. And it is erroneous because it presupposes that music is an irrelevance when becoming literate and numerate.

Pugh and Pugh (1998) offer an excellent analysis of why we should teach music, dividing it into two kinds of value: the utilitarian and the intrinsic. These writers do not underestimate the complexity of the arguments surrounding each of these aspects, but they feel that each is a valid reason for including music in every child's curriculum. Indeed, music has utilitarian value because:

- it is a vehicle for the transmission of culture;
- it contributes to social development;
- it is a form of enjoyment and source of pleasure;

- it is education for leisure;
- it contributes to preparation for adult working lives;
- it contributes to general scholastic development: physical development; moral and spiritual development.

Music also has intrinsic value because:

- it is an element of being human;
- it is a language;
- it is an expression of emotion.

Generally, it can be argued that both children and adults have music surrounding them constantly (from 'muzak' in the shopping centre and advertising jingles on the TV, to *Top of the Pops*, personal stereos and parties), and to omit the study of this phenomenon would be nothing short of criminal!

Despite an apparent take-over by literacy and numeracy within the National Curriculum, there is still cause for optimism. Music remains a requirement in law, although it is left to the discretion of individual schools as to when and how and how much to teach. In the Foreword to each subject in the National Curriculum orders, there are these words (DfEE/QCA 1999, p. 3, and my italics):

> The focus of this National Curriculum, together with the wider school curriculum, is [therefore] to ensure that pupils develop from an early age the essential literacy and numeracy skills they need to learn; to provide them with a guaranteed, *full and rounded* entitlement to learning; to foster their *creativity*; and to give teachers discretion to find the best ways to inspire in their pupils, a *joy* and *commitment* to learning that will last a lifetime.

The italicised words in the foregoing quotation do not indicate that children should receive an unrelieved diet of basic skills, nor do they indicate that literacy and numeracy should be taught in isolation from other subjects. It is less usual today to find examples of schools teaching literacy and numeracy through other subjects than in the past. In many primary and special schools, the morning is spent on literacy and numeracy while the rest of the curriculum must be fitted into the afternoons – echoes of pre-National Curriculum days.

However, on the optimistic side, the general message in the new orders (DfEE/QCA 1999, pp. 8–9) is that music offers important learning opportunities through promoting:

- pupils' spiritual, moral, social and cultural (SMSC) development;
- key skills;
- other aspects of the curriculum.

So there is no doubt that it will be taught (and inspected) as part of the new National Curriculum.

The programmes of study for music

All the different subject PoS start with a summary of the main aspects of the subject that pupils will learn during a particular key stage. For music, the wording of these make this particular subject accessible to all pupils whatever their learning needs. Although there are phrases that imply progression beyond what might be possible for many pupils with learning difficulties, there are still aspects of the order which mean that all pupils can be included at all levels. For example, in Key Stage 2 (DfEE/QCA 1999, p. 18): 'They improvise, and develop their own musical compositions, in response to various stimuli with increasing personal involvement, independence and creativity.'

Even pupils with SLD or PMLD can be involved in improvisation and composing, which one would hope would be achieved with an increasing amount of personal involvement, independence and creativity. I have written elsewhere about the possibilities for composing for pupils with profound and multiple learning difficulties (Lacey 1998), and the main thrust of my argument in that article is that pupils with PMLD, if given the right support, adequate resources and sufficient time, can compose simple improvisations or short pieces. These can be recorded in a variety of ways, probably utilising audiotape or videotape.

As in all the non-core foundation subjects (except citizenship), the PoS for music are divided into 'Knowledge, skills and understanding' and 'Breadth of study'. 'Knowledge, skills and understanding' is further divided into the four aspects of music: performing; composing; appraising; and listening and applying. The content of these sections is written in such a way that almost all pupils can be included in almost all aspects. There is a hierarchical element to music (as with any subject), which may not be achievable, either at the key stage in which it appears – or perhaps at all in the case of a few pupils with profound learning difficulties. For example, singing starts from using voices expressively and moves through singing in parts with clear diction to developing vocal technique and musical expression, none of which might be possible for pupils who do not use conventional language or who cannot use their voices. Some vocal pupils may be able to achieve singing expressively but not progress to part-singing, or perhaps can achieve singing in a round with others but do not progress to other forms of singing in parts.

The contents of *Planning, Teaching and Assessing the Curriculum for Pupils with Learning Difficulties* (DfEE/QCA 2001) offer much help to teachers who require adaptations of the subject orders to meet their pupils' needs. The music guidelines (QCA, 2001) demonstrate how the PoS can be varied to provide all pupils with relevant and appropriately challenging work at each stage. For example, staff may choose material from earlier key stages, or select just a single aspect from the age-related stage. They can spend time consolidating skills rather than pressing on with new-skill acquisition, or use music as a context for learning other skills such as social interaction or turn-taking.

There are many examples in the music guidelines that demonstrate how even youngsters with profound learning difficulties can learn through music. For example, there are mentions of using a Big Mack switch to 'participate in songs' or 'respond to own name in a song' or 'reach for instruments'. These are all activities that are recognisably intended for pupils at an early stage of development. There are other ideas for pupils who have learning difficulties with additional hearing or visual impairments.

The guidelines include suggestions for how to use the music schemes of work (QCA 2000a; 2000b) with pupils with learning difficulties – for example, proposing the selection of specific motivating aspects that are relevant to individual pupils, or consolidating learning through repetition and variety. The expectations at the end of each key stage are expressed, as in the schemes of work, in terms of what all pupils, most pupils and some pupils will do, recognising the different levels of engagement, response and ability to learn for pupils across the range of learning difficulties. The performance descriptions of attainment for music leading to Level 1 of the National Curriculum reinforce the different levels of engagement through providing 'best fit' descriptions at eight levels ranging from 'encountering' activities and experiences to 'pupils listening carefully to music'.

Planning and recording

Planning and recording are essential aspects of ensuring effective learning, and it can be helpful to conceive of this on four different levels: whole school, schemes of work, class lessons and individual objectives. The whole-school policy will contain the generalities of aims and how these will be met, as well as issues such as equal opportunities, resources and participation in music within the community. There will also be reference to the way in which pupils will be assessed and their achievements reported.

It is unusual to plan at the level of individuals in mainstream schools, but for many pupils with SEN it is necessary to consider exactly what is intended to be the learning opportunity if there is to be any sense of progression. There will be occasions when the objectives for individuals will be of a more fundamental nature than is included in the subject music, but these will be worked on during a music lesson. For example, for a pupil with PMLD, an objective may be: 'N. will have the opportunity to show awareness of a sound source presented directly in front of her.' For another, more able, pupil in the same class, an objective might be more overtly musical: 'N. will have the opportunity to discriminate between two very contrasting sounds by choosing the correct instrument to play in imitation of a demonstration behind a screen.' Other children in the same class will be able to join in a simple game such as this. Some may be able to discriminate between sounds closer in quality; others may be able to imitate specific rhythms played as a demonstration; and some may be able to take a turn playing an instrument behind the screen.

Planning at this level will originate from documents written for the whole school or department. The PoS offer the framework, but each school will have schemes of work through which these are translated and extended into specific learning opportunities. The documents published by the QCA already mentioned in this chapter can be the basis for planning at all levels. The schemes of work for Key Stages 1 and 2 (QCA 2000a) do not specifically include pupils with learning difficulties, although there are plenty of ideas that can be adapted and simplified. Progression is defined therein as having three dimensions: breadth, challenge/demand, and quality. This is helpful when considering pupils with SLD and PMLD, who may make little progress in a hierarchical way.

The schemes have been expanded upon in the QCA music-specific guidelines for the curriculum for pupils with learning difficulties (QCA 2001). For example, in the topic 'sounds interesting' (from the Key Stage 1 scheme of work), pupils are encouraged to explore a range of sounds in the kitchen. There follow several ideas for discriminating, matching and recording sounds, stories and songs, which are suitable for pupils with learning difficulties. There are several other publications that can contribute to planning at different levels (see the next section, giving details of resources).

Prior to the National Curriculum, detailed planning was unusual in music. It was often felt that the arts gave an opportunity for pupils to relax and enjoy themselves, and thus could be ad hoc in nature. In special schools especially, music was often a sing-song with drums and tambourines used to fill in moments between 'real work'. There was a feeling that singing could help to improve communication skills and give practice in counting, but music was not taken very seriously as a subject in its own right. There is still a very strong case for using music to support other parts of the curriculum, and this will be explored later in this chapter; but there is no doubt that it has much to offer as a separate subject.

If planning has been unsatisfactory, then assessment and recording have been almost non-existent. Level descriptions have already been considered, but these really only satisfy summative assessment. Formative records need more detail, and progress week by week can be noted down briefly to aid planning. It was never intended that music should demand lengthy record keeping, and so a balance will need to be struck between brevity and clarity. A note of class and group activities can be kept, as can any interesting responses from pupils. In the smaller classes of special schools, more detailed records can be kept of individual progress – which may vary tremendously within one group of pupils. For pupils with SLD and PMLD, most of what happens in a music lesson may be recorded elsewhere. For example, achievements in social interaction, discrimination between sound sources, and expressing choices may all be part of the early section of the English curriculum rather than music. Record keeping for music may merely consist of the experiences offered and examples of responses.

Resources

One of the most important aspects of planning, implementing and assessing in music is the part that staff play in the process. Many teachers feel that they lack experience and expertise and thus are unable to teach it sufficiently well. It is the most feared subject in primary or special schools, because people feel they cannot teach music if they cannot play an instrument themselves. There are, of course, a few people who are genuinely 'tone deaf' in that they cannot discriminate between sounds or they cannot hold a steady rhythm, but the majority of teachers have already got – or can be given – the basics of what they need in order to teach aspects of music effectively.

A specialist musician in a primary or special school is an undoubted advantage in helping to ensure that music is well taught. It can, however, be counterproductive to use such a person to take sole responsibility for all the teaching. A judicious mix of specialist and generalist teaching gives pupils a balance and ensures that music is not relegated to half an hour whenever the specialist is not covering for a sick colleague. Where no one on the staff has musical knowledge, a visiting musician may be an alternative, though dwindling LEA music services have reduced the number of visiting musicians over the last few years.

Here is an example of good specialist and generalist cooperation. One secondary special school had a visiting music teacher who came for one afternoon per week. The staff pondered how best to use this resource. There were too many classes for him to teach them all every week, and so it was decided that he would arrange his timetable to spend time with two teachers and their classes each week, teaching a lead lesson and giving ideas for follow-ups. He built in as much training for staff as he could and, once a term, reorganised his schedule so that he could lead an INSET workshop after school. He also checked the instruments and made sure that the guitars and chord harps were tuned correctly. He found an interested teacher who was keen to learn how to do this herself and gradually trained her to manage basic tuning. Finally, with this teacher, he organised a week-long residency for a local pop group who ran workshops for the older pupils.

Teachers may wish to consider planning focused-music topics as 'blocked' work, in the manner advised by the SCAA (1995, 1996). Finding imaginative ways of using staff – the most important resource available – is very important for a subject such as music. Classroom staff in primary and special schools have a crucial part to play, but they cannot do this without training. It is perfectly possible to teach music at Key Stages 1 and 2 without learning to read conventional notation, but there are many other aspects that present problems to non-musicians. Frequent workshops are necessary to help build confidence in teachers. It is probably better to teach the same thing several times – for example, simple chord progression using three chords, demonstrating how this can be used in many different ways – than to try to cover a lot of ground superficially.

There are, however, many aspects of music that can be taught with minimum specialist knowledge. Musical games are very useful and can supplement work done by specialists. There are many publications that give examples of games such as the following, from Birmingham Curriculum Support Service (1992):

Equipment: A variety of tuned and untuned percussion instruments.
Activity: Pupils sit in a circle.
The teacher chooses three different instruments and taps out messages in 'code' e.g.: sit still (two sounds on claves); stand up quietly (five sounds on tambour); stretch (long ring on Indian Bells).
The children respond to each coded message played in random order.
The pupils can then make up messages of their own and take turns to control what happens.

Training all class teachers to become competent music teachers is no small task. It is hoped that succeeding generations, who will have experienced National Curriculum music themselves, will be more capable than the present generation, but this enskilling is a lengthy process.

Although competent teachers are a vital resource, choosing and maintaining instruments is also very important. It is always better to have a smaller number of good-quality instruments than lots in poor shape. One orchestral-size cymbal on a strap will give a much more satisfying sound than six pairs of toy cymbals – often found in primary or special schools. Home-made instruments are rarely satisfying to play, although much can be learned from making them. Finding sound-makers from unusual sources can offer some interesting opportunities for learning and can perhaps be used to provide sound effects for stories. Many exciting percussion instruments have become available to schools over the last few years, such as the vibra-slap, the chocolo, the cabasa and sets of tongue drums. They are attractive to look at and give many opportunities to hear instruments with different timbres (i.e. sound qualities).

Some pupils with SEN will need adapted instruments, either because they have physical restrictions or because they find them too difficult to play satisfactorily. For example, hand chimes are useful for pupils who find the precision hard of hitting a chime bar with a beater, for hand chimes have a beater attached and need only to be rung like a bell. Tuning three guitars, one to each of the chords in a three-chord sequence, can enable pupils to play to accompany folk songs without having to learn where to put their fingers on the frets: each pupil plays only when her or his chord is needed in the song. Tuned percussion or keyboards can be colour-coded so that younger or less able pupils can follow a simple score.

A few books of songs and musical games have been written with pupils with SEN in mind, and these are listed at the end of this chapter. There are, of course, many others that have been produced for mainstream primary schools and that are very helpful for *all* abilities, particularly the series published by A & C Black. Some have accompanying cassettes, which unconfident teachers will find invaluable. You will also find listed at the end of this chapter three primary music courses, which are recommended for the mainstream and can be adapted for pupils with SEN.

It is at this point that teachers of secondary-age pupils with SEN sigh and say, 'There is never anything for teenagers.' They are right, of course. Very little has been written that combines simplicity with age-appropriate material. Teachers have to be very inventive, writing new words to well-known tunes and simplifying the words of pop songs. It might also be considered appropriate to move on with the kinds of instruments chosen for teenagers with learning difficulties. Keyboards, guitars, electronic drum machines, and a drum kit may offer a different challenge from the primary percussion instruments that they may well have been playing for many years. Progression can be built in to the opportunities offered to pupils, even if they do not make much progress musically. Listening to music can change a little too, though I do not subscribe to the belief that teenagers with SLD should not be allowed to listen to nursery songs even if that is what they like; I would encourage a wider repertoire, but would not want to deny enjoyment of the familiar. Generally, my attitude to age-appropriateness is more connected with the way in which one treats and values people with learning difficulties. It has very little to do with taking teddy bears and children's songs away from them.

Extension work with all pupils, but especially with teenagers with learning difficulties, can include working with visiting performers. There is a very useful guide to working with artists in schools (Sharp and Dust 1997), which can help make the most of interactions with professional musicians. The benefits for pupils and for teachers and schools are clearly discussed in that handbook, as are benefits for the artists themselves. Certainly, a workshop visit from local musicians can be very motivating for both children and their teachers, each reaching performance levels they did not realise were possible.

Finally, in terms of resources, teachers involved with pupils with PMLD will be interested in a book by Lambe and Hogg (2000) that brings together many ideas for resources and activities under the general umbrella of creative arts. There is a useful list of addresses at the end of the chapter therein on music, some of which also appear in the list at the conclusion of this chapter.

Some approaches to teaching music

Music lends itself well to a whole variety of different strategies for teaching. Sometimes teachers will lead and direct closely what is happening, but there will be other occasions when they will stand back and encourage pupils, giving them advice and facilitating their efforts. Equally, there will be times when pupils are working alone, in pairs, or in small groups, as well as the whole class together. Finding space for several small groups or pairs to work at once is very hard in some schools, especially those that are open-plan in design. If space is difficult, then it might be necessary to stagger composition classes. Using headphones for keyboards is another possibility.

Infant classes have traditionally had the 'music corner' where instruments and other sound-makers are available for experimentation, or tapes can be listened to, or simple work-cards can be left to encourage the practice of skills taught in lessons. Some special-school classrooms would find this difficult to emulate because of the presence of a few pupils whose behaviour precludes leaving out expensive equipment. It might, however, be possible to provide this independence at particular times or in particular places – for example, through centralised-resource or interactive-display areas.

Many class teachers find it difficult to teach the use of tuned percussion instruments. Often, they feel reasonably comfortable with untuned percussion, but xylophones, glockenspiels and chime bars present considerable problems. This may be where music specialists can be best used, so that class teachers can concentrate on practising skills already learned. However, there are many activities that are possible with minimal musical knowledge. Helping pupils to compose simple tunes using the five notes CDEFG or the pentatonic scale CDEGA, or even the whole octave C to C, can be about what sounds 'right' or 'interesting', 'scary' or even 'terrible'. Everyone's view is valid. Tape-recording the results can provide a permanent record of the tune if pupils are not able to devise notation of their own.

Music is essentially a practical subject. There is knowledge to be gained concerning the musical elements, resources, musical character, styles and traditions, and also about how music is communicated and how it reflects its historical and social context. But all these must be learned through experience rather than by didactic instruction (Stephens 1995). Movement and dance are very useful for experiencing a variety of styles, traditions and cultures. Often, pupils can express what they feel about a piece of music through their movements, which they would find difficult to express in words. I will return to movement and dance in the final section of this chapter's text, which will consider the relationship of music to other parts of the curriculum.

It has often been said that class music is not primarily about performance and that producing school concerts is not time well spent. I both agree and disagree with the sentiment. Certainly, giving over the whole of the half-term before Christmas to rehearsing for the nativity play may well put the balance of the curriculum into jeopardy, but judicious use of performance is essential in music. Some of this may be given over to pupils performing their own compositions to each other, but some will be given to performing the work of others. The opportunity to rehearse and refine songs and pieces is a good discipline and will be echoed in other parts of the curriculum, especially in drafting and redrafting written work in English. Putting on a concert can be an excellent topic for any age and ability group. There are opportunities for English, mathematics, technology and art as well as music if the pupils are encouraged to engage in sending out invitations, painting posters and making props, as well as composing and performing.

Performance is also about listening to others perform. Many community musicians, orchestras and bands have educational aspects to their work and are available to lead workshops and give concerts in schools. This is most effective when school staff can be involved in planning and follow-up work, meeting with professional musicians to decide on a focus, organising concert visits, taking part in workshops with pupils in school and reinforcing what has been covered in subsequent music lessons.

Music therapy

One aspect of music associated with special education is music therapy. This should not be confused with classroom music, although I would claim that as a teacher of pupils with SLD I used music in a therapeutic manner. Music therapists, however, draw a clear distinction between teaching and therapy, maintaining that in therapy they are using music to reach children's emotions, to arouse and engage them more effectively with the world around them. Music is the means through which communication is made, but the intention is not to teach the children music skills. Often, though, considerable musical progress is made as well as progress in communication. Music is chosen as the medium because it is claimed that the ability to appreciate and respond to music is inborn and is frequently unimpaired by disability, injury or illness (Association of Professional Music Therapists 1988).

Music therapy training is open only to music graduates, and it might be said that, because of its exclusivity, it has become a much-desired service. There are not many therapists around the country, and some teachers and parents feel somewhat cheated that their children cannot benefit from something that is so obviously 'a good thing'. There are a few LEAs that offer INSET to teachers who are not music graduates, so that they gain further understanding of the therapeutic uses of music and learn some techniques for practice (Mills 1991). This is a welcome initiative and seems to be the most sensible way forward so that more pupils with SEN can benefit from what music therapy has to offer.

There have been recent developments in using music therapeutically, particularly with the most profoundly disabled and deaf-blind youngsters. The work of Russ Palmer (2000) on the philosophy behind 'feeling the music' demonstrates that even profoundly deaf children can enjoy music. He writes of feeling music through vibration, suggesting that:

- low tones can be felt in the feet, legs and hips;
- middle tones can be felt in the stomach, chest and arms;
- high tones can be felt in the fingers, head and hair.

The work of Anne Nafstad and Inger Rodbroe is available on video, showing how people with multisensory impairment can be reached through using simple shared rhythms in a manner that those two authors call 'co-creating communication' (Nafstad and Rodbroe 1999). The implication is that, although the child may not be able to communicate very effectively on his or her own, together with an adult who is sensitive to the slightest attempts at interaction they can create the communication together. Music is seen as a powerful medium through which this co-creativity can be developed.

Soundbeam has developed over the last few years, and the work of Phil Ellis (1996) on 'sound therapy' using Soundbeam and electronic keyboards is available on video (*Incidental Music*). Soundbeam utilises a beam of light that can be broken by the slightest movement to create a sound effect on a synthesiser or keyboard. Ellis claims that children have been motivated by being able to control sounds even though their ability to play an instrument in the conventional way is severely impaired. He shows how, over time, children have learnt to control their movements sufficiently to be able to produce the sounds they prefer.

Managing sessions

Returning to music teaching, one of the most difficult aspects for staff who lack musical confidence is managing lessons. There is enormous potential for mayhem in terms of noise, and many teachers are wary of what might happen if they allow pupils to compose and perform freely. While this is quite understandable, it is important to find a way to organise sessions other than class singing and playing controlled solely by teachers. Encouraging pupils to work in pairs is a good place to begin. A lead lesson can be taught to the whole class, and then pairs of pupils can work on their own responses. Several pairs can work at once in different corners of the room and corridor. The rest of the class can be working on a different subject while they await their turn, which may not come for several days. A time can be arranged to share what they have been doing.

It is a little easier in special schools, where the classes are smaller, but certainly in schools for pupils with SLD there may be very difficult pupils who disrupt the class. Often, in these circumstances there are two or more members of staff in the class, in which case it is relatively easy for one to take a small group of pupils and support their efforts at exploring sounds and composing simple pieces. The pentatonic scale (CDEGA) mentioned earlier is very useful for pupils with learning difficulties because, even played randomly, pleasant sounds can be made. The teacher can accompany these sounds on, for example, just C and G, varying the rhythm to encourage awareness of differences.

Another problem facing the less confident teacher of music is how to manage whole-class percussion sessions. Everyone wants a turn and, if rules are not made, chaos can soon reign. Enabling the pupils to make their own rules is a good place to begin. How many do they think it would be sensible to have in the band? What is the fairest way to allocate places? How often should rotation happen? Pairing pupils can be helpful here too, so that everyone knows to whom they are handing on their instrument. Try dividing the class into two, pairing everyone within each half. One half will be this week's players, taking half the playing each. The other half of the class are either critical listeners or singers, depending on the piece being performed. For the next lesson, the roles will be reversed.

Again, in the small classes of a special school this is less of a problem. With pupils with PMLD it may be necessary to work individually with each pupil because they have few skills for interacting with others. A large drum or cymbal are good instruments to encourage reactions even from these pupils. The cymbal is particularly good as it resonates for some time, giving someone who may react very slowly ample opportunity to respond. Another useful sound-maker for giving time for listening is a microphone attached to an electronic digital delay (e.g. a Boss SE50 or an RSD10). Every sound made into the microphone can be repeated several times. It can also be slowed down and speeded up, altering the pitch – useful not only to attract attention but for creating interesting sound-effects for stories.

For pupils with MLD and SLD, music can be very useful for encouraging social interaction. There are a wealth of activities aimed at this, and the following are a few ideas:

- Sit in a circle. One person begins a simple rhythm such as 'fish fingers and chips' (with or without the words to help). He then 'throws' this rhythm across the circle to someone he can see, who 'catches' it and performs it herself. She then 'throws' this to another person across the circle, and so on.
- Sit in a circle. One person walks (or wheels) across the circle to play a cymbal to another person. She plays a 'message' to that person, perhaps indicating 'hello'. That person then takes the cymbal and greets someone else. He must find a different way to play the instrument from the first person. It can be different in dynamics, style, rhythm or speed. The game continues until the participants have run out of different ways to play it or have all been involved.
- Sit opposite a partner. The pair has one instrument between them. They have a 'conversation' using the instrument to speak for them. They take it in turns to 'speak' using the instrument to represent their mood.

- In pairs, using two instruments that are contrasting in timbre, compose a short sequence of rhythms. This could be made more difficult by asking for contrasts in dynamics or speed.

Music and other subjects

From these activities it can be seen that, although it has a valid life of its own, there are many ways in which music can be taught in combination with other subjects. Performance arts are probably the most natural to combine. Movement and dance have already been mentioned, but drama, puppetry, mime, poetry and prose all have moments when they can support and be supported by music. A simple example demonstrates how music and movement can influence each other: a pair of pupils (A and B) has one instrument between them; person A plays the instrument to control the way in which B moves; alternatively, B leads and her movements influence A's playing of the instrument.

Adding sounds to a story can give opportunities to learn more of both music and stories. Teenagers with learning difficulties particularly enjoy bringing life to the picture book *Haunted House* by Jan Pienkowski (1979). This is a young-children's book with doors to open and tabs to pull, all depicting horror scenes. There is no written story but much to imagine. The first page, for instance, has a staircase, a mouse, a pair of moving eyes, a door, a spider and a cat. Each one can be represented by a sound chosen from those available – an instrument, a voice, some part of the body, or something concocted electronically. The whole can be made into a musical piece by composing a suitable beginning, middle and end, and the performance can be led by a pupil who points to the different parts of the picture in turn. Other pages can follow, depending upon the concentration span of the pupils involved. This could be developed further through moving away from the original picture stimulus into a specific horror story acted out by a group of pupils and accompanied by a score. Combining performance arts is not only sensible in today's crowded curriculum but it also gives many opportunities for pupils to experience and use a set of expressive tools that support each other naturally.

Music can support other aspects of the curriculum, especially English and mathematics, because both language and patterns are integral parts. Music from different times and cultures relates easily to history, geography and modern foreign languages, and explorations of the properties of sound relate to science. Instrument-making contributes to design and technology, and recording music demonstrates ICT capability. Music has enormous potential, especially in the topic work found in primary and special schools, although dragging it into *every* topic is not advisable. Merely singing a song that has words fitting into the theme may actually be a poor choice in terms of the musical ability of the class, and listening to music for its representation of the sea or spring can mask the real musical aspects of the composition (Glover and Ward 1993).

Personal and social education is another aspect of the curriculum that can be well served by music. Social skills have already been mentioned, especially learning the basics of social interaction. Music can be made alone, but there are also plenty of opportunities to come together, share, take turns and listen to each other. This leads naturally into choir, band and orchestra work.

Building self-esteem through taking part in musical activities is another important aspect, and teachers have often been aware of pupils' successes that are not necessarily reflected elsewhere in the curriculum. Those who have difficulties in basic reading and writing are not necessarily disadvantaged in the field of expressive arts – although, equally, it must be remembered that not everyone finds them easy. Skilled teaching can ensure a measure of success for almost everyone. Gone are the days when children are banished from singing groups because they 'growl' and spoil the sound; everyone is encouraged to sing and, through practice, almost all can improve. Using the voice is like playing any other instrument: it needs technique, practice and regular use.

Conclusions

Although music, along with other arts subjects, has been neglected during the time devoted to implementing the Literacy and Numeracy Strategies, I am convinced that it will eventually take its proper place in the curriculum. Schools and teachers are hard-pressed at the moment and cannot give priority to training and support for musical activities. I have been involved in a private organisation called 'Special Music Courses' over the past five years, and the drop in numbers of teachers wishing to come on the INSET courses that we run, over those years, has been enormous. People who *do* come are full of enthusiasm and express tremendous regret that music does not have a higher profile in schools. For the immediate future, there will be no more training from 'Special Music Courses'. But there is great hope that the tide will turn, staff will have more time to devote to the arts in their schools, and they will want to increase their knowledge, skills and understanding of music.

References

Association of Professional Music Therapists (APMT 1988) *Music Therapy in the Education Service: A consultation document.* London: APMT.
Birmingham Curriculum Support Service (1992) *Implementing Music in the National Curriculum,* 2nd edn. Birmingham: Birmingham City Council Education Department.
DfEE/QCA (1999) *Music: The National Currriculum for England.* London: HMSO.
DfEE/QCA (2001) *Planning, Teaching and Assessing the Curriculum for Pupils with Learning Difficulties.* London: DfEE/QCA
Ellis, P. (1996) *Sound Therapy: The music of sound.* Bristol: Soundbeam Project (plus video, *Incidental Music*).
Glover, J. and Ward, S. (1993) *Teaching Music in the Primary School.* London: Cassell.
Lacey, P. (1998) 'Composing with pupils with PMLD', *PMLD–Link* 32 (Winter 1998/9), 25–7.
Lambe, L. and Hogg, J. (2000) *Creative Arts and People with Profound and Multiple Learning Disabilities: Education, therapy and leisure.* Brighton: Pavilion.
Mills, J. (1991) *Music in the Primary School.* Cambridge: Cambridge University Press.
Nafstad, A. and Rodbroe, I. (1999) *Co-creating Communication.* Dronninglund: Forlaget Nord-Press.
Palmer, R. (2000) 'Feeling the music philosophy' at http://www.kolumbus.fi/riitta.lahtinen
Pienkowski, J. (1979) *Haunted House.* Oxford: Heinemann.
Pugh, A. and Pugh, L. (1998) *Music in the Early Years.* London: Routledge.
QCA (2000a) *Music: A Scheme of Work for Key Stages 1 and 2.* London: QCA.
QCA (2000b) *Music: A scheme of work for Key Stage 3,* London: QCA.
QCA (2001) *Planning, Teaching and Assessing the Curriculum for Pupils with Learning Difficulties: Music.* London: QCA.
SCAA (1995) *Planning the Curriculum at Key Stages 1 and 2.* London: SCAA.
SCAA (1996) *Planning the Curriculum for Pupils with Profound and Multiple Learning Difficulties.* London: SCAA.

Sharp, C. and Dust, K. (1997) *Artists in School: A handbook for teachers and artists*. Windsor, Berkshire: NFER.
Stephens, J. (1995) 'The National Curriculum for music', in Pratt, G. and Stephens, J. (eds) *Teaching Music in the National Curriculum*. Oxford: Heinemann.

Other useful sources

Allen, A. and Coley, J. (1995–6) *Dance for All (Books 1–3)*. London: David Fulton Publishers.
Childs, J. (1996) *Making Music Special*. London: David Fulton Publishers.
Levete, G. (1982) *No Handicap to Dance*. London: Souvenir Press.
Perry, T. M. (1995) *Music Lessons for Children with Special .Needs*. London: Jessica Kingsley.
Peter, M. (1997) *Making Dance Special*. London: David Fulton Publishers.
Streeter, E. (2001) *Making Music with the Young Child with Special Needs*. London: Jessica Kingsley.
Wills, P. and Peter, M. (1995) *Music for All*. London: David Fulton Publishers.
Wood, M. (1983) *Music for People with Learning Disabilities*. London: Souvenir Press.

Song and musical activity books

Baxter, K. (1994) *Fundamental Activities*. Nottingham: Fundamental Activities. [PO Box 149, Nottingham NG3 5PU (includes video)]
Bean, J. and Oldfield, A. (1991) *Pied Piper*. Cambridge: CUP.
Clark, V. (1991) *High Low Dolly Pepper: Developing music skills with young children*. London: A & C Black.
Holdstock, J. and West, M. (various dates) *Earwiggo 1–6*. North Yorks.: Ray Lovely Music. [17 Westgate, Tadcaster, North Yorks. LS24 9JB]
Lennard, C. (1987) *Body and Voice*. Wisbech: LDA (includes tapes).
Mortimer, H. (2000) *The Music Makers Approach: Inclusive activities for young children with special educational needs*. Tamworth: NASEN.
Ockelford, A. (1996) *All Join In*. London: RNIB.
Pearson, D. (1987) *Up, Up and Away*. Oxford: OUP.
Powell, H. (1983) *Games Songs with Prof. Dogg's Troupe*. London: A & C Black (includes tape).
Thompson, D. and Baxter, K. (1978) *Pompaleerie Jig*. London: Arnold/Wheaton.

Addresses of disability arts groups/providers of training

Amber Trust, Garrow House, 190 Kensal Road, London W10 5BT.
Beat That!, Rose Cottage, Pound Lane, Stanton St. John, Oxon OX33 1HF.
Birmingham Centre for Creative Arts Therapies, The Friends Institute, 220 Moseley Road, Highgate, Birmingham B12 0DG.
Entelechy Arts Ltd, The Albany, Douglas Way, Deptford, London SE8 4AG.
Interact Performance Group, Ashbourne House, 2 Park Street, Harrogate HG1 5QU.
Orcadia Creative Learning Centre, 3 Windsor Place, Portobello, Edinburgh EH15 2AJ.
Sonic Arts, Francis House, Francis Street, London SW1P 1DE.
Soundbeam, Unit 3 Highbury Villas, St. Michael's Hill, Bristol BS2 8BY.
Soundabout, 12 Alfred Terraces, Chipping Norton, Oxon OX7 5UB.
Special Music Courses, Greenacres, Birdingbury Road, Marton, Nr Rugby CV23 9RY.

Chapter 10

Modern Foreign Languages

Keith Bovair

The only 'disabling' conditions that our pupils have are low expectations and assumptions made by adults.

(Bovair and Robbins 1996)

Introduction

In the late 1980s, the editors of this book met to collaborate on a work entitled *The Curriculum Challenge* (Ashdown *et al.* 1991) It was their firm belief that, with the onset of the National Curriculum, entitlement of *all* pupils should be met within the new framework being proposed. Since that time and since the first edition of this book, educators in the field of special education have risen to the challenge and are continually extending our knowledge and ability to access subject areas that were once considered only the domain of the mainstream of education.

The debate we are now having relates to the establishment of accreditation systems, which recognise the efforts, experiences and abilities of pupils who are on the continuum of education. Within the legal requirements of the National Curriculum for England within modern foreign languages (DfEE/QCA 1999a), there is a clear statement on inclusion to 'meet the specific needs of individuals and groups of pupils'. Segments from the three principles on which the National Curriculum is based are set out next (DfEE/QCA 1999a).

A Setting suitable learning challenges

1. Teachers should aim to give every pupil the opportunity to experience success in learning and to achieve as high a standard as possible. The National Curriculum programmes of study set out what most pupils should be taught at each key stage – *but teachers should teach the knowledge, skills and understanding that suit their pupils' abilities.* (my italics).
2. For pupils whose attainments fall significantly below the expected levels at a particular key stage, *a much greater degree of differentiation will be necessary.* (my italics)

3. For pupils whose attainments significantly exceed the expected level of the attainment within one or more subjects during a particular key stage, teachers will need to plan suitably challenging material.

B Responding to pupils' diverse learning needs

1. When planning, teachers should set high expectations and provide opportunities for all pupils to achieve, including boys and girls, pupils with special educational needs, pupils with disabilities, pupils' from all social and cultural backgrounds, pupils of different ethnic groups including travellers, refugees and asylum seekers, and those from diverse linguistic backgrounds.
2. To ensure that they meet the full range of pupils' needs, teachers should be aware of the requirements of the equal opportunities legislation that covers race, gender and disability.
3. Teachers should take specific action to respond to pupils' diverse needs by:
   a. creating effective learning environments;
   b. securing their motivation and concentration;
   c. providing equality of opportunity through teaching approaches;
   d. using appropriate assessment approaches;
   e. setting targets for learning.

C Overcoming potential barriers to learning for individual pupils and groups

1. During end of key stage assessments, teachers should bear in mind that special arrangements are available to support individual pupils.
2. Curriculum planning and assessment for pupils with special educational needs must take account of the type and the extent of the difficulty experienced by such pupils.
3. Teachers should take specific action to provide for pupils with special educational needs by:
   a. providing for pupils who need help with communication, language and literacy;
   b. planning, where necessary, to develop pupils' understanding through the use of all available senses and experiences;
   c. planning for pupils for full participation in learning and in physical and practical activities;
   d. helping pupils to manage their behaviour, to take part in learning effectively and safely, and, at Key Stage 4, to prepare for work;
   e. helping individuals to manage their emotions – particularly trauma or stress – and to take part in learning.
4. Not all pupils with disabilities have special educational needs. ... Teachers must take action, however, in their planning to ensure that these pupils are enabled to participate as fully and effectively as possible within the National Curriculum and the statutory assessment arrangements.
5. Teachers should take specific action to enable the effective participation of pupils with disabilities by:
   a. planning appropriate amounts of time to allow for the satisfactory completion of tasks;
   b. planning opportunities, where necessary, for the development of skills in practical aspects of the curriculum;
   c. identifying aspects of programmes of study and attainment targets that may present specific difficulties for individuals.
6. Pupils for whom English is an additional language have diverse needs.

7. The ability of pupils for whom English is an additional language to take part in the National Curriculum may be ahead of their communication.
8. Teachers should take specific action to help pupils who are learning English as an additional language by:
   a. developing their spoken and written English;
   b. ensuring access to the curriculum and to assessment.

It should be noted from the above that point C3b should be exploited by teachers because it allows for a multisensory approach that gives greater opportunity for a multidimensional curriculum among those with special educational needs. Furthermore, it should be noted that the use of ICT and alternative communication systems are now actively encouraged, which is demonstrated in the following section.

Teaching pupils with severe learning difficulties

There has been much scepticism about introducing a modern foreign language to pupils with severe learning difficulties. Typically, the argument goes something along the lines of 'We should not be teaching a foreign language to these pupils when they still have significant language deficits in their own language.' Although it is understandable that teachers may show caution, some schools have had a positive experience of teaching a foreign language and have found that it has the potential to be interesting, enriching and a great deal of fun. Moreover, it provides a new and effective experience of learning language skills (which are common to all languages) that is untainted by past failure, and students can find themselves delighted to discover that they are studying a subject studied by their peers.

At George Hastwell School, Cumbria, the introduction of a French week was so successful that French now occupies a regular weekly position on the timetable for secondary-aged pupils. Throughout the French week, lessons were planned with a French focus; in mathematics they learned to count up to ten in French and to compare French and British money; in geography they looked at books and maps of France; in physical education they played *boules*; in music they listened to the work of French composers; in art they painted French flags and produced posters; in design and technology they planned typically French meals, compiled menus and searched for French food at the supermarkets. The highlight of the week was the conversion of one classroom into a French café, which displayed their work and allowed visitors to select drinks and snacks made by the pupils.

In particular, the use of ICT has been a major factor in making the modern foreign languages curriculum accessible at George Hastwell School (McKeown 1993). Communication devices that can digitise and store sounds have been programmed with simple French phrases that pupils with communication problems or less confident pupils can produce by touching the appropriate part of the overlay of pictorial symbols on the keyboard. The overlays may be changed depending on the lesson content and may contain, say, pictures of food or clothes, or symbols that represent common phrases (see Figure 10.1 for an example of symbols for basic phrases).

Individualised worksheets may be prepared using symbols from, say, the 'Rebus Symbol Collection' from Widgit Software in WRITING WITH SYMBOLS 2000 (see resources list at the end of this chapter), and the worksheets can be associated with general topic areas. Using this software and an overlay keyboard, pupils may produce pieces of their own French writing accompanied by the appropriate symbols (see Figure 10.2).

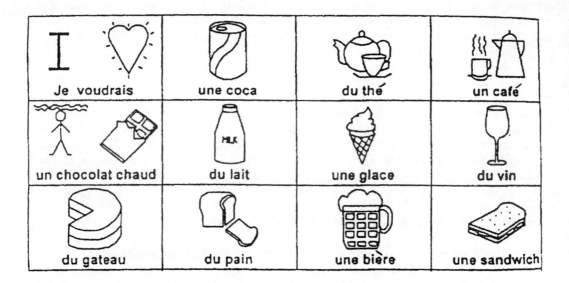

Figure 10.1 Symbol overlay for basic phrases

Figure 10.2 Writing in French with symbol software

Computers can also be set up with a number of programs that may help pupils practise their French vocabulary. For instance, pupils may have access to slide-shows created using KID PIX COMPANION, which is a program that allows pictures, including digitised images, to be placed in a sequence and accompanied by the sound of somebody labelling the image. At George Hastwell School, a popular slide-show contained digitised photographs of each pupil accompanied by his or her voice announcing '*Je m'appelle*'. And of course, when a pupil could not speak, the rest of the group recorded the greeting '*Bonjour*' for when his or her picture appeared.

'I suppose you are going to try to teach these kids French.'

The author of this chapter thrives on challenges and was confronted by the previous statement. Since the challenge, which was made in the early 1990s, the development of an accredited course has borne fruit. In 1999, 13 Year-11 pupils (the full class) obtained 12 merits (M) and 1 pass (P) in the French course offered by the relevant examining board. The pupils exhibited a full range of individual needs, as described in the following pen portraits taken from their Statements of Special Educational Needs – see Table 10.1 – and yet achieved some outstanding results.

The following year's (2000) attainment has been such that, out of a class of nine Year-11 pupils, there were nine distinctions. Again, the population of pupils were on a wide continuum of special educational needs. The grades predicted for 2001 are, out of 11 Year-11 pupils, 9 distinctions and 2 merits. (It should be noted that none of these results will show up on any league table as the system stands at present.)

This work in modern foreign languages was seeded in the early 1990s by the Rauzet Restoration Project at Durants School, Enfield, North London. It was set up to restore the fine Romanesque Church of Rauzet in the village of Rozet, France. A main task was the restoration of a mediaeval fishpond within the grounds. In this experience, the skills of learning a new language, self-sufficiency, practical problem-solving, enterprise, team-building skills, work experience, community/school links and extension of the National Curriculum all arose.

In 1993, Durants School was invited to join an existing work experience and community project in France. The project had been established the year before between White Hart Lane School, Le Lycée de L'image et du Son in France, the Craswell Grandmontine Society and the local community of Rozet. Essentially, the project focused on the restoration of the Priory at Rozet. Durants School was invited to work on the site, restoring part of the grounds. This built on an established programme of pre-work-experience skills based at Durants School and Capel Manor College in Enfield. The programme had been identified and established at Durants School to answer pupils' needs in helping them cope with emerging independence, practical problem-solving and the successful transference of skills into different work settings.

The work at Rozet was an extension of this requirement, and it was also designed to complement the archaeological work undertaken by the other groups. Durants School staff developed wider objectives for their students, encompassing a European-awareness programme and self-sufficiency. These included a European food project, funded by North London Training and Enterprise Council. Initially the work was planned and coordinated between White Hart Lane School (who liaised with the Lycée in France) and Durants School. All three schools liaised with the Grandmontine Society.

Table 10.1 Pupils successful in French

Pupil A:	a healthy, friendly polite and well-behaved boy who learns more slowly than many children of his age and is rather immature socially. (M)
Pupil B:	a healthy girl who has experienced learning difficulties in the mainstream setting and has exhibited some emotional and behavioural difficulties, possibly in consequence of this. (M)
Pupil C:	a physically healthy boy who, despite the highest level of support available in school, has made very little progress and is unable to cope with the demands of a mainstream curriculum nor the social demands of a large school. (M)
Pupil D:	a lively, friendly girl ... [who] has behavioural and learning difficulties related to William's Syndrome, [and] particularly delayed learning and language skills. (P)
Pupil E:	a girl whose original learning and behavioural difficulties identified her thus: 'Her development seemed to be relatively immature and slow, particularly in the areas of language, behaviour and general personal abilities.' (M)
Pupil F:	a boy who ... experiences clear learning difficulties and his needs are complicated by an emotional fragility. (M)
Pupil G:	a fit and healthy boy whose ... word knowledge is quite restricted and his verbal responses are often rambling . (M)
Pupil H:	a generally healthy girl who has moderate learning difficulties and has some difficulties communicating with adults. (M)
Pupil I:	a physically healthy and well-coordinated girl who is making steady progress at a school for children with moderate learning difficulties ... [she] has a slight speech impediment. (M)
Pupil J:	a healthy agile and generally responsive boy who has in the past experienced difficulties acquiring language skills, in learning and in behaviour. (M)
Pupil K:	a healthy boy who ... experiences difficulties regarding his relationships with other children. (M)
Pupil L:	a healthy, polite and well-behaved girl who has experienced learning difficulties for a number of years. (M)
Pupil M:	a generally healthy girl of below average ability ... who had been under-achieving in all areas of the mainstream curriculum. (M)

Outcomes of the project could be seen in the growth of pupils' self-esteem. This in turn helped them to develop many skills towards becoming independent young adults and extended their confidence in their academic learning. The project supported curriculum development in French, European awareness, mathematics, technology, history, geography and art; and it was continued at the school through Team Enterprise, which allows pupils to experience setting up a business. The skills of management, accounting, product design and selling were learnt through the framework of this aspect.

Pupils from Durants School, with assistance from the Enfield Chamber of Commerce and the Safeway supermarket chain, set up an English market stall in and around Nantes, France. They spent a whole week in the region, learning a variety of skills, in French, to make the work a success. This success was due to the experience of the previous project, as well as the skill and confidence of the staff who saw, along with the pupils, the benefit of learning another language. Thus, Team Enterprise, which generally provides a mainstream educational opportunity, was enhanced by relocation to France and added a dimensional element to the subject that has now been identified as an acceptable means of enhancing a subject area.

Re-signification

In all this, a key outcome for these pupils and their parents/guardians has been their re-signification as learners. It has been their 'resurrection' to receive recognition for their efforts. This is in a subject area that has often been denied to them by either well-intentioned or ill-informed adults. It should be noted that, often, our intent to be considerate of the needs of a learner by discouraging entry into a subject has placed – subtly – the pupil and the parent in distress. The messages they receive by either dis-application or non-inclusion, together with the Statementing process itself, often places them in a position of 'grief' (Bovair 1993).

The pupils involved in the project described above were not individuals who presented themselves as being compliant. The generalisations of their Statements often disguised the greater complexity of their needs. If they were a straightforward populace, the mainstream of education should have been capable of meeting their educational entitlement.

The next challenge is to transfer this style of practice into the mainstream.

The current context

In the mid-1980s the teaching of modern foreign languages to pupils with learning difficulties was a rare event. As previously stated, they were often withdrawn from lessons in order to deal with their first-language difficulties. Gradually, evidence was established that teaching another language was exciting and rewarding for pupils with special educational needs (Bovair 1995; Bovair and Bovair 1992; Bovair *et al.* 1992; Robbins 1995). It required the understanding that pupils with learning difficulties need what all pupils need, which is (Bovair 1995, p. 32):

- to know what is expected of them;
- to understand how to go about their work;
- to achieve success;
- to have opportunities for reinforcement;
- to see and record progress.

Also, teaching modern foreign languages requires a particular style of teaching. The teaching of modern languages lends itself to a multisensory approach, which suits the type of students we are discussing. This style of teaching will be familiar to all teachers of modern languages and will typically include (Bovair 1995, p. 32 again):

- *visual elements* – realia, flashcards, overhead projector (OHP), etc.
- *aural elements* – teacher, LSA [special support assistant], tapes, language masters, etc.
- *oral elements* – repetition, pair work, songs, conversations, etc.
- *kinetic elements* – action, mime, plays, games, etc.

Before all these elements were recognised as a means to establish access to a subject that was often exclusive, the confidence of teachers had to be established to enable them to develop appropriately differentiated material. The debate about entitlement had to be won, and the doors to experiential learning had to be opened in order to establish motivation to teach and to learn another language. And, by learning another language, the European dimension in a pupil's life becomes more accessible. As stated (Robbins 1995, p. 16):

> Young people with special educational needs, like all other young people, are growing up in a world of instant communications, within an economy that crosses national and even continental boundaries. If education is truly preparation for life, we should not deny them knowledge of the world as it is today and will be tomorrow.
>
> Each pupil has a right of entitlement to the curriculum, to life experiences, including speaking French, German, Spanish, etc., and to be able to visit the countries that have these languages as their national language. It is an equal opportunities issue.

The following anecdote illustrates the opportunities which should exist as a matter of course. In a school for moderate learning difficulties, the modern-foreign-language teacher set up a system by which she would give points every time she heard a pupil speak French. There was an award for the pupil with the highest number of points. At the same time, a new pupil joined the school. Asked by the head teacher after the morning break (which was supervised by the modern-foreign-language teacher) how he was getting on, the new pupil quickly replied, 'Fine, but they all speak French here!'

In 1988, the Council of Education Ministers of the European Community passed a resolution to strengthen the 'European dimension' in their respective school systems. The European dimension is not a subject but something that permeates the whole curriculum. Its purpose is to raise awareness of Europe's common historical and cultural heritage, to give pupils perspectives that stretch beyond national frontiers and to prepare them better for life in an interdependent Europe. This is currently being well embedded with the establishment of citizenship in the UK curriculum (DfEE/QCA 1999b). I am suggesting here that the European dimension – although cross-curricular and having its place in other subjects – may be subsumed into the modern foreign languages curriculum.

Original work in this area for pupils with moderate learning difficulties was established at Halmoor School, Birmingham, in the 1990s. The Eurotech Project 1995 was a technology-based project within Key Stage 3. It was developed over two terms. In the autumn term pupils were asked to:

- investigate signs in the community, such as shop signs, road signs and everyday signs;
- investigate information found on packaging such as weight, number of units, serving suggestions, country of origin, manufacturers, price, nutritional information and shape of packaging and materials;

- compare home packaging to foreign packaging to see whether the same information could be gathered despite language barriers;
- look at how packaging is put together, by dismantling and assembling different types;
- explore different shapes and packages and their suitability for a range of foods;
- visit local shops and a variety of markets;
- research pricing and availability;
- design both an item that was small and cost less than 25 pence and (given a design brief) one that was a quick-to-eat snack;
- design packaging for their snack food, market it and sell it.

During the following spring term, links were made with nine schools in Europe and a joint food project was initiated. The countries involved were Germany, Denmark, England, Northern Ireland and Holland. The project involved pupils recording their food intake on a specific day and recording the types of shops that they purchased in and the prices they paid. They then sent the information to the other schools and exchanged examples of packaging with each other. Those schools that had a fax were able to exchange information rapidly. They produced a video of the snack food that they had designed in the previous autumn term.

The pupils then set up a mini-enterprise scheme to raise money to sponsor some pupils for a residential visit to France. They had to develop the following skills:

- survey techniques within the school;
- safe food-handling procedures;
- recipe development;
- food tasting;
- recording and handling data;
- evaluation skills.

The two terms' work culminated in a residential visit to France continuing the theme of communication and marketing. As was stated by one of the teachers involved in the project (Robbins 1995, p.16):

> To watch one of our girls, who is normally very shy, helping one of the boys to buy an ice-cream at Mont St Michel was an object lesson in the growth of self-confidence. With their growing confidence we have seen improvements in other areas of the curriculum. The progress shown by pupils in reading and writing English is due in no small measure to their increased awareness of signs, interpreting another language and taking notice of written information in their environment.

Aims and challenges

It is suggested here that the aims of a modern foreign languages curriculum may be:

- to develop pupils' self-esteem;
- to develop pupils' ability to communicate in another language;
- to develop general language skills through a new learning experience, leading to a positive achievement;
- to develop pupils' capabilities in their own language;

- to provide intellectual stimulation and to promote skills of more general application;
- to learn about the countries where the target languages are spoken and to encourage positive attitudes towards different cultures;
- to ensure that all pupils achieve a degree of understanding that their village, town or city, and the United Kingdom as a whole, are part of the European Union;
- to give pupils the opportunity to appreciate similarities and differences in lifestyles and customs, and to learn that differences and diversity are an asset rather than a threat to living as a community;
- to establish links with other European countries;
- to appreciate the implications for everyday life of the single European market;
- to play an active part in developing professional understanding and collaboration in the field of special education.

The challenges for the teacher of modern foreign languages is to overcome the following difficulties identified by learning support teachers for pupils with learning difficulties:

- copying from the board.
- writing things down;
- following oral instructions;
- following written instructions;
- developing the confidence to participate;
- learning and remembering vocabulary;
- coping with grammar;
- coping with assessment.

As commented on by McColl (2000, p. 22):

> These lists suggest that some modern-language teachers may be unaware of the true nature of the problems some students experience in their classrooms. It seems likely, for example, that the difficulties faced by some students are not linguistic ones. This raises the possibility that some students do not, in fact, have particular problems with language learning itself, but only with the way in which languages are sometime taught.

Below Level 1: the beginning

As stated at the beginning of this chapter, what has been set out above is supported by the statement 'Inclusion: providing effective learning opportunities for all pupils' within each National Curriculum document (DfEE/QCA 1999a). It is now to be underpinned by *Planning, Teaching and Assessing the Curriculum for Pupils with Learning Difficulties* (DfEE/QCA 2001), which covers each subject area.

The subject-specific guidance for modern foreign languages in the last-mentioned publication (QCA 2001) concisely recognises a place for the subject. It recognises that through the learning experiences of a modern foreign language, all pupils, including those with learning difficulties, are enabled to develop their interest and curiosity in the similarities and differences between themselves and others – other countries, other cultures, other people and other communities. A key point, and one that has been made by teachers of modern foreign languages through the 1980s and 1990s, is that such subjects are introduced at Key Stages 3 and 4. Therefore, pupils enter this subject with no history of failure.

The same document recognises the curriculum development and design that has taken place since the inception of the National Curriculum. It identifies the use of ICT for direct contact, for working with materials from other countries (food, artefacts, art, etc.), for meeting and communicating with native speakers, for cross-curriculum opportunities, for work at each pupil's own pace, etc.

The guidance presents the variations that are afforded to educators, allowing for the selection of materials from earlier key stages – which in the teaching of modern foreign languages means non-statutory guidance at Key Stages 1 and 2. (DfEE/QCA 1999a) It allows for dimensional materials, use of alternative and augmentative communication, and the use of audio and video recordings and photographs rather than written material. Developing language and cultural awareness are central to this work, for the guidance also recognises that as citizenship is promoted within the National Curriculum, pupils with learning difficulties need to extend themselves if they are to be global citizens. What better way than through a modern foreign language?

Identified clearly and succinctly are opportunities and activities for Key Stage 3 and Key Stage 4. They are prefaced and sectioned by the terms 'all', 'most' and 'some' in order to indicate how pupils with learning difficulties could cope with the material presented. The guidelines – in what this author sees as a major step in a once marginalised subject area – offer descriptions of attainment that are similar to the P-levels in English and mathematics. In the generic sections, the language used in one of 'encounter', 'reflex responses', 'awareness', 'focus', 'intermittent reactions', 'respond', 'react', 'show interest', 'co-active exploration', 'proactive', 'communicate', 'remember', 'operate', 'communicate intentionally', 'seek attention', 'participate', 'sustain concentration', 'explore', 'observe', 'conventional communication', 'initiate', 'anticipate', 'actively explore' and 'apply'. These are all dynamic words that identify the dimensional, cross-curricular and physical elements of this subject area. It is not just eating a croissant at a table – an image that detractors often used to undermine modern foreign language experiences for pupils with learning difficulties.

Acknowledgements

The author wishes to acknowledge the contribution of the staffs at Durants School and Hallmoor School to the development of the curriculum described here. He is also very grateful for the material supplied by Clare Martin of George Hastwell School.

References

Ashdown, R. Carpenter, B. and Bovair, K. (1991) *The Curriculum Challenge*. London: The Falmer Press.

Bovair, K., Carpenter, B. and Upton, G. (1992) *Special Curricula Needs*. London: David Fulton Publishers.

Bovair, M. (1995) 'Only the top sets did French'. *Special* 4(1), 31–2.

Bovair, M. and Bovair, K. (1992) *Modern Languages for All*, London: Kogan Page.

DfEE/QCA (1999a) *Modern Foreign Languages*. London: HMSO.

DfEE/QCA (1999b), *Citizenship*. London: HMSO

DfEE/QCA (2001) *Planning, Teaching and Assessing the Curriculum for Pupils with Learning Difficulties: General Guidelines*. London: DfEE/QCA.

McColl, H.(2000) *Modern Languages for All*, London: David Fulton Publishers.
McKeown, S. (1993) 'French connections', in the pullout supplement 'Key Issues and Key Stages; Keeping track of the National Curriculum', *Times Educational Supplement,* 30 April.
QCA (2001) *Planning, Teaching and Assessing the Curriculum for Pupils with Learning Difficulties: Modern Foreign Languages*. London: QCA.
Robbins, B. (1995) 'Links across Europe', *Special* 4(1), 15–17.

Further reading

Bovair, K. and Robbins, B. (1996) 'Modern Foreign Languages' in Carpenter, B. *et al.* (eds) *Enabling Access*. London: David Fulton Publishers.
Edwards, S., (1998) *Modern Languages for All*. Tamworth: NASEN.
Kenning, M. (1994) 'Foreign languages and special needs: implications for teacher support', *British Journal of Special Education* **21**(4), 152–6.
Lucas, S. (no date) *Communication in French: A Package Developed for Use with Students with Severe Learning Difficulties*. Metropolitan Borough of Wigan Education Department.
National Curriculum Council (1993) *Modern Foreign Languages and Special Educational Needs: A new commitment*. York: NCC.
NFER (1995) *Small Steps of Progress in the National Curriculum: Executive summary*. Slough: NFER.

Other resources

Information sheets on activities and materials are available from the Centre for Information on Language Teaching and Research, 20 Bedfordbury, London WC2 4LB.
Widgit Software Ltd, 26 Queen Street, Cubbington, Leamington Spa CV32 7NA.

Chapter 11

Design and Technology

Rob Ashdown

The nature of design and technology

Design and technology is still a relatively new subject and, indeed, was introduced into many schools only in 1990 when it was first included in the National Curriculum. The fact that it is well established in the curriculum of mainstream and special schools is a tribute to the hard work of teachers and their advisers, but successive reports on the outcomes of school inspections by Her Majesty's Chief Inspector suggest that the subject continues to be among the least secure of the foundation subjects, especially in primary and special schools (OFSTED 2000). As regards developing a whole-school rationale for the subject, there is a statement about the importance of design and technology in the current booklet that sets out the guidance and legal requirements for the subject (DfEE/QCA 1999).

However, this last document places a lopsided emphasis on enabling all pupils to become discriminating and informed users of products and to become innovators themselves. These intentions are laudable since we live in a so-called 'technological society': pupils need to be made aware of the social and environmental effects of technological changes; pupils benefit from being better informed about both the development and the advantages and limitations of the products that they use in their daily living; and our society needs a steady supply of recruits to a variety of professions associated with design and technology, such as engineers, interior designers, furniture makers, fashion designers, food technologists, and so on. However, these possible outcomes of the teaching of design and technology have far less relevance for younger children and for children with complex learning difficulties of all ages.

Additional positive reasons for the place of design and technology in the school curriculum are offered by Ritchie (1995). For Ritchie the subject can provide many opportunities for developing:

- cognitive and manipulative skills, as well as understanding of the world, in the context of developing practical solutions to problems encountered in daily living;
- personal and social skills, in that activities should encourage collaborative working, interdependence, communicating ideas and information, toleration, and the appreciation of other perspectives;

- curiosity, creativity, originality and perseverance;
- problem-solving skills and strategies that have application in all subject areas of the curriculum.

Ritchie argues that good design and technology activities provide opportunities for children to tackle problems in contexts that have relevance, importance and meaning because they are related to their daily living environments and interests.

As regards pupils with complex learning difficulties, particularly those with profound and multiple learning difficulties, Ouvry and Saunders further enhance our views about the importance of the subject – see their Chapter 17 in this book. They regard the essence of the subject as about finding solutions to problems encountered and meeting identified needs in the best possible way. Good teaching should help pupils with PMLD to identify problems and to show them that they can be solved; it should help them realise that they have the power to change things in ways that benefit them; it should help them to express opinions; and it should help them to experience the consequences, both positive and negative, of decisions which they make. For Ouvry and Saunders, the roots of design lie in making choices, and teachers should be encouraging PMLD pupils to communicate their choices.

Similarly, evaluation at its most basic level involves expressing likes and dislikes. Therefore, teachers must provide pupils with opportunities for developing problem-solving and communication skills in contexts where they are supported in their attempts to find different ways of doing things when faced by a problem, and for expressing acceptance and rejection, in appropriate ways, of situations that they experience. In this sense, design and technology as a subject has a relevance to all pupils because it involves teaching them to think and intervene creatively to improve the quality of their life, as is actually stressed in the official statement about the subject's importance (DfEE/QCA 1999).

The requirements of the National Curriculum

Design and technology has had a rather chequered history as a National Curriculum subject, as exemplified by a number of changes in the programmes of study and attainment targets as successive versions of the National Curriculum attempted to introduce greater curriculum flexibility and reduce the level of prescriptive detail. In the first version of the National Curriculum, the four processes of identifying needs and opportunities, generating a design, planning and making, and evaluating were explicitly identified with their own attainment targets; however, it was stressed that the four processes should not be treated as separate entities but as elements of one interdependent process. In the 1995 version of the National Curriculum, design and technology was presented in a more straightforward way, with only two attainment targets (Designing and Making). In the current (2000) version, there is just one attainment target. This final reduction has been presented by the QCA as a way of emphasizing the interdependence of designing and making rather than as a process of simplification (QCA 1999).

There has been a concerted attempt over the years to slim down the programmes of study for the subject. For instance, in the earliest version of the subject there was a requirement to make three different types of products in five different contexts at each key stage, using at least five different materials. This requirement was dropped in the

1995 version because it was practically impossible to achieve, particularly at the early key stages, and, overall, the subject was reduced by about one-third. This reductive process has continued, and the current version requires coverage of a reduced range of materials at Key Stages 1 and 2, and work with food and compliant materials (i.e. plastics and textiles) remains optional at Key Stage 3.

The PoS state that teaching should ensure that knowledge and understanding are applied when developing ideas, planning, making products and evaluating them. The knowledge skills and understanding to be fostered are described under several headings:

- developing, planning and communicating ideas;
- working with tools, equipment, materials and components to make (produce) quality products;
- evaluating processes and products;
- knowledge and understanding of materials and components;
- knowledge and understanding of systems and control (at Key Stages 3 and 4 only).

The first in the list above, *developing, planning and communicating ideas*, for Key Stage 1 pupils focuses on generating ideas based on their own and others' experiences, sharing these with others, shaping plans, and developing their ability to communicate their ideas, including by drawing and making models. With Key Stage 2 pupils, the emphasis is upon developing ideas with target users and uses in mind, identifying outcomes and developing sequence actions and alternative actions as necessary. In the secondary-school years, there is much emphasis on using ICT resources for research purposes, responding to design briefs from others, developing design specifications and design proposals that meet them, producing plans that use advanced graphical techniques, including computer aided design (CAD), and producing practical designs for industries for manufacturing in quantity.

Working with tools, equipment, materials and components at the primary phase covers selecting appropriate tools, techniques and materials, skills of measuring, marking out, cutting and shaping materials, assembling, joining and combining materials and components, and using simple finishing techniques to improve appearance. For secondary-school pupils, there is an introduction to computer-assisted manufacture (CAM), the need to take account of the working characteristics of materials, the possibilities presented by modern materials (which are being developed at an astounding rate) and consideration of industrial applications including simulations of production and assembly lines. At all key stages there is an emphasis on the development of safe working practices.

Evaluating processes and products for Key Stage 1 pupils is described in terms of talking about their ideas, saying what they like and dislike, and identifying what they would do differently next time. Key Stage 2 pupils are to be encouraged to reflect on their work as it progresses, to carry out tests before making improvements, and to recognise the all-important link between the quality of a product and the skills of the person making it. The programmes of study for Key Stages 3 and 4 emphasise developing criteria for judging quality and devising and applying tests at critical stages in development.

Knowledge and understanding of materials and components starts at Key Stage 1 with developing awareness of the working characteristics of different materials and how mechanisms can be used in different ways. At Key Stage 2, pupils are taught how materials and components can be mixed and combined; they are also introduced to the use of ICT in mechanisms and how electrical circuits and simple switches can be used in systems. At Key Stages 3 and 4, pupils examine in more detail the physical and chemical properties of materials, classify materials and components according to properties, explore new ways of combining materials and components, and investigate manufacturing processes and their exigencies

Knowledge and understanding of systems and control is developed at Key Stages 3 and 4 only. The programmes of study cover: inputs, processes, and outputs; the need for feedback mechanisms; mechanical, electrical, electronic and pneumatic control systems; the uses of sophisticated switches sensors; the use of electronics, microprocessors and computers in control systems; and the uses of ICT in the general design of systems.

The development of knowledge, skills and understanding is to be achieved in three ways: through opportunities to investigate and evaluate products in terms of how they work, how they are used, and the views of people who use them; through 'focused practical tasks' (FPTs) that develop particular techniques, skills, processes and knowledge; and through 'design and make assignments' (DMAs) using a range of materials. Earlier versions of the National Curriculum for design and technology expected teachers to develop opportunities to disassemble products (although that requirement has now been dropped) and referred to 'investigative, disassembly and evaluative activities' (IDEAs).

The range of materials broadens as pupils get older. At Key Stage 1, food, textiles, and items that can be put together to make other items are explicitly mentioned. At Key Stage 2, reference is made to electrical and mechanical components, food, mouldable materials, stiff and flexible sheet materials, and textiles. At Key Stage 3 the emphasis is upon control systems, a range of contrasting materials, including resistant materials, compliant materials (i.e. plastics and textiles, including composites) and/or food. Modern materials, including so-called 'smart' materials that change in response to differences in environment or experience, are to be introduced. At Key Stage 4, activities have to be related to industrial practices and applications of systems and control.

Planning and teaching from the programmes of study

Each school's scheme of work for each key stage should provide full access to the content specified in the design and technology PoS. The rest of this chapter seeks to illustrate some of the 'job aids' and teaching strategies that are available to help teachers achieve this goal with pupils who have complex learning difficulties. Readers will also find helpful the non-statutory guidance on the design and technology curriculum for pupils with learning difficulties (QCA 2001) and the teachers' guides for optional schemes of work for pupils at Key Stages 1, 2 and 3 produced by the QCA (2000a, 2000b). These are available as guides, but, inevitably, the approach to developing a scheme of work will differ from school to school depending upon its individual circumstances (e.g. the ability and age range of the pupils, the physical resources and accommodation, the expertise and interests of teachers).

In the first edition of *Enabling Access*, Helen Mount (1996) described one particular approach, which was probably adopted by many primary and special schools when first faced with the introduction of the National Curriculum. Schemes of work often consisted of a number of planned 'topics' that addressed elements from the programmes of study for different subjects. Many hours of staff meetings nationwide must have been spent on generating ideas and information that could form the basis for a plan for each topic in the early years of introducing the National Curriculum. The main features of this approach are summarized by Mount thus:

- the whole school's staff meet to agree a topic and brainstorm ideas, perhaps setting on paper a 'topic web' to illustrate the interrelationship between the variety of sub-themes or activities identified;
- activities may then be related to the whole curriculum, including the National Curriculum, such that cross-curricular links are incorporated;
- if the whole school has planned together, individual class teachers might take one aspect of the topic and develop it further;
- activities should then be differentiated to make them accessible and suitable for pupils of different ages and with different abilities.

Mount also commends a 'modular approach', which was also described by Rose (1994). This whole-school approach to curriculum planning has resulted from one special school developing a series of modules that are effectively short courses designed for specific groups of pupils. Each module lasts for 6 to 12 weeks (approximately) and uses the same standard format (outlining the progression from previous work, as appropriate), some suggested activities for the lesson, the equipment needed, and cross-references to other curriculum areas. Although the initial development of documentation for each module is time-consuming, the sharing of good teaching practice that results, as well as the avoidance of unnecessary repetition, the positive management of time and resources, the development of differentiation strategies, the cross-curricular coverage, and a whole-school agreement on recording and assessment, all make this a worthwhile approach when developing new plans.

DATA support material

Since 1995, a range of support material for schools has been produced by the Design and Technology Association (DATA) with the active support of the DfEE. DATA has produced helpful guidance for teachers in both primary schools and secondary schools. For instance, there is a Primary Coordinators' File, which addresses all of the major aspects of planning, monitoring and evaluation that subject leaders are expected to address in the development of their subject (DATA 1996). The file also includes much practical detail about teaching techniques, equipment, and health and safety considerations. DATA has also produced a start-up pack of 30 units of work that provide a balanced scheme of work for Key Stages 1 and 2 (DATA 1995). And DATA has subsequently produced a booklet containing case studies describing how some of the units of work were delivered to children in different primary schools, together with nine additional units of work that focus on the more challenging areas of mechanisms and control systems and structures (DATA 1997). The units of work offer a good range of design and technology activities from which to choose.

Schools may use a unit of work exactly as set out in the DATA packs, or they may choose to adapt them to suit their specific requirements. This enables schools to shorten considerably the laborious processes described by Mount (1996) and Rose (1994), who had no such models available. For each unit of work, there is a clear description of several elements: the materials focus; potential learning outcomes; links with other subject areas; a list of all of the resources required; statements of the designing and making skills required; the knowledge and understanding to be developed for the unit;

the work that children will undertake in interlinked IDEAs, FPTs and DMAs; suggestions for extension activities that may be introduced at some later point to build on the knowledge and skills acquired; and the assessment opportunities available.

A sample unit of work

The following is an example of how one of the DATA units of work might be used with pupils with moderate to severe learning difficulties. The unit of work is aimed at designing and making of a pop-up card for a special occasion.

There are several potential outcomes: a variety of cards suitable for various occasions may be produced (e.g. Christmas, Easter, Mother's Day or a birthday), all of which incorporate a folded pop-up mechanism made from paper or card and have a good-quality finish using collage techniques. Various cross-curricular links may be identified – to religious education (celebrations), mathematics (measurement, properties of shape and symmetry) and art (paper collage, experimenting with colour and shape). The resources required for the unit are cheap and readily available: a collection of pop-up cards, exemplar pop-up mechanisms made by the teacher, coloured paper and card, scissors, safety rulers, PVA or similar glue or glue sticks, and examples of printed posters or picture books showing simple shapes that serve as models for designs.

The IDEAs involve providing a collection of pop-up cards for the children to explore, with the teacher encouraging talk about the suitability of cards for different people. The children should be asked to express likes and dislikes about the cards. They should be directed to examine how their preferred cards are decorated. The FPTs use the chosen pop-up cards and the exemplar mechanisms to focus the children's attention on the folded mechanisms. The teacher should demonstrate the task of folding and scoring thin card using the scissors and safety ruler and should assist the children in making different folding mechanisms with card, masking tape and glue. Sufficient time should be allowed for trying out some simple collage ideas suitable for a card.

The actual DMA is to design and make a pop-up card for a specific occasion. The children must be asked to think carefully about who the card would be for and about an appropriate design. They should be encouraged to keep their design simple. Rather than try to draw a design, the children may be helped to cut out or tear paper shapes and experiment with positioning these in different ways on the card. Next, the children should be shown again the pop-up mechanisms they have examined or made previously, and they should be asked to choose the most appropriate format for their design. With everything in place, the children may now be helped to put together their own cards. Finally, the children should be encouraged to evaluate their cards, indicating what they like about them and talking about improvements that could be made.

The whole process will take several sessions, lasting some six hours or more in total. Aspects of the process may be captured with a digital camera to create a project file. Indeed, sequences of photos of the process or instructions employing printed words and/or simple, stylised pictures (e.g. Makaton symbols or rebuses) might help with task completion for children who have learned the appropriate skills but who experience sequencing difficulties. Demonstration, explicit feedback and physical help will be needed from the teacher, but each child should be able to participate at his or her particular level of ability in the design, construction and evaluation of the cards.

QCA support material

Building on the work of DATA, the QCA produced optional schemes of work for Key Stages 1 and 2 (QCA 1998). Subsequently, an exemplar scheme of work for Key Stage 3 was produced (QCA 2000a). Also, in light of changes to the National Curriculum, updates were issued for the schemes of work intended for Key Stages 1 and 2, in terms of a modified teachers' guide, alterations to some existing units of work and production of some new units (QCA 2000b). The teachers' guides for these schemes of work not only introduce the units of work but also illustrate how the units can be sequenced across each key stage, how the three types of activity (IDEAs, FPTs and DMAs) are integrated within each unit, and the ways in which the units are interwoven and build on work that has already taken place.

The descriptions of the QCA units of work have certain advantages over the DATA units of work: they suggest specific vocabulary and phrases to be taught and used; they indicate the prior learning that children must have if they are going to benefit from the unit; they clarify expectations of the progress that most children will have made by the end of the unit and give expectations for some more able and some less able children; and they indicate health and safety issues to be addressed and other points to note. In addition, the units are available on the DfEE standards website (www.standards.dfee.gov.uk) and, therefore, can be downloaded, saved, read and edited to produce units of work that suit a school's particular needs.

EQUALS support material

The QCA and DATA documents are very useful, but they have been designed for the average learner. For instance, the teachers' guide for the QCA schemes of work for Key Stage 1 and 2 makes certain assumptions about the knowledge, skills and understanding that children will have acquired at the Foundation Stage (QCA 2000b): it is assumed that most children will have a degree of awareness about the world in which they live; they will readily ask questions about things, including their uses and how they work; they will talk with adults and one another about what they are doing and what they have discovered; they will respond to drawings and pictures and produce their own; they will know how to use a variety of tools and do so with increasing dexterity and safely; they will have experienced and used different materials and products; they will have developed some making skills, such as folding, cutting, mixing, joining; they show creativity; and they are motivated and interested to participate in activities. In short, there are a set of assumptions that children will have the language skills, problem-solving skills, learning strategies and positive attitudes to learning that simply cannot be taken for granted in the case of many pupils with complex learning difficulties.

Of course, the general 'inclusion' statement for the National Curriculum, as well as additional information in relation to design and technology for pupils with special educational needs, together recognise potential barriers to learning and suggest some general strategies for enabling all pupils to have access to learning opportunities. However, the onus is clearly upon schools to determine in detail how these exemplar schemes of work may be modified to suit individuals or groups of pupils who have special educational needs.

There are some published schemes of work giving access to design and technology for pupils with severe learning difficulties (SLD). EQUALS is a national organisation for teachers of pupils with SLD, and it has published an 'Access' curriculum setting out programmes of study for pupils with severe, profound and multiple learning difficulties (EQUALS 1997). One of the areas of learning in this proposed curriculum is described as 'Knowledge and understanding of the world', and this includes design and technology.

In 1999, EQUALS produced schemes of work for all curriculum areas for pupils with SLD, pupils with PMLD and pupils with moderate learning difficulties, including units for design and technology (EQUALS 1999a ,1999b, 2000). The units tend to focus on helping pupils to understand the properties of a range of common materials and certain mechanisms, to use a range of simple tools, to make simple products from materials provided, and to design and make their own products after selecting appropriate materials and techniques.

The units in the SLD scheme of work provide access to activities involving simple construction kits (e.g. Lego), foods, a range of battery-operated toys, computers, mouldables, fabrics, and sheet materials such as paper and cardboard. An intended progression is discernible, ranging from experiencing and responding to materials and equipment through to selecting, using and evaluating the use of materials. For instance, the activities connected with food have expectations starting with basic tasting and commenting on foods, moving on to comparing foods, then planning and making simple snacks, following recipes and evaluating what they have produced. Incidentally, food technology receives relatively more direct teaching in these units than work with other materials, on top of which there are opportunities for food technology within other areas of the Access curriculum.

Problem-solving and creative work with other materials is evident in some other areas of the Access curriculum, notably in units of work for PSHE, science and art. Nevertheless, schools might want to strengthen and add to the design and technology units to provide a broader range of activities and allow pupils to develop skills in using textiles, stiff and flexible sheets, mouldables and electrical circuits. Moreover, the EQUALS schemes of work give little or no consideration to ways of giving access to opportunities outlined in the Key Stage 3 and 4 PoS for design and technology, which require that pupils be taught about the effects of technologies on our lives, the work of designers and processes in industry, the use of computers in design work, and the use of compliant materials and modern materials.

The units in the scheme of work for pupils with PMLD offer a range of experiences of different materials and equipment: water, papers, dough, dry and messy materials, hard and soft materials, activity centres, battery-operated toys, computers, fabrics, wheeled toys, construction kits, etc. An expected progression is evident, starting with passive acceptance or toleration of activities involving different experiences, to making consistent responses and showing preferences and, eventually, to actively manipulating materials and activating cause-effect equipment.

The EQUALS units of work are written deliberately in a format that is similar to the format used by the QCA schemes of work. Thus, each unit helpfully contains details about:

- the unit's particular focus;
- where the unit fits in with other units and other curriculum areas;
- the key vocabulary that pupils should encounter;
- the resources required;
- the expectations of what pupils should know by the end of the unit;
- the learning objectives;
- possible teaching activities and learning outcomes, which are indicators of progress by pupils.

In the foregoing respects, the units are a very good resource. However, they are perhaps more suitable for use by schools as stimuli for staff debate and for the development of the school's own units and scheme of work, because there are reasons why they should not be adopted without alteration. Firstly, the range of activities suggested for each unit tends to be limited and there is no attempt to delineate IDEAs, FPTs and DMAs. Secondly, the EQUALS curriculum has been developed to provide a foundation for learning in the National Curriculum rather than as a set of activities that ultimately derives from and extends the programmes of study for each key stage so that they are made more inclusive. Finally, the units in the three schemes of work bear no simple relationship to each other – for example, Year 6 units in the PMLD scheme are not extensions of the Year 6 units in the SLD scheme.

Furthermore, the choice of scheme of work should be straightforward where the pupil population consists wholly or predominantly of one of the three groups of pupils, but curriculum coordinators face planning dilemmas in schools where there is a complex mix of pupils. They have to decide whether all pupils should follow just the SLD schemes of work, with appropriate modifications for any pupils with PMLD and MLD, or whether to run two or three different schemes of work concurrently. Interestingly, EQUALS has decided to revise its schemes of work in the light of the new QCA curriculum guidelines in relation to pupils with learning difficulties and intends to address some of these issues.

The delivery of the curriculum

There has been much healthy debate about approaches to teaching and learning for pupils with learning difficulties since the introduction of the National Curriculum: for instance, see Chapter 15 by Byers in this volume and the book by Babbage, Byers and Redding (1999). Of particular interest here is the fact that design and technology activities can provide many opportunities for the development of personal and social skills in the context of group work on a shared task.

Pupils with learning difficulties are increasingly included in activities in mainstream schools, and inclusive practices are developing within the special schools themselves (e.g. the trend for disbanding segregated classes for pupils with PMLD or autism). However, there is a serious danger that pupils with complex learning difficulties only *encounter* activities and do not actually gain anything from them because they are on the margin of a group and not properly involved by the teacher. In practice, genuinely inclusive group work demands very careful preparation and skilled teaching if all pupils are to be full participants and if each individual's particular developmental needs are going to be properly addressed.

Working in pairs may be an initial step towards group work, but it can still be very difficult to find evenly matched pairs of pupils for whom the intended outcomes of an activity will be the same. A critical point is that teachers must recognise that the emphasis in design and technology activities must be on the *process* and not upon the final product; they must be very clear about the different levels of functioning of each pupil in a group and plan lessons carefully so that there are learning opportunities for each individual. The teacher's role in providing 'scaffolding' is crucial: it may involve breaking down a task into manageable bits, providing visual schedules of photos or pictures depicting the sequence of these bits, giving physical prompts or verbal reminders, and so on. However, the emphasis is on active learning by the individual pupil at all times, even though they may not be able to operate independently.

There are a number of strategies that may promote effective group work. Rose (1991) and Sebba, Byers and Rose (1995) each describe one potentially useful method that is called 'jigsawing'. In this method, the activity is broken down into several interdependent tasks and a task is assigned to small groups of children and to individuals according to their needs and abilities. Indeed, the tasks are defined as a result of careful thinking about the knowledge, skills and understanding that the individual pupils have to develop. Completion of the task depends upon regular communication between individual pupils and groups, because each piece of the jigsaw is dependent upon the others. Thus, jigsawing offers an opportunity for teachers to develop compatible groups and at the same time meet individual needs in the context of group work.

For instance, in relation to the activities surrounding the making of pop-up cards, described earlier in this chapter, one group of pupils could have focused on the design of the front of the card, which is less demanding technically, and another more-able group could have focused on the pop-up mechanism. Of course, both groups would have to be brought together at times: for initially discussing and showing what had to be done; for reviewing at intervals what progress had been made; and, finally, for evaluating the finished product.

These opportunities for group work provide opportunities for sensory experiences and communication, even for those pupils with PMLD. For instance, if a target for a pupil is that he should reach out and grasp objects, a range of design and technology activities could provide interesting and meaningful contexts for developing this skill. Pupils with PMLD have much to gain from being with and observing more-active children, from experiencing the sights, sounds and smells of a range of activities, and from having opportunities to express their likes and dislikes. There is no reason why they should not co-actively saw a piece of wood or drill holes in it, for instance. Their meaningful participation in the process is only precluded by a lack of careful planning and teaching.

Planning, assessment and recording methods should be a matter of whole-school policy, although many aspects of lesson planning may be left to the judgement of an individual teacher. Clearly, units of work can provide acceptable medium-term plans, particularly if modelled on the QCA units. The QCA schemes of work also provide an acceptable model for long-term plans. There will be a need for agreement about recording individualised targets in classes where some or most children have complex learning difficulties. And there is an expectation that assessment will be kept simple and related to National Curriculum Levels 1–8 of attainment described in the curriculum handbook (DfEE/QCA 1999). However, in the case of pupils with complex learning difficulties, assessments will have to be made in relation to individualised targets and a fine-grained analysis of progression towards Level 1.

The guidance on the design and technology curriculum for pupils with learning difficulties (QCA 2001) includes eight levels of performance descriptions leading to Level 1 of the National Curriculum. EQUALS have also produced similar progress indicators in relation to all curriculum areas leading to Level 1 (EQUALS 1998). Of course, many schools will choose to develop their own pupils records, perhaps in terms of checklists of designing and making skills, but also through keeping annotated portfolios of products and/or photographs. Digital cameras and video cameras also make it possible to capture relatively cheaply the key elements of the designing and making process. Pupils' own recording and other written evidence may also be used. Lawson (1998) provides helpful suggestions to guide teachers on the sorts of plans and records they might keep.

Learning is a complex phenomenon that is not easily defined or described. In the case of pupils with complex learning difficulties, great care has to be exercised in planning for progression in learning and in describing what each pupil has learned from an experience. This task is not made any easier by the fact that much learning takes place without there being any observable outcomes. Indeed, the available methods for assessing levels of attainment in terms of pupils' interaction with their environment and performance on tests and tasks can provide only approximate indicators of learning. In the case of a minority of pupils with PMLD, the difficulties in gauging what learning is taking place are exacerbated by the fact that even fine-grained analyses of their behaviour may show no obvious response to an experience.

Performance levels P1–P3

Much useful guidance is contained in the descriptions of levels for National Curriculum design and technology, but these do not adequately convey the nature of attainments of pupils below Level 1 and how these relate to the specific progression in knowledge, skills and understanding that has been detailed for the subject at Levels 1–8. Nevertheless, it is possible to discern developing patterns of learning ranging from emerging awareness of aspects of the design and technology process to active learning without a need for much support from others. These extensions to the conventional level descriptions are described in the subject-specific guidance on the curriculum for pupils with learning difficulties (QCA 2001). These show that it is even possible to delineate knowledge, understanding and skills related to design and technology of pupils with profound learning difficulties even though it is clear that elements may be common to other subjects. That is why the published DfEE performance criteria for pupil attainment below Level 1 are stated in exactly the same way for all strands of English, mathematics etc. through the so-called P-levels (DfEE 1998) – particularly, in this context, levels P1–P3.

It is also important to be aware that pupils may appear to 'plateau' at a particular level in that there is no discernible 'vertical' progression. Yet, there may be 'lateral' progression, and this should be encouraged by planning to focus on the same knowledge, understanding and skills either by introducing new experiences or by extending existing experiences through introducing new objects, new environments, new people and new activities appropriate to the pupils' age, interests and prior achievements.

A minority of pupils with profound learning difficulties may show no obvious response at all to an experience. Indeed, they may require full prompting to participate in the experience. This could be taken to mean that they are not registering the experience at all, but this is unlikely. They may appear to be learning nothing, but systematic and frequent repetition of specific experiences over time may well be helping them to remember and recognise crucial elements. The fact that they may show no overt responses cannot be taken as a sign that they are not actively organising the incoming sensory information. However, at this developmental level, records can only show that they encounter the learning experience in a totally passive way. Plans would probably focus on describing with clarity the experiences rather than any expected outcomes.

Some pupils may show resistance, which provides evidence of learning even though it may not be desirable behaviour. The behaviour of other pupils with profound learning difficulties may show that they are dimly aware of the experience. The evidence may be slight and it may be difficult to tell whether their reactions are reflexive or deliberate. Such reactions will be observed intermittently, rather than all of the time, when an experience is repeated. Thus, for example, a child may only sit still momentarily or look up briefly when they are prompted to handle materials placed in their hands. Some pupils may begin to tolerate activities that had previously evoked apparent distress or resistance.

Other pupils may react more consistently and regularly as they become familiar with particular experiences; for instance, their behaviour may be more easily interpreted as indicating an affective response of enjoyment or displeasure, even though they may still not be intentionally communicating. They may begin to actively focus their attention on things seen and sounds heard. They may engage in co-active exploration when adults physically prompt them to hold, manipulate and look at objects and participate in activities. Planning should ensure repeated opportunities in experiences for such pupils to develop and demonstrate likes and dislikes of stimuli in a responsive environment and in a range of activities with different materials.

A good proportion of pupils with profound learning difficulties are seen to be not merely passive or reactive when exposed to experiences. They actively engage in them and show evident recognition and enjoyment of particular activities and the objects and people involved in them. They cooperate when physically prompted to explore things and generally require progressively less prompting to become involved, to the extent that, eventually, they might reach out for and grasp materials or objects and they might explore and examine them. Such pupils are likely consistently to communicate likes and dislikes, even though some may still be doing so without an obvious intent. Some might signal requests for objects or repetitions of activities through their actions and vocalisations. Generally, they will respond positively to attempts initiated by others to engage them in activities and show an ability to concentrate for short periods. Planning should ensure opportunities for these pupils to communicate needs as well as preferences for objects and activities, and it should foster shared or independent exploratory behaviour.

Many pupils with severe to profound learning difficulties and young children at the Foundation Stage show a preparedness to become actively involved in experiences. They anticipate familiar events with support from adults – perhaps with the visual clues given by the use of signs, 'objects of reference' and 'symbols' to indicate the imminence of an activity. They communicate in more conventional ways, using vocalisations, gesture and a few signs, symbols or objects of reference. They might show comprehension of some words for things and might respond to simple questions and instructions in clear contexts. They might imitate actions modelled by the teacher, but they will probably require some physical prompting as well. They are likely actively to explore things during activities and will do so in a sustained way for more than just a few minutes: for instance, tearing, bending, squashing and squeezing different materials, or banging them with a hammer. Planning should ensure opportunities for these pupils to develop language and communication skills, cooperative skills, and an ability to follow instructions and sustain concentration.

Performance levels P4–P8

Pupils who are operating at levels P4–P8 of the performance descriptions of attainment before National Curriculum Level 1 will move on at differing rates from the earlier levels described above to higher levels of attainment. At these later levels, the focus of teacher assessment switches away from the quality of interaction with people and objects in activities and onto the pupils' performance in more conventional tests and tasks of their specific design and technology knowledge, skills and understanding. Planning should ensure opportunities for pupils to develop key skills in the context of a variety of experiences, especially communication and problem-solving skills.

The value of repetition in both familiar contexts and new ones must be stressed. In addition to vertical progression, planning should allow for maintaining, consolidating, refining and generalisation, and there should be opportunities for functional application of learned skills in a range of environments. According to performance descriptions for levels P4 and P5, pupils should be able to clearly communicate choices about what they want to make in DMAs, perhaps identifying chosen items from pictures. With appropriate adult support, they should be able to use some basic tools and be able to assemble simple components; they should also be able to indicate likes or dislikes about their products and others when asked. At levels P6 and P7, they should be able to indicate, by communication or demonstration, what they would like to make and what its purpose will be. They will show increasing ability to handle a range of basic tools and choose the right tools for a task.

By level P8, which broadly equates to the early learning goals of the Foundation Stage for most children at five years of age, pupils should be able to generate and follow a simple plan. They should be able to select and use familiar tools and techniques that are appropriate, and they should be able to pass comment on what they are doing and what they have made. Even at this level and because of their language and memory problems, pupils with SLD may still require the support of visual communication systems using signs and symbols. Visual systems may be used to enable them to make choices, express ideas, record evaluations, recall the sequences of tasks involved in a making process and gain other important information needed for success in a project.

Conclusions

Although there have been many changes in the requirements for design and technology in the National Curriculum since 1990, the concept of a process (actually, several interdependent processes) has been retained throughout. It is a process of identifying needs, generating and developing ideas, planning, implementing and evaluating. Successful design and technology activities do not concentrate on the final product but on children being active participants in the process leading up to completing the product and its subsequent evaluation.

The skill of the teacher lies in providing the right degree of support for each pupil in generating ideas, in choosing what to make and how to make it, in making the product, and in evaluating both the end-product and all of the processes used in creating it. If teaching is imaginative and responsive, the subject can convey knowledge, skills and understanding that are of benefit to all pupils in many settings and that can be functionally related to their daily lives. Indeed, teachers are engaging in a comparable process when they teach design and technology.

Teachers who lack confidence and schools that need to develop their schemes of work further will find that they have much to gain from examining and reviewing the model schemes of work for delivery in schools and the small but developing literature. The DATA, EQUALS, QCA and other publications provide much useful guidance for planning in design and technology, which individual teachers and whole-school teams can use to build up what they are doing already and their experiences to date. It is hoped that this chapter has offered some assistance to people who are still seeking inspiration or who have moved on further and want to review their practice.

References

Babbage, R. *et al.* (1999) *Approaches to Teaching and Learning: Including Pupils with Learning Difficulties.* London: David Fulton Publishers.

DATA (1995) *Guidance Materials for Design & Technology: Key Stages 1 & 2.* Wellesbourne, Warwickshire: Design and Technology Association.

DATA (1996) *The Design and Technology Primary Coordinator's File.* Wellesbourne, Warwickshire: Design and Technology Association.

DATA (1997) *Planning into Practice: Design and Technology in Primary Schools.*, Wellesbourne, Warwickshire: Design and Technology Association.

DfEE (1998) *Supporting the Target Setting Process: Guidance for Effective Target Setting for Pupils with Special Educational Needs.* Nottingham: DfEE.

DfEE/QCA (1999) *Design and Technology: The National Curriculum for England.* London: DfEE/QCA.

EQUALS (1997) *The Access Programmes of Study Setting: Knowledge and Understanding of the World.* North Shields, Tyne and Wear: EQUALS.

EQUALS (1998) *Baseline Assessment and Curriculum Target Setting.* North Shields, Tyne and Wear: EQUALS.

EQUALS (1999a) *Schemes of Work – Knowledge and Understanding of the World (Part Two) for pupils with PMLD – Design and Technology Learning.* North Shields, Tyne and Wear: EQUALS.

EQUALS (1999b) *Schemes of Work – Knowledge and Understanding of the World (Part Two) for pupils with SLD – Design and Technology Learning.* North Shields, Tyne and Wear: EQUALS.

EQUALS (2000) *Schemes of Work – Knowledge and Understanding of the World (Part Two) for pupils with MLD – Design and Technology Learning.* North Shields, Tyne and Wear: EQUALS.

Lawson, H. (1998) *Practical Record Keeping: Development and Resource Material for Staff Working with Pupils with Special Educational Needs,* second edn. London: David Fulton Publishers.

Mount, H. (1996) 'Design and technology', in Carpenter, B. *et al.* (eds) *Enabling Access: Effective Teaching and Learning for Pupils with Learning Difficulties,* first edn. London: David Fulton Publishers.

OFSTED (2000) *The Annual Report of Her Majesty's Chief Inspector for Education: Standards and Quality in Education 1998/99.* London: The Stationery Office.

QCA (1998) *Design and Technology: A Scheme of Work for Key Stages 1 and 2.* Sudbury, Suffolk: QCA Publications.

QCA (1999) *The Revised National Curriculum for 2000: What has changed?* Sudbury, Suffolk: QCA Publications.

QCA (2000a) *Design and Technology: A Scheme of Work for Key Stages 3.* Sudbury, Suffolk: QCA Publications.

QCA (2000b) *Design and Technology: A Scheme of Work for Key Stages 1 and 2.* second edn. Sudbury, Suffolk: QCA Publications.

QCA (2001) *Planning, Teaching And Assessing The Curriculum For Pupils With Learning Difficulties: Art And Design.* London: QCA.

Ritchie, R. (1995) *Primary Design and Technology.* London: David Fulton Publishers.

Rose, R. (1991) 'A jigsaw approach to group work', *British Journal of Special Education* **18**(2), 54–7.

Rose, R. (1994) 'A modular approach to the curriculum for pupils with learning difficulties', in Rose, R. *et al.* (eds) *Implementing the Whole Curriculum for Pupils with Learning Difficulties.* London: David Fulton Publishers.

Sebba, J. *et al.* (1995) *Redefining the Whole Curriculum for Pupils with Learning Difficulties,* second edn. London: David Fulton Publishers.

Chapter 12

Information and Communication Technology

Tina Detheridge and Chris Stevens

This chapter begins by setting the context for the educational uses of information and communication technology (ICT) for pupils with special educational needs. It will discuss the requirements and recommendations of developing ICT capability in the National Curriculum as far as it affects pupils with learning difficulties and disabilities. It will look particularly at the role of ICT in providing access to learning. This will be illustrated by a number of examples where ICT has made a significant contribution to pupils' achievements. It will finally discuss some of the issues facing schools on identifying solutions and effective implementation. Readers who are interested in the historical development of ICT and SEN will gain useful information from OFSTED (1999), Abbott (1995) and Hawkridge and Vincent (1992).

Why ICT is important

That information technology forms a significant part of life is undeniable. It is essential to our communications systems, to industry and also to many of the services that individuals require. The rate of development in the application of ICT over the last decade of the twentieth century has had a fundamental impact on our life-styles. As Stevenson (1997) puts it:

> The best analogy we have heard for ICT is the analogue with the invention of Electricity. Electricity – once regarded as a strange, almost frightening wonder of the age – has come to serve almost every aspect of society. So also with ICT.

At a personal level, ICT is also taking an increasingly important role, filtering into the everyday life of the whole of the Western world. The cost of personal computers for private, educational and social purposes is bringing ICT within the realms of most people in society. For this reason, the development of the skills to use and manage ICT is essential for both employment and personal benefit. For many of us who grew up before the firm establishment of ICT, it has seemed a difficult and daunting task to develop the associated skills. This is certainly not the case for children currently passing through the educational system. The aim of ICT capability in the National Curriculum is to develop skills and confidence in the use of ICT so that, as pupils mature, they can take their place in all aspects of society.

The benefits of ICT go beyond the simple automation of processes, and today the subject offers new horizons, adding to the learning agenda. For example, it is no longer necessary to develop fine handwriting skills, since most formal writing is increasingly performed on a word processor. This is not to say that handwriting is redundant, but its principal purpose is increasingly for personal use. Furthermore, it is no longer necessary to have a great facility in long multiplication or long division because a hand-held calculator can accomplish this more quickly and accurately. What is necessary, however, is to acquire higher-order skills of estimation, understanding the concept of number, and logical thinking, so that the right calculations are made. In this way, users develop an intuitive understanding of the necessary processes and can apply their knowledge in generalised situations.

Access by means of ICT to large information sources through CD-ROM, online databases and the Internet are bringing personal research skills within the reach of everybody. Children exploring topics at school will have significantly wider access to information than the physical confines of the school library. The new technologies will 'enrich curriculum content by improved access to resources' (DFE 1995). The skills that pupils need will be to assess the quality of information they find, to analyse, and to discuss findings.

These same features, offered by ICT to everyone, have particular benefits to those with various special needs. The features can facilitate access to learning for those with physical or sensory impairments; they can provide a range of mechanisms that bring complex processes within the reach of pupils with learning difficulties. With the support of various technologies, many of the difficulties experienced by those with learning disabilities or difficulties can be overcome, putting them on a more equal footing with their peers and providing the means to engage in the same educational, work-related, social and personal opportunities as everybody else.

IT capability and the National Curriculum

The programmes of study relating to ICT at Key Stage 1, as published by the DfEE (2000), states (p. 27) that 'pupils should explore ICT to use it confidently and with purpose to achieve specific outcomes'. This may have a range of specific applications for pupils with learning difficulties and disabilities. The essence behind guidance for pupils with special needs is that ICT provides opportunities for pupils to work with increasing independence in key learning areas such as communication, language and literacy.

The section in the National Curriculum documents of guidance entitled 'Inclusion: providing effective learning opportunities for all pupils' (DREE/QCA 1999) gives a clear indication of the issues to consider when planning the ICT curriculum and the role of ICT in supporting learning throughout the curriculum. In particular, there is an emphasis on the need to create effective learning environments, secure motivation and concentration, provide equality of opportunity through teaching approaches, use appropriate assessment approaches, and set targets for learning. There has been a tendency in the past for the use of ICT in a passive yet receptive manner for pupils who cannot read text, with less attention to its role in supporting communication and creativity. The advent of software that allows pupils to receive information and to communicate using pictures, symbols, sounds and the spoken word has created new opportunities for access for pupils who have not reached the stage of using standard orthography. This is reflected at all key stages in the guidance on developing ICT capability for pupils with SEN.

It is also very clear in the National Curriculum that the development of ICT capability should be practical and useful. There is strong reference to the use of ICT across subjects to overcome potential barriers to learning. The inclusion of the performance descriptions (QCA 2001), for pupils with more severe disabilities, demonstrates the empowering role of ICT.

Access technology and a Code of Practice

In 1994, the DFE established the concept of a Code of Practice (DFE 1994), which recognised the important role that IT could play in assisting access to learning. This principle has been carried forward and strengthened in both practice and subsequent official guidance: in *Excellence for All* (DfEE 1997a) and *Connecting the Learning Society: The National Grid for Learning* (DfEE 1997b), for example, an LEA is guided to ask whether, in addressing a child's learning difficulty, a 'school has explored the possible benefits, and where practical secured access to, appropriate information technology' (DfEE 1997b, p. 56). A similar question was raised with respect to each area of special need.

To date, much of the guidance has been aimed at providing examples of the types of technologies that could be particularly appropriate, giving useful suggestions on the application of ICT to support pupils with SEN. Where used appropriately, this may avoid the need for further, more formalised measures to ensure that pupils' needs are met. The emphasis, because of its use across the curriculum, has been on tools for communication: word processing, spell-checkers, painting and drawing packages, and the use of a range of alternative input devices such as overlay keyboards, which can simplify the process. To explore the benefits, a school will need to take time with each pupil to assess his or her response to a range of strategies. If the child, teacher and any supporting adults 'are not able to use the equipment effectively, then the advantages of an IT solution are lost' (Day 1995). This has implications to the policy and management of IT, which will be discussed later.

In the past, ICT access has relied on the specialist knowledge of an ICT or SEN coordinator. A range of new initiatives aim nowadays to give all teachers confidence and competence in the use of ICT in the curriculum. In particular, these will focus around the standards for all newly trained teachers, the standards for specialist SEN teachers (Teacher Training Association, in press) and the expected outcomes of the training arising out of the New Opportunities Fund. If these initiatives succeed, then by 2003 the United Kingdom will have a highly skilled ICT-literate teaching population. Even if it takes longer or even only partially succeeds, there will be considerable improvement in the general quality of provision.

Securing access to ICT presents schools with a number of questions of management, including prioritising the availability of resources between different children and different classes. Wherever possible, it is desirable that the solutions should be found through the management of the same resources as those available to all other pupils. With the increased emphasis on inclusion, these management issues become increasingly important. For example, where the same piece of software can be used by all pupils, through its inbuilt flexibility or through the use of additional utilities, such as an on-screen selection grid (see Figure 12.1), the pupils are gaining in at least one of two ways: the software facilitates equality and inclusion, and it might also allow the teacher to differentiate activities more easily.

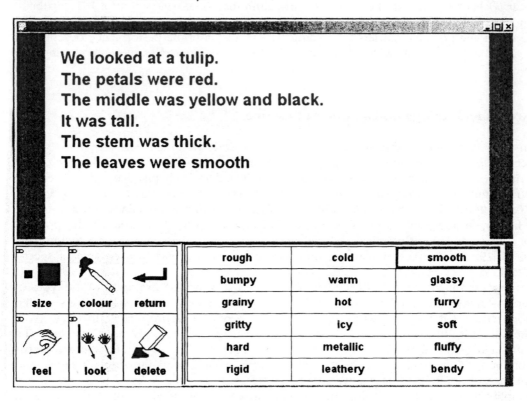

Figure 12.1 On-screen selection grid

In discussing access technology, Day (1995) identifies three types of access: physical, cognitive and supportive. *Physical access* 'is technology at its most dramatic, liberating the pupil from the physical barriers to learning' (p. 4). *Cognitive access* is aided where the IT is used to present the curriculum in a variety of ways that may make it more accessible to pupils with special needs, such as presenting information in small steps. *Supportive access* is where the technology can assist the pupil with tasks and skills that are difficult – for example, help for the pupil with poor handwriting who becomes demotivated by lack of presentation skills, or for the pupil with spelling difficulties who, by hearing her or his own writing/typing read back may be helped to identify and correct mistakes. Across each of these types of access there will be a continuum of need. At one extreme, the technology will be a lifeline; without it, a pupil might be unable to communicate or engage in the learning process. For example, a pupil without speech may use a communication aid with the help of switches. At the other extreme, the technology will act as a facilitator. In these cases it will not be essential for a pupil but will make the process easier or help to raise a pupil's motivation and self-esteem.

To identify a pupil's need, teachers have to be able to identify the type of access required and where on the continuum of need a pupil's use of technology lies. Chapter 2 in *Access Technology* (Day 1995) provides a useful checklist to help teachers in this process. In the checklist, teachers are led to consider the context and purpose behind the intended use of technology, the resourcing and support implications, and then to consider the expectations both by the learner and by staff and parents. This raises questions of management, monitoring and transition.

Examples of ICT used to enhance access to learning

This section presents a number of examples where ICT has been used to provide or enhance access to learning. Its purpose is not as a training manual but as an illustration of the variety of approaches available to build on different elements of IT capability. The majority of the illustrations are concerned with communicating ideas, which reflects the importance of communication for pupils with SEN – without the means to communicate, pupils are unable to demonstrate their understanding or receive recognition for their capabilities (Kiernan *et al.* 1987).

There are many pupils across the spectrum of learning abilities who have understanding, but are unable to demonstrate this through the normal channels. ICT has been shown to provide such a means for some pupils with profound and multiple learning difficulties (Detheridge 1996). Other pupils, with emotional and behavioural difficulties, may find that ICT provides some of the necessary conditions to motivate and enhance concentration, so that they are able to learn and to express their ideas (Howard 1991). Although Day (1995) identified three separate types of access, as described in the previous section, in practice many pupils will require support of more than one type. The child who, because of his or her physical disability, has missed many of the play opportunities to explore and manipulate objects may require cognitive support as well as physical support – for example, when working in the areas of mathematics involving shape and space. Despite this observation, for clarity the examples below have been put under the dominant heading.

Examples of ICT giving physical access

Veronica has cerebral palsy, no speech and severe physical disabilities. For her first few years at school she used a wooden communication board with symbols, which she selected by pointing with her fist. This gave her access to some 60 symbols and phrases at any one time. The symbols were chosen for her by a speech and language therapist to meet her most immediate needs. Interaction in class was mainly through a facilitator who read the symbols indicated and interpreted other gestural signals that Veronica made. Her means of communication now instead relies heavily on ICT. She uses a communication aid that gives her access to over 1,000 words and phrases. This extra flexibility means that she is no longer dependent to the same extent on the vocabulary that has been considered appropriate – she can choose her own. She can also type words, and so theoretically she is gaining access to unlimited communication. An integrated system that will bring speech communication, writing and mobility control into one device will soon give her a freedom that was unthinkable without ICT.

Ben is in a nursery class. He has no sight, has minimal physical movement and makes very few sounds. These disabilities made it very difficult for him to join in with group activities in the classroom and to play and make friends. He has been given a small device that can record several seconds of sound, which can be activated by a single press. As soon as he was given this very simple communication aid, he showed that he understood cause and effect and that he could participate in a game with his teacher. Ben works with a small group of pupils to play a version of 'Simon Says'. When he hits his switch, it says 'Clap your hands'; a friend has one that says 'Wave your hands'. Although neither of these pupils can physically respond to these commands, they can perceive the rest of the group doing it. This is clearly seen by their facial gestures and body language. Ben has shown that he can understand a game and take turns, but more importantly he is learning to be assertive – to make his presence felt.

Martha also has cerebral palsy, which, while not severe, makes writing and manipulating objects difficult. Many of the play activities in her Reception class involve manipulating objects, doing puzzles, sorting and building. She uses a computer program, which allows her to move shapes on the computer. She can do this easily with the help of a roller ball. She can move the object slowly to the area where she wants it and then press a button to put it in the right place – something she could not do with her hands. Given this tool, Martha has shown that she understands many mathematical concepts and, because this is a tool used by all of the class, she is not being singled out in any way.

Examples of ICT giving cognitive access

There are three major ways that ICT can enhance cognitive access to learning, and to communication in particular: through simplifying the writing process; by allowing pupils to explore ideas and try things out before committing themselves to a final outcome; and by presenting information in small quantities that can be easily assimilated.

Children who are full of ideas and excitement can be prevented or deterred from writing stories or expressing their own ideas because they have not acquired adequate writing skills. Overlay keyboards and on-screen grids can be used to give such pupils lists of words that they can use directly in their texts without having to learn to spell them first. It can give whole words and phrases as well as providing clearly defined topic lists or subsets of information, making selection much quicker and easier. (Figure 12.1 above showed the use of an on-screen grid set up so that a pupil could write with symbols as well as words.) The content of a grid is easily set up by the teacher. Clearly, pupils will be developing their finer skills in parallel, but will be practising creative writing at the same time.

James, who is 17 and has severe learning difficulties, is unlikely to acquire a high level of reading using standard orthography. To compensate, he uses pictorial symbols as an alternative and support for words. With software that allows him to write in symbols, James can record his experiences and what he has learned. His class teacher is confident that, by writing his ideas down, James has been helped to structure his thoughts. It has improved his thinking skills as well as helping him to show the extent of his ideas in a way that can be recorded. Detheridge and Detheridge (1997) have shown how this approach can create new opportunities, enhance self-esteem and promote autonomy.

Hawkridge and Vincent (1992) illustrate many ways in which children across the spectrum of learning difficulties can be helped to write and communicate their ideas. In particular, the facility offered by a word processor for writers to draft and redraft their work gives the chance to explore ideas and to develop thinking in the process at whatever pace they are able to work.

Talking books and multimedia CD-ROMs can provide material that is accessible to learners who have difficulty reading large amounts of material at a time. Information is presented in small chunks, often supported by pictures or moving images and with sound support. Like books but unlike videotape and audiotape, such media can be browsed and need not be followed in a strictly linear fashion. This can encourage pupils to search for information and to develop information-handling skills, at the same time as presenting material in ways that they can easily assimilate. McKeown and Thomas (1995) give many examples where multimedia has provided motivation and the right environment for pupils to maintain concentration for much longer periods than is their norm. The multisensory delivery makes information accessible to pupils with a range of difficulties, making it a particularly suitable medium for supporting differentiation in the classroom. Software that allows pupils to create their own multimedia presentations encourages collaboration, interaction and communication between peers. For instance, a group of deaf children in a first school created stories developed from previous reading. The ICT helped them to work together and to express their ideas in media that they could share with their hearing friends.

Examples of ICT giving supportive access

Speech output, either from pre-recorded speech or through speech synthesis, is one of the major ways in which the newer technologies can support cognitive access to learning. Pupils who find difficulty spelling and reading can gain reinforcement from their work by hearing it read. As well as the motivational effect, it can help pupils develop their own strategies for overcoming difficulties (Day 1994, Miles 1994).

Kate, who has severe spelling and reading difficulties, used a computer with a spell-checker to help her gain some independence in her writing. After a while using it, she was able to cope well with a hand-held spell-checker which she could keep in her pencil case. This was important to Kate because she did not want to be seen as different from her peers, as well as wanting a device that she could use in class and at home. The thesaurus facility on the spell-checker helps her find the meanings of words when she is reading. She finds using a dictionary for so many words slows her reading, but the thesaurus, by suggesting similar words that she might know, helps to keep up the momentum of the text.

Anthony, aged 11, has identified that his biggest problem is 'handwriting'. 'All of English, except talking, gives me trouble. I do not like writing, and I am not a good speller,' he says. It was decided to introduce him to Dragon DICTATE, a discrete or one-word-at-a-time speech recognition (SR) software package, in order to develop a positive approach to writing. Following a short enrolment process, he was very pleased with the extended story he wrote using SR. It was lengthier and more detailed than anything he had written before. Anthony says: 'Speech recognition is really good fun and I like working on it and learning how to use it. I found it a bit strange at first talking to a computer with all sorts of words coming up on the screen.'

For Anthony, the software had many advantages: he never saw mis-spelt words on the screen, so that no bad habits were reinforced; and some spellings were learnt through frequent use. Because he had to make a decision on whether to accept a word suggested by the software or to choose from the list of choices, he looked closely at the words and began to recognise words he could previously not read. He appeared more willing to experiment with content and layout, producing more elaborate and extended pieces of writing with a wider range of vocabulary and sentence structure. The software has helped him with inaccurate pronunciations and had improved his diction by drawing his attention to it. For example, he pronounced the word 'another' as 'an ever', and it wasn't until he saw it on the screen in this way that he realised his mistake.

For the teacher there were other advantages. After four months, Anthony was producing work on the computer that was far superior to work that he could produce by hand. In his case, quantity and content improved from producing no more than one or two paragraphs of simple sentences by hand, to producing two or three pages of complex yet readable sentences on the computer. Because he was writing at greater length, the content tended to show more depth of understanding of a subject, and he seemed to feel freer to play with vocabulary and phrasing.

Pupils at a school for children with emotional and behavioural difficulties use online chat as a way of exploring social relationships in a safe environment. The school uses software that makes it impossible for offensive words or descriptions to appear, and students have been taught to break off conversations if it appears that the topic is inappropriate. One student with communication difficulties likes this way of communication because he can take time to respond and can ask staff what is meant by the people he is talking with. The staff use these experiences as teaching opportunities for discussing what is and what is not acceptable in conversation (Abbott 1999).

Identifying solutions

To be able to identify appropriate solutions to meeting individual needs, a teacher has not only to be aware of the types of solution and strategies available but also requires training in their implementation. This has to be set in a context of limited budgets and realistic time-frames. The starting point must, however, be the identification of a *pupil's* learning needs and objectives; it is only when these have been clarified that particular strategies, including those involving IT, can be evaluated and proposed.

ICT solutions

The previous section gave a number of illustrations of the use of ICT to facilitate access to learning. Hopefully, a picture has emerged of the enormous range of solutions that may exist, many of which serve to develop ICT capability and to enhance learning for all pupils, not only those with special needs. Although some pupils will require specialised equipment, resources or strategies to give them the necessary access to learning, it is very desirable, as far as possible, for them to use generic tools that are used by all and sundry. By finding a means of accessing standard, commonly used equipment and software, pupils with particular needs can participate in the same activities as their peers. It facilitates inclusion and, importantly, gives them the tools required for use in further education and in the workplace.

In the early days of IT, specialist software was written so that pupils who could not manage a keyboard could write using switch-operated word processors. Much of the early learning software was designed specifically with this type of user in mind. Although useful, it encouraged separate provision. In the second half of the 1990s, specialist-software developers took on the agendas of inclusion and created tools to meet very flexible situations. For example, devices such as overlay keyboards, and on-screen grids have now become resources used day to day by teachers in raising standards for all pupils. It is disappointing to note that the converse is not true, and work still remains to be done in making mainstream software fully accessible. At the same time, access devices have increased in range and sophistication. Used in conjunction with the more flexible software, these technologies have created new opportunities for expression, leading to enhanced self-esteem, independence and autonomy for pupils at all stages of the continuum of learning difficulties. *The First Handbook of IT and Special Educational Needs* (Stanfield 1997) provides an early overview of these approaches.

As well as describing a continuum of need, Day (1995) discusses a continuum of provision across the pupil range. The needs of the majority of pupils will be met through the good use of existing resources that are available to all pupils in a mainstream class. At the other end of this continuum, a pupil may be provided with specified equipment for his or her sole use. It is likely that, in many mainstream schools that cater for such pupils, the teachers will need to consult specialists in order to ensure that technology is used to its greatest effect. As the severity of need becomes more acute, so the strategies, such as the selection of appropriate devices and the positioning of pupils and switches, becomes crucial.

Evaluation and review

Finding an appropriate access solution is not a one-off event. Not only do curriculum needs change but also individual capability develops. There needs, therefore, to be a continuous process of evaluation and review. Monitoring progress fulfils audit requirements and also gives detailed background information to identifying future provision. One of the hesitations behind review is a concern that expensive equipment will have to be replaced. The school will need, as part of its ICT and SEN policies, to develop mechanisms whereby equipment can be re-channelled to new pupils.

It is particularly important to review provision and training requirements at points of transition. Moving from one class to another will make one set of training demands on staff; transition between schools will make another. What might have been appropriate in one context may need revision in another. For example, access to a classroom computer may have given adequate support to a pupil with learning difficulties in a primary classroom, but the mobile life in a secondary school may suggest access to a portable computer.

Training and development

Whichever type of provision is made, in order for it to be most effective, pupils and anyone working with them need to be trained in the appropriate use. As mentioned above, in the first years of the new millennium the amount of training available is set to increase through initiatives such as the training of serving teachers funded by the New Opportunities Fund. But this in itself is not a total solution. Teachers and schools must build in these initiatives for training to take account of developing technologies and changing populations of schools. There have been too many examples of specific ICT equipment being underused or – worse – not being used at all because the first person trained in its use is no longer available. Ensuring that all participants are given the opportunity to become familiar with resources will go some way to ensuring continued effectiveness. It is also worth considering who needs what type of training. A classroom assistant working extensively with a pupil may require greater familiarity with specific equipment than the class teacher, while the SEN and ICT coordinators will require a greater understanding of the purposes and objectives behind each provision.

In addition, new approaches to training and professional development are required. The most interesting new approach to sharing information and expertise has come about through electronic communications. Electronic communication has shown itself to be a very valuable source of information as well as offering peer support through email forums and the Internet. The National Grid for Learning and allied initiatives will promote this; and, as individuals' skills develop, their willingness to participate will increase. And as the amount of material that is available on the World Wide Web increases, teachers – like pupils – will need to be discriminating about the quality (or otherwise) demonstrated in the wealth of material.

These technologies are offering new ways in which teachers can access professional development and training. It is no longer realistic for teachers to be released for postgraduate training. Distance learning and distance-supported training will eventually become the norm.

There are many sources of information available through the Internet. A good starting point for the newcomer is the National Grid for Learning site at www.ngfl.gov.uk.

Conclusion

ICT is an important medium for the whole of society. It provides powerful tools for expression, presentation, the exploring of ideas and the gathering of information. On its own, however, it cannot do any of these things. The resources and equipment have to be chosen to meet the need of the individual as well as the group. It is not a cheap option, and so school policies need to reflect matters of resource purchase, management, training and development. The most important factor in the successful use of IT to meet individual need will be the knowledge and sensitivity of the staff working with the pupils: sensitivity to recognise when intervention and help is needed; when to leave the individual to face challenges alone; and when it is more appropriate for pupils to work together. For pupils with learning difficulties, careful selection of resources can facilitate peer interaction as well as individual learning in ways that would not otherwise be possible.

Teachers are not going to acquire all of these skills easily or quickly, and plans need to be made for them to network with colleagues and to have access to specialist advice. There is, however, sufficient evidence to show that the use of ICT can facilitate access to learning when used appropriately to support other tried-and-tested educational strategies.

References

Abbott, C. (1995) *IT Helps.* Coventry: NCET.
Abbott, C. (1999) *Making Communication Special.* London: University of London (Kings College).
Day, J. (1994) *A Software Guide for Specific Learning Difficulties.* Coventry: NCET.
Day, J. (1995) *Access Technology: Making the right choice,* 2nd edn. Coventry: NCET.
Detheridge, T. (1996) 'The role of information technology in bridging the production/competence gap in severely disabled students' (unpublished MPhil thesis), Warwick: University of Warwick.
Detheridge, T. and Detheridge, M. (1997) *Literacy Through Symbols.* London: David Fulton Publishers.

DFE (1994) *Code of Practice on the Identification and Assessment of Special Educational Needs.* London: HMSO.

DFE (1995). *Superhighways in Education.* London: HMSO.

DfEE (1997a) *Excellence for All Children: Meeting special educational needs.* London: DfEE.

DfEE (1997b) *Connecting the Learning Society: The National Grid for Learning.* London: DfEE.

DfEE (2000) *National Curriculum for England (Key Stages 1–4): Information and communication technology.* London: DfEE.

DfEE/QCA (1999) *The National Curriculum: Handbook for Primary Teachers in England Key Stages 1 and 2.* London: HMSO.

Hawkridge, D. and Vincent, T. (1992) *Learning Difficulties and Computers.* London: Jessica Kingsley.

Howard, W. (1991) *IT Across the Curriculum: Supporting learners who display challenging behaviour.* Coventry: NCET.

Kiernan, C. *et al.* (1987) *The Foundations of Communication and Language.* Manchester: Manchester University Press.

McKeown, S. and Thomas, M. (1995) *Special Edition.* Coventry: NCET.

Miles, M. (1994) 'The Somerset talking computer project', in Singleton, C. (ed.) *Computers and Dyslexia.* Hull: University of Hull, Dyslexia Computer Resource Centre.

OFSTED (1999) *Special Education 1994–1998: A review of special schools, secure units and pupil referral units in England.* London: The Stationery Office.

QCA (2001) *Planning, Teaching and Assessing the Curriculum for Pupils with Learning Difficulties: Information and communications technology.* London: DfEE/QCA.

Stanfield, J. (ed.) (1997) *The First Handbook of IT and Special Educational Needs.* Nasen: Tamworth.

Stevenson, D. (1997) *Information and Communications Technology in UK Schools: An Independent Enquiry.* London: HMSO.

Teacher Training Agency (1999) *National Special Educational Needs (SEN) Specialist Standards.* London: Teacher Training Agency.

Further reading

Banes, D. and Coles, C. (1995) *IT for All.* London: David Fulton Publishers.

HMI (1990) *Education Observed: Special needs issues.* London: HMSO.

NCET (1993) *Opening up the Library for Visually Impaired Learners.* Coventry: NCET.

Wedell, K. and Detheridge, T. (1995) *Electronic Communications to Support Special Needs Co-ordinators.* Coventry: NCET.

Other resources

Dragon Dictate software: Words Worldwide Limited, Ash House, Bell Villas, Ponteland, Newcastle upon Tyne NE20 9BE.

Part II:
Access and Entitlement to the Whole Curriculum

Chapter 13

Religious Education

Erica Brown

Under the United Kingdom's Education Act 1996, schools must provide religious education for all registered pupils, although parents can choose to withdraw their children. Schools, other than voluntary-aided schools and those of a religious character, must teach religious education according to the locally agreed syllabus. In special schools, the requirements are detailed in the Education Acts 1993 and 1996:

> Every pupil attending a special school will, so far as is practicable, attend collective worship and receive religious education unless the child's parents have expressed a wish to the contrary. It is for the schools to decide what is practicable but, in general terms, the Secretary of State would expect the question of practicability to relate to the special educational needs of the pupils and not to problems of staffing or premises.

In September 2000, the revised National Curriculum was introduced in England. The legal status of religious education was not affected by this review. However, much curriculum development has taken place since the model syllabuses were published by SCAA in 1994; increasingly, members of faith communities have made a valuable contribution to producing new agreed syllabuses.

The principal world religions

Although legislation does not define which principal religions should be taught, it has come to be accepted that all principal religions in the United Kingdom should be included and that children should learn about, and from, the religions studied. Traditionally, there are six major world religions: Christianity, Islam, Hinduism, Buddhism, Sikhism and Judaism.

The place of religious education for pupils with special educational needs

The matter of religious education that is accessible to all pupils has not been documented in detail. Some agreed syllabuses produced after the Education Reform Act 1988 offer a very few lines of guidance, such as (the Agreed Syllabus for Religious Education in Avon): 'Special schools will be expected to implement the Programmes of Study and assessment arrangements of this Agreed Syllabus so far as is practicable.' Most agreed syllabuses for religious education are united in the view that, in the early years of pupils' religious and spiritual development, teaching should be relevant to children's life experiences while also encouraging an awareness and understanding of the belief and practice of religion.

Among the few educationalists who have written about religious education for all children is Flo Longhorn. Referring to pupils whom she calls 'very special', she says that special schools provide a relevant environment in which children can stretch, reach and attain their full individual potential (Longhorn 1993). Dowell and Nutt (1995), building on the work of Brown (1996), have emphasised the importance of helping children in special schools towards a greater awareness of themselves and other people. They believe this can be encouraged through activities 'in class, in the whole school and in the wider community'. Goss (1995) shares this view, and he charges teachers of pupils with profound and multiple learning difficulties (PMLD) 'to attempt to recognise emotional and spiritual needs within the curricular and social experiences provided'.

There is clear evidence that religious education already makes a distinctive and positive contribution to the achievement of high standards by many pupils. OFSTED inspection reports show that religious education plays the most successful role among all subjects in promoting the spiritual, moral, social and cultural development of pupils.

Religious education also promotes the values and attitudes needed for life in a diverse society, where similarities and differences are recognised and valued for the common good. For children with special education needs (SEN), religious education can help them to develop and express a conceptual understanding of faith and life issues that they are not always able to demonstrate in any other area of school life. It offers opportunities to explore religious concepts in ways that are not limited by the skills of literacy and numeracy, e.g. through discussion or through the creative or performing arts.

The spiritual dimension of religious education

The National Curriculum Council's discussion paper on spiritual and moral development (NCC 1993) argued that spiritual development is 'fundamental to other areas of learning'. In the context of religion, this may include beliefs and a sense of awe or transcendence. But spirituality is also concerned with the very essence of what it means to be human and, in this sense, it includes self-understanding and self-worth, creativity, emotional responses, a personal quest for meaning and purpose, and forming relationships. All recent agreed syllabuses charge teachers to introduce experiences that give pupils opportunities to respond with awe and wonderment. But they seldom suggest how this might take place within a busy classroom.

Recently, I joined a group of children with moderate learning difficulties as they explored the theme of 'New beginnings and springtime'. A large vase of daffodils on the table caught their attention. Selecting one of the flowers from the vase, Richie began to explore the frilled trumpet with his forefinger and then put the bloom to his face. The tip of his nose became covered in pollen. Ruth, who was sitting next to him, giggled and, selecting a flower for herself, she carefully pushed the entire length of her little finger into its centre. Withdrawing it, she admired the yellow dust and turned to her teacher and said: 'The bee collects that, and then the mummy and daddy bee do a miracle. They go to the bee house, and they make the dust into jam.' 'No they don't,' replied Richie. 'God does that for them, and then he turns it into honey.'

These children had discovered something for themselves. They brought their past learning experiences to the present time in an effort to make sense of what they were encountering. On one count we could argue that their understanding of bees is incorrect, but on another we can allow them to ponder on the wonderment of creation.

The ethos of a school

The joint QCA/DfEE publication entitled *Religious Education: Teacher's Guide* (2000) describes attitudes that are particularly relevant to religious education. Those such as respect, care and concern should be promoted through all areas of school life. Commitment, fairness, respect, self-understanding and enquiry are described as being fundamental in religious education. Encouraging pupils to develop these attitudes through religious education will contribute towards the practical application of these principles.

In order to encourage all pupils to develop their full potential academically and socially in religious education as in other subjects, the ethos of the school should promote:

- relationships based on mutual respect between all those who learn and work in the school;
- positive attitudes to learning – a philosophy that encourages purposeful learning, that celebrates effort as well as success, and that helps children to take responsibility for their own engagement in tasks;
- a safe, stimulating environment that recognises the individual needs of pupils and their families.

The access statement

Revisions to National Curriculum subjects (DfEE/QCA 2000) are accompanied by an access statement. This should be considered by Agreed Syllabus Conferences when drawing up guidance on religious education for pupils with SEN. It can be adapted, modified and used to include the importance of conceptualising pupils' experience, their interests and their family backgrounds.

Differentiation

The Education Act 1996 requires that all children are entitled to a broad and balanced curriculum. A wide range of ability and experiences exists within any group of pupils. Teachers need to be able to provide equal opportunities in learning through a flexible approach and skills that differentiate teaching and learning. The Code of Practice issued by the Department for Education (DFE 1994) required Individual Education Plans (IEPs) to be used in the planning, implementation and review of pupils' learning in order that they would be able to achieve at their highest attainable levels. In religious education this will include:

- an understanding by teachers of the ways in which children learn;
- matching work to children's previous experience;
- an understanding of factors that might hinder or prevent children learning;
- careful analysis of the knowledge and skills that comprise a particular learning task;
- structured teaching and learning that will help children to achieve and to demonstrate their learning outcomes;
- providing imaginative learning experiences that arouse and sustain children's interest;
- supporting the learning that takes place in religious education by what is taught in other curriculum areas;
- making judgements about gains in knowledge and understanding in order to inform future planning.

The DfEE/QCA non-statutory guidance for religious education (2000) describes a non-statutory assessment scale for religious education that sets level descriptors describing knowledge, skills and understanding that pupils are expected to have by the end of a key stage. The scale is structured around two attainment targets formerly used by the SCAA's model syllabuses in religious education (SCAA 1994) – 'Learning about religions' and 'Learning from religions'. Each attainment target has three strands, namely:

- AT1: Learning about religions:
  - knowledge and understanding of religious beliefs and teachings;
  - knowledge and understanding of religious practices and life-styles;
  - knowledge and understanding of ways of expressing meaning;
- AT2: Learning from religions:
  - skill of asking and responding to questions of identity and experience;
  - skill of asking and responding to questions of meaning and purpose;
  - skill of asking and responding to questions of values and commitments.

Planning from programmes of study in agreed syllabuses

Once schools are familiar with the requirements of their agreed syllabus and have made all the relevant choices that their syllabus allows (e.g. which religions are to be studied in which key stage) long-, medium- and short-term planning should include teaching and learning for pupils across the continuum of special needs.

Long-term planning for religious education is done in the context of the requirements of the locally agreed syllabus and of each school's overall curriculum plan, which reflects the needs of all children. Staff need to agree which parts of the PoS of the locally agreed syllabus are drawn together to make coherent, manageable teaching units. The long-term plan shows how these teaching units are distributed across both attainment targets in a sequence that promotes curriculum continuity and progress in children's learning. The units may be linked with work in other curriculum areas.

A medium-term plan identifies learning objectives and outcomes for each unit and suggests activities that will promote progression and an estimate of the time that each unit will take. In many schools, all staff are involved in the production of the medium-term plan, with the religious education coordinator ensuring that there is continuity within the units such that they promote progression.

Short-term planning is the responsibility of individual teachers, who build on the medium-term plan by taking account of the needs of children in a particular class and identify learning experiences and ways in which ideas might be taught. Short-term planning of religious education for pupils with SEN should:

- be based on an understanding of what pupils already know and understand;
- contain clear learning objectives linked to IEP targets;
- indicate expected learning outcomes and how these might be demonstrated by individual pupils;
- describe challenging and stimulating activities that have been carefully selected to teach the objectives;
- incorporate formative assessment procedures to inform future planning.

For special schools, there is the additional flexibility to modify the requirements of the local agreed syllabus to meet the needs of their pupils. This may be done, for example, by selecting materials out of the age-appropriate key stage or by making choices about the number of religions to be studied by the pupils, which may be influenced by the pupils' academic or social abilities. Schemes of work form the foundation for schools' medium-term planning and can be tailored to suit individual circumstances.

For short-term planning the development of pupils' IEPs provides information and a context to help teachers consider ways to provide religious education according to pupils needs. IEPs may require, for example, a focus on communication, social or other skills to which religious education can make a significant contribution. Some pupils may need additional experiences to consolidate or extend their understanding of concepts across the curriculum, and so the planning process needs to be flexible enough to allow for this.

Planning should be based on a set of sound principles and should consider:

- the range of pupil activity in the class/group;
- differentiated activities to teach the scheme of work appropriately;
- the past and present experience of pupils;
- the family background of pupils;
- the individual needs of pupils;
- a range of opportunities to assess progress and to report to parents;
- opportunities for pupils to recognise, record and celebrate (self-assess) their achievements.

Putting principles into practice

Although, in the early stages of pupils' religious education, study units may contain little that is explicitly religious, children's own life experiences should provide an essential framework for understanding religion. All children come to school with experiences of relationships with those who care for them. Within the school 'family', they will need encouragement to respond to their learning in a way that nurtures positive attitudes towards themselves and towards other people.

For children to begin to understand something about the belief that lies at the heart of religious practice, they will need to learn *about* religion as well as learn *from* religion. Although many children may come from homes where religion is not a way of life, others will learn about faith and practice in their families through such things as the clothes they wear, the food they eat (or don't eat), or the objects and symbols that surround them.

The QCA schemes of work (DfEE/QCA 2000) provide much that is relevant to pupils whose academic performance is within Key Stages 1–2. However, it is important that religious education also provides meaningful and relevant learning experiences for those pupils with PMLD and those who have very special educational needs. The framework that follows is, in the author's opinion, appropriate to such pupils.

Foundation experiences

In the very early stages of children's religious and spiritual development, it is necessary to provide a foundation on which to build an increasing awareness of themselves as individuals and of relationships with other people. This is particularly important for children with PMLD. Helping pupils to respond to different environments and giving them a wide range of opportunities to experience sensory learning will provide a framework for developing attitudes such as delight or curiosity, or skills such as reflection. Children should learn through using their senses and share experiences that enable them to become aware that people, objects, symbols, places, food and occasions can have special importance. The DfEE/QCA guidance (2001) provide some further insight into teaching pupils with PMLD.

A sensory approach to learning

All children use their senses to learn. A sensory approach is appropriate to all children's learning in religious education. The following list is not a definitive one; rather, it gives some examples for learning experiences that might be incorporated into schemes of work or study units using the sense of smell.

Learning objectives should be along the following lines:

- develop an awareness of different forms of religious expression;
- develop confidence in responding freely and appropriately;
- explore and share experiences and feelings;
- participate as a member of a group;
- develop preferences.

In relation to Christianity, these objectives could be met by:

- visiting a church decorated for a special occasion and smelling the perfume of the flowers;
- smelling the musty smell of a very old hymn-book or Bible;
- smelling the heavy smell of incense from a censer;
- smelling altar candles after they have been snuffed out;
- smelling the palm of palm crosses;
- smelling the spicy warmth of hot-cross buns.

Similarly, in Judaism the sensory approach could involve:

- smelling cinnamon, nutmeg and cloves in a spice box;
- smelling warm *challah* bread;
- smelling *Shabbat* and *havdalah* candles;
- smelling the leather of phylacteries.

In Hinduism:

- smelling spices used for the puja ceremony (e.g. saffron, cumin, haldi, turmeric);
- smelling warm ghee used in cooking;
- smelling ghee as divas burn;
- smelling joss sticks and incense.

In Sikhism:

- smelling the distinctive smell of dye used on a turban length or a sari fabric;
- smelling divas and joss sticks burning;
- smelling warm *karah parshad*.

And for considering Islam:

- smelling the wood of a Quran stand;
- smelling the fabric of a prayer carpet;
- smelling Muslim festival food.

Key Stage 1

At Key Stage 1, religious education should strive to build on children's understanding of themselves and their experiences of family life and relationships (see Figure 13.1). It is important that teachers take the variety of children's experience into account when planning schemes of work. All pupils should learn from the attitudes encountered in school that they are personally valued, while also beginning to discover the contribution that other people make. They should become increasingly aware of things that are special and important to themselves and other people, (Figure 13.2 shows a child's view of ourselves and our homes).

Children will benefit from opportunities to develop their awareness of the local environment through journeys (see Figure 13.3) and visits and by having a chance to experience awe and wonderment in the natural world. They should be introduced to symbolism in religion and hear stories about the lives of key figures and religious leaders. Pupils should be encouraged to celebrate their own achievements and milestones as well as joining in a variety of occasions when people meet together for worship and festivals. Some children will find it very difficult to enter imaginatively into the experience of other people, and they may need help in order to be aware of the needs and desires of their peers and their teachers.

IN FAMILIES CHILDREN LEARN ABOUT RELIGIOUS PERSPECTIVE ON
HUMAN EXPERIENCE AS THEY

GO SHOPPING
DRESS FOR THE DAY
VISIT PLACE OF WORSHIP
WATCH RITUALS AND CEREMONIES
SHARE IN FESTIVALS AND CELEBRATIONS
SEE RELIGIOUS OBJECTS AND SYMBOLS
ATTEND CHILDREN'S GROUP
LISTEN TO FAMILIAR SOUNDS
ASK QUESTIONS
HEAR STORIES

Figure 13.1

Ourselves and our homes

Figure 13.2

Our taxis take us home

Figure 13.3

Key Stage 2

Key Stage 2 should enhance the opportunities and experiences that pupils have already encountered in order that they may build on their knowledge and understanding of religion and increase their spiritual and moral development. Children should be developing a greater understanding of themselves and an awareness of the needs and feelings of other people from a variety of faiths and cultures. They should be given an opportunity to interact with the natural world and the local environment. By the end of Key Stage 2, pupils should have been helped to explore a range of religious ideas and themes, including how these are communicated through sacred writings and symbols. They should have heard stories about the life and teaching of Jesus and other religious figures and have been given opportunities to consider their own questions and concerns arising from the PoS. Their knowledge of religious belief and practice will grow through activities such as visiting places of worship and meeting people from religious communities.

Areas of learning, or study units

In order that children are given a broad and balanced curriculum, study units are suggested that develop dimensions of religion starting with each pupil's human experience (including lifestyle). The titles suggested are:

- Human experience;
- The world around;
- Special people/key figures and leaders;
- Special books/sacred writings;
- Special buildings/places of worship;
- Festivals and celebrations;
- Special times/rites of passage;
- Special journeys/pilgrimage;
- Language, symbol and communication.

The first two areas of study, namely 'Human experience' and 'The world around', lay the foundation for beginning to explore other dimensions of religion. (Figure 13.4 illustrates how a young child with special needs may visually interpret emotions). The remaining study units are concerned with 'Learning about religion' and 'Learning from religion'.

The scheme of work for religious education

In order that the religious education taught in a school reflects a curriculum that is broad and balanced while also being relevant to the life experiences and individual learning needs of pupils, the content will need to be planned carefully. This cannot happen unless teachers are prepared to stand alongside their pupils and to meet them at their point of learning. A scheme of work is an essential tool in the planning process, but if it is to meet the specific needs of individual children it will have to be interpreted and implemented creatively through the opportunities for learning that are provided.

The content of the school's scheme of work should be clearly identified and documented. It is important that what is taught contributes to a broad and balanced curriculum. In religious education, this will include the range of beliefs and practices of Christianity and other principal world faiths.

Recording pupil achievement

Understanding religion demands that children learn *about* and *from* the beliefs, values and customs that underpin the faiths studied. The use of attainment targets, statements of achievement and level descriptors will provide an important tool in enabling teachers to:

- plan future work, set tasks and provide learning experiences appropriate to pupils' ability and development;
- provide opportunities for pupils' learning;
- build on provided learning experiences, ensuring continuity and progression to the next key stage.

The author's framework of assessment uses the two attainment targets given earlier in the chapter, namely 'Learning about religions' and 'Learning from religions'. The attainment targets define the knowledge, skills and understanding that pupils of different abilities and maturities are expected to have gained by the end of each key stage. Both attainment targets are underpinned by the nine suggested study units that have been interwoven throughout the PoS, listed above and illustrated in the diagrams, (See Figure 3.5).

In addition, level descriptors have been selected in order that the achievements of *all* pupils may be recorded. They may be used as a guide to both the current performance of an individual pupil and as an indicator of how future progress may be made. They also indicate individual pupil reactions to the learning encounters provided through:

- experiencing an activity;
- being aware of an activity;
- responding to an activity;
- participating in an activity;
- being involved in an activity;
- demonstrating a learning outcome.

Figure 13.4 Emotions: a part of the 'Human Experience'

PUPIL RECORD	RELIGIOUS PERSPECTIVES ON HUMAN EXPERIENCE
Name: Darren Lewis **Half Term Ending:** Oct 96 **Key Stage:** 2 **Topic or Theme:** Sikhism	* Is encouraged to talk about people who are special to him. * Makes a collection of objects which are important to himself and to his peer group. * Reflects on special ceremonies and occasions in his own life.
KNOWLEDGE OF RELIGIOUS BELIEF AND PRACTICE	**Learning Experiences**

Special People/Key Figures and Leaders
* Is becoming aware of the importance of key figures and religious leaders eg. Guru Nanak, through hearing stories.

Language, Symbol and Communication
* Begins to understand the importance of artefacts as a focus of attention or as an aid an aid during prayer.
* Begins to use appropriate symbols for artefacts.

Learning Experiences
Darren has selected Sikh artefacts and printed the correct symbols from the computer programme to match the artefacts he has selected.

Statement of Achievement (including level)
Darren was involved in selecting symbols from the computer programme and he has completed the task he was set.
He participated in the acting of the story of Guru Nanak and the Needle.

Learning Experiences
Darren has joined in role-play in the home corner using Sikh cooking utensils and dressing up in Sikh clothes. He has made a card for Guru Nanak's birthday and listened to Indian music.

Statement of Achievement
Darren was actively involved in the celebration of Guru Nanak's birthday and he chose some symbols to express how he felt joining in with other pupils.

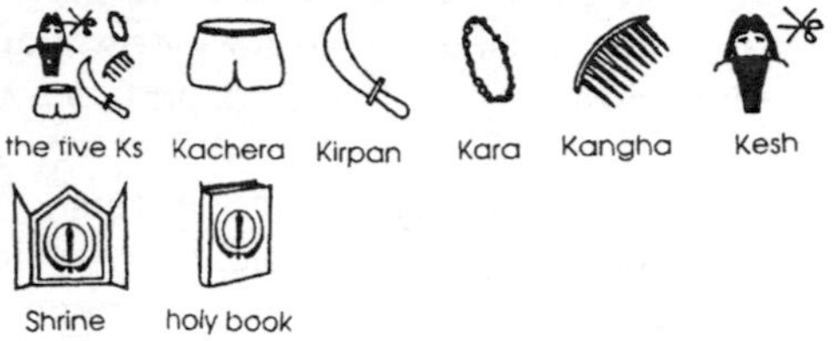

the five Ks   Kachera   Kirpan   Kara   Kangha   Kesh

Shrine   holy book

Figure 13.5 Pupil Record

For children with complex learning needs who may be at the extreme margins of the continuum of SEN, teachers will need to provide experiences that invite individual pupils to respond, for example, through:

- expressing emotions;
- developing self-awareness;
- responding to different environments.

Teachers will need to show how pupils have demonstrated their statements of achievement. In many cases, this will be supported by the level descriptors that describe pupils' involvement in the learning experiences provided. For example, the achievement of a pupil at the Foundation Stage for religious education within the study unit 'The world around', might be recorded as: 'Responds to the natural world', with the comment 'Has shown an awareness of the beauty and shape of a flower as she explored the trumpet of the daffodil with her fingers.'

Foundation for religious education: statements of achievement

Set out below are lists of possible statements of achievement that might be applicable for pupils at the foundation level in each of the nine study units listed for religious

education.
- Human experience:
  - A is beginning to develop an awareness of self;
  - A is beginning to develop an awareness of other people;
  - A is beginning to develop an awareness of belonging to a group;
  - A is beginning to develop self-control;
  - A hears a range of stories about human experience themes.

- The world around:
  - B experiences the natural world;
  - B responds to the natural world;
  - B responds to different environments;
  - B experiences situations that may evoke a sense of awe and wonderment – e.g. raindrops rolling down a window pane, watching baby chicks hatch, feeling the wind blow on face and through hair.

- Special people/key figures and leaders:
  - C recognises special people in own family;
  - C recognises familiar people in school environment;
  - C recognises familiar people in the local community.

- Special books/sacred writings:
  - D enjoys the tactile qualities of a book;
  - D shares a storybook with an adult;
  - D listens to a favourite story about everyday experiences;
  - D recognises favourite stories/books;
  - D begins to show an awareness of books that are special to other people.

- Special buildings/places of worship:
  - E responds to the atmosphere in different environments within school;
  - E recognises familiar environments;
  - E experiences a variety of different religious buildings in the local community.

- Festivals and celebrations:
  - F experiences sights, colours, smells, tastes, sounds associated with celebrations at home and at school;
  - F encounters a variety of religious celebrations.

- Special times/rites of passage:
  - G shares photographs of special occasions in own life with an adult;
  - G responds to a milestone or special occasion celebrated in own life.

- Special journeys/pilgrimage:
  - H responds to own experience of journeys and travelling;
  - H participates in a special journey.

- Language, symbol and communication:
  - J experiences signs and symbols in everyday life;
  - J begins to show an awareness of symbols in everyday life;
  - J recognises some symbols associated with religious festivals and celebrations.

End of Key Stage 1: statements of achievement

Set out next are lists of possible statements of achievement that might be applicable for pupils at the end of Key Stage 1 in each of the nine study units listed for religious education. Thus:

- Human experience:
  - K is developing an awareness of self in relation to others;
  - K is beginning to develop healthy self-esteem;
  - K is aware of the contribution that he/she makes as part of a group;
  - K demonstrates a degree of self-control;
  - K is beginning to demonstrate emotional responses to happenings in his/her own life, e.g. happiness/sadness;
  - K demonstrates an awareness of other people's emotions;
  - K listens to a range of stories with human-experience themes (e.g. families, friendship, loss or change) and is able to relate these to own experience.

- The world around:
  - L is able to identify different environments;
  - L expresses curiosity and interest at the world around;
  - L is beginning to be aware of how people care for living things and the local environment;
  - L has heard several creation stories.

- Special people/key figures and leaders:
  - M meets members of faith communities;
  - M is aware that some people follow a religious way of life;
  - M identifies the key figures from a Bible story and a story from one other sacred book;
  - M is aware some people believe God to be important.

- Special books/sacred writings:
  - N is aware that a story may be told for a specific purpose;
  - N is able to identify a story from the life or teaching of Jesus;
  - N is beginning to develop an awareness that holy books should be respected and handled carefully;
  - N can identify a Bible and knows the book comprises the Old and New Testaments.

- Special buildings/places of worship:
  - P understands there are special places where people go to worship;
  - P has been introduced to some of the key points in a place of worship, e.g. altar, pulpit, font; *quiblah, minbar,* ark; shrine; *langar;*
  - P begins to demonstrate an awareness of the distinctive atmosphere of a religious place;
  - P begins to demonstrate respectful behaviour when visiting a place of worship;
  - P has encountered a variety of sensory experiences in places of worship – e.g. heard music; touched different materials from which buildings are constructed; smelt incense; watched candles/sacred lights burning; looked at and touched fabrics and embroidery.

- Festivals and celebrations:
  - Q is beginning to recognise there are times that have special significance for some people;
  - Q helps to prepare and tastes a variety of foods associated with festivals from the religions studied;
  - Q begins to recognise the importance of preparing for a festival or celebration;
  - Q begins to show an awareness of the pattern of religious festivals for Christians and one other religion.

- Special times/rites of passage:
  - R begins to show an awareness of special events and milestones within his/her own life, e.g. staying away from home for a night; starting a school term; losing a tooth;
  - R begins to show an awareness of special events within family life, e.g. birth/initiation ceremonies; coming of age; weddings;
  - R is helped to make a pictorial chart of special times in his/her own life from birth to the present day.

- Special journeys/pilgrimage:
  - S experiences some different kinds of journeys and begins to recognise some of the reasons and motivations for these journeys;
  - S hears a first-hand account from someone who has been on a special journey or pilgrimage;
  - S brings to school a souvenir or memento of a special journey or a visit and explains to his/her peer group the significance of the item.

- Language, symbol and communication:
  - T is beginning to develop a sensitivity towards the special meaning conveyed by some religious symbols, e.g. dress; food;
  - T is able to recognise symbols representative of the religious group to which he/she belongs.

End of Key Stage 2: statements of achievement

Following the same pattern as above, set out here are lists of possible statements of achievement that might be applicable for pupils at the end of Key Stage 2 in each of the nine study units listed for religious education. Thus:

- Human experience:
  - U has increased knowledge of self;
  - U is able to reflect on his/her own sense of uniqueness;
  - U is able to make choices;
  - U demonstrates an empathy towards key characters in stories with human-experience themes;
  - U shows empathy towards the needs and feelings of people from a variety of faiths and cultures;
  - U shows sensitivity towards the life-styles of other people within the school family and the local community.

- The world around:
  - V demonstrates a sense of responsibility towards living things and the environment;
  - V participates in learning experiences that relate to environmental issues;
  - V is beginning to develop a concept of the interdependence of humankind and the created order;
  - V is beginning to recognise the commitment that religions have to the world in which we live;
  - V is beginning to appreciate the pain and beauty of the natural world;
  - V is beginning to reflect on existential questions of meaning and purpose.

- Special people/key figures and leaders:
  - W is becoming aware of the importance of key figures and religious leaders – e.g. Jesus, Moses, Muhammad, Guru Nanak and Siddartha Gautama – through hearing stories and through an increasing knowledge of religious belief and practice;
  - W meets and interacts with leaders from the Christian community and two other religions.

- Special books and sacred writings:
  - X can identify and name some holy books and recognise a story from the Christian Bible and one other story from another faith;
  - X shows awareness of the importance of religious books and sacred writings to some people;
  - X is able to identify and name holy books from the religions studied;
  - X is able to name some of the books of the Old and New Testaments in the Bible.

- Special buildings/places of worship:
  - Y has had opportunities to explore space within religious buildings;
  - Y has visited a variety of local places of worship from the Christian tradition and other religions studied;
  - Y demonstrates an ability for quiet reflection when visiting a place of worship;
  - Y is able to identify some of the key points in a place of worship and to sign/explain why they are of significance to worshippers.

- Festivals and celebrations:
  - Z is beginning to explore the significance of shared meals and special foods – e.g. Pesach; the Eucharist;
  - Z knows that Sunday is a special day for Christians and recognises the importance of a daily/weekly time of worship/reflection for some people;
  - Z is able to retell through words/pictures/signs/symbols the Easter and Christmas stories as recorded in the Gospel narratives, (see Figure 13.6);
  - Z is able to explain the significance of Easter for Christians.

- Special times/rites of passage:
  - AA has watched a video or experienced first-hand a baptism and wedding with the Christian tradition, and a wedding and an initiation ceremony from one other religion studied;
  - AA is able to talk about/sign/explain in symbols the importance of family photographs, visual reminders and verbal accounts as reminders of rites of passage;
  - AA begins to understand the importance of ritual and symbol in rites of passage

e.g. water in baptism; the exchange of rings during a marriage service; sacred thread; sharing special food; flowers and memorials at funerals.

- Special journeys/pilgrimage:
  - BB is able to identify several different reasons for making a journey;
  - BB begins to understand the significance of artefacts and mementoes as reminders of a special journey;
  - BB has visited a place of pilgrimage or a place that has special meaning for an individual or for a faith community – e.g. a cathedral, tomb or burial place;
  - BB is helped to find, in an atlas or on a globe, significant places of pilgrimage from religions studied.

- Language, symbol and communication:
  - CC has explored the symbol of the cross within Christianity and has encountered a variety of different crosses/crucifixes;
  - CC begins to understand the importance of artefacts as a focus of attention or as an aid during prayer;
  - CC is able to identify artefacts from own religious tradition (if appropriate) or the religions studied and is able to show how they might be used by a member of the faith tradition;
  - CC has experienced, either first-hand or through audiovisual aids, a variety of forms of worship from the religions studied;
  - CC begins to use appropriate language/signs/symbols for artefacts.

The QCA (DfEE/QCA 2000) lists several prerequisites for pupil success that are dependent on teachers being able to:

- set an appropriate classroom atmosphere;
- use subject knowledge confidently, employing questioning techniques effectively to elicit responses from pupils;
- be flexible in linking work in AT1 with work in AT2 as opportunities arise;
- be flexible in responding to pupils.

Example: scheme of work on Sikhism at Key Stage 2

Background

Guru Nanak was the founder of Sikhism. The name Guru means 'disciple'. Guru Nanak was born a Hindu, but he rejected the caste system and idolatry, and he taught that only one God should be worshipped. Guru Nanak is deeply admired by Sikhs as an example of piety and holiness; is regarded as a man who was chosen by God to reveal His message. The scheme of work suggested here centres on Guru Nanak's birthday and associated celebrations. See Figure 13.7).

Objectives

The objectives for our example scheme of work would be:

- to help pupils reflect on celebrations and occasions that occur annually;
- to develop an awareness of how religious beliefs and lifestyles are expressed through symbolism;
- to increase pupils' knowledge and experience of stories of key figures and leaders in religion.

Resources

The resources preferable to have to hand would be:

- a large, brightly coloured circular tablecloth;
- a collection of Sikh artefacts, including a framed picture of Guru Nanak and the five Ks;
- a Sikh garland used for decoration;
- divas or night-lights contained in brightly coloured holders;
- examples of symbols, badges and special clothes that are familiar to the pupils and representative of groups to which they belong (Figure 13.8 illustrates the artefacts to support Guru Nanak's Birthday).

Setting the scene

Invite several pupils to help put the tablecloth on the floor. Seat the group around the edge of the empty cloth. Have close to hand some examples of symbols and badges that are familiar to the pupils and a box of carefully wrapped Sikh artefacts.

The activity

Talk about the symbols, badges, clothing, etc. that belong to the pupils, emphasising their importance because they represent special places, groups, etc. Invite pupils to place their symbols on one-half of the cloth.

Introduce the five Ks by very carefully unwrapping them and explaining they are symbols that Sikh people use to show that they belong to the faith. Allow pupils to try on the *kara* and to feel the tactile quality of the wooden comb. Display the five Ks on the other half of the cloth and once again draw the attention of group members to their symbols.

Carefully unwrap the picture of Guru Nanak and talk about 'special' people and leaders within the pupils' experience. Explain that Guru Nanak is a special person for Sikh people and place the picture on the cloth close to the five Ks.

Ask how the pupils celebrate their birthdays. Encourage discussion about cakes and shared meals with families and friends.

Tell the Needle Story (see Brown 1995) and explain how Sikh people celebrate Guru Nanak's birthday. Invite a pupil to decorate the picture of Guru Nanak with the garland. Place a lighted diva on the cloth, emphasising how important candles and light are for festivals and celebrations.

At the end of the activity, pack the Sikh artefacts away carefully, reminding pupils of the importance of looking after 'special' objects.

Sensory learning experiences

Using the display described in the activities for Guru Nanak's birthday (Figure 13.9), pupils might be encouraged to explore Sikh artefacts:

- trace the shape of the *khanda* with your fingers;
- touch the coarse yak hair of the *chauri*;
- feel the tactile qualities of the wooden *kangha*;
- put the garland over your head and look at your image in a mirror;
- wear the *kara*; feel the coolness of the steel and its weight on your wrist;
- smell warm *karah parshad*;
- smell the candle wax of the diva;
- watch the curving diva flame;
- taste warm *karah parshad*;
- look at the rich embroidery on the *romalla* cover;
- feel the fringes of the *romalla* cover against your face.

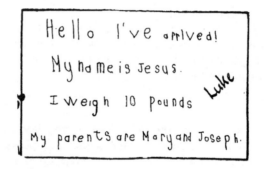

Figure 13.6 The Christmas Story

SIKHISM

KNOWLEDGE AND UNDERSTANDING OF SIKHISM (including belief and practice)

There is one God who is Creator.
All humans are equal before God.
Ceremonies: e.g naming, marriage, turban-tying.
Celebrations: e.g birthdays of Guru Nanak, Guru Gobind Singh; Baisakhi.
The lives of the Gurus.
The Guru Granth Sahib – its care in the Gurdwara.
Worship – led by the Granthi. Consists of: kirtan; ardas; langar.

LEARNING EXPERIENCES

Pupils could:
Hear Sikhs talking about themselves and their faith.
Listen to stories about Guru Nanak and other Gurus.
Observe a Sikh tying his turban.
Find out about the birthday of Guru Nanak and how it is celebrated.
Look at pictures or a video of the Golden Temple and find out where Amritsar is on a map.
Listen to the story of Baisakhi.
Share ideas about the importance of names and look up their own names in a dictionary of first names
Visit a Gurdwara and identify expressions of Sikh belief and practice.
Make a poster explaining the 5 Ks
Design their own symbol(s) to express something about themselves.

RELIGIOUS PERSPECTIVES ON HUMAN EXPERIENCE

Pupils should be encouraged to think about:
Times when it is easy to share and times when it is difficult.
Their own families and the activities which they enjoy.
Signs of belonging, e.g. uniforms, badges, symbols.
Ways in which people demonstrate respect, and how it feels to be respected.
Feelings which are evoked when visiting a place of worship.
The importance of community meals – meals which are special.
Books which are special to them.

SYMBOLS

The 5 Ks: kachera; kangha; kara; kesh; kirpan.
Karah parshad.
Khanda.
Nishan Sahib.

Figure 13.7 Sikhism

Guru Nanak's Birthday

1. Picture of Guru Nanak
2. Romalla cover
3. Chauri
4. Kachera
5. Kara
6. Kangha
7. Kirpan
8. Diva
9. Khanda

Figure 13.8 Guru Nanak's Birthday: supporting artefacts

GURU NANAK'S BIRTHDAY

KNOWLEDGE AND UNDERSTANDING OF SIKHISM (including belief and practice)

There is one God who is Creator.
Equality of humankind before God.
Truth revealed by the Gurus and the Guru Granth Sahib.
The community as a family.
The Gurdwara as a place of worship and a place for sharing.
Stories of the lives of the Gurus.
Worship in the Gurdwara – led by Granthi. Consists of: kirtan; ardas; langar.

LEARNING EXPERIENCES

Pupils could:
Dress dolls in 5 Ks.
Role play in home corner, using Sikh cooking utensils and dressing up in Sikh clothes.
Cook and taste karah parshad and Indian foods.
Experience different ways of celebrating birthdays.
Make cards for Guru Nanak's birthday.
Experience Indian music.
Visit a Gurdwara.
Make a class book about the life of Guru Nanak.
Bring to school/talk about things which are special to them.
Listen to stories about Guru Nanak.
Act out a story from the life of Guru Nanak.

RELIGIOUS PERSPECTIVES ON HUMAN EXPERIENCE

Pupils should be encouraged to think about:
How and why we share with each other.
How and why visitors are welcome to home and to school.
The importance of family life.
 Books which are special to us.
 People who are special to us.
  How we show concern for each other.
  Symbols in everyday life.
   Special clothes.
   Special ceremonies for special occasions.
   When and why people pray.

SYMBOLS

 Sikh appearance – the 5 Ks: kachera; kangha; kara; kesh; kirpan.
 Karah parshad.
 Khanda.
Nishan Sahib.

Figure 13.9 Planning for Guru Nanak's Birthday

Accreditation of religious education at Key Stage 4

The National Qualification Framework provides for entry-level qualifications to accredit the achievement of students whose attainment is below that of GCSE. Entry-level qualifications in religious education are available that will award grades of pass, merit and distinction equivalent to National Curriculum Levels 1, 2 and 3. The qualifications allow appropriate forms of assessment and provide entry paths to the Framework itself by offering progression to GCSEs and GNVQs.

Concluding remarks

It is a sobering fact that a child's view of what happens in the classroom is sometimes quite different from that of the teacher. As a profession, teachers often think that they are providing learning opportunities which are within the grasp of children, yet their reactions reveal that sometimes this is not so. However we choose to teach religious education, we should set ourselves high standards in order that we provide signposts to children's learning that will help them to reach milestones along the way.

References

Brown, E. (1995) 'Circles of growth'. *PMLD-Link*, 22.

Brown, E. (1996) *Religious Education for All.* London: David Fulton Publishers.

DFE (1994) *Code of Practice on the Identification and Assessment of Special Educational Needs.* London: DFE/Welsh Office.

DfEE/QCA (2000) *Religious Education: A scheme of work for Key Stages 1–2.* London: DfEE/QCA.

DfEE/QCA (2001) *Planning, Teaching and Assessing the Curriculum for Pupils with Learning Difficulties: Religious Education.* London: DfEE/QCA.

Dowell, J. and Nutt, M. (1995) 'An approach to Religious Education at Piper Hill School', *PMLD-Link* 22.

Goss, P. (1995) 'Opening up: the inner lives of individuals with PMLD', *PMLD-Link*, 22.

Longhorn, F. (1993) *Religious Education for Very Special Children.* Isle of Man: ORCA Publications.

NCC (1993) *Spiritual and Moral Development: A discussion document.* London: National Curriculum Council.

QCA (2000) *Supplementary Materials for Religious Education (Consultation)*, London: QCA.

QCA/DfEE (2000) *Religious Education: Teacher's Guide.* London: QCA/DfEE.

SCAA (1994) *Model Syllabuses for Religious Education.* London: SCAA.

Further reading

Brown, E. (1993) *Mixed Blessings: The special child in your school.* London: The National Society (Church of England) for Promoting Religious Education.

Brown, E. (1996) *Making R.E. Special in Gloucestershire.* Gloucester: Gloucestershire County Council/Westminster College.

Brown, E. (1998a) *Signposts and Milestones: Implementing the Agreed Syllabus in special schools.* Worcester: Westminster College/Worcestershire County Council.

Brown, E. (1998b) 'Things of the spirit: spiritual, moral, social and cultural education', *Support for Learning* 13(4).

Brown, E. (1999) *Loss, Change and Grief: An educational perspective.* London: David Fulton Publishers.

Brown, E. and Bigger, S. (1999) *Spiritual, Moral, Social and Cultural Education: Exploring values in the curriculum.* London: David Fulton Publishers.

Chapter 14

PSHE and Citizenship

Hazel Lawson and Ann Fergusson

Introduction

It is exciting to be writing a new chapter in this book to celebrate the addition of personal social and health education (PSHE) and citizenship to the National Curriculum framework for all schools. Many educators, but especially those involved in the education of children and young people with learning difficulties, will rightly protest that PSHE, or personal and social development, or personal and social education, has always been a crucial component of the curriculum they offer. It now has a high profile.

PSHE and citizenship are not new subject areas – Marland (1995) and Watkins (1995) each provide a detailed historical perspective. In 1990 the National Curriculum Council issued guidance for the whole curriculum (NCC 1990a), which included cross-curricular dimensions, skills and themes that together were intended to make 'a major contribution to personal and social education' (p. 2). *Health Education* (NCC 1990b) and *Education for Citizenship* (NCC 1990c) were two of the five cross-curricular themes, and the guidance concerned the place of these themes within the whole curriculum in addition to containing suggested knowledge, skills and understanding. However, the introduction of National Curriculum core and foundation subjects and the resulting time commitment to putting the programmes of study into practice meant that these cross-curricular themes, frequently viewed as a 'bolt-on afterthought' (Best 1999), were given a low priority by many schools.

The inclusion of PSHE and citizenship in the revised National Curriculum (DfEE/QCA 1999a, 1999b) has been influenced and developed by many groups and committees. The National Advisory Group on Citizenship, for example, produced *Education for Citizenship and the Teaching of Democracy in Schools* in September 1998 (QCA 1998) and the National Advisory Group on PSHE produced *Preparing Young People for Adult Life* in May 1999 (DfEE 1999a). Other groups met – for example, on sustainable development, careers education, the work-related curriculum and environmental education. Lees and Plant (2000) provide a comprehensive relationship map that illustrates the connections between the various contributing areas and the related guidance and publications.

It is easy to be cynical about the presence of PSHE and, particularly, citizenship within the National Curriculum. There is no escaping a political context with public and governmental concern for crime rates, truancy rates, disaffection among young people, exclusion from school and society, drug abuse, teenage pregnancy rates, voting patterns among young people, and equal opportunities. The danger lies in assigning responsibility for this wide array of societal issues: education, particularly through PSHE and citizenship, might aim to produce responsible active citizens but the burden cannot be solely attributed to teachers and schools.

Alternatively, we welcome the introduction of this curriculum area in an 'official' sense into schools, validating and extending the work on PSHE that has been developed and carried out over many years. PSHE has always been a 'core' curriculum area for pupils with learning difficulties and it now has a raised status for all pupils. Laterly, the QCA has produced specific guidance on PSHE and Citizenship for teachers of pupils with learning difficulties which the authors of this chapter were involved in preparing (QCA 2001). PSHE has also recently been recognised as a core area in special schools by OFSTED. The OFSTED *Handbook for Inspecting Special Schools and Pupil Referral Units* (OFSTED 1999) emphasises PSHE along with English and mathematics as priority areas in which to judge achievement of pupils and the quality of teaching. For example, in the area of standards the following instructions are given to inspectors (pp. 23 and 35, our italics):

> In judging achievement ... you must give priority to English, mathematics, and *personal, social and health education* and other academic targets set at annual reviews or in individual education plans (IEPs).

> The *personal development* of pupils should be a high priority in special schools and Pupil Referral Units. How well the pupils develop will reflect the extent to which they are independent and autonomous; feel personally fulfilled; achieve well and respond with optimism to challenges; develop social skills; and relate appropriately to peers and adults.

In the area of quality of provision, the instruction to inspectors is (OFSTED 1999, p. 44, our italics):

> You should pay attention to how the *skills* of communication, numeracy, *personal, social and health education* are taught ...

In this chapter we attempt to unravel some of the issues involved in teaching PSHE and citizenship to pupils with learning difficulties. We begin by looking at PSHE as a subject within the wider context of personal and social development. We offer interpretations of what PSHE and citizenship in the revised National Curriculum framework might mean for pupils with learning difficulties, and we suggest some approaches and strategies for translation into classroom practice.

What's in a name?

The terms 'personal social and health education', 'personal and social skills' and 'personal and social development' are not necessarily synonymous (Fletcher and Gordon 1994) although they are clearly closely related and interlinked. Figure 14.1 indicates a possible relationship between them. The broken lines indicate the changing and permeable nature of the divisions.

Personal and social development

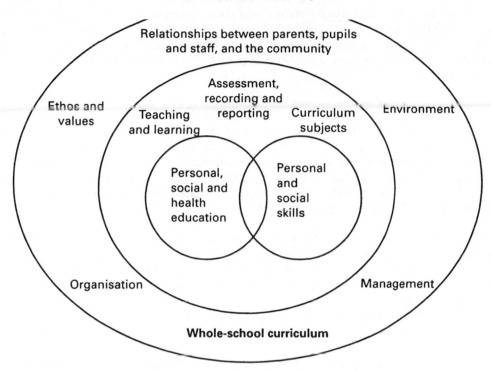

Figure 14.1 The relationship between personal social and health education, personal and social skills, and personal and social development

Personal social and health education

PSHE refers, here, to the curriculum subject. It is sometimes known more generically as personal and social education (PSE) or, reflecting a slightly different emphasis, personal social and moral education (PSME). It consists of skills, knowledge, attitudes and values, as shown in Table 14.1 (adapted from Lees and Plant (2000)).

Table 14.1 Knowledge and attitudes and values

Skills (can do)	**Knowledge** (be aware of, know)	**Attitudes and values** (think about, believe, value)
e.g. ● make choices ● give permission ● follow safety rules ● take turns	e.g. ● be aware of familiar people ● know their likes and dislikes ● understand the concept of growing from young to old	e.g. ● self-respect ● respect for others ● sensitivity to the environment

While being identified as a subject, PSHE includes 'all aspects of a school's planned provision to promote their pupils' personal and social development, including health and well-being' (DfEE 1999a, p. 2), and PSHE thus extends into other subjects and other aspects of school life. A keyword here is *planned* – referring to planned learning experiences and opportunities that take place in the classroom and in other areas of school experience.

Personal and social skills

Personal and social skills are cross-curricular and in common with other cross-curricular skills – for example, communication skills – they exist as part of a complex and sophisticated picture. Personal and social skills interrelate with the subject of PSHE and citizenship as illustrated in Figure 14.1, and part of PSHE and citizenship is about the development of a range of skills. They can also be planned for, promoted and developed across and within the whole curriculum. For example:

- *across the whole curriculum* – the ability of pupils to manage their own behaviour and emotions, reflect on personal experience, express their own views, make choices and decisions, work with others, and improve their own learning and performance (the latter two being identified as key skills in the revised National Curriculum documentation);
- *through PSHE and citizenship in particular* – personal care skills;
- *as discrete skill areas* – functional daily-living skills, leisure and recreation skills.

For pupils with learning difficulties, specific personal and social skills frequently feature in targets for individual education plans. This is partly because of their high priority for many pupils and also, in showing what pupils can *do* (rather than know, understand, believe or value), they are often observable, measurable and assessable and may be broken down into smaller steps for teaching and learning. However, many elements of personal and social skills cannot be reduced to an atomised concept (Sedgwick 1994). For example, the skill of cooking a meal can be broken down into its constituent tasks (perhaps through task analysis), but the skill of 'making a friend' becomes meaningless when analysed in this way.

Personal and social development

Personal and social development relates to *all* aspects of school life and should permeate all elements of the work of schools (Sebba *et al.* 1993). It thus requires a *whole-school approach* (Lees and Plant 2000) involving, for example, the management and organisation of the school; the physical environment; teaching and learning approaches; and relationships between staff, parents, pupils and the community. The ethos and culture of a school as a whole and the values that a school promotes have a crucial influence on the personal and social development of its pupils.

The values expounded in the 'Statement of Values by the National Forum for Values in Education and the Community', published in the National Curriculum handbooks (DfEE/QCA 1999a, 1999b) suggest commonly agreed values as a basis for teaching and a school's ethos. These values, concerned with the self, relationships, society and the environment, are closely related to many areas within PSHE and citizenship. Watkins (1995, p. 126) suggests that personal and social development is an 'aspect of learning to which every occasion in school has a contribution to make (albeit sometimes unplanned)'. Thus, drawing from Sedgwick (1994), personal and social development occurs, for example, when a pupil:

- helps another pupil who has fallen over;
- vocalises in response to another pupil tickling them;
- cooperates with others in a painting session;
- listens to his/her teacher reading;
- co-actively takes part in rolling over, with the support of a familiar adult.

This also occurs, for example, when a teacher:

- praises a pupil or group of pupils;
- asks a pupil if he/she wants more lunch and then waits for the pupil to respond;
- helps a pupil to face up to some difficulty;
- stands back and allows a pupil to complete a task unaided;
- physically prompts a pupil to take part in a turn-taking game during music.

Many of the above examples are unplanned, some are aspects of teaching approaches and relationships with pupils, and yet others may be planned experiences as part of the school curriculum.

Two broad aims for a school's curriculum are identified in the National Curriculum handbooks (DfEE/QCA 1999a, 1999b):

1. The school curriculum should aim to provide opportunities for all pupils to learn and achieve.
2. The school curriculum should aim to promote pupils' spiritual, moral, social and cultural development and prepare all pupils for the opportunities, responsibilities and experiences of life.

Personal and social development is, then, at the heart of the school curriculum and requires a *whole-curriculum approach* (Lees and Plant 2000) in that planned opportunities for personal and social development should be identified across the curriculum in addition to designated time for PSHE. These opportunities may be in other curriculum subjects and in additional aspects of the whole curriculum – for example, assemblies, sports activities, the literacy hour, work experience, school productions, residential trips, and wider community links. Personal and social development can also be located within the wide range of curriculum processes – for example, curriculum policy and guidelines; curriculum planning in long-term plans, schemes of work, individual education plans and short-term plans; delivery of the curriculum in teaching approaches and learning strategies; observation, recording and assessment; accreditation; and monitoring and evaluation.

At each stage of these processes the personal and social development of pupils is important, can be affected and should be considered. This might include, for example, matching stated values and aims with practice; considering ways of enhancing the development of confidence and self-esteem in pupils; or increasing pupil involvement, autonomy and empowerment through curriculum processes. Jelly *et al.* (2000) provide a useful list of questions about meaningful pupil involvement for pupils with special educational needs.

The academic and pastoral divide

The above discussion, with reference to Figure 14.1, serves to highlight a tension that has arisen since the introduction of the National Curriculum. This has been referred to as 'the academic and pastoral divide' (Best 1999) and pertains to a conflict between curriculum control, accountability and assessment on the one hand and pastoral aspects and concerns on the other.

The suggestion is that the PSHE curriculum, as other curriculum areas, has often been objectives-led, content-orientated and focused on 'facts' and discrete sub-areas (for example, sex education and drug education), and that this is at odds with a less formal and broader concept concerned with the affective (Murray 1998). Staff working with pupils with learning difficulties have, perhaps, been less caught up in such tensions because, for these pupils, the focus on the pastoral, the personal and the social has remained alongside an increasing emphasis on a subject-based curriculum. Nevertheless, the introduction of PSHE within the revised National Curriculum, and initiatives such as the National Healthy Schools Scheme (DfEE 1999b), may promote a focus on the wider personal and social needs and development of all pupils within such a content-led structure.

The framework for PSHE and citizenship in the National Curriculum

The framework for PSHE and citizenship in the National Curriculum is designed to build on the early-learning goals in the Foundation Stage (QCA 2000d) for personal, social and emotional development. The framework has developed from a broad consensus (DfEE 1999a, p. 2) that 'children and young people need the self-awareness, positive self-esteem and confidence to:

- stay as healthy as possible;
- keep themselves and others safe;
- have worthwhile and fulfilling relationships;
- respect the differences between people;
- develop independence and responsibility;
- play an active role as members of a democratic society;
- make the most of their own, and others' abilities.

There are three parts to the National Curriculum framework for PSHE and citizenship: PSHE and citizenship for Key Stages 1 and 2 (DfEE/QCA 1999a, pp. 136–41); PSHE for Key Stages 3 and 4 (DfEE/QCA 1999b, pp 188–94); citizenship for Key Stages 3 and 4, which is statutory from September 2002 (DfEE/QCA 1999b, and also available as a separate subject booklet).

PSHE and citizenship at Key Stages 1 and 2 and PSHE at Key Stages 3 and 4 are non-statutory. However, elements of them are statutory in the context of other subjects. For example, there are elements of PSHE in the science programmes of study relating to health, drugs and sexual development; there are aspects of citizenship in history, geography and RE; PE covers some aspects of health education; sex and relationships education (DfEE 2000) and is compulsory for secondary-age pupils; and careers education is compulsory for pupils in Years 9, 10 and 11. PSHE and citizenship can help in relating all these by providing a context in which to create a cohesive picture.

The framework consists of four strands:

- *personal development* – developing confidence and responsibility and making the most of their abilities;
- *active citizens* – preparing to play an active role as citizens, which at Key Stages 3 and 4 becomes a separate programme of study for citizenship;
- *health and safety* – developing a healthy, safer life-style;
- *relationships* – developing good relationships and respecting differences between people.

Knowledge, skills and understanding of PSHE are taught through a *breadth of opportunities*, where pupils have opportunities to:

- take and share responsibility;
- feel positive about themselves;
- participate and take part in discussions;
- make real choices and decisions;
- meet and talk and work with people;
- develop relationships through work and play;
- consider social and moral dilemmas;
- ask for help/find information and advice/provide advice;
- prepare for change.

Citizenship at Key Stages 3 and 4

At Key Stages 3 and 4, citizenship is given a more specific focus so as to enable pupils to develop a more informed and intentionally active part in life both in and beyond school. The programmes of study for citizenship at Key Stages 3 and 4 consist of three strands:

1. *Knowledge and understanding about becoming an informed citizen*, which includes content about legal and human rights and responsibilities, diversity of identities, the nature of government, the importance of democratic processes, the role of the media, conflict resolution, and challenges of global interdependence and responsibility.
2. *Developing skills of enquiry and communication*, which involves thinking about topical issues, problems and events, expressing and justifying opinions, and contributing to discussions and debates.
3. *Developing skills of participation and responsible action*, which is concerned with the consideration of the experiences of others, taking part responsibly in activities, and reflecting on the process of participation.

Guidance documents (QCA 2000a, 2000b, 2000c, 2001) provide ideas and suggestions for implementing the framework and for teaching, assessing and recording. Citizenship schemes of work are to be published in 2001 for all of Key Stages 1–4.

New ground?

In the boxes below, the elements of a PSHE curriculum in a school for pupils with severe learning difficulties (across the key stages) have been mapped against the new framework strands in order to identify parts of the curriculum that may be new (in bold type) or, alternatively, the parts of this curriculum that may be missing from the new framework. The PSHE curriculum areas in a school for pupils with severe learning difficulties (prior to the PSHE and citizenship framework) were:

- self-awareness, self-esteem and self-advocacy;
- personal care and personal skills;
- social skills (interpersonal skills and citizenship);
- community skills and daily living skills;
- health education (including personal safety and drug education);
- sex education;
- play, leisure and recreation.

Developing confidence and responsibility and making the most of abilities

From curriculum area self-awareness, self-esteem and self-advocacy:

- personal identity, positive self-image, self-respect;
- learning about themselves, appearance, abilities, strengths and weaknesses, likes and dislikes, own feelings, personal qualities;
- assertiveness and communicating own needs, rights, feelings and opinions; sharing opinions;
- determining own values within a moral framework (fair and unfair, right and wrong);
- learning to cope with loss and change and bereavement;
- developing processes of personal decision-making, personal choice, and self-determination;
- simple goals.

From careers education:

- careers choices.

New?   risk-taking, autonomy, facing new challenges;
managing praise and criticism;
influences, pressures and sources of help;
managing personal money, budgeting.

Preparing to play an active role as citizens (KS1 and 2) and in citizenship (KS3 and 4)

From curriculum area self-awareness, self-esteem and self-advocacy:

- making choices and decisions.

From social skills:

- learning about the need for rules and the responsibilities inherent in following those rules;

- recognising needs of others;
- own family, cultural setting, school;
- voting.

New? looking after the local environment, environmental sustainability; use of money, finite resources, the economy; legal and human rights, diversity; democracy, government, law; the media, topical, social, political, cultural and moral issues; participation, negotiation, decision-making; interdependence.

Developing a healthy, safer life-style

From personal care and skills:

- personal hygiene.

From health education:

- diet and healthy eating, exercise, sleep, basic first aid, health and safety;
- **personal safety**: awareness of danger; road safety; using equipment safely; respect for and ownership of body; dealing with different situations – e.g. being approached by stranger; peer pressure, saying 'no'; being aware of boundaries and appropriate behaviour; in connection with abuse and exploitation, who to approach when in need of help;
- **drug education:** drugs as medicines, safety rules and procedures when using medicines, people involved;
- with medicines, tobacco and alcohol, illegal drugs, the law, coping with peer influence, decision-making;
- assertiveness, getting help.

From sex education:

- body parts, male/female difference, physical/emotional changes with growth and puberty, menstruation;
- masturbation, relationships and friendships, love and sexual attraction, sexual intercourse and sexual relationships, contraception;
- babies: pregnancy, birth, child development, responsibilities of parenthood;
- sexual health and hygiene, sexually transmitted diseases, HIV and AIDS.

New? (nothing identified)

Developing good relationships and respecting the differences between people

---

From social skills:

- interpersonal skills, turn-taking, sharing, learning to wait, working with others – teams, partners, groups;
- cooperation, consideration, awareness of others, encouraging respect and sensitivity towards others, play;
- respecting differences and similarities between people, caring for others, bullying;
- 'appropriate' behaviour at different times, codes of behaviour (lunchtimes, fire drills, sporting activities, assembly, parties, queueing);
- interpersonal skills as a basis for developing positive relationships with others, importance of communication, humour, appropriate behaviour;
- different types of relationships – e.g. family, friends, staff, work colleagues, sexual. What do they mean? What do they involve? What social behaviour is appropriate in different relationships? What happens if relationships break down?

New?   awareness of stereotypes, racism, prejudice;

a range of life-styles;

support organisations and asking for help;

parenting.

It is apparent above that much of this PSHE curriculum that has been developed for pupils with severe learning difficulties is accommodated within the National Curriculum framework. Indeed, it is positive to note that the area of health and safety is all encompassed in this PSHE curriculum. Some areas that are perhaps new to this curriculum are identified, and many of these offer challenging opportunities for pupils with learning difficulties – for example, learning about prejudice, democracy, or influences and pressures on themselves. Many of these 'new' areas are within the strands of citizenship, particularly concerning greater participation in decision-making at various levels, as well as knowledge and understanding about the law, democracy and the government – the political literacy element of citizenship.

Retaining the important

Not included within the new framework are some aspects of personal and social development that are significant for pupils with learning difficulties:

- *personal care and personal skills*, such as toileting, privacy, dignity, modesty, dressing, personal appearance, eating/drinking, codes of behaviour at mealtimes, identifying and being responsible for one's own belongings;
- *skills for life/daily-living skills/community skills*, such as routes to local shops, social sight vocabulary, codes of behaviour in a range of settings outside school, use of amenities (e.g. cafés, parks, leisure centres, playgrounds, libraries, public toilets), use of public transport, shopping, kitchen and domestic skills, use of telephone (though use of money and budgeting is covered);

- *play, leisure and recreation skills*, such as hobbies, play, self-amusement/occupation, relaxation, making choices, use of indoor recreational activities, use of local community recreational amenities.

Although these elements may not be appropriate or necessary for mainstream pupils, who may learn such skills incidentally, it is crucial that these elements are retained for pupils with learning difficulties. They may be viewed as additions and extensions to the PSHE and citizenship framework, or as additional personal and social skills within the whole curriculum, with a clear overlap and relationship with particular elements of the PSHE curriculum (for example, personal care within the health and safety strand).

Citizenship

Three elements are identified that run through all education for citizenship (QCA 2000c, p. 4):

1. *social and moral responsibility* – pupils learning from the very beginning self-confidence and socially and morally responsible behaviour, both in and beyond the classroom, towards those in authority and towards each other;
2. *community involvement* – pupils learning how to become helpfully involved in the life and concerns of their neighbourhood and communities, including learning through community involvement and service;
3. *political literacy* – pupils learning about the institutions, issues, problems and practices of our democracy and how to make themselves effective in public life – locally, regionally and nationally – through skills and values as well as knowledge.

The first two of these, namely social and moral responsibility and community involvement, have often formed an implicit, if not explicit, part of the curriculum for pupils with learning difficulties, particularly at later key stages. Indeed, socially and morally responsible behaviour may have been overemphasised! The third element of political literacy, as noted above, contains newer and more challenging concepts, and it gains more emphasis at Key Stages 3 and 4.

The key concepts identified within education for citizenship (QCA 2000c, p. 20) are:

- democracy and autocracy;
- cooperation and conflict;
- equality and diversity;
- fairness, justice, the rule of law and human rights;
- freedom and order;
- individual and community;
- power and authority;
- rights and responsibilities.

These concepts are complex and apparently abstract for all pupils, and for pupils with learning difficulties require much interpretation to enable meaningful experiences and development for pupils.

Approaches to teaching and learning

For many pupils, particularly pupils with learning difficulties, it is probably unhelpful to separate PSHE and citizenship. Two of the three elements of citizenship listed at the end of the previous section, namely social and moral responsibility and community involvement, relate closely to PSHE, although they require a different emphasis in the context of citizenship. The third element of citizenship, political literacy, however, is quite distinct from PSHE content and concerns. It may therefore require separate coverage, where applicable and relevant, at Key Stages 3 and 4.

PSHE and citizenship can be planned for a variety of groupings: individual activity, group activity and whole-school activities. QCA guidance (QCA 2000a, 2000b, 2000c, 2001) suggests that a variety of forms of provision should be considered and a combination used. These are explored and extended below, with reference to pupils with learning difficulties.

Thus, PSHE and citizenship may be taught through:

- discrete curriculum time;
- other subjects/curriculum areas;
- cross-curricular topics or modules;
- regular routines;
- PSHE and citizenship activities and school events;
- pastoral care and guidance;
- incidental occasions – 'We're doing it all the time'.

An advantage of *discrete curriculum time* is that elements of PSHE and citizenship are easily identifiable. Discrete curriculum time may be necessary and appropriate for some aspects of the PSHE and citizenship curriculum – for example, sex and relationships education and political literacy – but is less likely in the early key stages. Discrete provision may also be necessary and appropriate for some pupils – for example, nurture groups (Bennathan and Boxall 1996) or 'quiet places' (Spalding 2000) for pupils with additional emotional difficulties.

It is unlikely that the whole of the PSHE and citizenship curriculum can or should be delivered through *other subjects/curriculum areas*. For pupils with learning difficulties where PSHE is, specifically, a core area, organisation in this way may weaken the emphasis and impact. However, as noted above, personal and social development needs to be promoted across the curriculum, and planned opportunities for PSHE and citizenship can be provided in other subjects. This may mean covering and enhancing particular elements in a specific subject – for example, religious beliefs and values in RE, moral or social stories in English, health education in science, cultural diversity in music, or environmental issues in geography. It also involves elements that should occur in all subjects – for example, reflection at the end of sessions, and opportunities to make choices or decisions.

Some of PSHE and citizenship is likely to be organised in *cross-curricular topics or modules* in early key stages – for example, projects based on the themes of 'Ourselves' or 'People who help us'. This may also be a useful approach at later key stages, where elements of PSHE and citizenship are integrated with other subject areas – for example, topics or modules focused on 'current affairs' or 'health and fitness'.

Regular routines may include, for example, personal-care routines, morning routines, lunch times, break times, or circle time. They represent an invaluable way of integrating

PSHE and promoting personal and social development in everyday school life. However, it is not sufficient to just be 'aware' that this happens; it needs to be specifically identified and planned for.

Again, it is unlikely that all of the PSHE and citizenship curriculum could be covered by *PSHE and citizenship activities and school events*. However, additional activities (for example, residential experiences, special days, charity fund-raising, mini-enterprise schemes, and assemblies) provide meaningful, interesting and relevant ways of extending the range of contexts, and for applying the curriculum to life beyond school.

Pastoral care and guidance may frequently be provided on an individual basis – for example, tutorial time. These occasions present opportunities for individuals to focus and reflect on their personal circumstances and personal development, which is an important part of relating the PSHE and citizenship curriculum to their own lives.

Many experiences that promote personal and social development will, of course, be *incidental occasions* and unplanned. For example: a playground incident leads to a discussion about fairness; the death of a pupil's pet requires sharing and consideration; and one pupil's expression of anxiety when trying a new standing frame leads to a classmate trying to comfort her and then develops into a class exploration of what worries and reassures pupils. To some extent, through the ethos of the school, the teaching approaches and attitudes adopted by the staff, the relationships between staff and pupils, and the dignity and respect afforded to the pupils, staff are promoting PSHE all the time and it is important to recognise that – PSHE and personal and social development do not only occur in the sex education lessons on Wednesday afternoon in the spring term in Year 8, nor is it only the PSHE coordinator who 'teaches' PSHE. Teaching and learning in all subjects is concerned with personal and social development, and it is necessary for all staff in all situations to be concerned with the personal and social development of pupils. This amounts to more than just ensuring coverage of all areas of the PSHE and citizenship curriculum.

An emphasis on the integration between subject-focused learning and cross-curricular elements, including key skills and personal and social development, is reinforced (as Byers, 1999, predicts) by the framework for PSHE and citizenship. This is reiterated in the curriculum guidelines for pupils with learning difficulties (QCA 2001).

Assessment

The QCA citizenship and PSHE update as at September 2000 (QCA 2000e) states:

> At key stages 1 and 2, there will be no requirement for end of key stage assessment. However, it is expected that schools will keep records of each child's progress and report this to parents.
> ...
> At key stage 3, there will be a requirement for end of key stage assessment in citizenship. This will take effect following the introduction of citizenship as a national curriculum subject in September 2002. ...
> As with other national curriculum subjects there will be no statutory arrangements for assessment and reporting at key stage 4.

It is sometimes suggested that it is invidious to assess PSHE because a large degree of it is bound up with values and it is morally wrong to assess the worth of a person. We agree entirely. However, there are elements of PSHE and citizenship – particularly those concerned with knowledge and skills, rather than values and attitude – that it is possible and worthwhile to assess. For example, knowledge on health issues, ability to make and communicate choices, strategies used in decision-making, or the ability to work with others are all areas where progress can be reviewed.

It is nevertheless very important, as Munby (1995) and Byers (1998) both purport, that the approach to, and methods of, assessment are themselves consistent with promoting personal and social development – for example, that pupils are involved in the assessment procedures and that positive achievements are highlighted (see Lawson 1998).

Creating opportunities for meaningful experiences

A very uncomplicated perspective of PSHE and citizenship may be a useful standpoint when considering strategies for delivery. If much of PSHE is viewed as having a very personal focus concerned with the development and understanding of the self (physically, emotionally, socially and sexually), citizenship can be perceived as an extension of this, as a means of looking beyond the self to the interdependence of individuals and the effect they as individuals have on the world (as a community and as an environment).

When developing the means by which to address and deliver the many aspects of PSHE and citizenship, there is much to take from strategies that are considered 'good practice' in mainstream and special schools. For example, the concept of matching the level of the activity to stages of development is not new and is advocated in relation to the delivery of citizenship education in mainstream settings (Lynch 1992). Lynch also highlights the need to plan for progression and suggests a 'phased introduction of materials' as a way of introducing increasingly complex ideas.

Start small: a familiar focus

Staff working with pupils with learning difficulties – and with profound and multiple or severe learning difficulties in particular – will be very accustomed to beginning new activities with a 'familiar focus'. This can be a very valuable strategy to adopt for many aspects of PSHE and citizenship and is advocated in the original national curriculum guidance for citizenship as a cross-curricular theme (NCC 1990c, p. 15):

> Pupils' own experiences provide the starting point in education for citizenship ... Curriculum provision should build on personal experience and encourage pupils to see citizenship as something which extends beyond their immediate experiences and relationship.

It might be helpful, for example, for pupils to be enabled to develop greater self-awareness in order that they can more meaningfully recognise the feelings and preferences of others. Much of citizenship has a focus on developing knowledge, skills and understanding about the wider community, not only locally but also nationally and globally. A starting point for some pupils is greater awareness and a more active involvement in their 'familiar communities' initially – their own family, class group or school can be a representative microcosm in which to develop many of the essentials, and to then generalise them to ever-increasing spheres.

Some suggestions for starting points for those at early levels of development are set out next:

- greater awareness of self and more active involvement:
  - awareness of self – e.g. preferences, dislikes, abilities and strengths, distinguishing features;
  - learning to control the personal environment – e.g. through switches or movement;
  - active involvement by developing anticipation and prediction – through familiar routines, repetition, enhancing specific features of activities or the use of cues (for example, objects of reference, physical prompts), an individual can be enabled to anticipate what is coming next and to respond intentionally and appropriately;
- the self and others:
  - awareness of self in relation to others and awareness of proximity of others;
  - recognition of familiar others (family, classroom staff, lunchtime staff, helper for horse-riding, *et al.*);
  - consolidating affective communication – learning that he/she can control situations through use of communication;
  - interaction – responding to and initiating interaction with familiar others and those who are not as well known;
  - similarities and differences between self and others;
  - making choices;
  - being part of a group and elements involved – taking turns, differing roles played and the value as part of the whole group;
  - being a member of different groups – family, class, school, neighbourhood, clubs;
  - individual roles and strengths – what each individual can offer or contribute;
- a mini-community – the classroom:
  - roles and rotas in the classroom – marking the register, taking dinner numbers to the office, watering the plants, tidying up;
  - class decision-making and planning – snacks, playtime activities, class outings, sharing resources, class rules, class councils;
  - working with other pupils – sharing skills and supporting others, for example by turning the pages of a book for another pupil, by moving a toy within reach of a child in a standing frame, by shadowing a new child at dinnertime to make sure he/she doesn't get lost;
- a mini-community – the whole school:
  - roles and rotas around school – being dinnertime monitor, taking messages to other classes, being a 'playtime pal' for younger pupils or those who need help to play appropriately or safely;
  - planning a school assembly;
  - school council – making decisions about whole-school issues, such as creating rules of conduct, fairly allocating time on playground apparatus, and issues related to school uniform, school dinners or homework;
  - project planning – developing school resources, designing a sensory garden, creating an effective way to store and access playtime equipment;
  - involvement in other decisions, such as the school's development plan and various policies;
  - whole-school events, e.g. drama and other productions for parents and the local community.

The above form a progression for pupils, starting from self-awareness and moving to an increasingly wider community context – from a small group, to a class, to the whole school, to the local community, and ultimately to a global perspective, where appropriate, at later key stages.

Real responsibility for pupils

The idea of learning by meaningful experience is reinforced here. By giving pupils opportunities for *real* responsibility, we are offering them the chance to become more actively involved and increasingly confident in their own learning and in the life of their school community. School and class councils are one example of this opportunity (Winup 1994). These 'real' responsibilities enable pupils to become aware of their rights and responsibilities and provide them with experience to generalise to a wider community perspective in adult life in balancing their rights and duties (Gould and Gould 1999). Whole-school special events have also been identified as having a valuable place in establishing the ethos of a school (Davies 1999), for they create opportunities for good models of working together by sharing roles and responsibilities, and they have the focus of shared goals as their outcome.

These types of direct and first-hand experiences offer a wealth of possibilities for pupils to develop many personal, social and life skills that are encompassed within both PSHE and citizenship. In particular, they provide positive and caring forums (Gould and Gould 1999) for pupils to work with others in order to explore differing needs and views and the need to respect each other by learning to listen, taking turns, trying to understand views or needs that are different to their own, resolving conflicts and making fair decisions.

The role of others

The development of some of the fundamental concepts inherent within these areas of the curriculum, for some pupils with learning difficulties, is dependent on the actions and responses of others (family, staff, peers). For example, the understanding of the differences between right and wrong or fair and unfair are normally developed by others (usually parents or other carers) alerting us to inappropriate behaviour and explaining the differences or modelling more appropriate ways of behaving. A consistent response to behaviour from others, over time, helps to shape an appreciation of such concepts.

This support role played by 'others' is crucial to the progress of pupils functioning at the earliest levels of development. For example, a pupil who is functioning at a pre-intentional level of communication (see Coupe O'Kane and Goldbart 1998) is almost entirely dependent on the consistency and sensitivity of response by others to their potentially communicative attempts, in order to develop meaning and intention for their actions. Similarly, some pupils will be dependent on staff to give them some responsibility and control over their environment and to present them with the opportunities to make genuine choices. Some schools involve pupils and staff in developing charters to describe rights, responsibilities and expected approaches towards each other.

The supporting role taken in the main by adults (and hopefully, with some direction initially, peers) is of great value across the learning continuum. The development of skills and understanding are based on experiences and influenced by others. Many pupils will need support to be made aware of others' views, feelings, preferences, differences – an awareness that we are not all the same and that we each bring our own set of experiences that in turn influence our individual perspective on life for reasons of differing life-styles, family structures, cultures or faith.

Access through creative contexts: 'storying'

Many of the ideas involved in these curriculum areas are of an abstract, conceptual nature and rely on concrete experiences for pupils to make sense of them. Some of these concepts, however, are not easy to access in real-life contexts without risk (for example, keeping safe, and saying 'no' to strangers); indeed, it may even be considered unethical to put pupils in these situations. Teachers need to create the necessary opportunities for pupils to have experience of situations in which to develop empathy for others or raise their awareness of differing perspectives in meaningful ways, in order that they can themselves develop the appropriate strategies, not only to cope but to take an active and informed part in (adult) life.

We have all been captivated and influenced in our upbringing by stories, whether folk or fairy tales or the retelling of events in our lives by members of our own family. As adults we constantly engage in 'storying' with friends and colleagues, sometimes exaggerating or fabricating features of the story to enhance its appeal. As well as providing amusement, we often sense that stories may offer us something of importance about our world and the ways in which we and others live.

MacIntyre (cited in Tandy 1998) believes that 'stories play a central role in our personal, social and moral development' and that storytelling plays a fundamental role for children in their sense of who they are and how they should live their lives. Tandy (1998) describes the idea of narrative being regarded as a 'primary act of mind', enabling us to organise our thoughts: by structuring and sequencing events, we can then store or retrieve information or experiences from our memory. He likens this type of 'semi-formal storying' to the way we encourage pupils to use 'stories' or news in circle-time activities (Curry and Bromfield 1994).

The Citizenship Foundation has also recognised the potential of stories as a vehicle for exploring topics that relate to social or moral issues (Rowe and Newton 1994). The impact and influence of media storylines is considerable, and the media see themselves acting responsibly by using topical social dilemmas as the focus of their storylines – for example, HIV, teenage pregnancy or drug abuse. In particular, we cannot help but be aware of the effect of TV 'soaps' on our pupils.

We could take the story theme one step further by reflecting on the 'stories' told in everyday life. Certain stories or pictures can be deduced, for example, from the uniforms that people wear. This information enables us to predict things about those individuals and how they might behave or act. For some of our pupils, stories may be an additional way by which they can make sense of the world they live in – for example, to understand that there are different ways of behaving, that not all people are trustworthy, or that there can be different consequences to actions. Stories can provide rehearsals or repetitions of events and their consequences (for example, what will happen on a visit to the dentist). They may even provide an indirect insight into things that particular pupils may never experience (for example, how it might feel to be bullied).

This notion of using story as a means of concept-building or illustrating new ideas is developed more specifically in the work of Gray (1998) and Howley (2000) and offers great potential for both the field of learning difficulties and the areas of PSHE and citizenship. The work of Gray and Howley independently, using what they term 'social stories', has been shaped through their research with people who are identified to be within the autistic spectrum of disorders. Personalised social stories are created with individuals, to enable them to recognise the effect that their behaviour has on others, and to illustrate more appropriate ways of behaving or coping in particular situations. The social story is produced in a format that pupils can 'read' by themselves – for example, using symbols or pictures as a bridge to the meaning of the 'text'. This strategy of social stories has much potential in enabling pupils to get an insight into more difficult concepts such as empathising with the feelings of others and into social skills.

However, stories do not always need to be so specific or individualised to be of value. A wealth of appropriate literature is easily available to use as a vehicle for addressing the many aspects of this curricular area or can be created by groups of pupils as illustrations. Commercially produced material to enable access and concept-building is available in the form of stories especially written (see, for example, Rowe and Newton 1994) or general fiction with moral or social themes (for example, 'The Smallest Whale' by Elisabeth Beresford (1997) on working together, or 'It was Jake!' by Anita Jeram (1991) on taking responsibility).

Below are further examples of activities in which to develop a 'storying' theme:

- scenarios and 'what if' situations – e.g. 'While out shopping you lose sight of your dad. What should you do?'
- simulation activities – e.g. spending time or carrying out a task as a wheelchair-user or wearing simulation glasses to experience a visual difficulty;
- drama/role-play;
- puppets;
- before and after' pictures or photos (perhaps taken by pupils);
- circle-time activities;
- props – e.g. the use of 'detective problem-solving' to find out information;
- visitors from diverse cultures, faiths, professions – telling stories, asking them questions;
- questioning – e.g. 'I wonder how ...?', 'Why ...?'

Each of these types of activity offers the chance to explore and understand actions and consequences, feelings, and how and why to do things differently or to improve them. As previously suggested, by giving pupils first-hand experiences in a safe environment, they are more likely to become more active and confident in their own learning and actions.

The way forward

We welcome the emphasis on PSHE in the revised National Curriculum, reinforcing its importance for all pupils. The new framework continues to remind us that PSHE is more than self-help, independence skills and sex education. Indeed, the *Preparing Young People for Adult Life* document (DfEE 1999a) states (p. 9) that for pupils with special educational needs 'the best practice is built on curriculum breadth, diversity and flexibility, rather than "special" curricular areas such as "social skills" or "training for independence"'.

We have attempted in this chapter to set PSHE and citizenship in the fuller context of personal and social development, including personal autonomy and self-determination. As Best (1999, p. 12) argues:

... interpretation and translation into practice are crucial. The generation of lists of facts, concepts, skills and dispositions which might be associated with citizenship ... can be seductive to curriculum designers, but the effectiveness of such schemes depends on the learning environments and pedagogical processes by which they are to be promoted.

In the light of such dangers, it is crucial to maintain the emphasis on personal and social development. The suggestions made by Sebba *et al.* (1993) and Byers and Rose (1994) relate to a 'drive to push forward … into territory concerned with pupils' personal and social development and specifically towards such targets as pupil autonomy, pupil self responsibility, pupil consultation and advocacy' (Byers and Rose 1994, p. 1). These have implications for the way we work with pupils at all levels (the whole-school approach noted earlier) and their involvement in the school, giving pupils a genuine voice. The values embedded in school organisation and practices need to be consistent with those we aim to encourage through PSHE and citizenship.

The revised framework for PSHE and citizenship offers challenges for staff working with pupils with learning difficulties. Some of these we have identified – for example, the need to consider ways of approaching the more challenging areas and to explore ways of making experiences meaningful for pupils with profound and multiple learning difficulties. This may mean uncertainties that appear to be in contradiction to the target structure of the National Curriculum and individual education plans. However, as Sedgwick (1994, p. 148) notes, 'empowering children involves risk above all else'.

Finally, all pupils now have an entitlement in school that should empower them to participate in society as active citizens. Together with Mittler (2000) and Ross (1999), we view PSHE and citizenship education as one means of enabling an inclusive society respecting and embracing diversity. If schools address the complete range of issues within PSHE and citizenship successfully, educational and social inclusion will be promoted – most importantly from the acceptance and support of the pupils themselves – as being the way forward.

Acknowledgements

The authors wish to thank Greenside School, Hertfordshire, for permission to use its PSHE curriculum, and acknowledgements are due to the staff of this school for their contribution to the development of this curriculum.

References

Bennathan, M. and Boxall, M. (1996) *Effective Intervention in Primary Schools: Nurture Groups.* London: David Fulton Publishers.

Beresford, E. (1997) *The Smallest Whale.* London: Orchard.

Best, R. (1999) 'The impact of a decade of educational change on pastoral care and PSE: A survey of teacher perceptions', *Pastoral Care*, June, 3–13.

Byers, R. (1998) 'Personal and social development', in Tilstone, C. *et al.* (eds) *Promoting Inclusive Practice.* London: Routledge.

Byers, R. (1999) 'Experience and achievement: initiatives in curriculum development for pupils with severe and profound and multiple learning difficulties', *British Journal of Special Education* **26**(4), 184–8.

Byers, R. and Rose, R. (1994) 'Schools should decide …' in Ros,e R. *et al.* (eds) *Implementing the Whole Curriculum for Pupils with Learning Difficulties.* London: David Fulton Publishers.

Coupe O'Kane, J. and Goldbart, J. (1998) *Communication Before Speech: Development and Assessment*, 2nd edn. London: David Fulton Publishers.

Curry, M. and Bromfield, C. (1994) *Personal and Social Education for Primary Schools through Circle Time*. Stafford: NASEN.

Davies, I. (1999) 'Citizenship education: what is to be done?', *Primary Teaching Studies*, spring, 11–14.

DfEE (1999a) *Preparing Young People for Adult Life*. Nottingham: DfEE.

DfEE (1999b) *National Healthy School Standard Guidance*. Nottingham: DfEE.

DfEE (2000) *Sex and Relationship Education Guidance*. Nottingham: DfEE.

DfEE/QCA (1999a) *The National Curriculum Handbook for Primary Teachers in England – Key Stages 1 and 2*. London: DfEE/QCA.

DfEE/QCA (1999b) *The National Curriculum Handbook for Secondary Teachers in England – Key Stages 3 and 4*. London: DfEE/QCA.

DfEE/QCA (1999c) *Citizenship*. London: DfEE/QCA.

Fletcher, W. and Gordon, J. (1994) 'Personal and social education in a school for pupils with severe learning difficulties', in Rose, R. *et al.* (eds) *Implementing the Whole Curriculum for Pupils with Learning Difficulties*. London: David Fulton Publishers.

Gould, J. and Gould, T. (1999) 'Citizens from the classroom: Learning by doing', *Primary Teaching Studies*, spring, 15–19.

Gray, C. (1998) 'Social stories and comic strip conversations with students with Asperger Syndrome and high functioning autism', in Schopler, E. *et al.* (eds) *Asperger Syndrome or High Functioning Autism?*. New York: Plenum Press.

Howley, M. (2000) 'An Investigation into the Immediate Impact of Social Stories on the Behaviour and Social Understanding of Four Pupils with Autistic Spectrum Disorder'. Unpublished MA dissertation, University College Northampton.

Jelly, M. *et al.* (2000) *Involving Pupils in Practice: Promoting Partnership with Pupils with Special Educational Needs*. London: David Fulton Publishers.

Jeram, A. (1991) *It was Jake!*. London: Walker.

Lawson, H. (1998) *Practical Record Keeping*, 2nd edn. London: David Fulton Publishers.

Lees, J. and Plant, S. (2000) *Passport: A Framework for Personal and Social Development*. London: Calouste Gulbenkian Foundation.

Lynch, J. (1992) *Education and Citizenship in a Multicultural Society*. London: Cassell.

Marland, M. (1995) 'The whole curriculum' in Best, R. *et al.* (eds) *Pastoral Care and Personal-Social Education*. London: Cassell.

Mittler, P. (2000) *Working Towards Inclusive Education: Social Contexts*. London: David Fulton Publishers.

Munby, S. (1995) 'Assessment and pastoral care: sense, sensitivity and standards' in Best, R. *et al.* (eds) *Pastoral Care and Personal-Social Education*. London: Cassell.

Murray, L. (1998) 'Research into the social purposes of schooling: Personal and social education in secondary schools in England and Wales', *Pastoral Care*, September, 28–35.

NCC (1990a) *Curriculum Guidance 3: The Whole Curriculum*. York: NCC.

NCC (1990b) *Curriculum Guidance 5: Health Education*. York: NCC.

NCC (1990c) *Curriculum Guidance 8: Education for Citizenship*. York: NCC.

OFSTED (1999) *Handbook for Inspecting Special Schools and Pupil Referral Units*. London: The Stationery Office.

QCA (1998) *Education for Citizenship and the Teaching of Democracy in Schools* (Crick Report). London: QCA.

QCA (2000a) *Personal, Social and Health Education and Citizenship at Key Stages 1 and 2: Initial Guidance for Schools*. London: QCA.

QCA (2000b) *Personal, Social and Health Education at Key Stages 3 and 4: Initial Guidance for Schools*. London: QCA.

QCA (2000c) *Citizenship at Key Stages 3 and 4: Initial Guidance for Schools*. London: QCA.

QCA (2000d) *Curriculum Guidance for the Foundation Stage*. London: QCA.

QCA (2000e) *Citizenship and PSHE Update*, September 2000. London: QCA.

QCA (2001) *Planning Teaching and Assessing the Curriculum for Pupils with Learning Difficulties: Personal, Social and Health Education and Citizenship.* London: QCA.

Ross, A. (1999) 'Some reflections on citizenship in the national curriculum' *Primary Teaching Studies*, spring, 20–23.

Rowe, D. and Newton, J. (eds) (1994) *You, Me, Us! Social and Moral Responsibility for Primary Schools.* London: The Citizenship Foundation.

Sebba, J. *et al,*. (1993) *Redefining the Whole Curriculum for Pupils with Learning Difficulties.* London: David Fulton Publishers.

Sedgwick, F. (1994) *Personal, Social and Moral Education.* London: David Fulton Publishers.

Spalding, B. (2000) 'The contribution of a "Quiet Place" to early intervention strategies for pupils with emotional and behavioural difficulties in mainstream schools', *British Journal of Special Education* **27**(3), 129–34.

Tandy, M. (1998) 'Values development in the early years' in Inman, S. *et al.* (eds), *Assessing Personal and Social Development: Measuring the Unmeasurable.* London: Falmer Press.

Watkins, C. (1995) 'Personal-social education and the whole curriculum' in Best, R.*et al.* (eds) *Pastoral Care and Personal-Social Education.* London: Cassell.

Winup, K. (1994) 'The role of a student committee in promotion of independence among school leavers', in Coupe O'Kane, J. and Smith B. (eds) *Taking Control: Enabling People with Learning Difficulties.* London: David Fulton Publishers.

Chapter 15

Classroom Processes

Richard Byers

Introduction

In *The Curriculum Challenge*, Ashdown *et al.* (1991) brought together a collection of chapters in which colleagues working with young people with learning difficulties raised a host of issues in response to the implementation of the original National Curriculum. Much has happened since. Most schools moved swiftly through a phase of shock and hostility into a period of development, testing out the hypothesis of the first set of orders against the reality of classroom experience. This process resulted in the energies of practitioners and policy-makers alike being monopolised by the National Curriculum for a period.

While some people concentrated for a time on mobilising an anti-National Curriculum backlash, most practitioners working with pupils with learning difficulties soon began to see the advantages of participation in a national movement. Among many such professionals, there is now a palpable consensus about balance in the curriculum, and a growing confidence about the development of teaching materials that manage to both challenge and meet the priority needs of pupils with learning difficulties. Schools experiencing an unaccustomed sense of relative calm should not allow themselves to become complacent, however. While some of the issues raised for debate in books, articles, professional development centres and staff-room discussions since 1990 have been resolved, many others, like the heads of the hydra, arise in their place to prompt fresh debate and reinvigorated development. This is a process to be welcomed; the school that stops and congratulates itself on having arrived is a school that is in danger of dying on its feet.

This chapter sets out to explore some of the issues, with their origins in classroom practice, that continue to provoke debate and prompt development. It is in the classroom, after all, at the interface between teacher and learner, that real development begins and ends. It is appropriate that outside influences should impinge upon these processes. All members of the school community – governors, parents, staff and pupils – should have their say in the creation and ratification of policy. But, in the end, schools are really all about teachers, learners and the curriculum that is an expression of the work that they do together.

In examining classroom processes, this chapter will discuss:

- whole-curriculum issues;
- pupils' individual priorities;
- sharing purpose and intention;
- providing appropriate tasks and activities;
- teaching approaches and learning styles;
- access, support and resources;
- interaction; and
- reflection and review.

In the spirit of perpetual development, which permeates this chapter, no attempts will be made to reach cosy conclusions. Staff in schools are only too aware of the complexity of many of the issues that continue to challenge them and to create real tensions. The following sections will, however, bring together some of the influences and ideas that inform curriculum development and will set out some of the implications of those ideas for classroom practice.

Whole-curriculum issues

Two of the central themes of Sir Ron Dearing's review of the National Curriculum in the early 1990s were to 'identify the essential elements of knowledge, understanding and skill within each subject' and to provide, for school staff, 'significantly greater scope for the exercise of professional judgement' (Dearing 1993). The Dearing review's themes (Byers 1994a; SCAA 1994) were pursued further in the review process that led to the publication of the revised National Curriculum (DfEE/QCA 1999a, 1999b). This version of the National Curriculum provides a 'national framework' that is described (p. 12) as:

> designed to enable all schools to respond effectively to national and local priorities, to meet the individual learning needs of all pupils and to develop a distinctive character and ethos rooted in their local communities.

The revised National Curriculum therefore places an emphasis on the entitlement of all pupils to engage with a shared curriculum while encouraging schools to use the range of available flexibilities in order to respond to local and individual differences. In this way, the revised National Curriculum builds on Stevens' (1995a) vision of 'a flexible framework which enables schools to plan their whole curriculum within a statement of minimum entitlement' and opens up further 'opportunities for debate' (Tate 1994) – a debate that had been inhibited by the original overloaded and over-prescriptive National Curriculum.

This new flexibility, and the increase in matters which are to be left to the discretion of members of school communities, is, of course, broadly to be welcomed, not least by those working among pupils with special educational needs. There is little doubt that the uncoupling of chronological age from the key stages, without the requirement to modify statements of special educational need (DfEE/QCA 1999a; 1999b) constitutes a major step forward. Similarly, the move, in the revised National Curriculum, away from statements of attainment, mechanical rules and checklists (SCAA 1994) and towards the use of level descriptions that entail professional judgements being made about the whole of a pupil's performance in a range of contexts and across time must be seen as positive (Byers and Rose 1996).

Although this more flexible framework – with its focus upon professional judgement and discretion at the classroom level and upon a vision of the curriculum being created, owned and maintained by school communities – has many benefits, it also has at least one major potential drawback. One impact of the original National Curriculum legislation upon schools catering for pupils with SEN was to force an increase in curricular breadth (Sebba and Byers 1992; Sebba and Fergusson 1991; Sebba *et al.* 1995). In part, this increased breadth concerned subjects and subject content. It required schools to take account of scientific discovery and technological innovation as well as teaching life skills and survival cookery. It enabled pupils to engage with story, verse and drama as well as acquiring a social sight vocabulary. It entailed learning about historical, geographical and cultural contexts as well as knowing how to use the bus route from school to the town library. All of these changes must be seen as bringing breadth and richness to a curriculum that had begun to be seen as narrow and impoverished.

If schools are to build honestly and productively upon the tradition of curriculum development over recent years, however, breadth in the curriculum must mean something more than simply 'extra subjects'. The National Curriculum Council's seminal work of guidance on whole-curriculum planning (NCC 1990) established a sound working definition of a whole curriculum, which is perhaps more effectively reflected in the revised National Curriculum than in previous versions. The NCC's definition encompasses:

- the subjects of the 'basic curriculum', with their associated assessment procedures;
- cross-curricular elements, including key skills, cross-curricular themes and pupils' personal and social development in a range of dimensions;
- extra-curricular activities;
- the spirit and ethos of each school community, which contribute to the intangible, or hidden, curriculum;
- strategies for the management of the school and its curriculum; and
- 'the most effective teaching methods'.

The document goes on to suggest that 'the wide range of skills which pupils must acquire must be reflected in an equally wide variety of approaches to teaching' (NCC 1990, p. 7) and that the responsibility for selecting those teaching methods that will ensure equality of opportunity for all pupils must remain with school staff. It may be seen as appropriate, therefore, that the revised National Curriculum does not prescribe teaching methods; that messages about how to teach have largely been removed from each programme of study.

The danger is that this revision of prescriptive language is seen as a justification for a return to a narrow range of classroom experiences for pupils with SEN. It is not simply the content of the whole curriculum that needs to be broad, balanced and relevant. With the review of the National Curriculum, there is even more of a requirement upon school staff to ensure that approaches to teaching, and the range of ways in which pupils are encouraged to learn, continue to evolve and develop in response to the changing needs of pupils.

As has been said before, 'it is not possible to implement the subject content of the National Curriculum without entering into the methodological debate' (Byers 1994b). The National Curriculum entitles pupils to experience learning in a new variety of styles as well as opening up new areas of subject content. It also secures the right of pupils to engage in a curriculum that sets out to meet their individual needs in the context of shared activities. Although the National Curriculum is organised under subject headings, there is no requirement for pupils to experience a curriculum that is concerned solely with subjects or schemes of work that are rigorously timetabled according to subject boundaries.

Pupils' individual priorities

Many practitioners now contend that the National Curriculum has led to a broadening of the whole curriculum for pupils with SEN, both in terms of knowledge, skills and understanding and in terms of the learning processes themselves. These professionals would not wish to return to times when pupils with learning difficulties were trained to plug in a kettle safely without any attempt being made to help them to understand the uses and dangers of electricity from a scientific point of view. Few people still argue that pupils with learning difficulties require an alternative, specialised curriculum. Indeed, Carpenter (1995) eloquently describes the ways in which pupils' varying individual needs can be met within inclusive activities that offer access to National Curriculum subject content.

The School Curriculum and Assessment Authority has proposed a vision of a whole curriculum that is indivisible, promoting learning for pupils in key areas of their personal and social development even as they encounter experiences founded in the subjects of the National Curriculum (SCAA 1996). This strand in planning has been enhanced by the emphasis on personal and social development in both the OFSTED (1999) *Handbook for Inspecting Special Schools and Pupil Referral Units* and the revised National Curriculum, which offers, for the first time, a national framework for the teaching of personal, social and health education and citizenship through the key stages. The revised National Curriculum also provides – again for the first time – a 'detailed, overarching statement on inclusion' (DfEE/QCA 1999a, 1999b). At a time when educational inclusion is so firmly upon the agenda (DfEE 1998), it would seem wholly inappropriate to exclude pupils with SEN from active participation in historical site visits and geographical fieldwork in peer groupings in order to revert to systems of one-to-one teaching and 'withdrawal for support'. Yet the challenge remains of maintaining a well-rounded and inclusive whole curriculum that provides access to the subjects and learning processes of the National Curriculum even as it also addresses the needs of the whole pupil.

There is no suggestion here that the subjects of the National Curriculum constitute a complete and sufficient whole curriculum, even with the addition of guidance on the teaching of personal, social and health education and citizenship. As has been shown above, the National Curriculum was only ever intended to constitute *part* of the basic curriculum, within a far broader whole curriculum for all pupils. For many pupils with learning difficulties, the task of addressing, as a priority, those particular targets and objectives that are expressed in individual education plans (DFE 1994) will mean working towards communication skills, interpersonal interactions or physical competencies that are not explicitly described in the PoS for any subject within the National Curriculum. This chapter argues that priorities such as these fall within the National Curriculum Council's definition of the whole curriculum (NCC 1990) and do not need to be addressed through the development of a separate curriculum. Indeed, the range of learning experiences inevitably provided in any honest attempt to implement the National Curriculum will also offer meaningful contexts in which to pursue pupils' individual priorities (Byers 1994c).

The OFSTED (1999) *Handbook* also suggests that classroom staff should employ a range of teaching methods in seeking to meet curricular requirements. Thus, pupils should sometimes experience whole-class teaching, which may involve listening to explanations, answering questions or participating in discussions. At other times and in other situations, staff may encourage smaller groups of pupils to work together on shared tasks or may set up individual activities. Whatever organisational strategies are selected – and there is no suggestion here that any particular methods are to be prescribed for any particular occasions – staff are encouraged (OFSTED 1999, p. 52) to evaluate whether:

● the choice of pupil grouping – for example, pupils working alone, in pairs, in small groups or all together – achieves the objectives for teaching and learning;
● the form of organisation allows the teacher to interact efficiently with as many pupils as possible.

In OFSTED's view, effective teaching has many facets and teachers should 'match the methods they use to the purpose of the lesson and to the needs of the pupils' (OFSTED 1999).

The UNESCO resource pack entitled *Special Needs in the Classroom* (UNESCO 1993) also emphasises that all pupils can be helped to learn when:

● school staff know pupils well and, through continuous assessment and evaluation processes, have a clear idea of what has already been achieved;
● pupils are helped to understand what they are learning and, through the negotiation of objectives (see DFE 1994), why it is significant for them;
● classrooms are organised and support deployed in such a way that all pupils are purposefully occupied for as much of the time as possible.

Building upon these principles and the OFSTED model, the following sections will explore some of the classroom processes that can help to promote effective learning.

Sharing purpose and intention

The UNESCO pack (1993) stresses the significance of ensuring that learning activities are meaningful for pupils. Bennett (1991) notes that there may often be a mismatch between the intentions of school staff and the reality of classroom tasks experienced by pupils. Frequently, Bennett proposes, the intention to challenge is reduced, in the transfer from teacher to learner, to the repetitious practice of established skills. Part of the solution to this problem lies in the accurate assessment of pupils' prior achievements and experiences (see below), but the deliberate sharing of purpose and intention between teacher and learner can also play an important role. Rose (1998) argues that this form of dialogue between teacher and learner will play a key role in preparing pupils 'for an included education'. Byers (1994c) argues that the meaning of activities should, wherever possible, be accessible to pupils from the outset, so that they are 'cued into the activity'.

This may be achieved, in some situations, by a clear verbal explanation given to the whole class. The UNESCO pack (1993) describes a dynamic relationship between teacher and learner whereby a clear demonstration of the task at hand leads to opportunities for pupils to engage actively in practical learning activities – food technology sessions might often begin in this way, with staff demonstrating the techniques that pupils will later use themselves. In other situations, it may be difficult to share the purpose of activities with whole-class groups; discussion of tasks with small groups of pupils may lead to clarity of intent, while the negotiation of shared objectives with individuals will assist staff in meeting the requirements of the SEN *Code of Practice* (DFE 1994) with regard to partnership with pupils. Fergusson (1994) gives a host of examples of strategies that staff can use to establish 'anticipation or intention' with pupils for whom the written or spoken word is problematic. These include the use of signs, symbols, objects of reference (Ockelford 1993) and tactile cues (Ouvry 1987).

Maintaining meaning and purpose for learners during classroom activity is likely to be as important as establishing shared intention at the outset. The provision of appropriate levels of support, together with carefully judged interventions, can keep pupils focused as well as guiding them towards new challenges. Staff may need to check pupils when they begin to 'drift', reminding them of previously established codes of conduct or shared performance criteria. Questions may be used to review, reaffirm or redirect activity. Options or points of decision that evolve during learning can be identified and discussed. Harris *et al.* (1996) suggest that the clarification of choices for pupils may have a positive impact upon behaviours that interfere with learning, as well as promoting self-esteem and self-reliance. Again, encouragement, guidance, negotiation and ongoing feedback during tasks can be non-verbal as well as verbal.

Providing appropriate tasks and activities

Well-focused learning opportunities are likely to be those that build upon pupils' previous skills, interests, experiences and aptitudes. Bennett (1991) and OFSTED (1999) stress the significance of the relationship between curricular intent, the reinforcement of previous achievements, and fresh challenge. Accurate assessment of pupils' prior learning is clearly of fundamental importance here and it is suggested that this is, once again, an aspect of classroom process that can – and should – meaningfully involve pupils (Fletcher-Campbell and Lee 1995; Lawson 1998; Jelly *et al.* 2000).

Designing and selecting tasks so that they provide pupils with challenge at an appropriate level is part of the differentiation process whereby educational experiences are adapted to take account of the differing needs, interests, aptitudes and previous experiences of different children. As Hart (1992) points out, differentiation must not become so extreme (constantly withdrawing individuals with particular learning difficulties for 'special programmes', for example) that pupils are marginalised, denied access to a broad range of curricular experiences or segregated from their peers. Viewed from the outset as pathways to access, inclusion and enhanced learning for *all* pupils, differentiation strategies of various kinds (Lewis 1992) can help staff to tailor class or group activities in order to provide opportunities to address both subject-focused learning and individual priorities.

In many instances, this will simply mean planning consolidation or enrichment activity for some pupils, while allowing learning to proceed at a slower pace for other members of the group. For other pupils, it may mean conceptualising a meaningful distinction between experience and achievement. Curriculum-related group experiences can offer relevant, purposeful contexts in which achievements are possible in terms of particular individual objectives. A modern-foreign-language lesson, for example, may provide opportunities for individual pupils to consolidate their communication skills in interaction with their peers, even though they could not be said to be learning French.

Brown (1996) argues that the notion of experience itself can be differentiated, and her ideas have informed the development of the Qualifications and Curriculum Authority's guidance on the assessment of outcomes for pupils with learning difficulties in relation to the revised National Curriculum (DfEE/QCA 2001). At one level, a pupil may simply be present during an activity and may be said to have encountered a learning opportunity without any discernible outcome – and, of course, for some pupils the willingness to tolerate shared activity may in itself be significant. At another level, it may be possible to note that a pupil is aware of, attending to, or focused upon an experience. For some pupils, again, this may constitute an important step on the road towards responding to experiences in positive ways. Smiles, enthusiasm communicated through body language, visual or aural attention redirected when activity shifts location, and even signs of frustration or dissatisfaction may all express early reactions that are worthy of note. These sorts of responses may, in turn, lead toward supported involvement and perhaps active participation in group experiences. As has been suggested, outcomes such as turn-taking, communicating or reaching and grasping in new contexts may themselves constitute very significant individual achievements for particular pupils.

The relationship between experience and achievement is therefore complex, but Byers (1999), building on guidance from the SCAA (1996), suggests that consideration of issues such as these will form a productive part of the process of designing well-differentiated activity. The recognition of the value of experience can help to promote meaningful involvement in group activity for all pupils, including those with profound and multiple learning difficulties. Indeed, Dearing (1995), Tate (1994), Stevens (1995b) and DfEE/QCA (2001) take this debate further. They emphasise that curriculum plans may themselves be differentiated, so that some aspects of subjects are treated in depth while others are offered in outline only. This means that pupils, by design, may encounter parts of the curriculum as experiences rather than as opportunities to gain knowledge, understanding or skills in depth.

Pupils with moderate learning difficulties who are studying English at Key Stage 3, for example, may explore a Shakespeare play in depth, reading scenes aloud together in the original language; watching video interpretations; visiting the theatre for a live performance; learning about the historical context. They may, in contrast, experience the narrative skills of Dickens and Hardy in outline only, by watching costume adaptations on video and listening to passages read aloud. In a similar spirit, the PoS for history in Key Stage 2 may be implemented in a school for pupils with severe learning difficulties by treating the study units concerning 'local history', 'a past non-European society' and 'Victorian Britain' in depth, as topics taught over extended time-scales. The remaining study units may then be treated 'with a lighter touch' (Dearing 1995), offering broadening and enriching experiences through site visits, museum trips, stories, drama and video.

Curriculum planners will arrive at decisions about which aspects of subjects to treat in depth and which to cover in outline in the light of considerations about their relevance to pupils, their accessibility, and the need to maintain breadth and balance in the whole curriculum.

Teaching approaches and learning styles

It is appropriate for teams of teachers, with the support of subject coordinators and senior managers, to come to corporate decisions about curricular intentions at the strategic, long-term planning stage (SCAA 1995). Individual classroom practitioners will, however, continue to shape those plans in the short term in response to the particular needs of particular pupils and in the light of the teachers' own interests and talents. Making learning interesting, exciting and engaging for all participants – staff and pupils alike – will remain a primary task for classroom staff. Indeed, however well-planned the curriculum – however successfully the big issues of progression, continuity, breadth and balance are addressed in schemes of work (Byers and Rose 1996) – pupils' experiences and achievements will be diminished by classroom activities that are dull, unimaginative, plodding and pedestrian.

In debating the task of 'mapping individual learning routes' through 'meaningful, relevant group activity', Sebba *et al.* (1995) stress intrinsic motivation. They describe ways in which pupils may be encouraged to pursue their individual learning targets by the creation of purposeful contexts within fresh experiences. These experiences, relating to well-founded curriculum plans that include the National Curriculum, may stand in contrast to the narrow, utilitarian programmes of one-to-one training in essential skills that have, in the past, characterised schooling for pupils with learning difficulties. The UNESCO pack (UNESCO 1993) emphasises the role of choice in providing classroom experiences that offer pupils a stimulating variety of learning opportunities. This is not to argue for an extreme form of *laissez-faire* education in which pupils 'do what they want', but to suggest that involving pupils in the direction that their own learning takes, with the planned generation of points of decision, or options, will be likely both to promote involvement and motivation and to teach young people to become self-managing, self-directing, self-responsible learners. This, surely, is what we ought to mean when we speak of an education for independence.

As has been shown above, OFSTED (1999) indicates that a range of teaching approaches will encourage a similar diversity of learning styles. No teacher in a mainstream setting would argue that pupils should undertake all their learning through a single means of accessing information – solely through reading, for example, or only by attending to 'chalk and talk', or always by practical investigation. A well-rounded education will provide all pupils with opportunities to learn in a variety of ways. Ouvry (1987) suggests that 'free exploration, trial and error, modelling and imitation, shaping, backward and forward chaining, or a combination' of such styles will also provide 'effective routes to learning' for pupils with the most profound difficulties. Byers (1994c) discusses the notion of 'whole pupil engagement' in learning opportunities that are relevant, purposeful – and fun.

Babbage *et al.* (1999) argue that teachers should adjust their approaches in order to take account of pupils' individual learning preferences. The contention here is that active participation and meaningful involvement can be positively encouraged through styles of learning that involve exploration, pupil initiation and problem-solving. Of course, passive – though attentive – watching, listening or experiencing might also constitute an appropriate way to learn for most pupils on certain occasions, and effective teachers will wish to take account of this variety in making decisions about their approaches to teaching a range of aspects for the whole curriculum.

The significance here of the notion of the match between methodology and curricular intent cannot be overemphasised. The OFSTED (1999) *Handbook* lists exposition,

222 *Enabling Access*

explanation, demonstration, illustration, practical activity, investigation, and problem-solving as potentially useful teaching methods, and it notes that the use and style of questioning should probe pupils' knowledge and understanding and challenge their thinking. It will be apparent here that these methods cannot all be used at once. The value of a problem-solving activity will be destroyed by prior demonstration and explanation. Exposition may follow practical activity but is likely to be an inappropriate way to support pupils' learning during an investigation. However, these examples give some idea of the range of approaches that can be employed, in balance, over time.

Access, support and resources

The revised National Curriculum (DfEE/QCA 1999a, 1999b) also encourages classroom staff to provide for pupils a range of adapted modes of access to learning activities. The general teaching requirements applying to all subjects suggest that pupils may need to use augmentative means of communication – involving signs, symbols or information technology, for instance – as well as adapted equipment and resources. While the lists of potential modes of access are not exhaustive, the message is clear. As well as supplementing worksheets with symbols or transferring writing tasks onto the computer, educators should feel free to adapt, extend, augment and interpret the PoS for National Curriculum subjects in any way in order to promote access for pupils to the concepts, knowledge, skills and understandings that lie behind the language of the orders.

It is also worth noting here that decisions about the availability to pupils of resources and equipment can have a significant impact upon their development as independent learners. While there are obviously some items of school equipment that, for safety reasons, will only be operated under supervision, it is possible to promote active participation, initiation and self-directed learning by opening up access for pupils to an increasing range of resources. On one level this may simply mean keeping items such as paper, crayons and glue in trays or on shelves at an appropriate height and accepting that pupils will only learn to become responsible resource users through experience. For many pupils, however, the ready availability of personal computers, tape recorders and communication aids may be of fundamental importance. These should not, therefore, be items that are shut away for supervised use at certain times of the week but considered, in many instances, as integral parts of general classroom activity.

If it is appropriate to adopt this flexible attitude to the use of resources, it is also important to consider the role of support staff. Ware (1994a), in her discussion of classroom organisation, draws attention to the need to plan for the targeting of support time in order to promote equality of opportunity for all pupils. This may not mean that all pupils receive the same amount of support but, rather, that the time available is directed equitably towards those pupils for whom adult support in particular learning situations is appropriate and productive.

Balshaw (1991) and Fletcher-Campbell (1992) argue that the effective use of classroom support is founded upon a whole-school policy for teamwork and cooperation, and in particular upon:

- shared understandings about pupils' needs and difficulties;
- shared intentions about curricular aims, priorities for individual pupils, classroom management issues and teaching approaches;

- shared development of skills, interests, awareness, expertise and collaborative attitudes between all members of staff;
- shared interpretations of professional roles, responsibilities and lines of management.

Steel (1991) notes the significant role that monitoring, evaluation and review by senior staff can play in securing progress towards the kind of collaborative approaches elaborated by Lacey and Lomas (1993). All parties agree that effective partnership between professionals is founded upon shared planning. Hornby (1994) and Gascoigne (1995) remind us that parents should also be seen as partners in the kind of 'social network system' (Appleton and Minchom 1991) model of collaboration since championed by the *Code of Practice* (DFE 1994).

Interaction

It is beyond the scope of this chapter to survey, in any kind of appropriate detail, work in the major field of communication and interaction. It may be worth noting, however, that experience in schools and during development programmes indicates that staff in schools for pupils with learning difficulties are pursuing, with vigour, interest and commitment, the kinds of interactive strategies described by Dunne and Bennett (1990), Rose (1991), Sebba *et al.* (1995) and Byers and Rose (1996). Expertise in planning sessions involving cooperative and collaborative groupings of pupils with MLD and SLD is acknowledged by many teachers as part of their repertoire of class- and group-management strategies. Pupils who are not yet ready for the challenge of working in a larger group may be given experience of paired learning as part of a process of development toward a team approach. Peer coaching, where pupils revisit, refocus and extend their understandings and achievements by supporting partners who are working at a slower pace, is seen as a useful method of promoting and consolidating learning for all concerned.

Planning group activities that meaningfully involve pupils with PMLD presents a greater challenge. Here, the role of staff in finding non-directive, empathic modes of interaction with pupils in order to facilitate contact, cooperation and communication between young people and their peers is crucial. Nind and Hewett's work (1994) on intensive interaction illuminates the territory in instructive detail. Although those authors suggest that many young people with very severe learning difficulties may never become 'sophisticated and subtle enough in their interactive abilities to learn to socialise and play together', and adhere to a position of 'tasklessness' in which interaction is an end in itself, many practitioners are finding that the techniques of intensive interaction can open young people up to the possibilities of contact with their peers and participation in the curriculum. Watson (1994) describes pupils who are 'relating better to other pupils', 'more involved socially' and making progress in terms of language and interpersonal behaviour after a programme of intensive interaction. Ware (1994b) notes that pupils who are encouraged to respond to adults within the classroom environment become more likely to initiate interactions themselves. This would bear out Nind and Hewett's evidence of 'students beginning to enter dialogue-like exchanges' and of their becoming less isolated after experiencing intensive interaction.

If staff are to play a part in developing young people's experiences of one another, they will be forced to consider subtle shifts of persona. The task of becoming a surrogate peer may not coexist comfortably with the roles of teacher, curriculum manager or disciplinarian. Just as staff who seek to become advocates on behalf of their clients experience a potential conflict of interest, so empathic interactors may feel uneasy slipping back into more traditional roles within the classroom. Adopting intensive interaction as another teaching technique may propel staff towards a profound review of the complex matrix of roles, rules, routines and responsibilities within the classroom.

Reflection and review

This sort of review of methodology will be familiar to the practitioner who has learned to become professionally reflective. Skrtic (1991, p. 35) argues that

> the invention of new [programmes] for unfamiliar contingencies through divergent thinking and inductive reasoning on the part of multidisciplinary teams of professionals engaged in a reflective discourse

is an inevitable and welcome part of life in a 'problem-solving organization' such as a school catering for a diversity of pupils. SCAA (1996), Byers and Rose (1996) and DfEE/QCA (2001) emphasise the significance of monitoring, review and evaluation in all phases of the work of schools. Thus, the review of short-term pupil priorities drives the process of revising long-term goals; pupil progress and achievement are used as measures in evaluating the effectiveness of schemes of work in terms of method as well as content; reshaping curriculum plans will lead to the revision of policy and the consideration of new strategies for the ongoing development of the school as a community endeavour. Whatever the future of the OFSTED inspection process, the creation of a culture of school self-evaluation and self-review, driven by a celebration of pupil diversity as a positive force, has to be seen as very healthy.

If schools are to move forward in this spirit, then the task of arriving, through assessment and diagnosis, at a view of the needs of individual pupils remains central (SCAA 1996). The design of appropriate tasks and activities, as discussed earlier in this chapter, is founded upon accurate assessment (among other things). If schools are also to meet the requirements of the *Code of Practice* (DFE 1994) and the mood of a revitalised process of recognising, recording and celebrating achievement, then the involvement of pupils themselves in this process will be pivotal (Tilstone 1991). Shining examples of imaginative and effective strategies for pupil self-recording can be found in most schools for pupils with learning difficulties. The task of further promoting self-assessment and self-review appears on many development plans for improving policy and practice in assessment, recording and reporting. Some colleagues are actively engaged in the task of creating routes of increased access for pupils to these reflective aspects of the learning process. It is perhaps less common to find schools that are encouraging pupils to assume increased responsibility for their own learning at all stages in the process and at a number of operational levels.

Mitchell (1994) describes a number of initiatives in which pupils and students of various ages are encouraged to become involved in sharing target-setting and negotiating performance criteria as well as actively participating in review and assessment. These ways of working, Mitchell suggests, 'allow pupils to take a degree of control over their learning – and, thereby, their lives' on an individual basis, just as the creation of student councils or committees (Winup 1994) can provide pupils with routes whereby their views can contribute to the generation of curricular options and whole-school development (Fletcher and Gordon 1994; Tyne 1994; Jelly *et al.* 2000).

Summary

It is the contention of this chapter that careful consideration of classroom processes must be seen as part of whole-curriculum planning for all pupils. Certainly, pupils with special educational needs will benefit from the levels of planning detail proposed here. What is suggested by the research (Ainscow and Muncey 1989) is that schools that provide effective teaching for those pupils who experience learning difficulties will be likely to be effective schools in general.

Of course, good teaching and effective learning do not occur in isolation. Ainscow (1991) notes the importance of:

- leaders committed to addressing the needs of all;
- staff who have confidence in their own abilities to meet a diversity of needs;
- an ethos in which all pupils are expected to be achievers;
- structures that provide support for individual members of staff;
- whole-school commitment to curricular breadth, balance and access for all;
- systems for monitoring and reviewing progress.

Best (1989), in advocating a whole-curriculum model for pupils' personal and social development, emphasises the role of school managers in providing inspiration, leadership and appreciative support, as well as opportunities for professional development, adequate resources and constructive appraisal. It is salutary, therefore, to reflect upon the lot of the many enthusiastic and committed teachers who become disillusioned, disenchanted and disaffected in the face of ongoing criticism; inadequate levels of resourcing; and mean-spirited approaches to the provision of opportunities for high-quality professional development.

If school staff are to devote the energy, forethought, intelligence, cooperation and effort that effective classroom processes inevitably entail, then they have a right to expect their work to be valued and supported in equal measure.

References

Ainscow, M. (1991) 'Effective schools for all: an alternative approach to special needs in education', in Ainscow, M. (ed.) *Effective Schools for All.* London: David Fulton Publishers.

Ainscow, M. and Muncey, J. (1989) *Meeting Individual Needs in the Primary School.* London: David Fulton Publishers.

Appleton, P. and Minchom, P. (1991) 'Models of parent partnership and child development centres', *Child Care, Health and Development* **17**(1), 27–37.

Ashdown, R. *et al.* (1991) *The Curriculum Challenge.* London: Falmer Press.

Babbage, R. *et al.* (1999) *Approaches to Teaching and Learning: Including pupils with learning difficulties.* London: David Fulton Publishers.

Balshaw, M. (1991) *Help in the Classroom.* London: David Fulton Publishers.

Bennett, N. (1991) 'The quality of classroom learning experiences for children with special educational needs', in Ainscow, M. (ed.) *Effective Schools for All.* London: David Fulton Publishers.

Best, R. (1989) 'Pastoral care: some reflections and a re-statement'. *Pastoral Care,* 7(4), 7–13.

Brown, E. (1996) *Religious Education for All.* London: David Fulton Publishers.

Byers, R. (1994a) 'The Dearing Review of the National Curriculum', *British Journal of Special Education* **21**(3), 92–6.

Byers, R. (1994b) 'Teaching as dialogue: teaching approaches and learning styles in schools for pupils with learning difficulties', in Coupe O'Kane, J. and Smith, B. (eds) *Taking Control: enabling people with learning difficulties.* London: David Fulton Publishers.

Byers, R. (1994c) 'Providing opportunities for effective learning', in Rose, R.*et al.* (eds) *Implementing the Whole Curriculum for Pupils with Learning Difficulties.* London: David Fulton Publishers.

Byers, R. (1999) 'Experience and achievement: initiatives in curriculum development for pupils with severe and profound and multiple learning difficulties', *British Journal of Special Education* **26**(4), 184–8.

Byers, R. and Rose, R. (1996) *Planning the Curriculum for Pupils with Special Educational Needs – A practical guide.* London: David Fulton Publishers.

Carpenter, B. (1995) 'Building an inclusive curriculum', in Ashcroft, K. and Palacio, D. (eds) *The Primary Teachers Guide to the New National Curriculum.* London: Falmer Press.

Dearing, R. (1993) *The National Curriculum and its Assessment – Interim report.* York: NCC/SEAC.

Dearing, R. (1995) 'Foreword', in SCAA, *Planning the Curriculum at Key Stages 1 and 2.* London: SCAA.

DFE (1994) *Code of Practice on the Identification and Assessment of Special Educational Needs.* London: HMSO.

DfEE (1998) *Meeting Special Educational Needs: A Programme of Action.* London: DfEE.

DfEE/QCA (1999a) *The National Curriculum: Handbook for Primary Teachers in England.* London: DfEE/QCA.

DfEE/QCA (1999b) *The National Curriculum: Handbook for Secondary Teachers in England.* London: DfEE/QCA.

DfEE/QCA (2001) *Planning, Teaching And Assessing The Curriculum For Pupils With Learning Difficulties.* London: DfEE/QCA.

Dunne, E. and Bennett, N. (1990) *Talking and Learning in Groups.* London: Macmillan.

Fergusson, A. (1994) 'Planning for communication', in Rose, R. *et al.* (eds) *Implementing the Whole Curriculum for Pupils with Learning Difficulties.* London: David Fulton Publishers.

Fletcher, W. and Gordon, J. (1994) 'Personal and social education in a school for pupils with severe learning difficulties', in Rose, R. *et al.* (eds) *Implementing the Whole Curriculum for Pupils with Learning Difficulties.* London: David Fulton Publishers.

Fletcher-Campbell, F. (1992) 'How can we use an extra pair of hands?', *British Journal of Special Education* **19**(4), 141–3.

Fletcher-Campbell, F. and Lee, B. (1995) *Small Steps of Progress in the National Curriculum – Final report.* Slough: NFER.

Gascoigne, E. (1995) *Working with Parents as Partners in SEN – Home and school: a working alliance.* London: David Fulton Publishers.

Harris, J. *et al.*. (1996) *Pupils with Severe Learning Disabilities Who Present Challenging Behaviours: A whole school approach to assessment and intervention.* Kidderminster: BILD.

Hart, S. (1992) 'Differentiation – way forward or retreat?', *British Journal of Special Education* **19**(1), 10–12.

Hornby, G. (1994) *Counselling in Child Disability – Skills for working with parents.* London: Chapman and Hall.

Jelly, M. *et al.* (2000) *Involving Pupils in Practice: promoting partnership with pupils with special educational needs,* London: David Fulton Publishers.

Lacey, P. and Lomas, J. (1993) *Support Services and the Curriculum.* London: David Fulton Publishers.

Lawson, H. (1998) *Practical Record Keeping: development and resource material for staff working with pupils with special educational needs,* second edn. London: David Fulton Publishers.

Lewis, A. (1992) 'From planning to practice', *British Journal of Special Education* **19**(1), 24–7.

Mitchell, S. (1994) 'Some implications of the High/Scope curriculum and the education of children with learning difficulties', in Coupe O'Kane, J. and Smith, B. (eds) *Taking Control – Enabling people with learning difficulties.* London: David Fulton Publishers.

National Curriculum Council (1990) *Curriculum Guidance 3: The whole curriculum.* York: NCC.

Nind, M. and Hewett, D. (1994) *Access to Communication: Developing the basics of communication with people with severe learning difficulties through intensive interaction.* London: David Fulton Publishers.

Ockelford, A. (1993) *Objects of Reference.* London: RNIB.

OFSTED (1999) *Handbook for Inspecting Special Schools and Pupil Referral Units: with guidance on self-evaluation.* London: The Stationery Office.

Ouvry, C. (1987) *Educating Children with Profound Handicaps.* Kidderminster: BIMH.

Rose, R. (1991) 'A jigsaw approach to group work', *British Journal of Special Education* **18**(2), 54–7.

Rose, R. (1998) 'Including pupils: developing a partnership in learning', in Tilstone, C. *et al.* (eds) *Promoting Inclusive Practice.* London: Routledge.

SCAA (1994) *Consultation on the National Curriculum – An introduction.* London: SCAA.

SCAA (1995) *Planning the Curriculum at Key Stages 1 and 2.* London: SCAA.

SCAA (1996) *Planning the Curriculum for Pupils with Profound and Multiple Learning Difficulties.* London: SCAA.

Sebba, J. and Byers, R. (1992) 'The National Curriculum: control or liberation for pupils with learning difficulties?', *The Curriculum Journal* **3**(2), 143–60.

Sebba, J. and Fergusson, A. (1991) 'Reducing the marginalisation of pupils with severe learning difficulties through curricular initiatives', in Ainscow, M. (ed.) *Effective Schools for All.* London: David Fulton Publishers.

Sebba, J. *et al.* (1995) *Redefining the Whole Curriculum for Pupils with Learning Difficulties,* 2nd edn. London: David Fulton Publishers.

Skrtic, T. (1991) 'Students with special educational needs: artifacts of the traditional curriculum' in Ainscow, M. (ed.) *Effective Schools for All.* London: David Fulton Publishers.

Steel, F. (1991) 'Working collaboratively within a multi-disciplinary framework', in Tilstone, C. (ed.) *Teaching Pupils with Severe Learning Difficulties.* London: David Fulton Publishers.

Stevens, C. (1995a) 'Foreword', in Byers, R. and Rose, R. (eds) *Planning the Curriculum for Pupils with Special Educational Needs.* London: David Fulton Publishers.

Stevens, C. (1995b) 'News from SCAA', *British Journal of Special Education* **22**(1), 30–31.

Tate, N. (1994) 'Target vision'. *Times Educational Supplement,* 2 December.

Tilstone, C. (1991) 'Pupils' views', in Tilstone, C. (ed.) *Teaching Pupils with Severe Learning Difficulties – Practical approaches.* London: David Fulton Publishers.

Tyne, J. (1994) 'Advocacy: not just another subject', in Rose, R. *et al.* (eds) *Implementing the Whole Curriculum for Pupils with Learning Difficulties.* London: David Fulton Publishers.

UNESCO (1993) *Special Needs in the Classroom – Student materials,* Paris: UNESCO.

Ware, J. (1994a) 'Classroom organisation', in Ware, J. (ed.) *Educating Children with Profound and Multiple Learning Difficulties.* London: David Fulton Publishers.

Ware, J. (1994b) 'Using interaction in the education of pupils with PMLDs (i). Creating contingency sensitive environments', in Ware, J. (ed.) *Educating Children with Profound and Multiple Learning Difficulties.* London: David Fulton Publishers.

Watson, J. (1994) 'Using interaction in the education of pupils with PMLDs (ii). Intensive interaction: two case studies', in Ware, J. (ed.) *Educating Children with Profound and Multiple Learning Difficulties.* London: David Fulton Publishers.

Winup, K. (1994) 'The role of a student committee in promotion of independence among school leavers', in Coupe O'Kane, J. and Smith, B. (eds) *Taking Control: Enabling people with learning difficulties.* London: David Fulton Publishers.

Chapter 16

Assessment

Ann Lewis

Introduction

There is a popular saying that 'weighing the pig doesn't make it any fatter'. I can still recall a school inspector some years ago repeating this to me, rather sternly, when I said that I thought we should be making more thorough assessments of children with learning difficulties. Times have changed, and rigorous and frequent assessments have become routine – perhaps too much so – in the English educational system.

In this chapter, I begin with a brief discussion of the political context of the assessment of children with learning difficulties. I then review thinking about the nature of such assessment, drawing on recent work in developmental and cognitive psychology. The final part of the chapter discusses a range of classroom approaches and strategies that might be used with pupils with learning difficulties; these range from broadly based classroom observations to focused pupil-adult conferences. The overall emphasis is on 'authenticity' in the contexts of the classroom and the school when assessing pupils with learning difficulties – a group of pupils that encompasses those with mild learning difficulties, for example in reading or mathematics, as well as pupils with severe and generalised cognitive difficulties.

Since the first edition of this book was published in 1996, there have been many changes in the context of, and general thinking about, the assessment of pupils with learning difficulties. These changes have been political (see next section) as well as related to developments in understanding about the psychological processes of assessment. Pertinent to both these areas is an increasing emphasis on the individual rights of children and the need to recognise each pupil's perspective with all its complex personal, social and emotional baggage (Lewis and Lindsay 2000). As Norwich (2000) notes, we can only assess what can be measured and that requires clear definitions about the nature of the attainment. The inevitable consequence is that the less easily measured slips out of the picture, particularly in a system in which there are strong political forces that give prominence to objective assessment. So, there is a potential conflict here. Seeing the world from the pupil's perspective may draw attention to what is not easily measured (e.g. feelings of self-worth or spirituality) yet forces for accountability push us toward a focus on making 'better' assessments of a narrower range of attainments.

The political context

The context of the educational assessment of children with learning difficulties is heavily politicised. Where once such assessments were strongly – often exclusively – oriented to diagnostic purposes, these assessments are now part of procedures with quite different objectives. (See Lewis (in press) for a review of successive ideologies in special education 1950–2000.) Concerns with benchmarking, target-setting, threshold performance indicators and value added reflect the system orientation of the assessments.

Furthermore, the development of Fair Funding in local education authorities has moved some of the responsibilities, and finance, for pupils with special educational needs from LEAs to schools. Increasingly the educational culture is shifting to one in which the assessment of pupils is explicitly tied to teacher rewards (indirectly through the repercussions of league tables of test results and directly through performance indicators and threshold payments). The political debates about these issues are beyond the scope of this chapter.

A seminal report on assessment (DES/Welsh Office 1988) described assessment as being at the heart of promoting children's learning. It emphasised the potential breadth of assessment instruments and noted that these might encompass interviews as well as various tasks and quizzes. One should add 'observation' as a key assessment tool in relation to pupils with learning difficulties (discussed further, below). The common goal of these various approaches is to obtain valid information about a pupil's attainments. Importantly, the above report stressed that the assessment process 'is the servant, not the master, of the curriculum' (para. 4). It is worth reiterating this stance: 'The assessment process ... should not be a bolt-on addition at the end. Rather, it should be an integral part of the educational process, continually providing both "feedback" and "feed forward"' (para. 4).

The subsequent National Curriculum, drawing on this report, can be seen as one way of fostering, through assessment, a matching of pupil and curriculum. There were many debates about the relative importance of formative and summative assessment for children with learning difficulties. Over time, summative assessments at ages 7, 11, 14 and 16 have gained prominence over more formative aspects of assessment. However, early documentation about these summative, end-of-key-stage assessments emphasised the links between teaching, learning and assessment. (See Lewis (1995a) for a discussion of National-Curriculum-linked summative assessment for pupils with learning difficulties.) For teachers working with pupils with learning difficulties, formative assessment remains a very important concern and focus of development. It is the prime concern in this chapter.

A major document for teachers working with pupils with learning difficulties is the Code of Practice concerning SEN (DFE 1994; DfEE 2000). This provides a five-stage assessment and monitoring procedure to be followed by all schools. The 1994 Code is under review at the time of writing, but changes are likely to be at the level of detail not of principle (DfEE 2000). The 1994 Code states (para. 2.1): 'At the heart of every school and every class lies a cycle of planning, teaching and assessing'. It lists the types of information relevant when learning difficulties are first identified. A key point (QCA 2000) is that assessment is carried out *with* the child not *on* the child.

The Qualifications and Curriculum Authority has been at pains to stress that assessment, record keeping, and acknowledging progress and achievement should be an integral part of teaching and learning for *all* pupils (DfEE/QCA 2001). The involvement of the pupils in this process is central to the approach advocated by the QCA project team. Some pupils may monitor and analyse their own strengths and weaknesses; others may indicate their preferences within and between activities; some may require help from advocates.

To help teachers recognise attainment below Level 1 of the National Curriculum, a framework is offered, building on some of the earlier work of Brown (1996). It describes possible changes in individual pupils' responses and behaviour as their early perceptions of experiences, and their increasing involvement in the learning process, develop into areas of knowledge, skills and understanding. The framework moves through encounter, awareness, attention, response, engagement, participation, involvement and understanding. It should not, however, be used mechanistically as a tool to measure hierarchical and linear progress. Rather, it is intended to enable staff sensitively to acknowledge the attainment appropriate to individual pupils as they move through a learning process. Schools are encouraged to develop their own assessment tools from this framework.

In each of the subject-specific materials offered by the QCA (DfEE/QCA 2001), 'performance descriptions' outline early learning and attainment. They chart progress up to Level 1 through eight steps: P1–P3, which show general attainment; and P4–P8, which show subject-specific attainment (P for 'pre'-National Curriculum targets). The performance descriptions for P1–P3 are the same across all subjects.

The 'performance descriptions' are a significant step forward in celebrating and articulating the attainment of pupils with a range of learning difficulties. They can be used by staff in much the same way as the National Curriculum level descriptions. They will provide more focused assessment evidence from which staff can refine and develop long-, medium- and short-term planning. Linear progress towards subject-specific attainment at Level 1 of the National Curriculum can be treated – and a pupil's overall development and achievement at the end of a year or key stage can be more clearly articulated – in a universally acceptable language. Moreover, teachers' professional judgements about which description best fits a pupil's performance over time and in different contexts can be stated in unequivocal terms. This development from the QCA gives value measurements for much of the excellent assessment practice already in place, and provides a framework for discourse regarding future developments.

The theoretical context

Motivation

Assessment in the context of special needs has traditionally emphasised behaviourist approaches. They are also typically found in some integrated learning systems based on computer-based packages used with SEN pupils (Lewis 1999). There is increasing evidence that such approaches hamper learning by encouraging avoidance of difficult tasks and a lack of persistence in the face of problems or unexpected results (see the review in Torrance and Pryor 1998). Those approaches have also been linked with a preference for performance goals ('How many did I get right?'; 'How can I, in future, avoid being seen to have failed?') rather than learning goals ('How can I get better at this?'; 'What strategies are helping me here?'). Moreover, a bias towards performance goals is encouraged by the use of extrinsic rather than intrinsic reinforcement. This bias has often been evident in the special-needs context in which classroom assessments have been linked with extrinsic reinforcers such as smiley faces on a chart, or the building-up of points to be exchanged for rewards.

Pupils' use of feedback

Increasingly, the literature in developmental and instructional psychology has been highlighting the importance of the nature and timing of feedback given to pupils (reflecting, in particular, constructivist approaches to learning). There is some evidence that there are systematic differences in the use that pupils of varying attainments make of feedback. For more able learners, feedback may interfere with, rather than aid, the learning process (Messer *et al.* 1996). In contrast, pupils with learning difficulties may need much reassurance, with frequent and specific feedback being given. It has been argued by some teachers that, for this reason, sensitive computer-based learning programmes are particularly valuable for pupils with learning difficulties (Lewis 1999). This view reflects a perceived rather than a demonstrated connection.

One type of feedback that may be particularly important for children with learning difficulties is self-monitoring. This relates to metacognitive strategies such as self-regulation as well as to self-efficacy beliefs. These may be valuable for children with learning difficulties in the areas of assessing and changing, poor cognitive strategies, emotional barriers to learning (such as task anxiety or low self-esteem) and behaviours interfering with learning (e.g. off-task behaviour). (See Black and Wiliam (1998) and Shapiro and Cole (1999) for discussion of these areas.) Techniques such as precision teaching, which involve specific daily short tests on a target skill in a manner that is allied to the charting of results, can be a very powerful way of helping pupils to see their changes in learning attainments and to develop understanding of the processes of having a learning goal. (See Ayers *et al.* (1998) for some more general practical ways to foster self-monitoring of learning.)

Some general guidelines

Throughout this chapter there is an implicit – and sometimes explicit – recognition that situated assessment is vital when working with pupils with learning difficulties. That is, assessment information needs to relate to particular contexts because learning and assessment are closely tied to ('situated in') specific contexts. Generalisation of learning from one situation to another is a well-recognised problem in the SEN context (Lewis 1995a). For example, a pupil may be able to add numbers in a workbook sum but not in a general problem-solving task; or may do so in the real world of a shop but not in the classroom. This connects with notions of authentic assessment (discussed by Cumming and Maxwell 1999) and also of dynamic assessment. Some versions of the latter aim to integrate assessment of home as well as school factors (reviewed in Elliott 2000).

Also, running through this chapter is a focus on fine-grained assessment. In the special-needs context, there have been concerns that the National-Curriculum-based assessments in England were not sufficiently finely graded to show progress for pupils with learning difficulties. The NFER (1995) identified some questions about assessment, reflecting these orientations, that schools might consider. These are summarised below:

- Is assessment sufficiently accurate and focused to inform future teaching and enable the setting of goals?
- Are assessment opportunities and activities built into schemes of work and/or programmes of learning?
- Do records include details of pupils' experiences or achievements and, if appropriate, the extent of support provided?

- Is assessment used to monitor progression towards short- and long-term goals?
- Is assessment used as a way of recognising and valuing all achievements and progress, however small, in all aspects of the curriculum and in whatever contexts?
- Is pupils' participation in self-assessment and recording actively promoted?
- What evidence is kept and collated to support teachers' assessments?

These questions provide a broad framework within which the ideas in this chapter can be located.

The NFER project (Fletcher-Campbell 1996; see also SCAA 1996) and subsequent work on the 'P' scales (DfEE/QCA 1998, DfEE/QCA 2001, DfEE 2001) have also supplied helpful evidence about what teachers look for in assessment approaches. Suggestions made in relation to accreditation of learning at ages 14–16 for pupils with learning difficulties (Fletcher-Campbell 1996) have relevance for other age groups. These features tie in with the questions posed above and highlight some particular characteristics that teachers were seeking in the accreditation of learning for pupils with difficulties. As teachers were looking for these features in externally derived assessment procedures, it is reasonable to suppose that they would also look for them in their own assessment procedures.

Some of the key features sought were:

- a small-steps approach linked with regular and frequent reviews and target-setting;
- recognition of the use of the same skill in various contexts;
- recognition of experience as well as attainment;
- use of a variety of means of assessment;
- flexibility of content and approach so that assessment methods suited pupils with various learning styles, interests and ages;
- focus on achievement;
- maximum pupil involvement in self-assessment.

These points are implicit in the following discussion. Types of assessment are divided into three broad levels, moving through broad classroom-based observations through focused observation to direct adult–child conferences.

Level 1: Assessment through general classroom observation

Observation of pupils is a vital first step in planning how their learning can be fostered. Observation can take many forms: structured or unstructured; and involving the teacher working with the pupil or remaining distanced. When and how teachers observe pupils will depend both on the aims of that observation and on what is realistic in a busy classroom. While teachers recognise that watching how pupils are learning is an important part of teaching, it requires careful planning to incorporate such activity into everyday classroom life. Croll and Moses (2000) draw attention to the high correlation between low overall achievement and emotional and behavioural problems. This highlights the need to assess a range of aspects of pupils' development.

Teachers may make time for observing pupils by doing more collaborative teaching. A variety of occasions arising unexpectedly (e.g. in the playground) might provide the opportunity for informal observational assessments. Adults, other than the teacher, might also carry out observations if given clear and detailed training about how to do this. I have worked with nursery nurses in primary schools who, using structured observation schedules, have monitored the integration of pupils from special schools (Lewis 1995b). This type of work can generate valuable data about whether pupils with difficulties in learning are isolated in mainstream school classes and about the types of activities in which they are engaged.

A variety of general observations helps the teacher to get to know individual pupils. They are also important in order to avoid unwarranted assumptions about apparent deficits needing to be taught specifically. Campione (1989) has referred to this as the 'leap to instruction'. Questions that a teacher might pose at this level include:

- In which kinds of activity does the pupil concentrate better or less well? What are typical periods of concentration for the pupil on particular activities?
- Which kinds of activity seem to be most meaningful for the pupil?
- In which kinds of activity is the pupil most confident?
- What are the preferred ways of accessing tasks?
- What are the preferred ways of responding to tasks?
- Does the pupil have a preference for certain kinds of materials (e.g. computer-based or linked with a particular piece of equipment such as a synchrofax or Language Master machine; trackerball, mouse, on-screen clicker or touch screen when working on a computer)?
- Does the pupil work better at certain times of the day (e.g. always tired in the first part of the morning or regularly livelier after the midday break)?
- Are there particular classroom friends with whom the pupil works well or poorly and/or prefers to be (or not be) near?
- Are there particular support staff or other personnel with whom the pupil works well or poorly?
- What motivates the pupil to learn?
- What special interests does the pupil have?
- In which kinds of classroom grouping does the pupil work better or less well?
- Does the pupil prefer a noisy or quiet working environment?
- How does the pupil respond if given scope for developing his or her own ideas?
- How do conclusions from the above points match with, or differ from, the perceptions of parents, therapists and other professionals who know the child?

All of the aspects of observation implied by the foregoing list relate to getting to know the pupil and, once identified, they can be built on constructively so that classroom experiences foster learning. In the longer term, pupils who favour a particular learning or thinking style (Sternberg 1997) or method (e.g. using computer-based materials) will need to have experience in using other approaches also but may benefit from a bias towards preferred modes.

The importance of motivation in influencing what pupils are apparently capable of is illustrated in the following account. A seven-year-old, Sarah, seemed unable to write even a sentence towards a story or 'news'. However, one day Sarah received a party invitation from a friend, Marie, in another class. She took the invitation home and showed it to her father, who wrote a reply saying that Sarah could come to the party. Sarah lost this note on her way to school the next day and became very upset about this. Her class teacher reassured her, saying that it would be all right as she would pass the message to Marie's teacher for her to give to Marie. However, later that day Sarah handed her teacher a carefully written note saying: 'To Marie, I am coming to your party. From Sarah.' Sarah had written the note and may have had help from other pupils with spellings but, highly anxious not to miss the party, she had been prompted to write a message. The message had a real purpose and brought out her writing abilities.

General observations might well alert the teacher to possible hearing, visual or motor impairments in a pupil (see Lewis (1995a) for further guidelines concerning these areas). If evidence about suspected difficulties is collected by caregivers and teachers, then health professionals have a useful supplement to medical diagnosis. This broader picture may help to rule out non-medical factors that appear to be influencing behaviour. For example, a pupil may show fear in physical education activities in school. If this goes alongside coordination problems at school and at home, then resultant action will differ from a situation in which this does not happen – fearfulness in school PE may, for example, seem instead to be more related to a lack of self-confidence in that particular situation.

Teachers may also have to respond to a range of pupils' medical problems, notably asthma, epilepsy and diabetes. A recent asthma-awareness campaign has suggested that teachers should not, as has apparently been common practice in many schools, keep inhalers in a 'safe place' which is inaccessible to the pupils. Instead, pupils who may need inhalers should have ready access to them at all times. Work by Michael Bannon *et al.* (1992) showed that few teachers in the United Kingdom had received information about childhood epilepsy, and they lacked confidence in dealing with pupils' epilepsy. However, the latter was not the case where teachers had a good general knowledge of the condition and adequate awareness of the likely difficulties experienced by a pupil with epilepsy. Bannon and colleagues concluded that local health authorities have an important role to play in providing appropriate training packages for teachers. There are a number of publications outlining the implications for teachers of pupils' medical conditions (e.g. Webster *et al.* 1994).

Level 2: Systematic observation

It may be appropriate to carry out some systematic observations of pupils, using structured observation schedules. Roffey *et al.* (1994) identified four means of structuring classroom observations, namely making a tally, taking field notes, using a checklist, and monitoring behaviour at time intervals. The last of the four involves recording pupils' activities by using a schedule based on pre-specified lists or categories of observed behaviours, often monitored over regular time periods (e.g. every 30 seconds). Systematic schedules are particularly useful for monitoring social behaviour; they can also be useful when monitoring a group of pupils in order to ascertain, for example, which pupils in the group contribute most to a conversation.

There are both benefits and disadvantages in using structured, systematic observation schedules within a classroom. If the schedule is clearly structured and appropriate for the aims, it can supply useful information. It can show whether or not a teacher's impression is justified, for example, that a particular pupil habitually concentrates much better on oral rather than on written activities, or that two pupils work more productively together than separately. However, a structured observation schedule may be difficult to use effectively. Pupils may interrupt or behave differently because they are aware of being monitored. The use of structured observation schedules also requires at least two adults to be present: one to carry out the observations and one to work with the class. Several detailed accounts of formal observational methods (e.g. Sylva and Neill 1990; Wragg 1993) expand on their use in classrooms.

Observational methods are useful ways in which teachers can build judgements about individual pupils and the dynamics of the classroom. They may also point to features of the classroom that the teacher could improve, such as making certain types of resources more accessible, or changing the location of some materials so that withdrawn pupils become more involved with other pupils.

So far in this chapter, identifying the point reached by a pupil has focused on observations of pupils' general development and behaviour. Observational methods need to be supplemented with assessments that focus on curricular tasks.

Level 3: Direct pupil–adult conferences

It is useful if a teacher can observe a pupil both working alone on a particular activity and working alongside the teacher. This is important because it enables the teacher to assess, first, the processes of learning and not just the end-products and, second, what the pupil can do alone compared with what he or she can do with some guidance.

Byers and Rose (1996) and Tilstone *et al.* (2000) give examples of starting points for assessment activities that could be used as part of pupil–adult conferences. For example, a pupil could be given two- or three-dimensional shapes for sorting and the following points considered. On what basis does the pupil sort the shapes when asked to sort them into 'the shapes that go together'? What does the pupil do when given a prompt (e.g. 'Look at the colours') – do they use this prompt profitably or treat it as an irrelevant cue? If the latter, does this seem to be because the word 'colour' has not been understood? How does the pupil explain his or her sorting pattern?

This apparently straightforward example can generate information about the pupil's hearing, vision, colour-blindness, vocabulary (receptive and expressive), manipulative skills, motivation, attention and distractibility, as well as the mathematical understanding being targeted. By talking through with the pupil (or communicating through sign), the observing adult may gain information about these diverse areas, rather than assuming that completion or otherwise of the task reflects strength/limitations specifically and exclusively in the targeted area of understanding.

There is a relatively strong tradition of pupil–adult conferences, in special needs contexts, for diagnostic purposes. This is illustrated in various approaches to assessing and helping pupils with reading difficulties. Pupil–adult conferences are widely supported in this context, although there are differing views about the best focus of the conference. Two contrasting focuses have been strongly advocated.

One focus, developed from formal testing of 'subskills', has been on the psychological subskills believed to underlie particular tasks, notably reading. This was based on the assumption that reading was composed of discrete and identifiable subskills that could be isolated and measured. Thus, for example, many 'reading readiness' tests have included assessments of a pupil's visual sequencing (e.g. identifying the next letter(s) in a regular sequence), auditory sequencing (e.g. recalling aural sequences of letters or numbers) and visual memory (e.g. drawing from memory a shape shown briefly). It then seemed logical to identify and remedy, by specific teaching, any weak subskills. Unfortunately, there was generally little transfer from resultant proficiency in the subskills to facility in reading (Adams 1990).

A second focus in pupil–adult conferences has been on analyses of pupils' errors in a particular activity. Systematic analyses of errors (or 'miscues') can provide useful clues for teaching. For example, there are different implications for teaching in the case of James, who repeatedly makes phonic errors in spellings (e.g. 'storiz' for 'stories'), compared with Toni, who fails to apply a common spelling rule (e.g. she writes 'storys' for 'stories', 'worrys' for 'worries', etc.). How the teacher chooses on which errors to focus and how these are analysed will reflect their (possibly implicit) theories on the nature of the knowledge/skills and the processes of acquiring these.

More generally, helping a pupil to articulate the processes engaged in a learning task might reveal the unhelpful models of learning to which the pupil is clinging. For example, it may become apparent that the pupil is convinced that speed is more important than accuracy when completing work; or that consulting a dictionary to check spellings is 'cheating'.

Communication between pupils can provide a valuable and unique basis from which to assess competence in various domains, particularly those of a linguistic nature. The task of tutoring another pupil can push the child tutor into explaining a task and so articulating thought processes. Thus the tutoring process can draw out social, cognitive and linguistic skills that may not otherwise be revealed. Pupils with severe learning difficulties who are placed in the position of tutoring non-disabled children have been found to produce unexpectedly complex linguistic structures and a variety of social skills (Lewis 1995b). If diagnostic procedures include pupi–pupil interaction as well as pupil–teacher interaction, there is a much broader base to the assessments.

Organising pupil–adult conferences

When organising pupil–adult conferences, the following points should be borne in mind:

- Acknowledge that it will be done relatively infrequently but in some detail for individual pupils.
- Acknowledge that some pupils will need this more frequently than do other pupils.
- Discourage other pupils from interrupting the activity.
- Avoid handing over this task to other adults in the classroom unless they fully understand its purpose and how to carry it out.
- Making time for pupil–adult conferences may (depending on pupil–adult ratios) require that teachers make more use of techniques in which pupils work without direct teacher involvement (e.g. collaborative work with classmates and self-checking games).
- It may be useful to record the conference on audiotape or videotape so that it can be analysed later. The tape will also provide evidence about the pupil's learning that could be kept as a record. Pupils often like to hear such tapes replayed and to comment on their learning and interaction with the teacher.
- Capitalise on occasions when the pupil is highly motivated and has a good relationship with the teacher, especially if this happens infrequently.

Key questions to maintain focus on the pupil

In pupil–adult conferences, it is important to maintain a focus on the *pupil*. The following questions, if used during an observation, should assist the adult in doing this:

- Can the pupil explain why he or she is carrying out an activity in a certain way?
- What can the pupil do alone, compared with prompting? (This is also very important for identifying able pupils who are doing work well below that of which they are capable.)
- What can the pupil do already on his or her own? (Teaching should extend not duplicate this.)

- Has the pupil retained earlier steps in learning? For example, a pupil who has difficulty in completing tens-and-units sums involving carrying across columns might have forgotten the 'base ten' concept underlying the activity.
- Can the pupil complete a given task in one context and transfer it to another context (e.g. add numbers using beads on a string *and* using a number line)?
- Can the pupil apply knowledge and skills in a new context (e.g. multiply numbers in a maths game *and* use multiplication facts to work out the numbers of rulers needed by groups of pupils in an art activity)?
- Can the pupil respond to a variety of question types (e.g. questions requiring recall, evaluation, speculation, problem-solving)? For example, after a science activity: 'What happened when we ...?', 'Could it have been done in a better way ...?', 'What might happen if we ...?', 'How did you feel about ...?'
- Does the pupil understand what he or she is being asked to do? For example, is the vocabulary of the teacher's question understood?

Will Swann (1988) gives a good example that illustrates this last bullet point. He describes talking to a five-year-old girl during her first week at school. The girl was drawing around flat, plastic shapes. He asked her, in the course of the conversation, how many sides the square had and in response the girl laid out, side by side, three other plastic squares. He put them back and asked the girl to show him a side of a square. She pointed to the centre of the top surface of one square. In his book, Swann goes on to discuss the various and ambiguous contexts in which the girl may have come across the word 'side' (sides of a team, sitting side by side, the side of a cupboard, etc.) and conjectures that the girl's responses reflected her thinking through different meanings of 'side'. He concludes that the pupil's 'difficulty' with the task was largely illusory and that the real problem was a failure of communication on his part, and not the pupil's.

Key questions for the teacher to maintain focus
The ambiguity of teachers' talk, particularly when pupils may not have become socialised into, or do not recognise, school procedures and expectations, has been documented by Shirley Cleave *et al.* (1982) and by Mary Willes (1983). Both sets of research provide salutary reading, for they indicate the potential for misunderstandings in classrooms. Examples include a pupil who interpreted the teacher's instruction, 'Would you like to join the story group now?' as an invitation ('No, thank you') and pupils being confused by the ambiguities of the teacher's request for them to 'line up'. Similarly, a friend was recently asked by her daughter for some sweets. My friend replied 'You want some sweets ... What's the magic word?'. Her daughter paused thoughtfully and then said 'Abracadabra?'

Pupils who find school learning difficult may be slower than other pupils to tune into the specific language conventions of the classroom. The following suggested questions for a teacher to consider when conducting pupil–adult conferences reflect these points:

- How am I presenting this task? Am I being clear and specific?
- Are particular linguistic features in instructions causing problems for the child (e.g. use of pronouns and prepositions; see Dockrell *et al.* 2000)
- What is the classroom environment like? Are there unhelpful distractions?
- How does the situation match the points noted from general observations (see earlier) about fostering productive learning contexts for this pupil?
- What are my expectations of this pupil? Am I inadvertently conveying low expectations (e.g. leaving too little time for the child to think about a response, or modelling a very limited range of possibilities)?

- What are the prerequisite skills and knowledge for this task? Have I checked that the pupil has these?
- How am I sustaining the pupil's awareness, attention and motivation?
- Am I giving feedback in a way that helps the pupil to use this, not just on a particular task but also more generally?
- How am I helping the pupil to recognise the type of progress made?
- How am I helping the pupil to be involved in setting targets for learning?
- How do my teaching strategies compare with those of other adults working with this pupil?

Conclusion

This chapter has examined the importance of trying to identify where pupils are in their learning. Several possible focal points and some ways of carrying out individual assessments have been discussed. Identifying pupils' starting points is the first step in planning teaching. Curriculum-based assessment is part of a continuous cycle of teaching and assessment. Recent theoretical work in the field is helping to explain why classroom practices, such as helping pupils to articulate learning strategies used, are fundamental to increasing attainments.

The ideas developed in this chapter are consistent with emerging ideas about whether the teaching and assessment of pupils with learning difficulties are essentially the same as, or different from, those used with other pupils. The argument put forward elsewhere (Lewis and Norwich 2000, Norwich and Lewis in press), and reflected here, is that a continuum of similar strategies is required, not a radically and qualitatively different approach.

References

Adams, M. J. (1990) *Beginning to Read: Thinking and Learning about Print.* Cambridge, MA: MIT Press.

Ayers, H. *et al.* (1998) *Assessing Individual Needs: A Practical Approach.* London: David Fulton Publishers.

Bannon, M. *et al.* (1992) 'Teachers' perceptions of epilepsy', *Archives of Disease in Childhood* 67, 1467–71.

Black, P. and Wiliam, D. (1998) 'Assessment and classroom learning', *Assessment in Education* 5(1), 7–73.

Brown, E. (1996) *Religious Education for All.* London: David Fulton Publishers.

Byers, R. and Rose, R. (1996) *Planning the Curriculum for Pupils with Special Educational Needs.* London: David Fulton Publishers.

Campione, J. (1989) 'Assisted assessment: a taxonomy of approaches and an outline of strengths and weaknesses', *Journal of Learning Disabilities* 22(3), 151–65.

Cleave, S. *et al.* (1982) *And So to School.* Windsor: NFER/Nelson.

Croll, P. (1986) *Systematic Classroom Observation.* Lewes: Falmer.

Croll , P. and Moses, D. (2000) *Special Needs in the Primary School: One in Five.* London: Cassell.

Cumming, J. J. and Maxwell, G. S. (1999) 'Contextualising authentic assessment', *Assessment in Education* 6(2), 177–94.

DES/WO (1988) *National Curriculum: Task Group on Assessment and Testing* (TGAT Report). London: HMSO.

DFE (1994) *Code of Practice on the Identification and Assessment of Special Educational Needs.* London: DFE.

DfEE (2000) *SEN Code of Practice on the Identification and Assessment of Pupils with Special Educational Needs: SEN Thresholds; Good Practice Guidance* (consultation papers). London: DfEE.

DfEE (2001) *Supporting the Target Setting Process: Guidance for Effective Target Setting for Pupils with Special Educational Needs.* London: DfEE.

DfEE/QCA (2001) *Planning, Teaching and Assessing the Curriculum for Pupils with Learning Difficulties.* London: DfEE/QCA.

Dockrell, J. *et al.* (2000) 'Psychological aspects of researching children's perspectives', in Lewis, A. and Lindsay, G. (eds) *Researching Children's Perspectives.* Buckingham: Open University Press.

Elliott, J. (2000) 'The psychological assessment of children with learning difficulties', *British Journal of Special Education* 27(2), 59–66.

Fletcher-Campbell, F. (1996) 'Just another piece of paper? Key Stage 4 accreditation for pupils with learning difficulties', *British Journal of Special Education* 23(1), 15–18.

Lewis, A. (1995a) *Primary Special Needs and the National Curriculum,* 2nd edn. London: Routledge.

Lewis, A. (1995b) *Children's Understanding of Disability.* London: Routledge.

Lewis, A. (1999) 'Integrated learning systems and pupils with low attainments in reading', *British Journal of Special Education* 26(3), 153–7.

Lewis, A. and Lindsay, G (eds) (2000) *Researching Children's Perspectives.* Buckingham: Open University Press.

Lewis, A. (in press) 'Charlotte's web: changing views of special educational needs', in Richards, C. (ed.) *Changing English Primary Education.* Stoke-on-Trent: Trentham Books.

Lewis, A. and Norwich, B. (2000) *Mapping a Pedagogy for Special Educational Needs.* Exeter: University of Exeter.

Messer, D. J. *et al.* (1996) 'Using computers to help tell the time: is feedback necessary?', *Educational Psychology* 16(3), 281–96.

NFER (1995) *Small Steps of Progress in the National Curriculum.* Slough: NFER.

Norwich, B. (2000) *Education and Psychology in Interaction: Working with Uncertainty in Interconnected fields.* London: Routledge.

Norwich, B. and Lewis, A. (in press) 'Mapping a pedagogy for special educational needs', *British Educational Research Journal.*

QCA (1998) *Supporting the Target Setting Process,* London: DfEE.

Roffey, S. *et al.* (1994) *Young Friends: Schools and friendship.* London: Cassell.

SCAA (1996). *Planning the Curriculum for Pupils with Profound and Multiple Learning Difficulties.* London: SCAA.

Shapiro, E. S. and Cole, C. L. (1999) 'Self-monitoring in assessing children's problems', *Psychological Assessment* 11(4), 448–57.

Sternberg, R. J. (1997) *Thinking Styles.* Cambridge: Cambridge University Press.

Swann, W. (1988) 'Learning difficulties and curriculum reform: integration or differentiation', in Thomas, G. and Feiler, A. (eds) *Planning for Special Needs: A Whole School Approach.* Oxford: Blackwell.

Sylva, K. and Neill, S. (1990) 'Unit 2: Assessing through direct observation', in Warwick University Early Years Team (eds) *Developing your Whole School Approach to Assessment Policy.* Windsor: NFER-Nelson.

Sylva, K. *et al.* (1980) *Childwatching at Playgroup and Nursery School.* London: Grant McIntyre.

Tilstone, C. *et al.* (2000) *Pupils with Learning Difficulties in Mainstream Schools.* London: David Fulton Publishers.

Torrance, H. and Pryor, J. (1998) *Investigating Formative Assessment.* Buckingham: Open University Press.

Webster, A. *et al.* (1994) *Supporting Learning in the Primary School.* Bristol: Avec.

Willes, M. (1983) *Children into Pupils.* London: Routledge and Kegan Paul.

Wragg, E. C. (1993) *An Introduction to Classroom Observation.* London: Routledge.

Chapter 17

Pupils with Profound and Multiple Learning Difficulties

Carol Ouvry and Suzanne Saunders

Introduction

Although the term 'profound and multiple learning difficulties' (PMLD) has now been in use for many years, it is still necessary to define what is meant by it for a particular purpose or document. In many schools for pupils with severe learning difficulties, the proportion of pupils with PMLD has increased in relation to the total school roll (Male 1996); over time, the criteria for placing pupils into this category appear to have changed.

On the one hand, advances in medical science ensure the survival of children with very extensive disabilities, thereby increasing the number of profoundly disabled pupils in schools (Carpenter 1994a). Some pupils who would, in the past, have been regarded as having PMLD are now perceived to be more intellectually able in comparison with other pupils. They may be regarded as having multiple disabilities but not profound intellectual impairment. Consequently the pupils who are now referred to as having PMLD may well be more disabled than would have been the case in previous decades. If this is so, the task for teachers of pupils with PMLD is now even more challenging than it has been in the past.

Ware (1994, p. 5) defines those with PMLD as 'having two or more severe impairments, one of which is profound learning difficulties'. She supports this definition by referring to research published in the 1980s that showed that comparatively few people with profound learning disabilities had no other severe impairments. However, the small number of pupils who have profound learning disabilities but do not appear to have additional impairments can be the most challenging to teach because there is no obvious focus to provide a starting point for the teaching process.

In *Planning the Curriculum for Pupils with Profound and Multiple Learning Difficulties* (SCAA 1996), a clear description is given (p. 8) of the pupils whose difficulties are the focus of the document. They are:

pupils with profound and multiple learning difficulties who, in some respects appear to be functioning at the earliest levels of development and who additionally have physical or sensory impairments. Some of these pupils may be ambulant and may also behave in ways that either challenge staff and other pupils or result in their isolation, making it difficult to involve them in positive educational experiences. Most experience difficulties with communication.

The curriculum for pupils with PMLD

All of these barriers to learning have to be addressed in the curriculum for pupils with PMLD and, prior to the introduction of the National Curriculum, the developmental curriculum provided the structure for creating an individual education plan for each pupil (Ouvry 1987). The introduction of the National Curriculum changed the focus of curriculum development towards issues of entitlement and access across all curriculum subjects for all pupils. Since then, individual schools and working groups throughout the country have undertaken a great deal of work to develop extended programmes of study for pupils with SLD and PMLD, and to incorporate the changes and accommodate the guidelines that have been produced since the National Curriculum was first introduced (SCAA 1994). Despite these changes, practitioners who work with pupils with PMLD are still striving to achieve a satisfactory synthesis between the subject-led National Curriculum and the developmental and learning needs of PMLD-affected pupils, (Aird 2001).

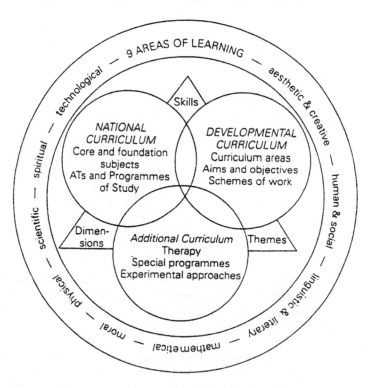

Figure 17.1 The whole curriculum for pupils with PMLD (from Ouvry 1991)

Figure 17.1 (from Ouvry 1991) shows a model of the whole curriculum, which includes the developmental curriculum, the additional curriculum and the National Curriculum. This demonstrates the overlap and interrelationship of these three aspects of the whole curriculum. The model has been modified (Sebba and Byers 1992; Sebba *et al.* 1995) by changing the relative size of the circles to indicate the different emphases that can be placed on the various aspects of the curriculum for each individual pupil or group of pupils.

This model demonstrates that the National Curriculum subjects alone cannot provide the whole breadth necessary for pupils with PMLD, who will need additional and very specific activities to cater for their individual needs. Greater flexibility in terms of time for work on priority areas within the National Curriculum resulted from the Dearing Report (Boyd and Lloyd 1995), but for pupils with PMLD the challenge remained of providing useful and meaningful, rather than tokenistic, access to the National Curriculum subjects (Kent TVEI (Technical, Vocational Education Initiative) 1995). The entitlement to balance and relevance indicates the need for time to be spent on elements of the developmental and additional curricula, which are not easily embedded into work derived from the National Curriculum.

These concerns were addressed in *Planning the Curriculum for Pupils with Profound and Multiple Learning Difficulties* (SCAA 1996). Indeed, the stated purpose of this document was (p. 1, our italics) 'to show how all the priorities for pupils' learning can be planned for, both *through* and *alongside* the revised National Curriculum orders'. Many of the priorities in IEPs for pupils with PMLD are likely to involve the acquisition of basic and fundamental skills that are not amenable to categorisation into subject-related knowledge, skills and concepts (Coupe O'Kane *et al.* 1995). Nevertheless, for pupils with PMLD the National Curriculum programmes of study can provide a structure and context for activities that offer opportunities for working on individual priorities. The SCAA document states (p. 12): 'Subject-specific contexts can be provided to teach skills identified in a pupil's individual targets, whether these are directly related to the subject or not.'

In this case, the pupil is not learning about the subject, but learning *through* the subject. Just as the National Curriculum can be a vehicle for general learning, other aspects of the whole curriculum (whether additional subjects that are traditionally regarded as part of the developmental curriculum, or alternative activities, such as therapies and remedial and innovative work) can be a vehicle for subject-related learning. Figure 17.2 shows in a schematic way how both focus on individual learning priorities and breadth of experience can be addressed through activities that are derived from different elements of the whole curriculum.

It would be a mistake to assume that subjects can only be used with pupils with PMLD as vehicles for learning basic and undifferentiated skills – the 'continuing work, comprising skills and processes that might permeate all learning experiences for pupils with profound and multiple learning difficulties' that is described in the SCAA document (SCAA 1996, p. 32). Each subject can be seen as providing a learning continuum, starting with the general basic concepts and skills acquired during the early stages of learning, which are the foundations for all future learning and progressing, through the teaching activities, toward subject-specific concepts, knowledge, skills and understanding. At some point along the learning continuum, each pupil will begin to grasp the subject-specific elements, and then the subject, as well as the activity to which it has given rise, will have meaning for the pupil. We are all of us at some point along this learning continuum, which extends to the farthest limits of human understanding – a point that very few of us

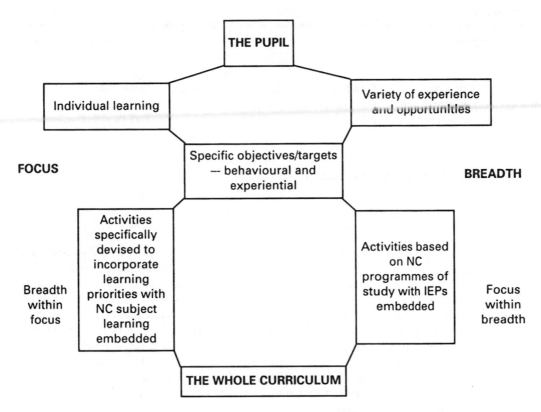

Figure 17.2 Focus and breadth in the curriculum (This section is adapted from Ouvry 1994.)

indeed will ever achieve. Figure 17.3 illustrates this learning continuum from basic general concepts and skills to highly specific subject-related skills, knowledge and understanding.

It is not possible to predict when or whether a pupil with PMLD – or, indeed, a young child, or a pupil with SLD – will reach a stage when learning changes from general to subject-specific. However, the use of subjects as vehicles for general basic learning ensures that no pupil is denied the possibility of making this transition, and, if it does not occur, ensures breadth and variety of experience while still focusing on learning priorities. A pupil can be said to be learning through the subject – the subject is part of the method rather than the content.

The SCAA's 1996 document gives an example in which pupils with PMLD were involved in a maths activity with their class group. The subject content was the estimation and measurement of distance, but the individual content for the pupils with PMLD was physical release of grip on a car and visual tracking as it rolled down a slope. All the pupils in the group would be at their own individual levels of understanding and achievement of the subject-related content. It is interesting to speculate how far along the continuum each pupil with PMLD might be, and whether the positioning of the pupils allowed opportunities to access both general and subject-related content. It is important

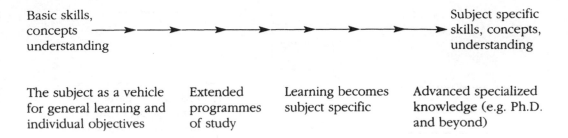

Figure 17.3 The learning continuum

to realise that pupils will only be able to achieve the more specific subject-related learning as and when the opportunities for this are made available and accessible.

This continuum from general to highly specific subject-related skills and understanding is reflected in the differentiated performance criteria identified to assist in the target-setting process (DfEE 2001). These criteria extend the level descriptions in some subjects of the National Curriculum, and provide criteria for personal and social development that did not have level descriptions prior to this document. The first three levels (labelled P1–P3) for all subjects are the same, and comprise basic skills, concepts and understanding, as shown in Fig. 17.3. The following levels (P4–P8) are extensions of, and lead into, Level 1 of the National Curriculum and represent a gradual move towards subject-specific skills and understanding.

The publication entitled *Planning, Teaching and Assessing the Curriculum for Pupils with Learning Difficulties* (DfEE/QCA 2001) is intended to underpin these earlier developments and to help ensure the inclusion of all pupils, including those with PMLD, in the full entitlement to the National Curriculum. In addition to guidance on the development of the whole curriculum, these guidelines provide supporting materials that extend the PoS in all the National Curriculum subjects including cross-curricular skills. The guidelines also provide supplementary materials for areas that were formerly regarded as being part of the developmental or additional curricula, which are particularly relevant to pupils with PMLD (such as personal, social and health education, and daily living skills). It is emphasised that the materials are not intended to represent a separate curriculum, but they extend and expand the PoS of the National Curriculum so as to accommodate the complex learning needs of pupils working significantly below age-related expectations and, in particular, those with PMLD. It is also recognised that some of the pupils will have other important individual priorities – such as various forms of therapy, or physical or emotional healthcare needs – that do not easily fall within the National Curriculum even in its extended form.

The sensory approach

The sensory approach has, for a considerable time, been widely used as a point of access to a wide range of subjects and experiences, including the National Curriculum

(Bowe 1994; Longhorn 1994). However, the current guidelines demonstrate, by identifying sensory awareness and perception as one element in the area of thinking skills, that this level of access should not be regarded as sufficient in itself.

Sensory experiences alone are not enough because they do not necessarily have any meaning for a pupil. It is only when they have an intrinsic meaning of their own, or are part of an experience that itself has meaning, that they will provide the opportunity for meaningful involvement in the learning process and the development of thinking skills, leading to more subject-specific understanding. As well as providing a broad range of sensory stimuli and facilitating the acquisition of perceptual skills, sensory experiences should also provide opportunities for conceptual learning and greater understanding of a pupil's surroundings and the activities and experiences of everyday life (Carpenter 1994b).

The sensory approach can be used in a number of ways (Moss 1994; Sims 1994). Firstly, there is the traditional approach, which is rooted in the developmental curriculum and is used to 'stimulate' the senses in order to:

- increase awareness of change in the surroundings;
- improve acuity;
- develop perceptual skills to gather information from the environment.

Activities are devised to provide sensory experiences that are usually based on stages of sensory development and the acquisition of basic skills identified as priorities in the pupils' IEPs. The equipment and materials used are frequently specialised and often have no inherent meaning of their own, or they are used in a way that is quite different from that for which they were made. Activities using this type of equipment are often carried out in situations that do not provide a meaningful context.

This approach is useful in assessment and training of sensory skills, in providing motivating experiences that a pupil at the earliest stages of learning can engage in, and can provide a starting point for the functional use of the senses; but it has limitations as a long-term teaching technique.

Secondly, sensory experiences may be incorporated into activities that have their own structure and meaning but that have been devised to provide opportunities for sensory work within the sequence of the activity. The sensory experiences will still be based upon individual priorities and will focus on the development and use of perceptual skills. Drama, games, music, art, massage and many other activities are used in this way, and there are an increasing number of 'resource packs' commercially available (such as 'Galaxies', sensory stories, etc.) that focus on sensory experiences within a structured activity.

Thirdly, sensory experiences are used as an access route to subject-based activities that have their own body of concepts, knowledge, skills and understanding, some of which may be accessible to pupils with PMLD (Moss 1994). The activity has its own meaning and also offers opportunities for sensory experiences (for example, handling artefacts or equipment relating to a topic under discussion) that may or may not have meaning for a pupil with PMLD. The difficulty here is that sensory experiences may seem quite random and meaningless to the pupil with PMLD when provided through a topic whose meaning is outside the understanding of the pupil.

The challenge facing teachers is how to create a meaningful sensory experience for pupils in all teaching contexts and one that provides the opportunity to progress beyond experience to understanding. The sensory experience has to be invested with its own

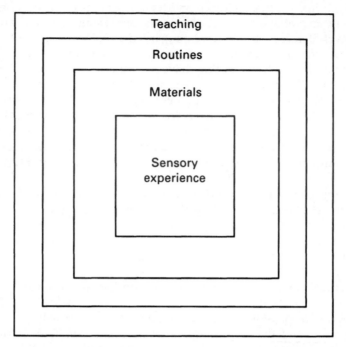

Figure 17.4 Aspects of an activity that provide meaning to sensory experiences

meaning for those pupils who are currently learning at that level, in addition to any meaning it may have in relation to the subject that forms the context for the activity. This applies equally to activities that are not specifically focused on the National Curriculum.

The experiences must provide opportunities for conceptual learning, as well as providing sensory experiences. There are a number of ways in which this can be achieved. A sensory experience can acquire meaning in relation to different aspects of any given situation or activity. Figure 17.4 shows how the different aspects of an activity provide ever-widening possibilities for creating meaning from sensory experiences.

Some of the youngest pupils, and a small number of older pupils with PMLD, will be at the earliest stages of learning, when the sensory properties are the focal point. McInnes and Treffry (1982) have called this the 'TRY' stage and describe it (p. 19) as providing a pupil with the motivation to reach outside of the self and to initiate interaction between himself/herself and the environment. Engagement and interaction with the materials lead to the earliest form of meanings with the development of preferences, and of early concepts of object permanence, cause and effect, and relationships with the ability to control events.

However, the sensory experiences can also contain conceptual elements such as similarity and difference, or specific concepts relating to a particular sense. For example, the sense of touch is used in many activities to explore artefacts related to a subject or used in an activity. In addition to the sensory properties of the materials used, concepts can be introduced through carefully chosen experiences that demonstrate: similarity and difference; contrasts of temperature, texture, weight, etc.; and the identification of objects relating to the activity.

Materials and equipment

Materials and equipment can acquire meaning by association with familiar activities – for example, items related to personal welfare, eating and drinking, food technology, design and technology, and information technology. Regular appropriate and specific use of objects can be built into the scheme of work, and this may enable objects of reference to be used to identify an activity in advance and to prepare a pupil for participation.

Progress can be seen in terms of:

- recognition of objects/materials used regularly;
- noticing the absence of objects/materials used regularly;
- expression of likes and dislikes, and an ability to make considered choices between different materials;
- differentiation of actions used in relation to materials;
- functional understanding of a range of materials/equipment;
- complexity of equipment/materials and their functions and properties;
- appropriate use of familiar objects/materials in other settings;
- using a range of actions with new materials in new activities.

In the history section of *Teaching Humanities to Pupils with Special Educational Needs* (Coupe O'Kane *et al.* 1995) there is an example of using objects that have a very personal meaning to individual pupils, such as outgrown boots or armbands previously used when swimming. By evoking a sense of personal history in pupils with PMLD, the opportunity is taken to introduce subject-related concepts such as the passing of time.

Routines, signals and cues

Familiarity with routines and sequences of events that form a regular part of an activity can also invest sensory experiences with meaning, because they become signals and cues for what is *going* to happen; meaning is derived from the structure of the activity.

Routines, signals and cues can be built into all teaching activities, whether this is personal welfare, classroom tasks, thematic experiences or subject-focused activities. Routines will allow not only the recognition of the sensory elements of the activity but also anticipation of what is coming next and thereby an opportunity for active participation. Within a routine, pupils can be given choices based on the sensory experiences themselves or their meaning for each pupil. The pupils can be given space for initiatives within the known routine, e.g. 'What comes next?', 'What shall we use next?' or 'This is not the usual way that we ...'. Distinct start and finish routines can give information about what an activity is about, the sequence of experiences within it, and what is going to happen next.

Progress can be seen in terms of:

- active engagement in the activity;
- demonstrating anticipation of the sequence of events;
- an ability to initiate within the routine;
- an ability to participate in the routine at any point in its sequence;
- an ability to recognise the routine in a different environment;
- increasing number of routines in which a particular pupil can take an active part.

The teaching environment

The teaching environment will also invest sensory experiences with meaning. Pupils learn how to 'read' their surroundings, using their senses and learning the familiar landmarks, signals and clues that tell them about a place, an activity or an event. Particularly as pupils move toward adulthood, there is a need for a variety of environments – including off-site and community environments – to be provided so that they can use and develop their skills in reading their environment and become familiar with a variety of different places.

Progress can be seen in terms of:

- a familiarity with learning environments;
- anticipation of a learning event/activity;
- an increased number and complexity of environments that are familiar;
- an ability to function and participate in an increasingly greater number of environments.

The history section in *Teaching Humanities to Pupils with Special Educational Needs* (Coupe O'Kane *et al.* 1995) includes a number of examples that show how sequences of events and consequences of actions can lead to a concept of change of time passing. The examples illustrate many ways of using sensory experiences and making them meaningful. They show ways in which the regular association of experiences can create meaning – for example, the linking of: a person with a particular experience; a symbol with a regularly occurring event; activities within the sequence of events; a place with a regular event. This culminates in generating a sense of personal history by the use of articles with a very personal meaning to each pupil (Park 1998): one object or experience on its own has no meaning, but in association with others it acquires meaning for an individual.

The following detailed example of the planning and carrying out of a project in design and technology will show how an activity generated by the National Curriculum can provide a context for learning at a number of levels, and how it can create meaning from sensory experiences.

Illustration of a context for learning: design and technology

As with all subjects of the curriculum, design and technology can be used as a context for learning fundamental skills and concepts and for working on individual objective. However, the practical nature of many aspects of the subject also means that it provides excellent opportunities for practising subject-specific skills and gaining subject-specific vocabulary, knowledge and understanding.

The curriculum for design and technology describes ways in which pupils develop their design and technology capability through the process of perceiving a problem or need, designing, adapting or modifying something that that will solve the problem or meet the need, making the article (which engages them in sustained practical effort), and evaluating the finished product. In Key Stage 1, pupils are: working with a wide range of materials to make products; experiencing elements of construction by assembling and dissembling products; and seeing how the characteristics of materials can be altered and used to suit different purposes. Pupils are also generating ideas about what to make and how to make it; designing, making and modifying products; reflecting on the process and finished product; and evaluating strengths and weaknesses. Throughout the process they are expanding their technological vocabulary and understanding, and developing their thinking in a technological way. As pupils move through the subsequent key stages, they are engaged in a similar process of designing, building and evaluating, but they are developing more complex practical skills and engaging in technological debate at an increasingly sophisticated level.

In thinking about how pupils with PMLD can be given access to as much of the design and technology curriculum as possible (see also Chapter 11 of this book), it is necessary first to consider the essence of the subject and discover what, at its most fundamental level, it is all about. We can then go on to consider how we may convey this essence to pupils and thereby give them experiences that will help them to extend their experience and develop their understanding of it.

Design and technology is, at its heart, about drawing on knowledge and understanding of the world, the products that exist within it, and ones own experience of them, to identify problems or ways in which things could be improved, and about effecting a change or constructing something in order to solve a problem. Thus, the subject is ideal for pupils with PMLD because it encourages greater awareness of their own physical environment and the development of the notion that they can act to improve their experiences within that environment, both of which are crucial elements of their learning.

To a large extent we, as teachers, are responsible for the environment in which our pupils learn, the ways in which staff relate to children, the activities and tasks that they engage in, and their experience of daily living while at school. Thus we have the opportunity to develop in our pupils the attitudes and ways of thinking that will be helpful to them as individuals, as well as encouraging the development of technological understanding. We can do this by teaching them to recognise the following:

- that problems exist but can be solved;
- that individuals have the power to change things and make them better through either action or communication;
- that pupils can express an opinion about how they would like something to be and then experience the consequences of that decision.

The 'design and make' aspect of the design and technology curriculum incorporates elements of: exploring a task to identify a problem or need; generating an idea and communicating it to others; testing out proposals; and planning and making a product. While it is easy to focus on the largely practical aspects of making something, the latest advice (QCA 2001) warns against reducing lessons to linear craft activities, where the design and outcome are prescribed by the teacher, because this will reduce opportunities for pupils to make the connection between designing and making. Different pupils within a group will have strengths in different areas of this process and, as part of a group experiencing elements of design, a child with PMLD may begin to appreciate the notion of planning even if he or she cannot yet personally generate the design.

The activity can also provide genuine contexts for communication – at whatever level – and for the pupil to experience the need to listen to and consider the ideas of other people. The roots of design lie in choice, and it is only when we can perceive the different ways that something might be, or might be used, that we can begin to think of the best or most suitable way to construct it. By experiencing and exploring all aspects of a task or product – trying out different options, making simple choices, and expressing opinions on the different options – a pupil can be said to be on the road to designing. Making choices and expressing opinions is fundamental learning that a pupil with PMLD needs to practise throughout the day in all contexts; by extending it in the subject-specific context of design and technology, the pupil might learn that personal choices can contribute in however small a way to the design of a product.

The actual making or adapting of a product also provides a wonderful focus for pupils with PMLD to engage in a wide variety of practical activities and to explore the properties of a wide range of materials – at whatever level and in whatever way possible. As well as experiencing the static properties of materials, design and technology also invites them to investigate how materials can be combined, assembled, disassembled and changed, in order to make them suit a given purpose. Additionally, pupils can experience, develop and practise skills in a range of focused practical tasks, such as: tearing, cutting, sawing, sanding, planing, sticking, nailing, stirring, mixing, dividing, etc. While these all offer plenty of opportunity for sensory exploration, they can also provide opportunities to lead pupils on from the purely sensory experiences to the development of skills and of concepts such as 'hard' and 'soft', 'rigid' and 'pliable', 'rough' and 'smooth', 'apart' and 'together'. As well as enjoying the practical tasks, pupils might also gain satisfaction from a knowledge that they are engaged in a meaningful activity that will lead to the development of a real finished product – be it a food item, a piece of art, or a product that can be used in their daily lives.

The final element of design and technology is product evaluation. This may be hard for some pupils with PMLD but, as with design, if such pupils are given the opportunity to engage in evaluative activities – perhaps as part of a group – then evaluative thought can emerge. At its most simple, evaluation involves expressing an opinion about something. It is therefore important that the projects chosen for pupils with PMLD should be as relevant to their daily lives and their practical experience as possible, so that the results of their efforts impinge in a genuine way on their lives. By asking pupils for their opinions or noting their instinctive or intended responses – even if it is simply by noting likes and dislikes – those pupils are being involved in evaluation. If they can go on to appreciate that their responses are acted upon and that something changes as a result – be it as simple as the fact that an activity is not repeated or as complex as a product being redesigned – then learning has taken place. This learning can dramatically improve every aspect of their lives, showing again how the subject of design and technology can provide a focus or context for generalised learning as well as giving opportunities for specific knowledge and skill development.

The following example shows how design and technology can be incorporated into a topic that the class may be studying and how an individual child's personal learning objectives as well as specific design-and-technology goals may be pursued.

An example project

Assume that we are in a school where the current topic is movement and that much work has been undertaken in different curricular areas to explore this subject. A design-and-technology component might focus on ways of moving things from one place to another, covering some or all of the following:

1. investigating familiar products and exploring materials;
2. designing and making;
3. undertaking focused practical tasks;
4. achieving individual objectives.

These four aspects are discussed further below.

Investigating familiar products and exploring materials
For example, pupils might:

- gather in one place all the items that they can identify within the school that help people move things or themselves around, e.g. a trolley, a large box or crate, a bookcase on wheels, a set of rollers or castors, a wheelchair, a motor car, the school bus, etc.;
- explore the properties of each through moving different things around in each one;
- experience different ways of moving things, e.g. pushing and pulling, sliding, carrying in the hands, carrying in the lap, throwing, rolling, tying to a wheelchair and towing, etc.

For some pupils, this stage of sensory exploration will provide opportunities to experience the different properties of the items and the contrasts between them. Many of them will already have meaning for them as they are familiar everyday objects that they see regularly though perhaps do not often use themselves.

The purely sensory experiences can be extended into concept development such as:

- 'heavy' and 'light';
- 'large' (bulky) and 'small' (non-bulky);
- 'wheeled' and 'non-wheeled';
- the moving of objects within a room or between rooms.

Designing and making
There could be opportunities to share in the design and construction of a wheeled trolley that could be used to transport objects from room to room (and perhaps to move people over short distances under close supervision). At its simplest, the trolley could be a piece of medium-density fibreboard (MDF) with castors at each corner. At its most complex it could include sides, handles, brakes, etc. The complexity of the task will need to be determined by the skills of the staff and the resources available. (A volunteer or the school caretaker may be willing to help if necessary.) While the degree of involvement of each child in the design process will vary according to ability, the important thing is that all pupils are given the opportunity to participate at their own level and to experience the results and consequences of their own design decisions, whether successful or not. Much can be learned from seeing the consequences of wrong decisions (e.g. a trolley with three wheels keeps tipping).

When the trolley is complete, the pupils should be involved in using it as much as possible and possibly be moved on it themselves. Ongoing use of it in the classroom will encourage them to make the association between the product they have made and its ultimate usefulness. Their responses to it may well develop over time.

Undertaking focused practical tasks

The example project gives opportunities for a whole range of practical tasks, each of which is a complete activity in its own right, but that together build a finished product.

The sounds, sights, smells and tactile experiences involved in handling woodworking tools and carrying out (or being helped to carry out) the tasks of sawing, planing, sanding, drilling, hammering, screwing, etc. are immense – and usually very different from other daily activities. Ideally, the activity should be carried out in a specific location, e.g. a garage or workshop, so that the atmosphere, smells, sounds, etc. that are specific to that area can help the pupils to place the activity in a specific context. Similarly, the special tools and materials that they work on can be used to cue them into the activity and help them to anticipate the task to come. Enabling pupils to use the tools and be as independent as possible within the constraints of safety and good practice should be a priority; they can gain satisfaction from the knowledge that they have been able to contribute meaningfully to a finished product, even if their task has been simply the sanding of the wood.

Achieving individual objectives

Consider an imaginary pupil, Asad, whose IEP shows that he needs to work on fundamental skills such as: turn-taking; grasping and releasing; making choices from picture cues; appropriate use of familiar everyday objects; and balance while sitting. All these can be addressed through the technology sessions. For example:

- Asad will participate in reciprocal games of pushing and pulling objects across a table with an adult; he will also throw objects to another person and catch them back with physical help;
- Asad will take objects out of wheeled vehicles and place them in a different vehicle when given the verbal instruction;
- Asad will choose which woodworking task he wishes to do from a choice of three photograph cards;
- Asad will use a sandpaper block to smooth a piece of wood without a verbal prompt and unaided;
- Asad will support himself in a sitting position when helped onto the trolley and maintain this posture as he is pulled the length of the corridor.

This example shows how a curriculum subject such as design and technology can be used to give pupils a different context in which to practise their generalised learning objectives, and also how it can give them a wide range of subject-specific experiences that, through sensory exploration, can lead to increased vocabulary, understanding and skills. The variety of experiences also expands the breadth of the curriculum, offering enjoyment and stimulation.

Record keeping

The keeping of records in an appropriate way is an important element of the teaching process as it enables the teacher to maintain an ongoing awareness of a pupil's current abilities and level of skills, so that future planning and teaching can be better focused and made more effective. Figure 17.5 shows the stages in this process.

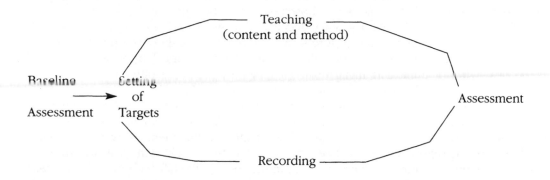

Figure 17.5 Stages in the assessment and recording process

Recording also meets the esteem and motivation needs of pupils, teaching staff and parents, who can see that a particular child is progressing. When, as with most pupils with PMLD, progress is slow and the steps made are small, effective record keeping is even more important to show achievement. However, devising an effective record-keeping system is not an easy task and, as Byers and Rose (1996) point out, many schools have struggled to develop a format that is usable, manageable and also meets the needs of all pupils and teachers in a school. It is important that a school has a coordinated approach to record keeping, with common systems and formats; but it is also essential that any system is flexible enough to meet the needs of a wide variety of pupils in a school.

There are many characteristics of a good record-keeping system, but when we are considering record keeping for pupils with PMLD the following features are particularly important. The record-keeping system should:

- allow for the recording of experiences given as well as responses or achievements made;
- be able to be completed by a variety of staff, not just the teaching staff;
- relate directly to each pupil's IEP;
- be able to take account of a wide variety of pupil responses to a situation;
- record achievement in subject-specific understanding and individual priorities;
- be capable of recording responses in whole-class and small-group sessions as well as in individual sessions;
- allow for the recording of process as well as final result;
- be simple to complete and analyse, leading directly to the assessment of progress and the planning of future work;
- lead directly and easily to the production of reports for a variety of interested parties.

A record-keeping system can easily become unwieldy and result in the production of volumes of paper that are never looked at again. In those circumstances, a teacher becomes a slave to the system, spending far too long filling out record sheets and thus leaving too little time to consider and analyse what the records show about each pupil's learning. *Planning the Curriculum for Pupils with Profound and Multiple Learning Difficulties* (SCAA 1996) stresses the requirement for a system that enables pupils' responses to be recorded as and when those responses are significant.

It is crucial, therefore, that a teacher decides what not to record, as well as what is significant to an individual and therefore should be recorded. Using each pupil's IEP as a guide as to what to include can provide a useful starting point. Surprising or unusual responses, when a pupil acts in an uncharacteristic or markedly different way, should always be noted and the reasons for the change should considered.

The SCAA document also emphasises the need to record each pupil's *experiences* as well as achievements. It is necessary to ensure that pupils have adequate coverage of the range of curriculum subjects and of the subject matter within them. However, showing evidence of curricular coverage need not involve the teacher in vast amounts of recording: general schemes of work, with an indication of whether the pupil was present for the session or not, may suffice. Of greater importance, and the point on which teachers should concentrate their efforts, are the records that show significant individual responses in relation to the priorities highlighted in IEPs. These records should lead a teacher to consider for each pupil:

- achievements;
- possible regression;
- lack of, patchy, or inconsistent progress;
- apparent difficulties;
- any need for support;
- learning style;
- personal interests.

All of the items in the preceding list should help a teacher to plan further work and to use teaching strategies best suited to each pupil's learning style.

It is also necessary to remember that, for pupils with PMLD, progress or achievement may not always equate with moving up a hierarchy of achievement that describes an ever-increasing level of skill or knowledge. While always working towards higher skill levels, teachers should also be looking to increase understanding of experiences, to provide breadth, and enable pupils to carry out existing skills in different circumstances. Figure 17.6 illustrates these two dimensions of progress.

increasing level
or complexity
of skills

familiarity and understanding
of increasing number of
environments and transfer of
skills to new situations

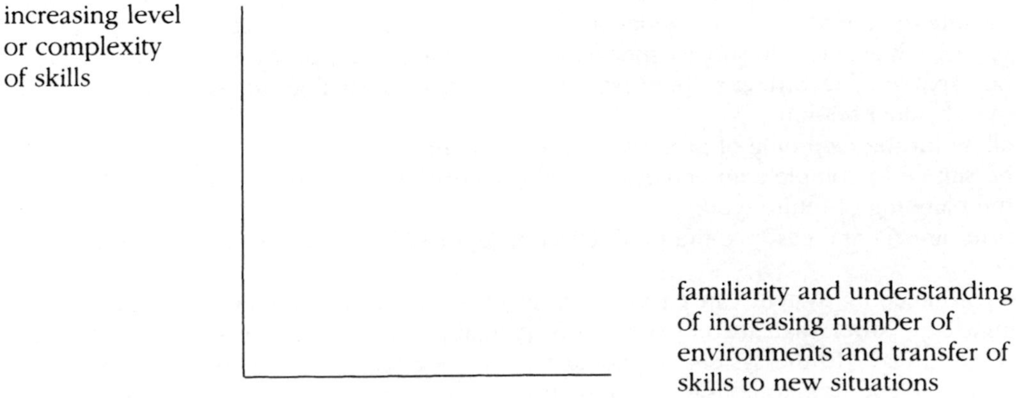

Figure 17.6 Two dimensions of progress

It is important that record-keeping systems are able to illustrate progress in both of the dimensions shown in the diagram. Here, the shortcomings of the checklist system of recording are apparent as, all too often, these are designed to record progress on the vertical axis only, so that pupils who have not developed new competences but have nevertheless had experiences (becoming tolerant of, and showing increasing ability to participate in, a variety of situations) are not given the recognition that they deserve. For pupils with PMLD, this dimension of progress may be the most achievable.

References

Aird, R. (2001) *The Education and Care of Children with Severe, Profound and Multiple Learning Difficulties*. London: David Fulton Publishers.

Boyd, C. and Lloyd, P. (1995) 'The school context for curriculum change', in Ashcroft, K. and Palacio, D. (eds) *The Primary Teacher's Guide to the New National Curriculum*. London: Falmer Press.

Bowe, A. (1994) 'The evaluation of the sensory curriculum for meeting the needs of pupils with PMLD', *PMLD-Link* 20, 7–9.

Byers, R. and Rose, R. (1996) *Planning the Curriculum for Pupils with Special Educational Needs*. London: David Fulton Publishers.

Carpenter, B. (1994a) 'Facing the future: the challenge of educating learners with PMLD', *Westminster Studies in Education* 17, 37–43.

Carpenter, B. (1994b) 'Finding a home for the sensory curriculum', *PMLD-Link* 19, 2–3.

Coupe O'Kane, J. *et al.* (eds) (1995) *Teaching Humanities to Pupils with Special Educational Needs: A practical resource*. Telford: Ergent Publications.

DfEE (2001) *Supporting the Target Setting Process: Guidance for effective target setting for pupils with special educational needs, revised edition*. London: DfEE.

DfEE/QCA (2001) *Planning, Teaching and Assessing the Curriculum for Pupils with Learning Difficulties*. London: DfEE/QCA.

Kent TVEI (1995) *Crossing the Bridge: Access to the National Curriculum for pupils with profound and complex learning difficulties*, Canterbury: South East Information Network.

Longhorn, F. (1994) 'Noses in action', *PMLD-Link* 23, 7–9.

Male, D. (1996) 'Who goes to SLD schools?', *British Journal of Special Education* **23**(1), 35–41.

McInnes, J. M. and Treffry, J. A. (1982) *Deaf-Blind Infants and Children*. Milton Keynes: Open University Press.

Moss, N. (1994) 'Assessment, recording and reporting of the sensory curriculum', *PMLD-Link* 20, 10–12.

Ouvry, C. (1987) *Educating Children with Profound Handicaps*. Kidderminster: British Institute for Mental Health.

Ouvry, C. (1991) 'Access for pupils with profound and multiple learning difficulties', in Ashdown, R. *et al.* (eds) *The Curriculum Challenge: Access to the National Curriculum for pupils with learning difficulties*. London: Falmer Press.

Ouvry, C. (1994) 'Approaches to intervention'. Course Unit in 'Strategies for working with people with profound and multiple learning disabilities' (EDSE 35), Birmingham: The University of Birmingham.

Park, K. (1998) 'Form and function in early communication', *The SLD Experience* 21, 2–5.

QCA (2001) *Planning, Teaching and Assessing the Curriculum for Pupils with Learning Difficulties: Design and Technology*. London: QCA.

SCAA (1994) *The National Curriculum and its Assessment*, London: SCAA

SCAA (1996) *Planning the Curriculum for Pupils with Profound and Multiple Learning Difficulties*, London: SCAA.

Sebba, J. and Byers, R. (1992) 'The National Curriculum: control or liberation for pupils with learning difficulties', *The Curriculum Journal* 3(1), 143–60.

Sebba, J. *et al.* (1995) (eds) *Redefining the Whole Curriculum for Pupils with Learning Difficulties*, 2nd edn. London: David Fulton Publishers.

Sims, J. (1994) 'Reflecting on the sensory curriculum', *PMLD–Link* 20, 4–5.

Ware, J. (1994) 'Introduction to working with people with profound and multiple learning difficulties'. Paper written for Course Unit 1, 'People with profound and multiple learning difficulties (Part A: The population)', Birmingham: The University of Birmingham.

Chapter 18

Teachers Researching the Curriculum

Sally Beveridge

This chapter is concerned with the ways in which teachers can undertake research into the curriculum for children with learning difficulties. The idea of teachers researching the curriculum may appear rather peripheral, given the range of pressing and competing demands that schools face in the current educational climate. It is important, therefore, to begin by addressing the question of *why* teachers can find it both relevant and useful to adopt a research role. The answer lies, in part, within the notion of teachers as reflective practitioners.

Teachers as reflective practitioners

When students entering the profession are asked why they wish to become teachers, two reasons they frequently give are:

- that they find children's development fascinating, and want to be involved in enhancing their learning;
- that they think teaching will not be dull or unchanging, but will provide them with a range of varying challenges.

These reasons relate directly to two major interacting facets of the teaching role, namely the promotion of children's learning, and the extension of teachers' own professional practice in ways most likely to facilitate this. It is central to teachers' work that they seek to ensure that the quality of the provision they make is as effective as possible in promoting children's learning. This emphasis requires that they become reflective practitioners, who evaluate the impact of what they do both at the level of individual classroom practice and at the level of whole-school policies.

At the level of classroom practice, teachers need to experiment with and evaluate many different aspects of their teaching. These aspects might include, for example, modes of explanation and feedback, organisational strategies, physical arrangements, different teaching materials, and the involvement of other children as a learning resource; the list is also likely to cover assessment, evaluation and record-keeping practices. It can be argued that there are a number of reasons why such experimental teaching becomes even more important when working with children who have significant learning difficulties. Firstly, children with learning difficulties require an approach that is as responsive as possible to their diverse, complex and possibly idiosyncratic patterns of needs. Secondly, because pupils can sometimes appear to 'get stuck' on plateaux of learning, they require inventive and creative help from their teachers if they are to maintain motivation and make progress. Further, wherever progress is slow or uneven, not only the pupils but also their teachers need strategies that emphasise forms of monitoring and evaluation that are sufficiently detailed to promote a sense of achievement. Finally, children with the most complex learning difficulties may be particularly vulnerable to the 'fads and fashions' that, as Robson (1993) argues, education is prone to. If this is so, then it is essential that teachers should assess the impact of new methods and materials as closely as possible.

Reflection upon their own practice can help teachers to extend the development of their professional skills, knowledge and understanding. While much of their evaluation must focus on what goes on at an individual classroom level, they can also work in cooperation with colleagues to monitor and appraise practices across the school. The focus of investigation at a whole-school level might include, for example, the channels of communication that exist among staff in a particular school, and between the school and the parents and/or professional support agencies, and the ways in which these affect the curriculum.

Whether they engage in exploration of classroom-based or of school-based issues, when teachers seek to follow more systematic approaches in their investigations, then they are extending their reflective practice to incorporate an element of research.

Research as an extension of professional skills

What is research? A dictionary definition of the verb 'to research' includes: 'to search into [a matter or subject]; to investigate or study closely' (*The Shorter Oxford English Dictionary* 1973). Synonyms include: to 'investigate, explore, delve into, dig into, enquire' and to 'examine, study, inspect' (*The Oxford Thesaurus* 1991). Moreover, Robson (1993) has described the personal qualities needed by researchers as follows (p. 162, my italics):

> having an *open and enquiring mind*, being a '*good listener*', general *sensitivity* and *responsiveness to contradictory evidence*.

It can thus be argued that the term 'research' embraces a range of exploratory and evaluative activity that is directly associated with teachers' reflective practice; and also that it involves attributes and skills that should be central to teachers' work. It would be misleading to conclude, though, that this means that research is always an integral part of teaching. It involves a more rigorous approach than is usual in teachers' practice, and the use of systematic methods of enquiry. Accordingly, the research role is best seen as an *extension* of professional skills.

Teachers are most likely to see a need to take on this extended role in order to:

● increase their understanding and awareness of their own practice and that of their school as a whole;

- gather relevant evidence about the effectiveness of their practice;
- enhance their confidence and skill for experimenting with new ways of working.

Whether teachers engage in individual or in collaborative study with colleagues, they benefit from having someone who can play the part of a 'critical friend' (Lomax 1991) to support them in their research role. By acting as a sounding board and by putting forward alternative perspectives, such critical friends can help researchers to articulate and clarify their thinking.

The role of teacher–researcher

Teachers have a number of advantages over outside researchers when it comes to the investigation of practice in their own school settings. For example, they have a wealth of background knowledge and experience of the context for their study. They are not only familiar with school policies and procedures, but they have usually also built up relationships of trust with those who may be involved in the research. As a result, they should be in a good position to ensure that the study is developed in ways that are sensitive to the perspectives of the pupils, staff and parents concerned.

However, there are also disadvantages that can arise from knowing the setting so well. Teachers may need to 'fight familiarity' (Vulliamy and Webb 1992) if they are to remain open to fresh perspectives, alternative interpretations and new insights into school-based practice. It is important to recognise, too, that teachers' status in relation to pupils, parents and colleagues may well influence the research role that they are able to adopt; a teacher may find it hard, for example, to sit back and take a non-directive classroom role in the same way that an outside researcher might. It is therefore necessary for teachers to give thought to the nature of the research role that they aim to adopt, and to communicate this clearly to others. In doing so, it is helpful to bear in mind the different sets of expectations that can be associated with teaching and research. Cooper (1995) suggests that while teachers are expected to make judgements and provide an active lead, researchers are required to be impartial and non-judgmental, following the lead of their 'subjects'. Perhaps what is most significant here is that researchers need to try to see things from a range of different viewpoints, rather than only those that fit with a teacher's perspective.

The role of teacher–researcher brings with it certain ethical considerations. Firstly, wherever evaluative research goes beyond personal and subjective practice to that of other people, then it is evident that teachers must be alert to the potential sensitivities that can be involved. Those who are to be affected by the evaluation need the information and the opportunity to discuss the purposes and motivation for the research, the ways in which research evidence will be gathered, and the use to which findings will be put. For example, if the research aims to promote some change in school practice, then colleagues need to feel that they will have some involvement in the decisions that are made.

Further, there are some well-established principles in research that require careful consideration by teachers who wish to conduct investigations in their own school context. Depending on the nature of the research, these can apply not only to colleagues but also to pupils and their parents. They relate to the protection of anonymity and of confidentiality, which can sometimes be difficult to ensure within a small and close staff group (Robson 1993); they also concern the extent to which the 'subjects' of the study have real choice about their participation (Clough and Barton 1995). As a general principle, researchers should seek to ensure that all participants are clear about the purposes of the investigation and that they are willing to be involved. There are issues here when pupils are the focus of study. These arise from both their understanding of and their relationship to teachers at school (Burgess 1995). The issues become more complex among children and young people who have significant learning difficulties, and in all cases it is important to communicate with their parents about pupils' participation.

Purposes and approaches in teacher research

The focus of teacher research must clearly be the curriculum in its broadest sense, and the aim must be to ensure that the curriculum experienced by the pupils is as effective as possible in promoting their learning and development. Table 18.1 illustrates the sorts of topics that teachers of children with learning difficulties might seek to investigate.

Table 18.1 Teachers researching the curriculum: some examples of research topics

	Individual children and class group examples	Whole-school examples
Range and quality of planned learning experiences	Curriculum audit; inclusive learning; specific teaching approaches; specific learning programmes; cross-curricular links; use of ICT; etc.	Process of curriculum planning, development and review; specialist curricular roles; specific policy development, for example in relation to inclusion; etc.
Processes of development and learning	Generalisation of skills; problem-solving; aspects of communication; involvement of children in target-setting, self evaluation and review; self-advocacy; classroom-based assessment; etc.	Whole-school approaches to assessment, recording and reporting; the involvement of children and parents in the process; the involvement of speech, physio- and other therapists; etc.
Classroom relationships and management	Cooperative learning; peer interactions; behaviour management; room management; etc.	Staff roles and responsibilities; working with support assistants; channels of communication; inclusion of pupils with complex needs; etc.

The table includes some examples focused on individual children and class groups and others that are concerned with whole-school policy and practice. Teacher research can also address wider issues, such as the way in which the curriculum might be enhanced by communication with parents, support agencies, other schools and colleges, the local community, and so on. Research topics may be identified as a result of factors outside school – for example, they may follow on from local or national government initiatives, or from attendance at a course that has stimulated staff interest in particular issues. On the whole, though, the impetus for undertaking an investigation will tend to be teacher concern that there are aspects of current practice that may be in need of change. The intention then is to explore current practice, identify possible improvements and, where these are implemented, monitor their effects. That is, the research is frequently of an evaluative and problem-solving nature.

Having identified a topic for research, the next step is to clarify what is to be investigated and why. Teachers can usefully develop their thinking about the specific research questions they wish to address in discussion with colleagues. They also need to seek out relevant sources of information, such as those coming to light through practitioner journals and professional contacts. It may well be that aims and intentions are only refined as the investigation gets under way, in a pilot phase or a period of 'progressive focusing' (Corrie and Zaklukiewicz 1985), in which research questions become more distinct as a result of the information that is gathered.

However, it is essential for the overall sense of direction that sufficient time is given to ensure that purposes are as clearly stated as possible at the outset. The range of purposes may include:

- exploration, experimentation and evaluation of particular teaching strategies and procedures;
- the enhancement of teacher awareness and understanding – for example of the perspectives of pupils, parents and colleagues from other disciplines;
- the development of professional skills, for example in observational assessment, involving pupils in target-setting, cooperative learning, the use of new technology, and so on.

Once the research questions and purposes are reasonably clear, it is possible to make decisions about the sort of research approach through which they might practicably be addressed. Robson (1993) has distinguished two main research approaches of particular relevance to teachers. When the research questions require a broad overview of evidence gathered in standard form from a number of different people, then a *survey approach* can be appropriate. For instance, perspectives might be sought from teachers within the local area who have a responsibility for coordinating ICT across the curriculum; or from the music therapists who have links with the region's special schools; or from the mainstream pupils who have experience of a particular inclusion initiative.

Frequently, though, teachers' research questions require an approach that offers less wide-ranging but more detailed evidence. A *case-study approach* allows an in-depth investigation, with (for example) an individual child or group of children, a group of school staff, an interdisciplinary team, or a single school, as the focus. One particular form of case-study approach, referred to as 'action research', is often recommended for school-based problem-solving (see, for example, O'Hanlon 1996). This involves a cyclical process through which schools can continually modify and refine their practice. Adelman (1985) has described four stages of the process in which school staff:

- identify their concerns and collect research evidence that will help them clarify what, if anything, needs changing;
- propose some changes that, on the basis of the evidence, provide possible solutions to their concerns;
- develop an action plan to implement those changes;
- monitor and evaluate their effects.

It is important to note that the choice between undertaking surveys and case studies does not have to be of an either/or nature, because for some evaluative studies it is helpful to combine the two approaches. For example, teachers can use a preliminary survey as a basis for identifying significant issues or examples of practice, which they then go on to investigate at greater depth through case studies. Conversely, they can use exploratory case-study observations and interviews as a basis for the development of a broader survey.

Contexts and methods of investigation

When the purposes and general research approach have been identified, then decisions need to be made about *who* is to be studied, in which *settings or contexts*, and in what sorts of *activities*, in order best to answer the specific research questions. Taking each of these in turn, the study might, for example:

- focus on individuals, groups or classes of children, and/or their parents and staff;
- take place in classrooms, staff rooms, playgrounds, homes, clinics, the local environment, or some combination of these;
- highlight particular sorts of events and activities, more or less structured learning opportunities, processes or products of interaction, and so on.

There are a number of texts that teachers can find useful in terms of the detailed guidance they provide on research methods (e.g. Bell 1999; Cohen *et al.* 2000; Robson 1993). The following discussion offers a brief overview of issues in the use of the three main types of method of investigation that can be chosen. They involve the researcher in observing behaviour; in asking people for information and for their views, feelings and perspectives; and in collecting written documentation or visual records. These are not mutually exclusive approaches and, particularly in case studies, it is appropriate to consider combining a range of different strategies.

Observation

Direct observation allows a researcher to gather evidence about overt behaviour. The behaviour might be that of children, observed in interaction with their teachers, with other children or with particular curricular materials; or it might be that of adults, in parent–teacher consultations or in curriculum-planning meetings.

All observers bring a set of attitudes, expectations and experiences to the act of observing, which must influence both what they notice and also how they interpret it. Accordingly, it is particularly important that researchers try to guard against bias, in the form of selective sensitivity to particular behaviours or types of behaviour. Helpful strategies in this regard include:

- aiming for precision in observational records;
- making clear distinctions between evidence (what exactly was observed) and interpretation (what was inferred);
- explicit reflection upon alternative possible interpretations.

Wherever possible, it is invaluable to share observations with others, in order to check whether they see the same behaviours and interpret them in the same ways. It is also important to ask colleagues and, where appropriate, parents, about the extent to which the picture that emerges from the observations corresponds with their experience.

There are a number of related questions that need to be considered when planning to use observational methods. These concern the observer role, the form of the evidence that is collected, and the length of time over which observations should take place. Researchers can act as participant or non-participant observers. As discussed earlier, it can be difficult for teacher–researchers to take on the non-participatory role if their investigation is focused on their own work contexts. However, the greater the degree of participation in events and activities, the harder it can be to gather detailed evidence at the same time. Participant observers may also find it difficult to retain sufficient detachment to allow them to keep an overview of what is going on. If practicable, it is worth considering the use of audio- or video-recordings to support the observation process. Although it takes time to transcribe information from such records, it can be helpful in providing a more complete picture than might otherwise be achieved.

When thinking about the form of the observational evidence that they wish to collect, researchers need to consider whether they want to try to observe and record *everything* that happens within a given time period, or whether they are only interested in sampling certain aspects, such as the frequency or duration of particular types of behaviour. The first of these options is more open-ended, and may potentially offer richer insights, but it poses obvious practical difficulties as far as accuracy and detail are concerned. The second option requires a more structured approach, perhaps using prepared schedules such as those described by Croll (2000). It may lend itself to more objective and accurate information-gathering, but it can only portray certain predefined aspects of behaviour. The extent to which researchers structure their observations to focus on specific aspects of behaviour has to be guided by the questions which they seek to address, but it must also be affected by practical considerations of how much can be noted down consistently and accurately within their research settings. (See Tilstone (1998) for a detailed exploration of the use of different techniques for classroom-based observation.)

Whatever form their observations take, researchers need to feel confident that they have gathered a representative picture of what usually happens. This means that they have to make decisions about the length of time over which they should continue to gather evidence. Their own presence in an observer role can affect what takes place, and this may be particularly apparent if they use an audio- or video-recorder with children or adults who are not used to this. It is important, therefore, to plan sufficient time within each observation period as well as a sufficient number of observation sessions overall, in order to provide a sound evidence base for the research.

Interviews and questionnaires

Interviews and questionnaires allow researchers to ask people directly for information. The information may be of a factual, knowledge-based kind, or it may also include feelings, attitudes and perceptions. For instance, case-study research into the effectiveness of a school's policy on managing difficult behaviour or on the integration of therapy within the curriculum might involve asking staff, pupils and parents questions that are designed to elicit their understanding and feelings about the policy in action as they experience it.

The relationship between researchers and the people from whom they ask information can, of course, have an effect on the answers they get to questions of a less factual nature. This is likely to be the case when teacher–researchers seek information from their colleagues, but it raises particular issues concerning parents and pupils, who may wish to give the responses they think are expected of them. When planning interviews or questionnaires, it is therefore important to give consideration to how best they can be introduced and their purposes explained in ways that will encourage openness in the expression of personal views; and how leading questions can be avoided.

It is only comparatively recently that researchers have attempted to access the views of children and young people with significant learning difficulties directly, rather than relying on the perceptions of their parents and teachers. A number of studies have been reported now that address some of the methodological issues concerned (e.g. Beveridge 1996; Christensen and James 2000; Clough and Barton 1998; Lewis 1995; Lewis and Lindsay 2000; Lloyd-Smith and Dwyfor Davies 1995; Minkes *et al.* 1995; Wade and Moore 1993). The strategies that they consider include, for example, the use of visual and practical aids to help the obtaining of a response, and ways of synthesising interviews or questionnaires with direct observation in order to build up as complete a picture of pupil experience as possible.

Decisions about whether to use an interview or a questionnaire procedure are likely to be based primarily on the type of information that a researcher wants to gather and the numbers of people who are to be approached. Sometimes both may be used: for example, unstructured interviews with a small number of people may provide the material to draw up a questionnaire for a wider survey of opinion; or, more frequently, a broader questionnaire survey may reveal issues to follow up in greater depth through interviews with a subgroup.

Interviews usually involve individual face-to-face discussion, although there are advantages sometimes in a paired or small-group context and, out of necessity, some teacher–researcher interviews may be conducted on the telephone. They can take the form of open-ended, unstructured discussions around the focus of the research concern, or they can have more structured formats. For most purposes, teacher–researchers tend to opt for a semi-structured approach in which they identify the main questions for discussion in advance but vary the sequence of these, as well as their use of prompts and requests for elaboration, in response to the way that the individual interview develops. At its most tightly structured, an interview schedule begins to resemble a questionnaire, to the extent that it has a standard sequence and wording of questions.

The greater the degree of structure, the more thought needs to be given to the wording of the questions to ensure that they are clear and that, while they are not leading questions, they relate clearly and constructively to the research focus. The design of a questionnaire – particularly one that is to be completed in the absence of the researcher – takes time and effort to get right: there are issues involved in layout, sequencing and response conventions, all of which affect the likelihood that people will complete it and that they will do so in the expected manner (see, for example, Robson 1993).

Written documentation and visual records

Written documentation can provide a very important source of information in school-based research. A range of forms of written material is likely to be generally available in schools, and others might be specifically generated for the purposes of a particular study. Material can include formal documentation – for example, the school prospectus, written policies, curriculum plans and records, IEPs, statement and annual reviews. It can also include less formal records such as home school books or other correspondence with parents, teacher and pupil diaries, and so on. Photographs provide a form of visual record whose potential, for example when compiling pupils' Records of Achievement, has been recognised by many schools for some time. More recently, researchers have also begun to report on the use of photographs as a source of evidence in their investigations (e.g. Burgess 1995; Prosser 1998; Walker 1993).

It is important that the evidence from documentary sources – just like that from observations, interviews and questionnaires – is linked very clearly to the focus and purposes of the investigation, and so the ways in which written or visual records are used will vary from study to study. For instance, written documents might be examined for their reference to pupil and parental involvement in decision-making processes, or for evidence of cross-curricular links in staff planning for the programmes of study. Photographic records might be analysed for reference to individual therapy objectives within particular curricular activities, or for evidence of the relationship between physical organisation and interactions in the classroom.

Turning planning into action

This chapter has focused primarily on the planning and preparation that teacher researchers need to consider prior to beginning their investigations. Table 18.2 summarises the stages involved; that table also incorporates an example that illustrates the way in which a case-study approach can appropriately draw upon a combination of research methods.

When moving into the implementation of their research plans, teachers can usefully think about beginning with a preliminary exploratory or pilot phase, in which they:

- try out the practicalities of their chosen methods of investigation;
- check that the information that they derive – for example from observation and interview – is what they actually need in order to address their research questions;
- undertake any fine-tuning to their plans and methods that seems necessary.

It is particularly important that researchers pay attention to the reliability, or what Robson (1993) refers to as the 'trustworthiness', of the information they gather during their studies. They need to have procedures in place that allow them, and others, to feel confident about its accuracy and its representativeness. Joint information-gathering with colleagues – for example in direct observation or from audio- or video-records – is a very helpful strategy, but it is not always possible or appropriate. Self-reflection and regular discussion with other staff should always be practicable, and these two approaches can have a useful monitoring function when they are structured to help researchers consider whether they are:

Table 18.2

Stage	Example
Identify the research focus	A teacher has concerns about the extent to which cooperative-learning approaches feature in the National Curriculum.
Clarify research questions and purposes (consult relevant reading and professional contacts; discuss with colleagues)	She wants to: evaluate the effectiveness of cooperative-learning approaches for the pupils with SLD with whom she works; provide structures that help her to develop cooperative learning within the classroom; develop her own skills in (i) the use of cooperative-learning approaches, and (ii) classroom-based research.
Decide on a research approach (e.g. survey, case study)	She chooses a case-study approach with an action-research element: her investigation will be shaped as it goes on by the information she gathers.
Decide on the context: who is to be studied, in what setting(s) and in what sorts of activity	The study will involve the senior group of pupils with SLD with whom she works most frequently, herself and two support staff. It will take place in the classroom, on a series of weekly sessions structured round cooperative-learning tasks.
Decide on the methods (e.g. observation, interview, questionnaire, written documentation, visual records)	She needs to use a combination of methods: (i) Participatory ongoing observations of the pupils by all three staff (also audio-recorded) to establish the frequency of requests for staff help, comments to staff, comments to other pupils, negotiation, conflict; duration of their on-task behaviour. (ii) Interviews in the form of structured feedback sessions with pupils, and weekly discussion with support staff. (iii) Written documentation where the teacher–researcher keeps a diary to include reflections on pupil responses to inform weekly planning, and reflections on own practice.

- being as consistent and rigorous as possible in the way they collect evidence;
- remaining open to alternative perspectives;
- demonstrating convincing evidence to support their interpretations and judgements.

The way in which teachers are able to use the results of their research will clearly vary according to its initial purpose and intentions. Most teacher–researchers undertake relatively small-scale studies within the contexts of their own classes or schools, and therefore it is important to be cautious about the extent to which their findings can be generalised more widely. Where the findings make sense, seem relevant and resonate with other teachers' experience and knowledge, then the research can communicate with and have an impact on a wider professional network. However, its main impact is always likely to be on the teacher–researchers' own practice, either as individuals or in collaborative whole-school developments. This impact may operate at a number of different levels, for example, on their:

- attitudes and understanding of differing perspectives;
- observational, listening and recording skills;
- analytical and informed approach to problem-solving;
- confidence and skill in experimenting with different teaching approaches.

It might be argued that professional development of this kind for teachers will be of benefit not only to the teachers themselves but also to the children and young people they teach.

References

Adelman, C. (1985) 'Action research', in S. Hegarty and P. Evans (eds) *Research and Evaluation Methods in Special Education*. Windsor: NFER-Nelson.

Bell, J. (1999) *Doing Your Research Project*, 3rd edn. Buckingham: Open University Press.

Beveridge, S. (1996) 'Experiences of an Integration Link Scheme: the perspectives of pupils with severe learning difficulties and their mainstream peers', *British Journal of Learning Disabilities* 24(1), 9–19.

Burgess, R. G. (1995) 'Gaining access to pupil perspectives', in M. Lloyd-Smith and J. Dwyfor Davies (eds) *On the Margins: The Educational Experience of 'Problem' Pupils*. Stoke-on-Trent: Trentham Books.

Christensen, P. and James, A. (eds) (2000) *Research with Children: Perspectives and Practices*. London: Falmer Press.

Clough, P. and Barton, L. (eds) (1995) *Making Difficulties: Research and the construction of SEN*. London: Paul Chapman.

Clough, P and Barton, L. (eds) (1998) *Articulating with Difficulty: Research Voices in Inclusive Education*. London: Paul Chapman.

Cohen, L. *et al.* (2000) *Research Methods in Education*, 5th edn. London: Routledge.

Cooper, P. (1995) 'When segregation works: pupils' experience of residential special provision', in M. Lloyd-Smith and J. Dwyfor Davies (eds) *On the Margins: The Educational Experience of 'Problem' Pupils*. Stoke-on-Trent: Trentham Books.

Corrie, M. and Zaklukiewicz, S. (1985) 'Qualitative research and case-study approaches: an introduction', in S. Hegarty and P. Evans (eds) *Research and Evaluation Methods in Special Education*. Windsor: NFER-Nelson.

Croll, P. (2000) *Systematic Classroom Observation*, 2nd edn. London: Falmer Press.

Lewis, A. (1995) *Children's Understanding of Disability*. London: Routledge.

Lewis, A. and Lindsay, G. (2000) *Researching Children's Perspectives*. Buckingham: Open University Press.

Lloyd-Smith, M. and Dwyfor Davies J. (eds) (1995) *On the Margins: The Educational Experience of 'Problem' Pupils*. Stoke-on-Trent: Trentham Books.

Lomax, P. (1991) 'Peer review and action research', in P. Lomax (ed.) *Managing Better Schools and Colleges: an Action Research Way*. Clevedon: Multilingual Matters.

Minkes, J. *et al.* (1995) 'Having a voice: involving people with learning difficulties in research.', *British Journal of Learning Disabilities* **23**, 94–7.

O'Hanlon, C. (ed.) (1996) *Professional Development through Action Research in Educational Settings*. London: Falmer Press.

Prosser, J. (ed.) (1998) *Image-based Research: a Sourcebook for Qualitative Researchers*. London: Falmer Press.

Robson, C. (1993) *Real World Research*. Oxford: Blackwell.

Tilstone, C. (ed.) (1998) *Observing Teaching and Learning: Principles and Practice*. London: David Fulton Publishers.

Vulliamy, G. and Webb, R. (eds) (1993) *Teacher Research and Special Educational Needs*. London: David Fulton Publishers.

Wade, B. and Moore, M. (1993) *Experiencing Special Education*. Buckingham: Open University Press.

Walker, R. (1993) 'Finding a silent voice for the research: using photographs in evaluation and research', in M. Schratz (ed.) *Qualitative Voices in Educational Research*. London: Falmer Press.

Part III:
The Context for the Whole Curriculum

Chapter 19

Enabling Partnership: Families and Schools

Barry Carpenter

Introduction

Parents are the children's first and most enduring educators.

(QCA/DfEE 1999)

'Partnership with parents' (a well-rehearsed phrase) has developed something of a hollow ring. How do we give it back its meaning? How do we breathe life back into this concept that is so crucial to our work in schools? Maybe the time is right for us to reconceptualise partnership – to rediscover its true meaning. We could abandon it as yet another lost educational cause, but would that bring any real benefit to children, their parents, their teachers and our schools?

By redirecting our focus, we may enable partnership to become a reality once more. Many schools have established excellent working relationships with parents, gently nurtured over many years, but in the recent past our major efforts have been toward the implementation of the National Curriculum and the raft of legislation that has hit schools during the 1990s and into the new millennium. If we are truthful, has 'partnership with parents' been given sufficient in-depth attention in our policy, planning and practice? Only in the last few years has there been a resurgence of texts that discuss parents and their children with special educational needs (SEN; Dale 1996; Carpenter 1997; Hornby 1995; Mittler and Mittler 1994; Randall and Parker 1999).

'Parent partnership' has remained a major theme in the Standards Fund, enabling LEAs, in collaboration with voluntary-sector disability groups, to establish Parent-Partnership Officer posts. In many instances, the clarity of information, advice and support on SEN for parents has improved considerably. The consultation document on the revised Code of Practice endorses and expands the role of 'partnership with parents' that existed in the earlier Code of Practice. The key message (DFE 1994, Section 2:28, pp. 12–13) remains that: 'Children's progress will be diminished if their parents are not seen as partners in the education process with unique knowledge and information to impart.'

It is in relation to children as learners that parents enter into a dialogue with their LEA and/or the local schools. In general, parents support and want to share in any holistic approach to their child's development, and thus the ground is established for the ongoing interaction between schools and parents. In the context of a school, a child's learning is set within the curriculum. That learning is supported by teachers, special support assistants, peers and associated professionals (speech therapists, physiotherapists, educational psychologists, etc.). In the home, it is the parents, siblings, grandparents, relatives and 'significant others' (i.e. friends, neighbours, etc.) who nurture the development of a child. The shared focus for both environments – home and school – is the child; the common language is based upon the child's needs, and the common goal is to enable the child to develop through quality learning experiences. The ground is set for families and schools to share in the child's learning – to share the curriculum.

Recently, there has been a welcome broadening of thinking from the UK government away from a focus solely on parents to the wider support offered by a family. The new Family and Parenting Institute has been established, founded on a core message: 'Families are at the heart of our Society and the basis of our future as a country.' Around the establishment of this Institute is a national policy based on three principles (Home Office 1999):

● children must come first;
● children need stability;
● families raise children.

These statements about children set their development within the family.

The child through the eyes of the family

> The most important thing that happens when a child is born with disabilities is that a child is born. The most important thing that happens when a couple become parents of a child with disabilities is that the couple become parents.
>
> (Ferguson and Asch 1989, p. 24)

Two American writers, Philip Ferguson (a parent) and Adrienne Asch (who is disabled) offer this powerful thought. They are affirming what is often not the case at all. Parents become 'Down's parents'; babies become 'deaf babies'; the child becomes 'the blind child'; the family becomes 'the disabled family'; and a completely different pattern to the family history is assumed. It is not what was hoped for or expected. Suddenly, in the eyes of some professionals and areas of society, that family is no longer an 'ordinary' family. However, while the family's journey through life might follow a different route from what was anticipated, the destination is the same. It is the child and not the disability that should be uppermost in people's minds.

But this is not always so, as Rod Wills, a parent, reminds us (Wills 1994, p. 249):

> Some of the roles assigned to parents cause great pain. What is imposed on parents is often based on mistaken belief, historical prejudice and myths. Negative attitudes towards disability have strongly shaped what we do to people who are disabled, how it is done, and the consequences for their family.

Do professionals have real insights into how the birth of, and life with, a child with a disability impacts on family life? At times, they may assume that they know what families need, but they do not understand the range of emotions experienced. Manuel (1996), a parent, states: 'What is often not recognised is that mums and dads and brothers and sisters have love for the child. They don't necessarily want to abandon that child. Because it's their child.'

In our civilised society, the term 'abandon' in the quotation from Manuel may seem inappropriate, but examples can still be found of situations where parents were put under pressure to relinquish responsibility for their children. Jan and Dave recall how their baby, Sarah, contracted meningitis when she was eight days' old and, after spending three months in intensive care, she was left with profound and multiple disabilities. Two professionals saw Sarah's parents before they took her home: one talked of disability benefit allowances (for which Sarah was not eligible until she was much older!); the other of immediate respite care for whatever period the parents chose. As Jan retorted: 'This is my baby. I look after my baby. I am not giving up my baby to anyone' (personal correspondence). The professional approaches made to Jan and Dave were insensitive and ill-timed, for they did nothing to enhance their quality of life or parenting confidence.

Despite everything that has been written about supporting families over the past decade, their needs are still not met. Researchers such as McConachie (1997) remain critical of professionals and claim that they are not good at giving parents the support they need during the first months after a baby has been found to have complex disabilities. These claims challenge professionals to reflect on their practice and their approaches to families, as well as their commitment to family-centred service. Their goal is given focus by Ritchie (1998, p. 4): 'What can services do to value and preserve an enriched family life [for people with disabilities]?'

Schools need to appreciate this perspective in working with families of children with SEN. There is, naturally, a range of emotions within families, any of which may influence how those families engage with a school. There is much debate around some of the associated theories (Dale 1996), but it would be true to say that some parents in any school population where there are children with learning difficulties will display some of the characteristics associated with grief or sorrow (Roll-Pettersson 2001). Indeed, other family members may also display such tendencies. Some reports have suggested that many grandparents have difficulty adapting to the situation and attempt to deny their grandchild's disability, and thus offer low levels of support to the family (Hornby and Ashworth 1994; Mirfin-Veitch and Bray 1997); other studies have expressed concerns about siblings and their perceptions of their brother or sister's disability, or their own interrelationship with their parents (Meyer and Vadasy 1997).

Some parents claim that they accept their child but appear never to accept the disability completely. This bereavement response may remain with some parents for many years and tinge their interactions with the local school. They may never seem to share fully the joy of their child's achievements, always grieving for that lost normality. While some have attributed these feelings of grief and mourning to the early traumatic period following the disclosure of diagnosis shortly after the birth of a baby with a disability, experience has also shown that a grief response is possible during the school years when parents are told that there is a possibility that their child has some learning difficulty. Usually, the confirmation of this comes in the form of a Statement of Special Educational Need, and again the shock of this may traumatise some parents in a similar way that a bereavement would, or it may affirm their own suspicions about their child's difficulties – and so they mourn. As one mother of a child with learning difficulties said: 'In realising his academic limitations, I realised the loss of my own dream for his future' (parent workshop, January 1998).

However much professionals may reassure, guide or offer support, these feelings cannot always be rationalised. We are far too dismissive of emotional responses; we need to acknowledge that they are an important feature of the adjustment process. If a child with learning difficulties is to be accepted as a full family member, then each family member must come in their own way to value and appreciate the many and diverse talents of such a child and, moreover, to acknowledge the child as a person in his or her own right. Some parents leave grief behind (if ever a bereavement response was a reality for them), but they may have periods of recurring distress. One explanation for this is the 'chronic sorrow model' (Olshansky 1962). This model has had various phases of popularity, and in both the 1980s and the 1990s it was the subject of some debate (Gabba 1994; Wikler 1984). Again, for some parents there may be some identification with this pattern of response. It is argued that parents may experience periods of grieving at later stages in their child's life without being poorly adjusted to their child. The parent who continues to feel sadness about a child's disability can still be confident and caring. The parent who is experiencing sorrow, however, may reflect this state of mind in the way they deal with their child's education.

Grief, or sorrow, may not be the state of mind for many parents, but 'chronic vulnerability' (Carpenter 1997) certainly will be. This may manifest itself in hypersensitivity, short temper and an inability to cope with criticism of their child or themselves. For the parent, it may be symptomatic of the dread of further unanticipated bad news, the desire to protect their child in the face of a social structure whose capacity to care for that child is being continually eroded, an over-protectiveness, or a desire to compensate. This may not be too far away from how *any* parents feel about their child; however, for the parent of a child with SEN, it is more accentuated.

Lessons from early intervention

> With other families, there were interests in common other than our children, and time spent with these families was for the same reasons one might spend time with any set of friends. What is unique about friendship with other families [of children with special needs] is the depth of understanding: they are more than the sincere, empathetic professional. They have been there too – through the endless hospital appointments, the perplexing behaviour patterns, the unanswered questions. This in no way diminishes the invaluable contribution of professionals, but to live with a child with a disability 24 hours a day brings lessons that no professional course of training can ever hope to teach.
>
> (A father, quoted in Carpenter and Herbert 1995)

Developments in the field of early intervention, and a knowledge of how it has moved to more family-based approaches of service delivery, may inform our thinking about how we can construct our partnerships between schools and families. In the past, early-intervention programmes tended to focus upon the child with SEN in relation to particular areas of skills development (Robinson 2000). The nature of such a programme may have become disorientating to the family; often, little attention was given to the quality of relationships being established between the child and the family members. This can actually have an adverse effect on the child/family relationship, with an unhelpful emphasis upon the provision of parents 'with teacher skills instead of strategies for communicating with their child in an optimal manner' (Basil 1994).

More recently, the move has been toward family-focused models of service delivery. Many researchers and practitioners feel that family-centred models are more humane and dignifying to a child with SEN and his or her family (Bentley-Williams and Butterfield 1996), although this is not to diminish the qualities that professionals working in the early-intervention phase should possess. Such approaches acknowledge a child's context, for children do not develop separately from this context but are always informed by their environment. Sue Buckley and Gillian Bird, in their guidance to parents on early intervention, emphasise (Buckley and Bird 1995, p. 1) that 'the most important gift parents can give their baby is to ensure that he or she is a much-loved member of a stable family group'.

An early-intervention team that, even in times of uncertainty and anxiety, has the family at its centre should be self-supporting and self-sustaining. Such approaches also increase the capacity of families to provide resources to other families to assist in solving problems. Hornby (1989, 1995) has written extensively on parent-to-parent schemes that illustrate this particular approach. Sensitive interaction within the early intervention team will enable a family to change its contribution over a period of time. The dimensions of family involvement might increase or decrease depending on how the family may be feeling at a particular time – as with any child-rearing process, there are problem periods. What we must acknowledge is that families of children with SEN are first and foremost *families*. While being positive in our focus, there should be space for, and acceptance of, the full range of emotions experienced by many families and their implications for the dynamics within the team.

Family-centred approaches in early intervention have been strengthened in the United States through legislation. Public Law 99/457 formally requires an Individualised Family Service Program (IFSP) to be prepared. This has been the subject of much debate regarding family inclusion, parent participation and professional role definition (Bailey *et al.* 1990). Ideally, an IFSP is designed by parents and includes areas of emphasis that reflect parental resources, concerns and priorities – for both themselves and their children. The IFSP in the United States marks a shift away from the Individualised Education Programme (IEP), which was professionally driven and developed on the basis of a process whereby professionals share with parents their evaluation information and divide goals from objectives. This shift is bringing with it a considerable need to present information in 'parent language' as opposed to professional jargon (Campbell *et al.* 1992).

There has been considerable debate around the efficacy of early intervention. Politicians and administrators have tried to apply cost principles to this strategy that are diametrically opposed to its fundamental purpose – the effectiveness of early intervention cannot be judged on child gains alone. Rather, we have to set the child within its family, and assess the gains of early intervention as a family-support strategy. Michael Guralnick, President of the International Society for Early Intervention, expressed this in the agenda for development he set at the beginning of the last decade of the twentieth century (Guralnick 1991). When we evaluate the outcomes, we will see that the facilitating foundations of early intervention made a crucial contribution to the lives of all family members, not just the child with a special need.

What constitutes 'the family'?

Professionals in families can work to eliminate the physical, cultural and social barriers that prevent families from attaining the best possible quality of life.

(Seligman and Darling 1989, p. 237)

So, what constitutes a family? Is the traditional nuclear interpretation valid? What of reconstituted families, or families with different cultural traditions or faith backgrounds? And what of the extended family? Our definition of an extended family could be quite crucial to helping schools interact with families. If we include only blood relatives, then we may be excluding other people who have a deep bond with the family and offer quality support at a variety of levels – social, emotional, psychological or practical.

In the Maori culture of New Zealand, they have a helpful concept known as a Whanau. A Whanau is a family's social structure incorporating all age ranges, interests and experiences (Ballard 1994). It constitutes an extended family in many respects. It incorporates a range of significant people who take a genuine and shared interest in each other's lives, and who will advocate for each other. Ought we to allow families to self-define their supporting social system? As individuals, most professionals recognise the importance of family-centredness, but within the outmoded structures of support services there is still discrimination against family involvement. Service guidelines often fail to recognise changes in society, including restructured family units, that as individuals we *would* acknowledge.

The stereotypical notion of 'the family' (two married parents of the opposite sex, with two children, who rely on the father's income) is a reality for only one family in seven in the European Union at the turn of the millennium (Roll 1991). Nevertheless, research indicates that, despite anxieties about the destruction of the family, it is the form rather than the function that has changed (Dahlstrom 1989). The patriarchal model of the family, which comprised blood relatives and included safety nets for the aged, infirm or other dependent kin, is far less a feature of modern life than it was at the beginning of the last century (Mitterauer and Sieder 1982). David (1994) has documented the changing gender roles in society that have also influenced the stereotypical roles assumed by key family members (e.g. mothers, fathers and siblings).

All of these influences indicate that our traditional role-definitions of the family are no longer valid and can hinder professional interactions. The definition from Winton (1990, p. 4) captures the essence of the family:

> Families are big, small, extended, nuclear, multi-generational, with one parent, two parents, and grandparents. We live under one roof or many. A family can be as temporary as a few weeks, as permanent as for ever. We become part of a family by birth, adoption, marriage, or from a desire for mutual support. A family is a culture unto itself, with different values and unique ways of realizing its dreams. Together, our families become the source of our rich cultural heritage and spiritual diversity. Our families create neighbourhoods, communities, states and nations.

The family, however, is still seen as the major vehicle within which to rear children, and its importance is persistently highlighted in European (Leskinen 1994) and international (Mittler 1995) studies. Following the birth of a child with disabilities, the need for the family, as well as the implicit emotional and practical means of support it can offer, becomes very great. But does that family have to comprise blood relatives? In our modern mobile society, is this the reality for many families? Demographic trends are a significant influence, as is the ever-increasing breakdown in marriages, which can lead to many reconstituted families. For any of these families the reality of support may be derived from a 'self-defined family': a flexible family comprising non-blood relatives carrying out the functions traditionally associated with the patriarchal, blood-related family.

Families are systems influenced by many factors: the ethnic and cultural background; the stage of the family life-cycle; environmental events; external factors; individual relationships; and the personal and collective experiences of family members. Individuals in a family develop roles, rules to live by, communication patterns, ways to negotiate and solve problems, and methods for completing tasks of daily living. Families provide social support and sustenance, and they share commitments and responsibilities. They are also contexts (Carpenter 1997) for learning and growth, and they have a particularly decisive influence on the social and emotional development of children.

The model below suggests an extended family-support network that reflects a more appropriate reality for many families than the traditional nuclear model. Patterns of interaction may vary within this group. Some may revolve around the triad of primary support – child, mother, father. They may also centre on a lone parent with a child with a disability, who seeks and receives various types of support from any of the identified groups.

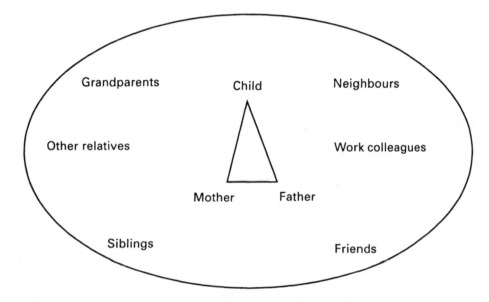

Figure 19.1 A triad-based extended family support network

When one of the children within a family has a defined disability, the need for that family to be an effective social structure becomes even more important. If support services do not allow them to function in this way, we have an obligation to make our criteria for inclusion more flexible. As Beckman and Beckman Boyes (1993), writing from the professional-parent perspective, remind us (p. 1): 'The news that a child has, or is at risk from, a developmental disability, is often among the most frightening and confusing pieces of information that parents will ever receive.' A family that has become 'divided by definition' will not be functioning at full strength when support is most needed.

The need for support from professionals is also crucial. As Davies (1998, p. 1) points out:

> If parents are overwhelmed by the extreme stresses of the situation, they will be unable to cope with the child's problems and will find it difficult to provide the love, security and responsive stimulation essential to the well-being and development of the child.

In order to provide effective services for our families, we must understand and respect them. Roles in families differ according to situation and culture, and they may not fit stereotypical assumptions. The key to providing support is to listen to the families themselves.

The impetus for partnership

> Parents should be partners in the planning and delivery of services ... parents are the informed experts on their children. (Wolfendale 2000, p. 149)

All schools desire to be effective schools. The OFSTED (1999) *Framework for the Inspection of Schools* actively promotes the soliciting of opinions of parents as to the effectiveness of a school. Good communication and collaboration with parents is one of the hallmarks of an 'effective school'. It is a subtle but significant shift to move our collaborative strategies to encompass the family rather than just the parents. Parents (plural) may not be the reality for many children: as Mittler (2000) cites, 25 per cent of children over the age of 16 will have experienced their parents divorcing. Families will, however, be a reality for the majority of children. Within those self-defined families, it is important that all family contributions are valued (Carpenter 2000).

What a family can contribute

Family dynamics may mean services need to build in an unaccustomed flexibility to their approaches to families. It is inappropriate for single parents to be consistently unsupported by either their partner or significant others in their meetings with professionals owing to the timing of, or the exclusion of non-blood relations from, these meetings. Mothers play a pivotal role in many families, and research and other studies have shown that they carry the bulk of household chores, and that childcare is normally carried out by them (Hornby 1995). Hautamäki (1997) has produced findings from a cross-Nordic study in which she contrasts the situation of over 1,000 mothers of children with Down's Syndrome with mothers of non-disabled children. She found that the mothers of children with Down's Syndrome had increased care-taking responsibility, had often revised their 'life project' goals, had more-restricted leisure activities and different work patterns, and, when they did work, they had high levels of sick leave. In her international study, Mittler (1995) found that mothers typically remained the major carers throughout all regions of the world.

In the case of fathers, Herbert and Carpenter (1994) suggest that if we are to include those whom McConkey (1994) has described as the 'hard-to-reach parents', support services need to take into account 'the life patters of fathers'. They need to be offered increased access to information and support, to be provided with opportunities to network with other fathers, and to have their need for information and emotional support within the family addressed. In order to achieve these aims, greater training and awareness among professionals is necessary. In his collection of essays by fathers, Meyer (1995) indicates how the birth of a child with a disability brings about life-transforming experiences. For some, it is a challenge that allows them to display aspects of their personality not previously acknowledged; for others, it causes 'relentless stress' that disorientates their life goals and affects their work patterns. In this new millennium, the nature of fatherhood has begun to undergo significant redefinition. Perhaps, as a result, some men will be released from the stereotypical definition of masculinity that impairs and restricts their natural fathering traits (Carpenter 2000a).

Bray *et al.* (1995) identified two main types of love within their cohort of fathers: 'unconditional' and 'transforming'. Firstly, there were those fathers who displayed utter devotion to their children by just accepting whatever they did and patiently standing by them through all of their endeavours. Secondly, there were others who felt that by their transforming acts (e.g. converting a room in the house, or building special play equipment in the garden) they could significantly transform their child and enhance their life opportunities.

Traditionally, it has been thought that siblings of children with learning disabilities suffer particular problems related to isolation, guilt or resentment. As with fathers, it is important that specific consideration is given to the needs of these family members, as a study by Newson and Davis (1994) has demonstrated. Their workshops with brothers and sisters of children with autism led to some considerable attitudinal adjustments in the siblings who were part of that group. Glynne-Rule (1995) found in her survey that few siblings experienced bullying and teasing, and that, after the parents, the siblings of the child with learning disabilities were the main relatives providing help, care and education. Similarly, other studies (Byrne *et al.* 1988; Tritt and Esses 1988) have shown that siblings of children with disabilities show no difference in emotional and behavioural disturbance to siblings of 'normal' children. Brothers and sisters have often been found to be well-adjusted and mature, and to show a responsible attitude that goes beyond their chronological age (Dale 1996; Meyer and Vadasy 1997).

Meyer (1997), in a collection of writings by the siblings of children with disabilities, included humorous, thoughtful stories offering insights into the needs and perceptions of those growing up with a brother or sister with special needs. Justin, aged 10, wrote (p. 23):

> There are good parts about having a brother who has autism. My brother, Jacob, is old enough to play with, and he understands some things. But, unfortunately, there's a bad part. Sometimes my brother gets out of hand and hits people – even me!

A disabled child's grandparents are a common source of support for the family (Hastings 1997). In cases where grandparents have difficulty in adapting to the family's situation, breakdown in the relationship between them can occur. However, Mirfin-Veitch and Bray (1997) have shown that grandparents offer support that is both emotional and practical. They are the people to whom parents feel most able to disclose their full range of emotions, and they may also offer direct assistance to the family through shopping, babysitting and financial support.

The literature on 'significant others' in the lives of children with disabilities is sparse. Mittler notes (1995, p. 51) that the support that is available to families, particularly in the locality in which they live, is 'crucial in determining their quality of life'.

What do we know about partnership?

> We have to learn together about our children.   (parent)

There have been various phases in the growth of the parent–professional relationship. For many years, parents of children with special needs were left largely unsupported and received little help from professionals. Then the 'professional as expert' became an accepted way of working with parents of children with special needs. In this approach, the professional used their position and expertise to make judgements and take control of what needed doing. This approach was based on some unfortunate common attitudes to parents: that they were problems, adversaries, in need of treatment, causal, or needing to be kept at a professional distance (Hornby 1995). Many teachers would claim that they are not comfortable with the role of expert, but it is acknowledged that some parents push teachers into that role. As one parent said recently in her child's annual review: 'I am most comfortable with the notion of you [the teacher] as an expert.' Naturally, she deserves to have this viewpoint respected.

The 'transplant' model of parental involvement emerged in the early 1970s, where the home was acknowledged as a potentially important learning setting but one in which professionals could transplant their skills and expertise on parents. Workshops for parents to train them to use professional techniques were a common feature of this approach, particularly in relation to behaviour modification. While parents are individually valued in this approach for their interactive role, it is a professionally led approach, with professionals transmitting skills to parents rather than parents ever taking a lead for themselves. It clearly does not bear out Wolfendale's (1989) definition of 'equivalent expertise'.

The 'consumer' model developed by Cunningham and Davis (1985) marks the beginning of true partnership. There was a shift in power from the professional to the parent, with the parent exercising control over the selection of services for their child. At a recent parent workshop, 'mutual respect' was the phrase used time and time again to express the key principle that should apply to the working practices between schools and families. This is very much a feature of the consumer model, which went some considerable way to achieving what Warnock described as 'a partnership, and ideally an equal one'.

The consumer approach requires professionals to display genuineness, respect and empathy toward parents. The working relationship between parents and professionals can be characterised as:

- a shared sense of purpose;
- a willingness to negotiate;
- sharing of information;
- shared responsibility;
- joint decision-making and accountability.

In the late 1980s, the rights of parents came to the fore. Parents have, in the United Kingdom's education legislation, remained the focus. This has been in parallel to service development in other public sectors, and in the sociological perspectives in the literature, which has recognised the family as the context for the child's development. These models of family-centred, family-oriented, family-focused service delivery have emerged (Leskinen 1994; Randall and Parker 1999). The Children Act 1989 went some way towards stressing the importance of families and of the views of those families and the children themselves. If we are to develop partnerships with families, then we need to realise who it is, apart from blood relatives, that families themselves consider important (Carpenter 1998).

A series of semi-structured interviews (Carpenter 1997) with 20 families of children with severe learning difficulties (aged 5–16 years) revealed that the following non-blood relatives offered support:

- neighbours;
- friends;
- work colleagues;
- church members;
- teachers and assistants;
- link families;
- volunteers (from charitable organisations).

The main types of support offered (i.e. reported by more than five families in the sample) were:

- babysitting and child-minding;
- transport;
- respite care;
- social activities;
- meals out for child and/or family;
- practical help in the home (household chores, maintenance tasks);
- empathetic listening.

All families in this study reported that, without the help of their 'self-defined' family, their patterns of living would have been severely disrupted and, moreover, that their capacity to function effectively would have been damaged.

Other recent models, which guide professional working practices, have also placed an emphasis on the family and its effectiveness as a support network. The 'empowerment' model (Appleton and Minchcom 1991) gives us a strong indication of how the emphasis is beginning to shift from parents to families. The key points of this model can be summarised as:

- the rights of parents as consumers;
- choice of service and level of engagement;
- recognition of the family as a system;
- recognition of the family's social network.

More recently, Dale (1996) has produced the 'negotiating' model, which focuses on negotiation as a key transaction for partnership work and builds upon the consumer and empowerment models. As his work states (p. 14):

> [The model] offers a framework for exploring a partnership practice that can embody or respond to the constraints and reality of actual power relations and positions of the parent and professional within present or future societal contexts.

The 'negotiating model' endeavours not to discriminate against the parents' rights to be involved and consulted, and it aims to advance, through collaboration and negotiated decision-making with all parents and families, to a point where all are mutually happy with outcomes. The key features of this particular model are:

- negotiation as a key transaction for partnership;
- joint decision-making;
- resolution of differences;
- shared perspective.

The lessons to be learnt from these various models and the last two decades of endeavour on all parts in parental involvement can be summarised in the following six-part list of recommendations to families, schools and also professionals working with either or both parties.

1. Be honest with each other.
2. Be willing to learn from each other.
3. Treat each other with respect and dignity.
4. Be willing to admit you make mistakes.
5. Work collaboratively and cooperatively.
6. Be yourself.

The context for partnership

If we are to work effectively with families, it is important that they know that we value their context – the home. Parents and professionals grow and change. Families also grow and change. The constitution of a family in one particular year might not be the same the next – an older sibling may have married, gone out to work or moved away to university – and such changes can have a major impact on a family. A child with learning difficulties might not understand where his or her much-loved sibling has gone; a key supporter in the family might no longer be around to help with babysitting; the person who listened to a mother's anxieties might no longer be available to 'counsel'. Schools need to be sensitive to such changes in a family's balance. Listening to and understanding each other's points of view is critical. Schools can do much to strengthen parent–child relationships.

Many researchers and practitioners feel that family-centred models are more humane and dignifying to the child and the surrounding family. The researchers acknowledge the context applying for each child, with its associated demands and limitations, and they introduce appropriate and sustainable interventions. Such approaches are also aimed towards increasing the capacity of families to provide resources to other families, to assist in problem-solving and to build self-supporting and self-sustaining practices. Sensitive interactions between families and professionals are also crucial if the family is to be allowed to make its contribution in the ever-changing, uncharted scenario of their child's development.

Ways of working

> No attempts by teachers to communicate with parents about their children are a waste of time.
> (parent comment in response to a questionnaire about home–school links, 1992)

There are many practical ways for schools to develop relationships with families and offer them support. Many others have cited ways in which it is possible to work with parents (Hornby 1995; Wolfendale 1989). The following list offers some practical suggestions, which schools may like to use as starting points for evaluating their current approaches for working with parents/families:

- home visits;
- shared planning and recording;
- circles of celebration (achievement certificates etc.);
- playgroups;
- parent-support groups;
- home–school diaries (handwritten, by audio means – for instance, using an Echo 4 machine – or in symbols);
- telephone contact;
- child's profile;
- parents' library;
- shared training;
- sensory activities;
- events for all the family.

Further discussion of these suggestions can be found in Carpenter and Herbert (1994). Ways of supporting families demand a broader consideration of the type of activity that will encompass all family members.

The Sunfield School example

Family support is crucial to the well-being of a child. As McConkey (1999) discusses, family support can take many different forms. An example of this would be the work of Sunfield School in Worcestershire. There, instead of developing a policy for working with parents, they wrote a 'Family Charter'. this was developed and ratified by a consultation group of families. The charter opened two-way channels of communication and enabled the school to establish a partnership that was based on shared aims, principles and aspirations.

The 'Family Charter' opens with a clear statement:

Sunfield welcomes all our children's families, friends and others significant in their lives.

It goes on to articulate what families can expect: respect, honesty and integrity, confidentiality, regular communication, empathy, supportive listening, information, partnership, and a safe environment. This is fulfilled by the school through a variety of means, as set out in the Family Charter:

- valuing the (self-defined) family's opinion and knowledge of their child;
- respecting their need for privacy and confidentiality;
- making regular contact;
- care and concern for parenthood;
- being non-judgemental and giving time;
- working together for the benefit of their child;
- providing a Family Centre.

Clearly, these ideals need to be expressed in concrete ways – the 'tangibility factor' needs to be strong. The Sunfield Family Charter concludes by listing some of the ways in which the school will attempt to fulfil these goals: regular reporting, home–school diaries, systematic telephone calls, the provision of a parent-based information, siblings weekends, family fun days, half-termly newsletters.

Monitoring and evaluating, with the families themselves, the effectiveness of the Family Charter is important to the school. Every two years, the school commissions an independent consultant to conduct a family survey (Carpenter and Woodgate 1999). The survey aims to obtain feedback from families in four main areas:

- communications;
- feelings about the services the school provides;
- involvement in the life of the school;
- overall attitudes to the school.

The responses received from families have so far been invaluable in evaluating provision and planning future services. School staff had never before received such systematic feedback from families on their work. There were some amazingly straightforward suggestions that were easy to implement (e.g. 'Whom do we contact to reorder school uniform?'); other ideas demanded long-term planning, but were equally worthwhile and could be incorporated into the school's development plan. What the exercise has shown to the school staff is that they have much to learn from families; the letter's perspective is vital.

Conclusion

For us, the priorities for the home–school partnership are communication, information and involvement.

(feedback from a parent-support group meeting to discuss and evaluate home–school links)

Dale (1996) talks of a 'whole-family' approach – how could we apply this to the shared curriculum links that we might embark upon with families, or the dialogue of learning they might establish with us? This may not require significant modification of the usual approach. Rather, we will need to reappraise the target audience. (Our traditional focus would have been mother and father – or, in reality, mother.) What is the potential contribution of the significant others? Mirfin-Veitch and Bray (1997) point out the increasing role that grandparents are playing in the care of their grandchildren. If they are the receiver of the child when they arrive home, is it they who will read the home diary, discuss the school day with the child, and share paintings, books and news?

What of brothers and sisters? Glynne-Rule (1995) discovered in her study that after the parents it was the siblings who provided the most within-family support. In the time they spend with their sibling, is there some constructive medium for interaction that can be provided by the school? A more holistic overview would enable us to determine 'learning partners' according to task/experience, to match the most appropriate supporter to the naturalistic context, in order to bring maximum benefit to the child. Children need families; children need schools. By empowering each other, we can empower our children. As one parent stated to me:

The greatest gift we can give to our children is a caring, supportive family. Parents are often very unsure of the best ways to help their child, and I believe if they are given flexible, responsive and sensitive support, this will not only strengthen their role in the short term but will also increase their capacity for the future. It is the parents and families who usually provide the most constant ongoing interest and support in a person's life, so any investment of time and energy, by schools and professionals, I believe is well spent.

References

Appleton, P. L. and Minchcom, P. E. (1991) 'Models of parent partnership and child development centres', *Child: Care, Health and Development.* 17, 27–38.

Bailey, D. B. *et al.* (1990) 'Preservice preparation of special educators to work with infants with handicaps and their families: current status and training needs', *Journal of Early Intervention* **14**(1), 43–54.

Ballard, K. (ed.) (1994) *Disability, Family, Whanau and Society.* Palmerston North, NZ: Dunmore Press.

Basil, C. (1994) 'Family involvement in the intervention process', in Brodin, J. and Bjorck-Akesson, E. (eds) *Methodological Issues in Research in Augmentative and Alternative Communication,* Jonkoping. South Africa: Jonkoping University Press.

Beckman, P. J. and Beckman Boyes, G. (eds) (1993) *Deciphering the System: A guide for families of young children with disabilities.* Cambridge, MA: Brookline.

Bentley-Williams, R. and Butterfield, N. (1996) 'Transition from early intervention to school: a family-focussed view', *Australasian Journal of Special Education* **20**(2), 17–28.

Bray, A., *et al.* (1995) 'Fathers of children with disabilities: some experiences and reflections', *New Zealand Journal of Disability Studies* **1**(1), 164–75.

Buckley, S. and Bird, G. (1995) 'Early intervention: how to help your child in the preschool years', *Down's Syndrome Trust Newsletter* **5**(1), 1–5.

Byrne, E. A. *et al.* (1988) *Families and the Children with Down's Syndrome: One feature in common.* London: Routledge.

Campbell, P. *et al.* (1992) 'Enhancing parent participation in the individual family service plan', *Topics in Early Childhood Special Education* **11**(4), 112–24.

Carpenter, B. (ed.) (1997) *Families in Context: Emerging trends in family support and early intervention.* London: David Fulton Publishers.

Carpenter, B. (1998) 'Defining the family: towards a critical framework for families of children with disabilities', *European Journal of Special Needs Education* **13**(2), 180–8.

Carpenter, B. (2000) 'Sustaining the family: meeting the needs of families of children with disabilities', *British Journal of Special Education* **27**(3), 135–44.

Carpenter, B. and Herbert, E. (1994) 'School-based support', in Mittler, P. and Mittler, H. (eds) *Innovations in Family Support for People with Learning Disabilities,* Lancashire: Lisieux Hall.

Carpenter, B. and Herbert, E. (1995) 'Including fathers: parent–professional considerations of the role of fathers in early intervention', *Network* **4**(4), 4–11.

Carpenter, B. and Woodgate, A. (1999) 'Market solution', *Special Children,* 119, 16–18.

Cunningham, C. and Davis, H. (1985) *Working with Parents: Frameworks for collaboration.* Buckingham: Open University Press.

Dahlstrom, E. (1989) 'Theories and ideology of family function, gender relations and human reproduction', in Boh, K. *et al.* (eds) *Changing Patterns of European Family Life.* London: Routledge.

Dale, N. (1996) *Working with Families of Children with Special Needs.* London: Routledge.

David, T. (ed.) (1994) *Working together for Young Children: Multiprofessionalism in action.* London: Routledge.

Davies, H. (1998) 'The benefits of psychological support for parents', *Opportunity* 16, 1–5.

Detheridge, M. (1995) *The Writing Set: An overview and rationale,* Leamington Spa: Widgit Software Ltd.

DFE (1994) *Code of Practice on the Identification and Assessment of Special Educational Needs*, London: HMSO.

Ferguson, P.M. and Asch, A. (1989) 'Lessons from life: personal and parental perspectives on school, childhood and disability', in Biklen, D. *et al.* (eds) *Schooling and Disability.* Chicago: NSSE.

Gabba, M. (1994) 'Some things are unacceptable', *Special Children*, February, 19–20.

Glynne-Rule, L. (1995) 'Support for the disabled', *Times Educational Supplement*, April.

Guralnick, M. (1991) 'The next decade of research on the effectiveness of early intervention', *Exceptional Children*, **58**(2), 174–83.

Hastings, R. P. (1997) 'Grandparents of children with disabilities: a review', *International Journal of Disability, Development and Education* **44**(4), 329–40.

Hautamäki, A. (1997) 'Mothers – stress, stressors and strains: outcomes of a cross-Nordic study', in Carpenter, B. (ed.) *Families in Context: Emerging trends in family support and early intervention.* London: David Fulton Publishers.

Herbert, E. and Carpenter, B. (1994) 'Fathers – the secondary partners: professional perceptions and a father's perceptions', *Children & Society* **8**(1), 31–41.

Home Office (1999) *Supporting Families.* London: Government Offices

Hornby, G. (1989) 'Launching parent to parent schemes', *British Journal of Special Education* **15**(2), 77–8.

Hornby, G. (1995) *Working with Parents of Children with Special Needs.* London: Cassell.

Hornby, G. and Ashworth, T. (1994) 'Grandparent support for families who have children with disabilities: a survey of parents', *Journal of Family Studies* 3, 403–12.

Leskinen, M. (ed.) (1994) *Family in Focus.* Jyväkylä, Finland: Jyväkylä University Press.

Manuel, P. (1996) 'A parent's perspective'. Paper to the National Children's Bureau Conference, London (December).

McConachie, H. (1997) 'Do UK services really support parents?', *Opportunity* 15, 1–2.

McConkey, R. (1985) *Working with Parents: A practical guide for teachers and therapists.* Beckenham: Croom Helm.

McConkey, R. (ed.) (1999) *Family Support*, Kidderminster: British Institute of Learning Disabilities.

Meyer, D. J. (ed.) (1995) *Uncommon Fathers: Reflections on raising a child with a disability.* Bethesda, MD: Woodbine House.

Meyer, D. J. (ed.) (1997) *Views from our Shoes: Growing up with a brother or sister with disabilities*, Bethesda, MD: Woodbine House.

Meyer, D. and Vadasy, P. (1997) 'Meeting the unique concerns of brothers and sisters of children with special needs', in Carpenter, B. (ed.) *Families in Context: Emerging trends in family support and early intervention.* London: David Fulton Publishers.

Mirfin-Veitch, B. and Bray, A. (1997) 'Grandparents: part of the family', in Carpenter, B. (ed.) *Families in Context: Emerging trends in family support and early intervention.* London: David Fulton Publishers.

Mitterauer, M. and Sieder, R. (1982) *The European Family.* Oxford: Basil Blackwell.

Mittler, H. (1995) 'Families speak out: international perspectives on families', in *Families Speak Out: International perspectives in families' experiences of disability.* Cambridge, MA: Brookline.

Mittler, P. and Mittler, H. (1994) *Innovations in Family Support for People with Learning Difficulties.* Lancashire: Lisieux Hall.

Mittler, P. (2000) *Working towards Inclusive Education: Social contexts.* London: David Fulton Publishers.

Newson, E. and Davis, J. (1994) 'Supporting the siblings of children with autism and related developmental disorders', in Mittler, P. and Mittler, H. (eds) *Innovations in Family Support for People with Learning Disabilities.* Lancashire: Lisieux Hall.

OFSTED (1999) *A Framework for the Inspection of Schools.* London: HMSO.

Olshansky, S. (1962) 'Chronic sorrow: a response to having a mentally defective child', *Social Casework* 43, 190–93.

QCA/DfEE (1999) *Early Learning Goals.* London: DfEE/QCA.

Randall, P. and Parker, J. (1999) *Supporting the Families of Children with Autism.* Chichester: John Wiley.

Ritchie, P. (1998) 'Quality of life issues and the role of services'. Keynote address to the Mencap National Focus Group (PIMD), Manchester (June).

Robinson, C. (2000) 'Transition and change in the lives of families with a young disabled child: the early years', in May, D. (ed.) *Transition and Change in the Lives of People with Intellectual Disabilities*. London: Jessica Kingsley.

Roll, J. (1991) *What is a Family?*. London: FPSC.

Roll-Pettersson, L. (2001) 'Parents talk about how it feels to have a child with a cognitive disability', *European Journal of Special Needs Education* **16**(1), 1–14

Seligman and Darling, R. B. (1989) *Ordinary Families, Special Children: A system approach to childhood disability*. New York: The Guildford Press.

Tritt, S. G. and Esses, L. M. (1988) 'Psychological adaptation of siblings of children with chronic medical illness', *American Journal of Orthopsychiatry* 58, 211–20.

Turnbull, A. P. and Turnbull, H. R. (1986) *Families, Professionals and Exceptionality*, Columbus, OH: Merrill.

Wikler, L. (1984) 'Chronic stresses of families of mentally retarded children', in Henninger, M. L. and Nesselroad, E. M. (eds) *Working with Parents of Handicapped Children*. Lanham, MD: University Press of America.

Wills, R. (1994) 'It is time to stop', in Ballard, K. (ed.) *Disability, Family, Whanau and Society*. Palmerston North, NZ: Dunmore Press.

Winton, R. (1990) *Report of the New Mexico Home Memorial 5 Task Force on Young Children and Families: Report 1*. New Mexico: The New Mexico Home Memorial 5 Task Force on Young Children and Families.

Wolfendale, S. (1989) *Parental Involvement: Developing Networks Between School, Home and Community*. London: Cassell.

Wolfendale, S. (2000) 'Special needs in the early years: prospects for policy and practice', *Support for Learning* **15**(4), 147–51.

Chapter 20

Access to the System: The Legislative Interface

Philippa Russell

Introduction: the context for policy and practice

There are an estimated 1.6 million children in England and Wales with special educational needs. The past few years have witnessed significant changes to the statutory and policy framework for SEN. The Government's Green Paper, *Excellence for All Children: Meeting Special Educational Needs* (DfEE 1997) set out six key themes (including raising expectations and standards for children with SEN). A key objective of the report was to promote the inclusion of children with special educational needs within mainstream schools wherever possible, and obtain 'good value for money' from SEN expenditure through 'shifting resources from expensive remediation to cost-effective prevention and early intervention' (DfEE 1997). The Green Paper was followed in 1998 by the Government's programme of action (DfEE 1998), designed to deliver the key themes.

It is estimated that 285,000 children in England and Wales currently have a Statement of SEN. There is a continuing marked upward trend in numbers of children with statements who are educated in mainstream schools. Between 1995 and 1999, the proportion of pupils in special schools – as a percentage of the total statemented population – decreased from 40.6 per cent to 32.5 per cent. But, even so, around 97,000 children are educated in 1,200 special schools in England and Wales. There are wide variations (from 0.3 per cent to 1.5 per cent) in the numbers of pupils in mainstream settings across local education authorities. Expenditure on SEN forms a major element (approximately 35 per cent) within LEA budgets. A major challenge for the future in terms of strategic planning for SEN will be the increased delegation of the budget to schools. In order to meet the 90–per-cent targets for 2002/3, it is probable that LEAs will delegate some provision for children with statements directly to schools.

Overall, the use of independent or non-maintained provision fell during the three calendar years 1998–2000, but it has been estimated that there are more than 300,000 children under the age of 16 in England and Wales who have one or more disabilities (British Medical Association 1999; Office of Population Censuses and Surveys (OPCS) 1989). As at early 2001, around 16,500 children with SEN are attending residential schools, with the largest number – 8,000 – in schools for children with emotional and behavioural difficulties. Many residential schools are under increasing pressure to provide 52–week-per-year residential care. This trend has to be offset against gradual but encouraging increases in mainstream school placements for all children with disabilities, and a recognition that parents are expecting more community-based services that enable them and their children, in the words of the Children Act 1989, to lead lives that are 'as ordinary as possible'.

There has been growing concern about the impact of disadvantage, family problems and health issues both on the education of children with disabilities and/or statements of SEN and also on the education and development of children 'in need' under the Children Act 1989. The current acrimonious debate about difficult and disruptive children, and the growth of exclusions from the mainstream and special-school sectors, highlight the need for better understanding between health, education and social services departments and the need to adopt 'whole-child' approaches, based on a clear understanding of the legal basis for entitlement to services and the purchasing arrangements within different agencies to meet individual needs.

The Children Act 1989 marked a watershed in terms of attitude toward, and expectations for, disabled children and their families. For the first time, disabled children were brought within a common legislative framework with other children. In effect, the 'social model' of disability was firmly acknowledged, and decades of residential care within health settings was ended. But the inclusion of disabled children within overarching legislation for all children created challenges as well as opportunities.

Over the past decade, since the early 1990s, we have seen major steps forward in terms of the inclusion of disabled children within early years, education, play and leisure provision. There has been a new and positive commitment to the involvement of disabled children in decision-making about their lives – and more proactive planning for transition to a valued active life in the community. However, there is ongoing evidence of the pressures of caring experienced by many families, and there are challenges in promoting genuine disability awareness across all children's services.

Developments in provision for young children with SEN

The United Kingdom, like the USA, has seen an ongoing debate over several decades about what constitutes effective early identification and intervention strategies for young children with SEN or disabilities. An evaluation of strategies such as the USA's High Scope Programme have indicated that the benefits of early intervention can be long-term and can have significant impact upon the adult lives of the children (and families) concerned. The UK government's Programme of Action on SEN (DfEE 1998) acknowledges the importance of the early years and promises to provide high-quality early years education and childcare, including support for parents, and encourage earlier identification of difficulties and appropriate early intervention.

These goals are to be achieved progressively through Early Years Development and Childcare Partnerships, which integrate childcare and education and which place a greater emphasis upon earlier identification, with appropriate interventions from the earliest stages to tackle difficulties and provide effective support (including independent advice) for parents. Baseline assessment should offer a planned transition from pre-school to the school stages of education. There is a new and welcome emphasis upon multi-agency planning and provision for children with SEN (with Early Years Excellence

Centres offering models for such collaborative working and for the inclusion of children with a range of disabilities and special needs within mainstream provision).

Early-years provision in the United Kingdom has always reflected diversity, with education, health, social services departments, and the independent and voluntary sectors all making a range of provisions. Local authorities have varying levels of direct maintained education provision in the early years, with some authorities relying heavily upon the voluntary and independent sectors.

The integration of care with education within the Early Years Partnerships, and within a growing range of providers, offers both challenges and opportunities. The introduction of the Early Learning Goals and a new Foundation Stage have led to a powerful debate about:

- definitions of *excellence and inclusion* in early years services;
- the *purpose* of early years education;
- the need to ensure that children have access to *play* and other developmental activities;
- concerns about *SEN expertise in early years provision* and the *sources of advice and support* that will be available to the increasingly diverse early-years sector.

The education of young children with SEN cannot be achieved without active participation of parents and a wider range of community services. Definitions are still challenging. The current debate about what constitutes *inclusion*; the role of *specialist* provision and support services and the interface between *play* and early years education is still unresolved.

But there are real opportunities for the development of a more proactive approach to the planning and delivery of services for young children with SEN across early-years services. The Health Act 1999 introduces 'partnership in action', which offers new flexibilities in joint commissioning, and pooled budgets between education and child-health services in many authorities. New integrated inspection arrangements within the Care Standards Act, 2000 extend the Government's key theme of quality and regular audit and review. Importantly, the theme of partnership with parents runs across all the strands of the Government's early-years projects. With specific reference to SEN, proposals to extend the role of Parent Partnership Services to the early-years sector are a reminder of the potential isolation of parents with young children with SEN, and of the importance of strengthening parents' confidence and competence in helping their young children to learn and develop. Finally, and by no means least, the advent of Human Rights legislation and the creation of a Disability Rights Commission in 2000 have reminded many providers of their new responsibilities under Part III of the Disability Discrimination Act 1995 (DDA) – and the need to ensure that early-years services are truly accessible and as far as possible inclusive for children with disabilities, for disabled parents, for carers and for staff.

The UK government announced its broad policy approach to early-years services in May 1997. The key element within the new policy direction was the requirement that every local authority should create a broad-based Early Years Development Partnership, which would draw up an Early Years Development Plan for the region. In response to the National Childcare Strategy, planning arrangements for childcare and early-years education were integrated within Early Years Development and Childcare Partnerships. Their statutory basis is contained within sections 117–124 of the School Standards and Framework Act 1998.

The emphasis upon local partnerships and strategic direction was put firmly within the context of targets and 'strategic principles' for Early Years Development and Childcare Partnerships. The 1999–2000 planning guidance (DfEE 1999a) sets as targets:

- good affordable childcare for children aged 0–14 in every neighbourhood;
- provision for children with SEN or disabilities within inclusive settings wherever possible and appropriate;
- a clear framework of qualifications for both early-years education and childcare workers;
- active involvement of parents and family in early education and childcare, with the opportunity to improve skills.

Sure Start

Sure Start, a major initiative to target early intervention services to the young children and families most 'in need', has been rightly described by David Blunkett, when Secretary of State at the DfEE, as 'one of the most ambitious early intervention programmes ever created in the United Kingdom ... a cornerstone of the Government's drive to tackle child poverty and social exclusion, based on firm evidence of what works' (DfEE 1999b, p. 1). The government intends to invest £450 million to set up 250 Sure Start projects across England within the life of the Parliament that commenced in 1997 with Labour coming to power. The programme aims to improve the health and well-being (and thereby the life chances) of families and children before and after birth through providing new and often pioneering services offering:

- family support;
- advice on nurturing;
- better access to healthcare;
- new opportunities for early learning.

The first trailblazer Sure Start programmes have been established in 60 areas, and a further 69 districts are submitting proposals, with the objective of achieving (DfEE 1999b, p. 1) 'the promotion of the physical, intellectual and social development of pre-school children – particularly those who are disadvantaged – to ensure that they are ready to thrive when they get to school'. Key targets for Sure Start areas include:

- ensuring that 90 per cent of children have normal speech and language development at 18 months and 3 years;
- ensuring that all children have access to good-quality play and early-learning opportunities;
- helping progress toward the early-learning goals for children when they get to school.

An analysis of the first project plans indicated the need for greater clarity in guidance about disability and SEN, and programmes are now expected to set out:

- the different provisions and services that are available for children with disabilities or SEN and their families;
- details of arrangements made by service providers for the early identification and assessment of children's SEN;

- details of any specialist provision and services (and the assessment and referral arrangements to such services).

There is a strong emphasis on preventive services, with a Sure Start guide to evidence-based practices (DfEE 1999c) to offer examples of how early identification and assessment services or support for children with complex needs might work in practice.

A new framework for the assessment of children in need and their families

The Children Act 1989 marked a radical change in policy and practice for children's services by including children with disabilities within a common framework for *all* 'children in need'. Importantly, with the advent of a Disability Rights Commission in 2000 and a national policy thrust towards greater inclusion in education, Schedule 2 of the 1989 Act requires local authorities to provide services for children with disabilities that are designed to minimise the effect of their disabilities and to give them the opportunity to lead lives that are as normal as possible (Department of Health (DoH) 1991).

In practice, the achievement of these objectives has been challenging. Since 1996, local authorities have been required to produce Children's Services Plans, which should provide inter-agency strategic planning for children in need within all local authorities. The planning requirement has highlighted the challenge of producing accurate and relevant information on local populations of disabled children. More recent guidance on children's services planning (DoH 2000) broadens the responsibility for the planning and delivery of services by expecting more 'joined-up thinking' and better integration of planning activities across service boundaries.

Since the implementation of the Children Act 1989, there have been growing aspirations across all three statutory services (education, health and social services) to provide more timely, accurate and evidence-based assessment of need. There has been corresponding recognition that no single agency can carry out an effective assessment, and that effective outcomes for children who are regarded as being 'at risk' or who have developmental, social, health or educational difficulties will depend upon the skilful analysis of a wealth of accumulated experience and expertise across all agencies and within the family itself.

As a consequence of the new policy commitment to *joint and integrated* assessment protocols and procedures, the Department of Health, the Department for Education and Employment (DfEE) and the Home Office have jointly developed and published a *Framework for the Assessment of Children in Need and their Families* (DoH/DfEE/Home Office 2000). The new framework is accompanied by practice guidance, and it offers a new and holistic approach to 'whole child, whole family' assessment that both recognises and contributes to educational assessment.

The statutory basis for assessment of children 'in need' rests in section 17 and Schedule 2, Part 1 of the Children Act 1989. The Act gives local authority social services departments the powers to assess children's needs 'where it appears to a local authority that a child in their area is in need', at the same time as any other assessment of the child's needs is made under the Education Act 1996, the Chronically Sick and Disabled Persons Act 1970, the Disabled Persons (Services, Consultation and Representation) Act 1986 or any other specified legislation.

Historically, such joint assessments have often been linked to LEA responsibilities for safeguarding children under the procedures laid down in *Working Together to Safeguard Children* (DoH 1999a). But there is growing evidence that many children with disabilities or SEN and their families also have a wide range of needs for which social services and health interventions may be important in order to maximise educational progress and opportunity. The new requirements on schools and education providers to take steps to prevent educational discrimination against disabled pupils and to make 'reasonable adjustments' under the SEN and Disability Act, 2000 is likely to raise awareness of the importance of more holistic assessment procedures and the exchange of information and advice between agencies to promote access and inclusion.

The new framework for assessment (DoH/DfEE/Home Office 2000) is seen as providing an *ecological* approach. In effect, it sees assessment as covering three 'domains', namely:

1. the child's developmental needs;
2. the parent's or other care-giver's capacities to respond appropriately;
3. the wider family and environmental factors.

In assessing these three domains, the framework recognises that education services have a vital role to play, in particular providing (DoH/DfEE/Home Office 2000, para. 5.43): 'important information on the child's development, their level of understanding and the most effective means of communicating with the child'.

Succeeding in school is seen as a 'major protective factor' in children's lives; the Practice Guidance describes education as 'the key service for children' and advocates strong partnerships (DoH 2000). The Practice Guidance includes a specific section on disabled children, recognising the discrimination and fragmentation of services that they and their families frequently experience. It hopes (para. 3.78) that 'the use of the Assessment Framework will mark a radical departure in assessment, moving from a single agency and service-led assessments to assessments of the whole child by a co-ordinated group of professionals'.

The new approach is particularly relevant for the assessment of children with SEN or disabilities. It emphasises the need to:

- listen to, value and support parents and members of the wider family;
- ensure that each child has access to appropriate and adequate healthcare;
- recognise the interface between disability and social disadvantage;
- involve children and young people in assessment and decision-making, with appropriate support, and respect their priorities;
- take account of any cultural or personal preferences related to the child's ethnicity or other family factors;
- avoid multiple assessments.

The new approach has important implications for schools and for LEAs. The consultation document on the revision of the SEN Code of Practice (DfEE 2000) similarly reflects the need for 'joined-up assessment' and shared planning for children and young people with SEN or disabilities.

The Assessment Framework stresses the importance of asking disabled children and young people what they want and of seeing them as active contributors to any programme of activity. The Assessment Framework recognises the challenge of encouraging such participation. Children's own priorities will vary and are likely to change over time. It is also important to be sensitive to any fluctuations in children's abilities. Tiredness, distress, illness or an unfamiliar environment can temporarily wipe out a skill. Real participation requires ongoing respect, support and a willingness to listen to and value children's perspectives

As the Assessment Framework notes, the genuine involvement of children in decision-making will necessitate changes in policy and practice. The Framework suggests that there are five 'critical components' in working directly with children, namely (DoH 2000, para. 3.42):

- *seeing the child* who is the focus of an assessment (i.e. not relying upon paper records alone);
- *observing the child* (including observing children in school settings where appropriate);
- *engaging the child* (i.e. developing a relationship and communication system with the child so that he/she can make real choices);
- *talking to the child* (i.e. recognising that time, confidence, advice and support, and careful preparation are essential for a genuine dialogue);
- *undertaking activities with the child* (i.e. sharing activities that enable the professional to gain a better understanding of the child's responses and needs).

Butler and Williamson (DoH 1997), asking a group of children and young people with disabilities and a range of SEN what they saw as key elements in good professional practice in assessment, identified some key qualities (pp. 1–2):

- listening seriously and believing;
- being available and accessible;
- being non-judgmental and non-directive (i.e. explaining and suggesting options and choices);
- having a sense of humour;
- 'straight talking' – not making any false promises;
- being trustworthy – not breaking any confidences.

The young people wanted positive relationships with the adults in their lives. They were anxious to play an active role in assessment but frequently felt unable to do so.

Protecting vulnerable children

There are likely to be two positive outcomes of the use of the Assessment Framework: firstly, greater participation by social services departments in educational assessment; and, secondly, stronger partnerships between education and social services in protecting vulnerable children.

Children with disabilities and some SEN will be particularly at risk of abuse in many settings (Crosse *et al.* 1993; Westcott 1993). The increased vulnerability is due to a range of factors including:

- multiple carers and service settings;
- the limited communication skills of the children;
- disbelief that certain children could be abused;

- children feeling 'out of control' over their lives, care and bodies;
- a greater likelihood of spending time outside the family home (e.g. in respite or other care) and of that care being removed from family and community.

The Practice Guidance (DoH 2000) stresses the importance of assessments considering the safety of different settings and services in a child's life. Marchant, in the Practice Guidance, cites the example of the possible abuse of a six-year-old girl (DoH 2000, para. 3.88):

> Concerns were raised about the possible sexual abuse of a six-year-old girl with learning disabilities. School and residential staff felt initially that she could not be abused because she resisted nappy changing with such violence.

In reality, the school and residential care staff were seeing appropriate behaviour by the girl, who anticipated abuse taking place and had no other communication skills with which to express her fear and anxiety. The case illustrates the importance of honest and open exchange of information about children with complex needs, where the accurate interpretation of behaviour in an educational setting may need to be made in partnership with health or social services. As the DoH (1999a) notes in *Working Together to Safeguard Children*, safeguarding children must be seen as a corporate responsibility, within which all three statutory services have a critical role. Education is the universal service for the majority of children and it will have a unique perspective on the lives of children with disabilities or special educational needs.

The Protection of Children Act 2000 provides a background legal framework for the above guidance and in particular lays a corporate responsibility upon all children's services (including schools and the LEA) to have regard to child-protection policies, practices and procedures, both in the recruitment and deployment of staff and in the keeping of children safe across all environments.

Families from minority ethnic groups

A particularly disadvantaged group of families with disabled children in all studies (Beresford 1995; Chamba *et al.* 1999; Emerson and Azmi 1997; Shah 1996) are those from minority ethnic groups. Beresford, in her analysis of Family Fund data, found families from minority ethnic groups among the most disadvantaged in the survey. Shah (1996) refers to the 'silent minority' of families with disabled children who experience the multiple prejudices of racism, poverty and misunderstanding about the wishes and feelings of families in the Asian community. Like Emerson and Azmi (1997), she notes the barrier of inadequate information and lack of interpreters, the reluctance to offer some services such as respite care because of misunderstandings about the role of the extended family, and the poor housing and poverty that exacerbate any problems of care.

Emerson and Azmi (1997), in a study of Asian carers in the north-west of England, found that 65 per cent of families with a disabled child had difficulties in paying basic bills. Only a minority could speak (37 per cent) or write (24 per cent) English, and hence had little knowledge of services that might have supported them. On a formal measure of health-related stress, four out of every five carers reported levels of stress that indicated a real risk of developing mental health problems in the future. Over 40 per cent of carers reported back or sleep problems, depression, or chest pains. But, notwithstanding high levels of social deprivation, families were anxious to help their children and to participate in any therapy or other programmes. Messages for future action lie within the Quality Protects initiative (see below), which requires local and health authorities to take account of the needs of families from minority ethnic groups in their areas and through the Government's Children's Task Force and Health Improvement Plans.

Quality Protects: improving the 'life chances' of vulnerable children

Social services have a crucial role to play within the UK government's wider social-inclusion strategy (DoH 1999b). Children's social services work with some of the most disadvantaged families and some of the most vulnerable children in our society. Children's social services need to provide the right targeted help to ensure that all children and young people are able to take maximum advantage of universal services, in particular education and health. Good assessment of the needs of children and families plays an important role here, enabling needs to be identified at an early stage so that services and support can be provided (DoH 1999b).

A three-year Quality Protects initiative was launched in September 1998 and was extended for a further two years in 2000. The programme arose from widespread concerns about the safety and quality of care offered to vulnerable children (in particular, those looked after by the LEAs), as raised in the Utting Children's Safeguard Review (Utting 1997). The programme has five key elements, as listed below:

1. *New national objectives*, setting standards and outcomes for services for children in need across the UK. One such objective will necessitate close partnerships with education and child health services and has implications for policies across early-years services; namely, that children with specific social needs arising out of disability or a health condition should be living in families or other appropriate settings in the community where their assessed needs (for education, health or social care) are adequately met and reviewed;
2. *Annual management action plans* (QMAPs), which set out how each local authority (social services and education) and the relevant health authority will strengthen and jointly improve their services so that they meet the new objectives;
3. *User consultation with children and young people and with parents*, to inform them of the development of local services;
4. *A new Children's Grant*, to fund improvements;
5. *A new and important role for elected members* in setting standards and ensuring that local authorities meet them.

The first round of Quality Protects QMAPs were jointly developed and signed up to by education and social services departments. The second round has required participation by the relevant local health services. All planning arrangements under Quality Protects must address services and support for disabled children. The analysis of the first two years of QMAPs (Khan and Russell 1999, 2001) indicates some creative new thinking about children with disabilities and SEN within a more holistic local-authority planning system.

There are clear and positive messages about inclusive planning within early-years provision and within some transition-planning arrangements. However, the same analysis indicates the challenges in planning across education and social care and in ensuring that the necessary supports are available for the greater inclusion of children with a range of special needs within mainstream services. The programme has probably been underutilised by education services, but it offers considerable potential for 'joined-up planning' at local level and, from 2001, will have dedicated additional funding for services for disabled children.

Child health services

Child health services have seen significant changes in recent years. In the NHS, more accessible screening and surveillance and the development of specialist community child-health services have raised expectations about the contribution of health services to educational assessment. However, there is ongoing concern (British Medical Association 1999; House of Commons Health Committee 1997a and 1997b) that positive partnerships have been difficult to achieve and that fragmentation of services is common.

Health authorities and Primary Care Groups (shortly to become Primary Care Trusts) have an important role in contributing to inter-agency planning and in cooperating in the development of QMAPs. The health authorities have a responsibility to agree *how* the local health services should contribute to inter-agency assessments (including the appointment of the designated medical officers, to whom the SEN Code of Practice (DFE 1994; DfEE 2000) allocates the role of managing and coordinating the health input to educational assessment and statements.

Health Improvement Plans form part of a jointly agreed strategy between the local authority, NHS Trusts and the Primary Care Groups/Trusts. They were introduced to improve the quality of life of vulnerable people, and education services will have an important role in ensuring that they reflect local priorities and improve the quality of inter-agency working to safeguard children and promote their welfare.

NHS Trusts and Primary Care Groups/Trusts are responsible for the direct provision of community health services in hospital and community settings, including a range of provision from the school health service to therapy services. A major review of mental-health services has also underlined the importance of stronger partnerships with Child and Adolescent Mental Health Services (CAMS) and earlier identification of any mental-health difficulties that may affect children's progress.

The NHS Plan, the Health Act 1999 and the Health and Social Services Act 2000 provide a framework for health services of the future. The Health Act 1999 is of particular relevance to education services, as it permits new flexibilities in pooled budgets, joint commissioning and direct health-service contributions to joint initiatives led by local-authority or other providers. Consultation on the principle of 'partnership in action' suggests that the flexibilities, when implemented, could have major and positive implications for:

- the joint commissioning and funding of therapy services;
- pooled budgets for equipment;
- joint commissioning and purchasing of residential education.

'Partnership in action' is likely to be taken forward actively in the future through proposals to create new joint Health and Social Services Trusts, thereby increasing the possibility of more inclusive services and – for schools – the likelihood of easier access to advice and input to assessment.

The Health and Social Services Act 2000 and the Carers and Disabled Children Act 2000

The United Kingdom's Health and Social Services Act 2000 takes 'partnership' further forward and makes it a requirement for local authorities to introduce direct payments for parent carers and young disabled people aged 16–17 in lieu of services otherwise provided by a local authority. Although introduced in a Health and Social Services Act, the new arrangements primarily relate to social care, and will enable parent carers and young people (subject to assessment of need and of their ability to manage such payments – with support if necessary) to purchase a much more flexible range of support services. Direct payments cannot be used to purchase direct educational provision, but they can be used for personal support or transport to enable a young person to go on a school trip, to attend an after-school club or leisure activity, or (in the case of a further education college) to provide extra practical support during the day.

Local authorities will be expected to set up support arrangements (possibly linked to a relevant voluntary organisation or Centre for Independent Living). The guidance on the Carers and Disabled Children Act 2000 emphasises the importance of direct payments for young disabled people aged 16–17 (which can be extended into adult life under the Direct Payments Act 1998). They can offer an important tool in transition planning for some young people, providing real opportunities to acquire skills in managing personal assistance, a budget for the direct payments, and use of a wider range of services.

Fit for the future? New developments in transition planning and the role of the Connexions Service

The SEN Code of Practice (DFE 1994) introduced the 'transition plan' as part of a process of planned progression from children's services to adult life for young people with SEN or disabilities. Growing interest in strategic transition planning is reflected within both the revised SEN Code of Practice (DfEE 2000) and the Learning and Skills Act 2000. However, the reality is more often lack of coordination, poor information about options for further education and training, and very little real participation by the young people concerned.

To address concerns about transition planning, the Government is to introduce a new Connexions Service in April 2001, which will provide all 13–19–year-olds with access to advice, guidance and support through the creation of a network of personal advisers. These personal advisers will take responsibility for ensuring that the needs of all young people (including those with disabilities or SEN) are met in an integrated and coordinated manner.

Connexions personal advisers will work under the aegis of the Connexions Partnerships. The responsibilities and roles of the Connexions Partnerships are set out in the Learning and Skills Act 2000 and are designed to ensure more-effective transitions for all young people (including those with SEN) on leaving school and moving through post-16 education and training. The partnerships will develop agreements between the service and each relevant school in their area, with schools having an important role in determining the most relevant deployment of personal advisers within their own service.

Connexions personal advisers will attend the Year 9 annual reviews for young people with statements or significant levels of SEN, and those advisers will work with the school and any relevant agencies in order to draw up and implement a transition plan. Each

Connexions Partnership must ensure that there are sufficient personal advisers with the appropriate skills, experience and training to work with young people with disabilities or SEN, and to act as their advocates or mentors as appropriate. The emphasis is upon flexibility, and the personal advisers can work as one-to-one mentors or in peer support or group activities.

Connexions Partnerships will have responsibility for arranging a review of young people with a learning disability in their nineteenth year (in partnership with the local Learning and Skills Council and the Employment Service). Where a young person is not yet ready to use adult guidance services, social-services departments may be involved and the Learning and Skills Council and Connexions Partnership may determine that the young person should continue to be supported by the Partnership up until his or her twenty-fifth birthday. Hence, transition-planning arrangements for young people with complex disabilities or SEN should have more continuity and a more informed transition into appropriate adult provision.

The Connexions Service will be expected to evaluate its performance both by surveying users (including schools) and reviewing progress towards national and locally set targets. The transition planning process itself will be expected to follow the framework set out in the revised SEN Code of Practice (DfEE 2000).

Connexions, if successful, has major implications for pupils and for schools. If effective, it will provide individualised mentoring and support, and assist in the more effective targeting of often scarce resources. The local partnerships should assist in developing more strategic partnerships between education, careers, health and social services in planning for the future. But the programme will also pose challenges in requiring assurances not only that the local partnerships and personal advisers are sufficiently experienced, informed and trained to be effective partners and advocates, but also that the Connexions Service can establish sound working relationships with schools, SENCOs and local parents and voluntary organisations.

The Human Rights Act 1998

The implementation of the Human Rights Act 1998 in October 2000 has raised considerable interest (and some concerns) across education and other statutory services. The 1998 Act implements Article 14 of the European Convention on Human Rights, to which the United Kingdom has been a signatory for some years. It has broad applicability across all legislation and is binding on public authorities. The definition of a 'public authority' includes voluntary organisations, schools and others that provide services on behalf of a local or similar authority.

Protocol 1 of Article 2 of the European Convention on Human Rights sets out the right to education, namely:

> No person shall be denied the right to education, in the exercise of any functions that it assumes in relation to education and to teaching. The State shall respect the right of parents to ensure such education and teaching in conformity with their own religious and philosophical convictions.

However, the UK Government has entered a reservation to this right, namely:

> In view of certain provisions of the Education Acts in the UK, the principle affirmed is accepted by the UK only in so far as it is compatible with the provision of efficient instruction and training and the avoidance of unreasonable public expenditure.

It is important to recognise that this reservation limits the impact of Article 2 upon UK education legislation. It is also important (with particular reference to the SEN and Disability Act, 2001) that the Court of Human Rights defines education very broadly thus:

> The education of children is the whole process whereby, in any society, adults endeavour to transmit the beliefs, culture and other values to the young, whereas teaching or instruction refers in particular to the transmission of knowledge and intellectual development.

Article 2 refers to the education of children, but is likely to cover the continuance of their education in further or higher education. Under the Human Rights Act 1998 and its related Convention, states do not to have to provide a particular *type* of education. Rather, Article 2 of the Convention gives a right of access to educational facilities already in existence and a right to draw benefit from that education.

There has been considerable interest as to whether parents can use the legislation to require inclusive education for their children. Test cases in other European countries suggest that this is not likely to be possible. A case in the Netherlands (De Klerks v. Netherlands) decided that whereas the parents had a conviction that 'inclusive education was right for their child, the local authority had considerable discretion as to how it provided appropriate services and was able to consider efficient use of resources in deciding that the girl should remain at a special school' (Dawe 2000).

The 1998 Act is most likely to have an impact in strengthening the right of children to be consulted and involved in assessment (including longer-term conciliation and appeal arrangements) and in considering whether there is equity within local arrangements for assessment, eligibility criteria and allocation of resources.

Disability on the agenda: the DDA and the SEN and Disability Bill

The DDA is still little-known in children's services. The 1995 Act's core objectives are to ensure that disabled people (including children) are not treated less favourably because of their disability than other people. It therefore requires providers of services (whether in the business community or the voluntary or statutory sectors) to change any policies, practices or procedures that make it impossible or unreasonably difficult for disabled people to use a service. Providers are similarly expected to provide auxiliary aids or services and overcome physical features that make it impossible or unreasonably difficult for disabled people to access a service through a 'reasonable alternative method'.

From 2004, providers of services will be required to make changes to the physical environment to promote access and prevent discrimination. All duties are subject to the test of 'reasonableness' in terms of the nature and cost of the changes required and the first years of implementation of the 1995 Act indicate two things: firstly, that 'reasonable' adjustments are usually possible without undue expenditure and relate more to planning, staff training and attitudes than to major capital expenditure; and, secondly, that capital expenditure to buildings (i.e. ramps, lifts, etc.) can usually be built into longer-term refurbishment plans. In the case of schools, the Schools Access Initiative will provide important 'pump-priming money'.

Currently, the DDA covers discrimination in:

- employment;
- land and property;

- education (limited coverage at present – see below);
- transport vehicles;
- goods and services (including statutory services).

Education is currently excluded from the DDA except for employment requirements, the provision of information on how a school or college proposes to prevent discrimination, and buildings (when used for 'non-educational' purposes). Schools and LEAs should note that when an educational property is used for after-school clubs, play activities or parent evenings, it is subject to the DDA.

The exclusion of education from the DDA (this exclusion being linked to concerns that its *in*clusion might interfere with the effective implementation of the Education Act 1993 and SEN Code of Practice (1994), thus causing the creation of a 'dual system') attracted widespread concern. Additionally, the DDA was not backed by a Disability Rights Commission with enforcement powers, and there were concerns that discrimination would persist.

In 1998 the Government appointed a Disability Rights Task Force to consider the potential role and structure of a Disability Rights Commission and, within this consideration, to discuss whether education should now come under a disability discrimination framework. The Task Force (DfEE 1999b) strongly recommended the inclusion of education and did not see difficulties with dual definitions of disability and SEN. In 2000 the UK Government launched the Disability Rights Commission and announced that it would introduce a SEN and Disability Act which would effectively implement the Task Force recommendations (DfEE 1999d) and bring disability discrimination and SEN issues together.

The Act (2001) addresses a number of wider policy issues relating to disability and SEN, including:

- the need for greater clarity about a child's right to inclusive education (i.e. amending section 316 of the Education Act 1996);
- the requirement that all LEAs provide parent-partnership services (but replacing the requirement to provide a 'named person' for all parents going through statutory assessment with a requirement instead to provide an 'independent parental supporter' to those who want one);
- the requirement that all LEAs provide arrangements for 'dispute resolution' (i.e. mediation or conciliation) so as to facilitate early settlement of any disagreements between parents and the LEA, and to reduce the number of sometimes very adversarial appeals to the SEN Tribunal;
- the extension of the role of the SEN Tribunal so that it can hear disability as well as SEN cases.

The SEN and Disability Act, 2001 imposes a range of new and important duties on all education providers (including early-years providers, schools, colleges, institutes of higher education, and LEAs) to avoid discriminating against disabled students and to make reasonable adjustments to policies, practices and procedures where these prevent a student from accessing educational services. The emphasis, as in the DDA, is upon ensuring that disabled students are not treated less favourably because of their disability. Cases in dispute can, as noted above, go to the SEN and Disability Tribunal.

At the request of the Government, the Disability Rights Commission will provide a formal educational conciliation service and will produce two Codes of Practice on the school and post-school stages of education to provide guidance on the new arrangements.

The SEN and Disability Act , 2001 has major implications for all education services. Part II of the Bill, addressing disability discrimination in the school stages of education, makes it unlawful to discriminate against disabled pupils in admission arrangements to schools or in access to education or associated services. 'Discrimination' is described as treating a pupil less favourably than other pupils would be treated because of his/her disability, unless it is possible that to demonstrate that different treatment is justified.

Schools must now take reasonable steps to ensure that they do not discriminate against disabled pupils and to ensure that such pupils are not put at 'substantial disadvantage' in comparison with pupils who are not disabled. However, schools are not required to remove or alter physical features of their buildings and land or to provide auxiliary aids or services. The presumption is that the existing arrangements for statutory assessment will ensure that any individual pieces of equipment or specialist services (such as therapy) are made available to those individual pupils who need them.

There is ongoing debate about how the above requirements will work in practice. Schools are still permitted to take into account a number of factors in determining how they might meet the needs of a disabled pupil and what adjustments they might make, for example 'the need to maintain academic, musical, sporting and other standards; the financial resources available to the responsible body and health and safety requirements' (Clause 12 of the Act). However, implementing a recommendation from the Disability Rights Task Force (DfEE 1999b) and drawing on the experience of implementing the Individuals with Disabilities Education Act 1997 (IDEA) in the USA, the Act introduces two important requirements:

- *Accessibility strategies*: all LEAs must prepare written strategies for improving over a prescribed period the physical environment of the schools for which they are responsible. The purpose of this strategy is to require LEAs to plan incrementally, taking account of present provision and resource levels, in order to increase the accessibility of their education services.
- *Access plans*: all schools (including maintained, non-maintained and independent schools) must similarly prepare written plans for improving, over a prescribed period, the physical environment of the school in order to improve the extent to which disabled pupils can take advantage of the education and associated services offered.

The requirement for written plans, which must cover specific periods of time and be regularly reviewed, offers a powerful steer towards: better consultation with local services for disabled children and adults, as well as the voluntary sector; the use of access audits in order to plan incrementally for enhanced access; and better use of new monies available through the Schools Access Initiative.

With reference to schools, governors will be required to report annually on:

- arrangements for admission of disabled pupils;
- the steps being taken to prevent disabled pupils being treated less favourably than other pupils;
- the facilities offered by the school to assist access by disabled pupils;
- their access plan (see above), prepared in compliance with the new legislation.

The new legislation raises a range of challenges. Firstly, it will require schools and LEAs to work with a wide range of partners in order to ensure that their plans are positive, practical and based on sound advice. Secondly, there are concerns that the focus is upon physical access rather on access to the curriculum. Thirdly, few schools have thought through their obligations with regard to the full range of education services covered by the Act. In the United States, a large number of early cases were related to the exclusion of disabled pupils (usually on inadequate evidence) from school trips and journeys, a refusal to include disabled pupils in musical or drama activities (often through misunderstandings of health and safety regulations), or an unwillingness of the school and related health services to administer medication on the school premises. There have also been a growing number of cases brought in the USA relating to bullying and harassment by other pupils.

More positively, the use of mediation in the USA (introduced in IDEA, mentioned above, with schemes now required in all US states) has led to very positive understandings and adjustments by schools to existing policies and practices prior to formal hearings. Additionally, a significant 'knowledge gap' has been identified with regard to practical advice for schools on what constitute 'reasonable adjustments' and how they can develop short-, medium- and longer-term access objectives. In the UK, the Disability Rights Commission will be offering such advice through Codes of Practice, its Conciliation Service and through its wider advice and information roles.

The SEN and Disability Act, 2001 has excited considerable anxiety in some education services. But messages from South Australia and the United States (where disability discrimination legislation has always included education) indicate that there are few problems. Most disabled children already have statements of SEN and hence are already within the 'SEN system'. The emphasis upon 'reasonable adjustments' has in general led to practical and often creative solutions to including disabled pupils within the full life of the school. Very importantly, the new legislation (which covers education literally 'from the cradle to the grave') complements the inclusion statement within the revised National Curriculum, the principles and practice of the SEN Code of Practice (both 1994 and 2000) and the UK government's commitment to maximising the potential of all pupils.

Challenges for the future

The past decade has seen a range of new initiatives to improve the quality of life of all children and families. Early Years Development and Childcare Partnerships, Sure Start, Quality Protects, Connexions and the new arrangements for care leavers all include specific references to the additional needs of children and young people with disabilities or SEN. The UK Government's Programme of Action on SEN (DfEE 1998) prioritises stronger partnerships between education, health and social-services departments. The Health Act 1999 offers new opportunities for the flexible funding that is crucial for the optimum care of many disabled children with multiple and often complex needs.

The SEN and Disability Bill, together with the advent of a Disability Rights Commission, raise important questions about the equitable allocation of resources to disabled children within overall local planning arrangements – and the likelihood of challenges from parents and special interest groups over eligibility criteria and access to services.

How effective will the new initiatives and legislation be in ensuring that children with disabilities or SEN (and their families) achieve their maximum 'life chances' and avoid the social exclusion that has affected so many disabled children over the past decade? This first analysis of Quality Protects, from a disability and SEN perspective, indicates that there is a more proactive and integrated approach towards the development of better-integrated, and more inclusive, services in a number of authorities. Very importantly, the analysis finds evidence of exciting and innovative work around consultation with parents and disabled children as 'partners in policy-making' at local level.

A small number of authorities are developing more transparent and accessible assessment arrangements and eligibility criteria. There are real possibilities of greater synergy between the Assessment Framework set out in the revised SEN Code of Practice and the Department of Health's new framework for assessment for children in need (DoH/DfEE/Home Office 2000). Most importantly, there is a strong principle of access and achievement within the revised National Curriculum, with a new emphasis upon citizenship and participation in society – which both challenges and recognises the importance of developing a partnership approach across a wide range of agencies in helping children with disabilities or SEN.

The principle is closely linked to that of rights and access as expressed within the DDA and the role of the Disability Rights Commission. As David Blunkett commented, when launching the report of the Disability Rights Task Force (DfEE 1999b, p. 1):

> Education is vital to the creation of a fully inclusive society, in which all members see themselves as valued for the contribution they make. We owe all children – whatever their particular needs and circumstances – the opportunity to develop their full potential and to play a full part as active citizens.

References

Beresford, B. (1995) *Expert Opinions: Families with severely disabled children*. York: Policy Press/Joseph Rowntree Foundation.

British Medical Association (1999) *Growing up in Britain*. London: BMJ Publications.

Chamba, R,. *et al.* (1999) *On the Edge: Minority ethnic families caring for a severely disabled child*. Bristol: Policy Press.

Crosse, S. *et al.* (1993) *A Report on the Maltreatment of Children with Disabilities*. Washington, DC: National Centre on Child Abuse and Neglect.

Dawe, R. (2000) *The Human Rights Act: Implications for disabled people*. London: Disability Rights Commission and the Royal National Institute for Deaf People.

DFE (1994) *The Code of Practice on the Identification and Assessment of Special Educational Needs*. London: DFE.

DfEE (1997) *Excellence for All Children: Meeting special educational needs*. London: DfEE.

DfEE (1998) *Special Educational Needs: A Programme of Action*. London: DfEE.

DfEE (1999a) *Early Years Development and Child Care Partnership: Planning guidance 1999–2000*. London: DfEE.

DfEE (1999b) *Sure Start: Making a difference for children and families*. London: DfEE.

DfEE (1999c) *Sure Start: A guide to evidence-based practices*, London: DfEE.

DfEE (1999d) *From Exclusion to Inclusion: Report of the Disability Rights Task Force on Achieving Civil Rights for Disabled People*. London: DfEE.

DfEE (2000) *SEN Code of Practice on the Identification and Assessment of Special Educational Need (consultation document)*. London: DfEE.

DoH (1991) *The Children Act 1989: Guidance and regulations (Vol. 6): Children with Disabilities*. London: HMSO.

DoH (1997) *Turning Points: A resource pack for communication with children*. London: DoH.

DoH (1999a) *Working Together to Safeguard Children*, London: DoH.
DoH (1999b) *Mapping Quality in Children's Services: An evaluation of local responses to the Quality Protects programme. National Overview Report*, London: DoH.
DoH (2000) *Consultation on New Guidance for Planning Children's Services*. London: DoH.
DoH/DfEE/Home Office (2000) *Framework for the Assessment of Children in Need and their Families*. London: The Stationery Office.
Emerson, E. and Azmi, J. (1997) *Improving Services for Asian people with Learning Disabilities and their Families,*. Manchester: Hester Adrian Research Centre.
House of Commons Health Committee (1997a) *Second Report: The specific health needs of children and young people (Vol. 1)*. London: The Stationery Office.
House of Commons Health Committee (1997b) *Third Report: Health services for children and young people in the community, home and school*, London: The Stationery Office.
Khan, J. and Russell, P. (1999) *Quality Protects: First analysis of management action plans with reference to disability and SEN*. London: Council for Disabled Children.
Khan, J. and Russell, P. (2001) *Quality Protects: Second analysis of management action plans with reference to disability and SEN*. London: Council for Disabled Children.
OPCS (1989) *The Prevalence of Disability amongst Children (OPCS Surveys of disability in Great Britain, Report 3)*. London: HMSO.
Shah, R. (1996) *The Silent Minority: Children with disabilities in Asian families*, 2nd edn. London: National Children's Bureau.
Utting, W. (1997) *People Like Us: Report of the review of the safeguards for children living away from home*. London: DoH/Welsh Office.
Westcott, H. (1993) *Experience of Child Abuse in Residential Care and Educational Placements: Results of a survey*. London: NSPCC.

Further reading

Audit Commission (1994) *Seen but not Heard: Co-ordinating child health and social services for children in need*. London: HMSO.
DoH (1997) *Government Response to the Reports of the Health Committee on Health Services for Children and Young People*. London: DoH.
DoH (1999) *Quality Protects: First analysis of management action plans with reference to disabled children and their families*. London: Council for Disabled Children/DoH.
DoH/Council for Disabled Children (1998) *Disabled Children: Directions for their future care*. London: DoH.
Dobson, B. and Middleton, S. (1998) *Paying to Care: The cost of childhood disability*. York: York Publishing Services.
Family Fund Trust (1995) *What Would Be of Most Help to You in Caring for Your Disabled Child?*. York: Family Fund Trust.
Gordon, D. *et al.* (2000) *Disabled Children in Britain: A re-analysis of the OPCS disability surveys*, London: The Stationery Office.
Hall, D. (1996) *Health for All Children*, 3rd edn. Oxford: Oxford University Press.
Marchant, R. and Page, M. (1993), *Bridging the Gap: Child protection work with multiple disabilities*. London: NSPCC.
Mental Health Foundation (1997) *Don't Forget Us: Children with learning disabilities and severe challenging behaviour*. London: Mental Health Foundation.
Morris, J. (1995) *Gone Missing: A review of research and policy for disabled children living away from their families*. London: Who Cares? Trust.
National Society for the Protection of Children (1996) *Childhood Matters: Report of the national commission of inquiry into the prevention of child abuse*. London: HMSO.
OPCS (1993) *Mortality Statistics: Perinatal and infant, social and biological factors (Series DH3/25)*. London: HMSO.

OPCS (1995) *The OPCS Monitoring Scheme for Congenital Malformations (Occasional Paper 43)*. London: HMSO.

Russell, P. (1996) *Positive Choices: Services for disabled children living away from home*. London: National Children's Bureau.

Russell, P. (1999) *Having a Say: Involving disabled children in decision-making*. London: Council for Disabled Children.

Schweinhart, L. J. and Weikhard, D. P. (1993*) A Summary of Significant Benefits: The High-Scope Perry Pre-school Study through Age 27*, Ypsilant. MN: High-Scope Press.

Social Services Inspectorate (1995) *Report of the First National Inspection of Services for Disabled Children*. London: HMSO.

Social Services Inspectorate (1998) *Report of Second National Inspection of Services for Disabled Children*. London: DoH.

Sylva, K. (1996) *Evaluation of the High-Scope Programme*. Oxford: Oxford University Press.

Chapter 21

Issues in Teacher Training and Development

Jill Porter

Introduction

Important national developments have taken place since the previous edition of this book. Most notably, the UK Government has reiterated its commitment to developing inclusive provision with a pledge, set out in the Green Paper, that by 2002, 'special and mainstream schools will be working together alongside and in support of one another' (DfEE 1997, p. 52).

Local education authorities are required to produce Education Development Plans (EDP) that include their policy on inclusion and any planned action to promote it, as well as how they will raise standards in schools. These twin priorities of inclusion and raising standards will together place new demands on teachers, along with the implementation of the literacy and numeracy strategy and the revised National Curriculum, including *Planning, Teaching and Assessing the Curriculum for Pupils with Learning Difficulties* (DfEE/QCA 2001).

The nature of these demands will be revealed more clearly with time. For those working in special schools the populations are likely to continue to change towards those with increasingly complex needs – a trend identified in surveys of both schools for pupils with severe and moderate learning difficulties (Male 1996a and 1996b). DfEE statistical information suggests that the numbers of pupils attending special schools remained broadly constant between 1992 and 1997 (DfEE 1998), and we cannot assume that the population is likely to fall dramatically in the short term.

Research suggests that LEAs are uncertain about what is meant by the term 'inclusion' (Ainscow *et al*. 1999). Many LEAs have not yet brought about significant changes to special-schools provision and, although some have made quite radical reorganisations, others seem content with a small-steps approach (Croll and Moses 2000). The latter's survey of primary schools reports (p. 42):

> The principle of an all-inclusive mainstream education system has made very little ground among teachers and both teachers and heads were unanimous in seeing a continued role for special schools.

It is therefore difficult to be certain about training needs, although there are some very strong indications from government agencies. The Programme of Action (DfEE 1998) highlights the need for special schools to be flexible in the way in which they work, to act as a source of 'expertise, advice and professional development' for mainstream colleagues. For mainstream teachers, the pattern of provision is likely to be varied and uncertain as LEAs are likely to have different policies for the way that provision is organised. The implications for both groups are therefore that, given the variation in provision, training needs to be flexible and varied.

A major concern of the past has been that there are insufficient numbers of teachers gaining training in learning difficulties (Miller and Porter 1994, 1999; Mittler 1995; Porter 1996). Courses have closed, full-time training has largely disappeared, and there has been a diversification of training providers. These trends seem largely set to continue. A recent survey by Julian and Ware (1998) to investigate the qualifications of teachers in schools and units for children with learning difficulties concluded that there had been little progress in preparing adequate numbers of teachers since the Advisory Committee on the Supply and Education of Teachers (ACSET) report of 1984, which brought about the demise of specialist initial teacher training. Consistent with other research, the survey reveals that 60 per cent of teachers in SLD schools have relevant qualifications, compared with 30 per cent of teachers in MLD schools and those catering for the range of learning difficulties. Across the provision, only one in five teachers had gained a specialist qualification through in-service training. This reveals that the vast majority of teachers were trained prior to 1984 on full-time initial training courses. Indeed, only half the teachers in the survey felt able to access INSET, and head teachers expressed concern about getting cover for teachers or relying on the goodwill of teachers to attend twilight courses. Many head teachers also added that their learning support assistants were in some instances more experienced than teachers entering special schools. Teachers therefore appear to be unevenly placed to contribute to the new role for special schools.

The last five years have seen many new developments brought about by the Teacher Training Agency (TTA). Its brief has been to raise standards in schools through the development of the teaching profession. In addition to introducing strategies to attract more able and committed people into the profession, it has set about improving the training that is already being provided. A particular feature of this has been the introduction of a set of standards or expectations of teachers at different points in their career. There has therefore been identifiable expectations of teachers having *some* understanding of special educational needs from the initial award of qualified teacher status, through induction, to becoming subject leaders and head teachers. The latest to be introduced are those originally intended for SEN specialists – teachers of pupils with severe/and or complex needs.

National SEN specialist standards

There have been notable shifts in thinking during the development of national SEN specialist standards, largely as an outcome of a consultation process. While the standards were initially conceived as 'standards for specialist teachers', this has been seen as incompatible with a more inclusive approach to education provision. Consequently, they are now presented as 'providing a more structured approach to gaining specialist knowledge, understanding and skills in SEN, for any teacher, SEN specialist or not' (Grant 2000, p. 10).

While this change of emphasis diverts attention from the difficulty of defining a 'specialist teacher', it does not detract from the difficulty of defining 'specialist'. What depth and breadth of knowledge, skills and understanding are required? Debates about what constitutes distinctive elements in a pedagogy of SEN (Lewis and Norwich 2000) reveal that there is no simple definitive answer that can be provided by a checklist approach.

The standards as currently laid down are divided into three sections – core, extension and role-related – and are described as an audit tool for teachers, head teachers, managers and training providers 'to identify priorities for training and development in relation to the effective teaching of those pupils with severe and/or complex SEN' (TTA 1999, p. 1). The group of pupils referred to in the quotation is described as including those with: autistic spectrum disorder (ASD); physical and sensory disabilities; acute emotional and behavioural difficulties; severe and profound learning difficulties; specific learning difficulties; and speech, language and communication difficulties. Those pupils with MLD do not appear to be included, although conversations with the TTA during the development of this document suggested that the needs of these pupils would be addressed by teachers who had attained the core standards.

The use of these disability categories has been seen as 'too simplistic', given the variety of educational needs that pupils with a designated label may experience. (This has been well borne out by Male's (1996b) survey of MLD schools.) Thus, whereas previous drafts of the TTA (1999) document grouped standards around impairments, implying a deficit-centred view of SEN, the revised document adopts a broader approach, which reflects areas of required teacher expertise. There is an expectation that the standards will be 'applied and implemented differentially' (TTA 1999, p. 2), depending on the needs of staff and pupils in particular contexts. The research cited earlier suggests variation in LEA policy, leading to individual teachers having differing training and development needs.

The three aspects of the TTA standards

As mentioned above, there are three aspects to the TTA standards: core, extension and role-related. Each of these is described further next.

The core standards are described as a starting point and are seen as common across the full range of pupils. It is therefore anticipated that all teachers of pupils with severe and/or complex SEN will have this foundation from which to build particular areas of expertise. The core standards are listed under five headings, the first providing a context and the other four relating directly to the skills, knowledge and understanding that are required by teachers in the classroom. The five are:

- strategic direction and development of SEN provision, both nationally and regionally;
- identification, assessment and planning;
- effective teaching, ensuring maximum access to the curriculum;
- development of communication, literacy and numeracy skills, and ICT capability;
- promotion of social and emotional development, positive behaviour and preparation for adulthood.

Although these five are described as a starting point, it is unclear whether in fact the broad perspective is always better-acquired first. For example, teachers of pupils with profound and multiple learning difficulties might more readily acquire knowledge, skills and understanding that directly relate to their daily work before standing back to gain a broader picture. (Indeed, they may feel that the core standards contribute little to their professional expertise.) In contrast, newly qualified teachers working in a mainstream classroom may target the acquisition of these foundation areas more readily.

Section 2 of TTA (1999) presents extension standards – summary statements of more specific specialist skills, knowledge and understanding that might be acquired. The organisation of these reveals a partial attempt to move away from types of special need with the use of four headings that are indicative of aspects of difficulty:

- communication and interaction;
- cognition and learning;
- behavioural, emotional and social development;
- sensory and physical development.

Mindful that these broad statements may under-represent particular difficulties, the document also contains additional specific knowledge skills and understanding that teachers of children with ASD, deafness, visual impairment or deaf-blindness will need.

Section 3 of the TTA (1999) document contains standards in relation to the types of roles and responsibilities of teachers – particularly their advisory, curricular and managerial roles. Skills and attributes are described as illustrative only, as they do not necessarily describe all the activities carried out by a specialist SEN teacher. In many ways they provide an important adjunct to much specialist training, which does not always provide many opportunities for *specialist* managerial training other than for SENCOs.

A final section briefly describes skills and attributes of teachers that in other contexts might be referred to as the attitudes needed by *all* teachers.

Other considerations

A number of case studies are set out in the document to illustrate how this auditing procedure might work. The case studies highlight the complexity of the process and the likelihood that it cannot easily be carried out by individual teachers without consultation with their 'line managers'. This indicates that the process should be well linked to performance management (DfEE 2000b).

A number of headings suggest that the auditing is determined by the context in which the teacher is working, together with a consideration of their role and previous experience and their contribution to the school's or service's priorities for development. Thus, the trend outlined for a shift in professional development from being individually determined to school- or even LEA-determined (Porter 1996) seems, on the face of it, set to continue. Having determined priority areas for development, an audit is carried out using the standards to identify areas of need. However, the gap between identifying broad needs and establishing which standards will meet those needs may not be so easily addressed. It is perhaps unsurprising that 'line managers' play a fundamental role in this process. It is likely that they too will need to identify important development priorities if they are to enable teachers to set the course of their professional development.

To illustrate the complexity further, we might consider a teacher who has a particular concern about the challenging behaviour of the pupils that he or she teaches. It is important that this is understood in relation to the broader needs of the group, namely their learning difficulties (Harris 1995; Porter and Lacey 1999). Thus, in addition to identifying the need for additional specialist knowledge, understanding and skills in relation to 'behavioural, emotional and social development', it will also be important to consider 'cognition and learning'. However, given the well-documented links between challenging behaviour and communication (e.g. Bott *et al.* 1997; Carr *et al.* 1994; Thurman 1997), it will be essential to look at this aspect of the document. (One might also recognise the higher incidence of sensory impairments among these pupils (Emerson 1995) and target standards from the fourth area.) Despite the claims that no teacher will require all the specialist standards, there may well be groups that have considerable needs.

It remains to be seen how course providers decide to package courses, although it is likely that, as with initial teacher training, they will have to indicate clearly which standards are being addressed as part of any training programme. Such individuality of need is difficult to meet without forgoing other characteristics of provision. If teachers are enabled to link standards flexibly to training, then courses are likely to be short, have a mixed and wide group of participants, and forsake notions of fixed prerequisites and therefore progression. While provision of this nature may be flexible, the depth of knowledge, understanding and skills taught could be severely restricted. Providers will need to find ways of clustering standards together in a way that provides an appropriate curriculum. This is likely to be most successfully achieved around notions of role, as has been achieved with SENCO courses and the newly conceived Behaviour Coordinator (BECO) courses.

Funding the training

Historically, the DfEE has funded INSET through grants earmarked for national priority areas to which LEAs make annual bids. Currently this fund is called the Standards Fund (previously referred to as GEST). Over time, LEAs have been asked differentially to make up the amount of money required for a particular activity. Money for training has therefore depended firstly on government priorities and the allocation of funding, and secondly on LEA policy, both with respect to the areas targeted and also how the money is used. In some instances, this was devolved directly to schools but, in other areas, substantial parts of the fund were kept centrally and decisions were made at LEA level about what training and development opportunities would be provided. Teachers and schools were therefore dependent on the priorities and insights of personnel within a particular LEA to access funding for training.

Changes to the Standard Fund for 2001–2 suggest that there will be greater flexibility in the way that it operates, including allowing longer periods of time to spend the money and a degree of freedom to move the money between categories (DfEE 2000c). Most notably, however, it is expected that high priority will be given to the professional development of teachers and other staff in all categories, including in the subject of 'inclusion'. Additionally, a greater proportion of the funding is expected to be allocated directly to schools.

The DfEE has set out a number of important new initiatives, directed largely at individuals and with a commitment to promoting professional development as an entitlement for all teachers (DfEE 2000a). Career planning and performance management lie at the heart of this process, with the expectation that teachers will keep a career portfolio. Access to a diversity of opportunities is encouraged through the allocation of professional bursaries, the development of learning partnerships and the award of Best Practice Research Scholarships.

There is a further source of funding, this time for providers. One of the key objectives of the TTA corporate plan for 2000–3 is 'ensuring that teachers of pupils with SEN receive high-quality training' (TTA 2000a). Course providers will therefore bid to the TTA for funding to support courses against stated criteria. The TTA has also reviewed the mandatory courses, which are to remain 'in the 'foreseeable future'. Again, course providers will bid to the TTA for recognised national training against specific criteria using the SEN specialist standards. The criteria give good indications of the characteristics that accredited training courses may be expected to have in the future – as set out in the next section.

Future characteristics of funded training

Taking the criteria set by the TTA for funded INSET, it is likely that there will be greater involvement of a number of agencies collaborating together (TTA 2000b). As stated in the Programme of Action (DfEE 1998a, p. 29):

> We will encourage LEAs, higher education institutions, career services, voluntary bodies and health and social services to work together in developing and delivering specialist training.

This mirrors the greater involvement of schools in initial teacher training. The strength of the suggestion is that courses can reflect local needs and is seen as a way of ensuring the relevance of the course. However, INSET provision is a slightly different proposition. While LEAs may make an important contribution in designing courses, they cannot always guarantee that those teachers who apply for a place are part of the intended group. Indeed, it is not unheard of that trainers are given one brief and teachers are given another when attempting to fill places on a course that they have designed together but that teachers perceive as untimely, inappropriate or unattractive.

One of the TTA's funding criteria is that courses include teachers in identifying their own training and development needs within the context of the aims and outcomes of the provision. This is a positive move and puts appropriate emphasis on the active element of learning, as teachers are encouraged to articulate their needs and think about how and where in the course these will be met. It helps to ensure that trainers set clear parameters to the course but, equally, build in flexibility to meet differing needs, and demonstrate how these will impact on course content and assignments. Teachers can be better assured that courses will have a strong practical element, in that learning will be centred around the application of knowledge and understanding to developing practice (and policy) within their workplace. Furthermore, course evaluation takes place against teacher-identified needs. In this way there can be greater transparency in the negotiation of course design and delivery.

Other criteria include the requirements for courses to reflect data from research and inspection, and to develop schoolteachers' skills in using evidence and conducting research. This reflects the TTA's concern that if teaching is to be recognised as a profession, not only must teachers take responsibility for their professional development but teaching must be seen as evidenced-based and courses must address 'nitty gritty pedagogic issues' rather than 'the trendy topic of the moment' (Millett 1999). This is an important development because it helps to highlight what has been one of the key features of much accredited training and suggests a return (by the UK Government) to recognising the importance of the reflective practitioner. It must also be recognised that examining the evidence base will highlight the complexity of decision making rather than leading to simplistic conclusions of good practice (see Lewis and Norwich 2000).

Additional TTA criteria include the importance of internal and external quality control and assurance mechanisms, including how they impact on practice (again, building the evidence base). This will provide a challenge to course providers whose evaluation of courses is limited to questionnaires filled in by course members (Porter 1996). These measures must be complemented by others that detect changes in teacher behaviour. Ware and Porter (1996) describe a small-scale study carried out in Ireland on the impact of an induction course. The study investigated both changes in teacher behaviour and the consequence of these changes on pupil behaviour. Such detailed workplace observations are not frequently perceived as a viable option for course providers.

An alternative to these objective measures would be through the use of portfolio assignments, where the teacher has reflected on practice and provided his or her own evidence on the ways in which the practice had developed. This would be a learning tool for course members and tutors alike, provided that a system of overview was introduced to look across portfolios and supply information for course evaluation. The use of standards could occur selectively in order to audit the impact of the course. There is a proposed inspection programme of training provision by LEAs, higher education institutions (HEIs) and other providers, and one assumes that, as with initial teacher-training courses, the outcome of these evaluations will directly effect future levels of funding.

A final criterion set by the TTA is that funded courses must lead to postgraduate accreditation, and therefore HEIs are assured of some continued involvement even if it is limited to the validation of training programmes. This, however, may prove to be a double-edged sword, for it presumes that *all* teachers want to study (and be assessed) at masters level. For a variety of reasons, this may constrain the delivery and design of training, and it is not necessarily compatible with the checklist approach to standards, where breadth or numbers of standards covered, rather than the depth required by masters-level study, may be the driving force.

There is also a draft Code of Practice for those providing development and training opportunities funded through government money (DfEE 2000a). It is targeted at any organisation that provides training or development, and potentially it provides a much-needed mechanism for promoting quality assurance across a range of activities. Essentially, it reflects the expectations and criteria of the TTA but is set out in a more readily accessible checklist.

Training and LSAs

One of the key ways of promoting inclusion has been the use of learning support assistants (LSAs) as an important classroom resource (Moore 2000), leading to a sharp increase in their numbers. This has occurred in both mainstream and special-school settings as a way of facilitating access by learners with complex needs, including those with challenging behaviour (Male 1996a; Porter and Lacey 1999).

The roles of LSAs are varied and demand a whole range of different skills (Mencap 1999). Furthermore, although there is 'a clearly understood distinction' about how their responsibilities differ from that of teachers, the practice suggests something rather different (Farrell *et al.* 1999). This results in considerable inequalities within the system, and although such flexibility could be seen as a strength, it nevertheless raises important questions about the management of LSAs at all levels – classroom, school and LEA.

The DfEE stated in the 1997 Green Paper its aim for 'a national framework for training learning support assistants', and it commissioned a survey of effective practice in the management, role and training of LSAs in mainstream and special schools. This revealed a need for a national programme for LSAs where training leads to accreditation and the development of a career path and salary scales (Farrell *et al*. 1999). The picture is not, however, straightforward. The report found few barriers for LSAs getting on courses and successfully completing them – with a very commendable pass rate of almost 90 per cent, suggesting that the issue was not in fact about providing training. Indeed, a parallel report commissioned by Mencap (1999) points to the fact that training was only one element that would enable LSAs to work effectively.

LSAs saw a number of other measures as very important, including: opportunities to learn from others through observing and talking with them; the development of lines of communication to facilitate joint planning; support from others; and positive and consistent approaches to special needs throughout a school. It would appear that teachers cited training as more important than LSAs who 'felt ... that learning through watching and talking to other people was even more important, as this was part of their everyday job' (Mencap 1999, p. 22). This outcome echoes the broader survey by Farrell *et al*. (1999, p. 6):

> LSAs want opportunities to pursue competency-based training which has maximum relevance to their work and work context ... they require, in the main, training that is aimed at supporting them in doing a better job in the classroom.

It is perhaps indicative that teachers think in terms of more formal training such as access to courses that are traditionally linked to a broader plan for career development, while LSAs recognise the value of simply being able to do the job better. Moreover, the majority of LSAs don't aspire to becoming teachers (Farrell *et al*. 1999). It is important that training providers are cognisant of *their* perspectives to their work.

There are a number of unpursued discrepancies within the DfEE-commissioned report by Farrell *et al*. (1999). LSAs were found to prefer LEA courses to those based in further or higher education establishments, but schools' INSET programmes were felt to include topics of limited relevance. Farrell *et al*. (1999) point to the need for INSET to have 'a differentiated carefully planned curriculum' where training is shared. Their report also points to the importance of improved induction, and the DfEE has commissioned introductory training material for LEAs to use with recently recruited assistants to help to ensure they have a clear understanding of their roles and responsibilities. Good-practice materials on effective deployment of LSAs are also being developed.

These initiatives will be frustrated if support is not also provided in parallel for teachers to develop their management skills. As Farrell *et al*. have reported (1999, p. 61): 'Feedback from LSAs in this study suggested that teachers can lack confidence and competence in managing another adult in the classroom.' This is likely to be a particular issue for *established* teachers working with pupils with learning difficulties in mainstream settings, because it is included in the training standards for newly qualified teachers (TTA 1998).

Access to training

The availability of funding, together with developments in technology, have already had an important impact on access to training and professional development. This trend looks set to continue.

It has been argued that different modes of training – full-time, part-time and distance-learning – have different strengths, and that mixed modes of training have much to offer (Porter 1996). Teachers and other staff need to be well placed to select the mode of training that is best suited both to their own needs and to the types of knowledge, skills and understanding they wish to acquire. The SEN specialist standards document has reinforced the variety of routes to acquiring new professional skills in the outline of the case studies quoted. However, both exemplars that refer to pupils with learning difficulties contain references to the teacher needing to develop new areas of skill and understanding and, in the case of the teacher working in an MLD school (ironically, given the availability), the text refers explicitly to training.

The biggest new development is the growth of independent learning through using digital multimedia, either through self-contained CD-ROM or interactive programs on the Internet. We are already witnessing these changes – for example, in the setting up of the National Grid for Learning and the use of CD-ROM by the TTA. In support of this and other ICT developments, the UK Government is investing through the National Opportunities Fund to ensure that the existing teaching force develop the ICT competencies expected of newly qualified teachers.

The strengths of conventional distance learning have been well-documented (Miller 1994 and 1996) with respect to the increased flexibility it provides for deciding on the place, time and pace of study. It is, however, vital to recognise the significance of the social dimension of learning. Teachers frequently cite the importance of sharing experiences and the growth of confidence as particular success factors in a taught course (Miller 1996; Watson 1988). Indeed, discussion and debate is an integral part of the learning process as teachers clarify and question their understanding of course material and relate it to their own classroom experiences. These elements ensure that teachers are engaged in the learning process and not purely passive spectators of presented ideas. Clearly, this process is easier to orchestrate in a live situation. The development of multimedia material presents particular challenges if this interactive element is to pervade all learning. People working in other fields of education have highlighted the need to shift attention from a focus on the presentation of content to the development of learning activities and supports, including the role of human interaction (Chambers 1999). The ability to access multimedia courses suggests a number of advantages over traditional distance material. The use of video material to support professional development is well noted (Jaworski 1990), and there is a growing understanding of how their use can be best tailored to encourage reflective practice (Potter and Richardson 1999). It is also likely to be more accessible to those teachers who also have SEN.

There are a number of online tools that provide opportunities for collaborative activities across the group of students and that also promote debate and discussion, problem-solving, and reflection on practice. In the field of learning difficulties, changes in access to courses have largely come about through difficulties of funding. These new course developments are, however, costly for the provider and require a considerable investment in time and resources. It is unlikely, therefore, that their use will proliferate overnight – at least, not if high-quality training is to be supplied.

There is also another consideration: how many providers will be appropriately placed to make this investment? Tait and Mills (1999, p. 3) paint a bleak view of the future in making a distinction between:

> successful educational institutions using a range of teaching and learning strategies substantially centred on ICTs, and less successful institutions which ... will be taken over or will go bankrupt.

There is an irony here that while people may be increasingly well placed to access training and 'ride the changes which family and work bring throughout life' (Tait and Mills 1999, p. 3), in minority areas, such as where learning difficulties apply, there could actually be even less choice and a further diminution of training.

Summary

In this chapter I have outlined some of the current changes that are taking place within the field of staff training and development. In many ways the trends give rise to cautious optimism with:

- the focus by the TTA and DfEE on developing teaching as a profession;
- the national outlining of a set of specialist SEN standards;
- the return of reference to the reflective practitioner and the importance of research;
- recognition of the needs and importance of LSAs;
- expectation of cross-agency collaboration in providing training;
- further emphasis on issues of quality assurance;
- technological developments with the potential to increase access and flexibility of training opportunities.

However, the success of these changes is dependent in no small measure on:

- support by line managers and others to enable teachers to audit their needs and identify how they can best be met;
- recognition of the perspective of LSAs in providing appropriate opportunities to acquire relevant expertise;
- recognition of the not inconsiderable resource implications for technological developments in training;
- access to appropriate levels of funding.

The previous edition of this book set out arguments about the limitations to training, and these still hold true in the main. It would be easy to generate a number of concerns about the existing situation (Miller and Porter 1999; Porter and Miller 2000), but it is important to look forward so as to capitalise on those opportunities that exist already and to develop flexible pathways to support the continuing professional development of staff.

References

ACSET (1984) *Teacher Training and Special Educational Needs.* London: ACSET.

Ainscow, M. *et al.* (1999) *Effective Practice in Inclusion and in Special and Mainstream Schools Working Together.* Sudbury: DfEE.

Bott, C. *et al.* (1997) 'Behaviour problems associated with lack of speech in people with learning disabilities', *Journal of Intellectual Disability Research* **41**(1), 3–7.

Carr, E.G. *et al.* (1994) *Communication Based Intervention for Problem Behavior.* Baltimore: Paul Brookes.

Chambers, M. (1999) 'The efficacy and ethics of using digital multimedia for educational purposes', in Tait, A. and Mills, R. (1999) (eds) *The Convergence of Distance and Conventional Education: Patterns of flexibility for the individual learner.* London: Routledge.

Croll, P. and Moses, D. (2000) 'Resources, policies and educational practice', in Norwich, B. (ed.) *Specialist Teaching for Special Educational Needs and Inclusion: SEN Policy Options Steering Group policy option paper 2* (3rd series). Tamworth; NASEN.

DfEE (1997) *Excellence for All Children: Meeting special educational needs,* London: HMSO.

DfEE (1998a) *Meeting Special Educational Needs: A programme of action,* Sudbury: DfEE.

DfEE (2000a) *Professional Development Support for Teaching and Learning.* www.dfee.gov.uk/circulars/dfeepub/feb00

DfEE (2000b) *Performance Management in Schools,* Sudbury: DfEE.

DfEE (2000c) *Changes to the Operation of the Standards Fund 2001–2.* www.dfee.gov.uk/circulars/dfeepub/sep00

DfEE/QCA (2001) *Planning, Teaching and Assessing the Curriculum for Pupils with Learning Difficulties.* London: Dfee/QCA

Emerson, E. (1995) *Challenging Behaviour: Analysis and interventions in people with learning disabilities.* Cambridge: Cambridge University Press.

Farrell P., *et al.* (1999) *The Management, Role and Training of Learning Support Assistants.* Nottingham: DfEE.

Grant, A. (2000) 'The national SEN specialist standards', in Norwich, B. (ed.) *Specialist Teaching for Special Educational Needs and Inclusion: SEN Policy Options Steering Group policy option paper 4.* Tamworth: NASEN.

Harris, J. (1995) 'Responding to pupils with severe learning disabilities who present challenging behaviour', *British Journal of Special Education* **22**(3), 109–15.

Jaworski, B. (1990) 'Video as a tool for teachers' professional development', *British Journal of Inservice Education* **16**(1), 60–65.

Julian, G. and Ware, J. (1998) 'Specialist teachers for pupils with learning difficulties?: A survey of head teachers in schools and units', *British Journal of Special Education* **25**(1), 28–32.

Lewis, A. and Norwich, B, (2000) 'Is there a distinctive SEN pedagogy?', in Norwich, B. (ed.) *Specialist Teaching for Special Educational Needs and Inclusion. SEN Policy Options Steering Group policy paper 4.* Tamworth: NASEN.

Male, D. (1996a) 'Who goes to SLD schools?', *Journal of Applied Research in Intellectual Disabilities* **22**(1), 2–5..

Male, D. (1996b) 'Who goes to MLD schools?', *British Journal of Special Education* **23**(1), 35–41.

Mencap (1999) *On a Wing and a Prayer: Inclusion and children with severe learning difficulties.* London: Mencap.

Miller, C. (1994) 'Professional development and distance education'. Paper presented to the SENTC Working Group, April.

Miller, C. (1996) 'Relationships between teachers and speech and language therapists: Influencing practice by distance education', *Child Language Teaching and Therapy* **12**(1), 29–38.

Miller, C. and Porter J. (1994) 'Teacher training: setting the bill', *British Journal of Special Education* **23**(1), 7–8.

Miller, C. and Porter J. (1999) 'Standards for specialists? A review of the proposals for teacher training for SEN specialists', *British Journal of Special Education* **26**(1), 55–8.

Millett, A. (1999) 'Teaching tomorrow: Challenges and opportunities'. Valedictory speech at the Teacher Training Agency Annual Review. London, March 2000.

Mittler, P. (1995) 'Professional development for special needs education', in Lunt, I. *et al.* (eds) *Psychology and Education for Special Needs*. Aldershot: Ashgate.

Moore, J. (2000) 'Developments in Additional Resource Allocation to Promote Greater Inclusion', in Norwich, B. (ed.) *Specialist Teaching for Special Educational Needs and Inclusion: SEN Policy Options Steering Group, policy option paper 2* (3rd series). Tamworth: NASEN.

Porter, J. (1996) 'Issues in teacher training', in Carpenter, B., *et al.* (eds) *Enabling Access: Effective teaching and learning for pupils with learning difficulties*. London: David Fulton Publishers.

Porter, J. and Lacey P. (1999) 'What provision for pupils with challenging behaviour?', *British Journal of Special Education* **26**(1), 23–7.

Porter J. and Miller, C. (2000) 'Meeting the Standards?', *British Journal of Special Education* **27**, 72–5.

Potter, C. and Richardson H. (1999) 'Facilitating classroom assistants' professional reflection through video workshops', *British Journal of Special Education* **26**(1), 34–6.

Tait, A. and Mills, R. (eds) (1999) *The Convergence of Distance and Conventional Education: Patterns of flexibility for the individual learner*. London: Routledge.

Thurman, S. (1997) 'Challenging behaviour through communication', *British Journal of Learning Disabilities* **25**, 111–16.

TTA (1998) *National Standards for Qualified Teacher Status*. London: TTA.

TTA (1999a) *National Special Educational Needs Specialist Standards*. London: TTA.

TTA (2000a) *Teacher Training Agency Corporate Plan 2000–2003*. London: TTA.

TTA (2000b) *Principles and Criteria for the Second Interim Bidding Round for TTA Inset Funding*. www.teach-tta.gov.uk/inset/principles, June

Ware, J. and Porter, J. (1996) 'Evaluating teacher training'. Paper presented at IASSID Conference, Helsinki, Finland, July.

Watson, J. (1988) 'One-year courses: The teachers' views', *British Journal of Special Education* **15**(2), 79–82.

Chapter 22

Changing Public Attitudes

Christina Tilstone

Introduction

As far back as December 1995 Bengt Lindqvist, the UN Special Rapporteur of the Commission for Social Development on Disability, wrote:

> In all societies of the world there are still obstacles preventing persons with disabilities from exercising their rights and freedoms and making it difficult for them to participate fully in the activities of their societies.
>
> (Lindqvist, 1995, p. 2).

Since then, people with disabilities themselves have campaigned vigorously to break down the many obstacles or barriers to full participation. Consequently, there has been a great improvement in the United Kingdom, and others in the world, in providing access to buildings, services, transport and leisure activities including theatres, cinemas and museums. Modern technology has also enabled the development and provision of aids and appliances that help a person with a disability to live more efficiently and happily in a community. It is, however, recognised by those with a disability that the creation of a consequent 'disability industry' can perpetuate discriminatory practices by highlighting the limitations to which disabled people are subject (Oliver, 1996; Mason and Reiser, 1994), and Oliver (1996) strongly argues that the obstacles and barriers are not created by the limitations of individuals but are due primarily to society's failure to take account of the needs of the disabled in its social organisation.

In response to this failure, the disability movement has identified a long list of barriers to full participation in society, of which access to the physical environment is only one element. Others include the passing and enforcing of anti-discrimination legislation; increased awareness of the rights and responsibilities of those with a disability; and their involvement (or the involvement of their chosen representative) in decisions relating to their participation in society (Mittler, 2000). A much more serious barrier, which keeps those with disabilities or learning difficulties apart in society, is the attitude of members of the general public toward them.

Unfortunately, historical events have not helped the so-called 'able-bodied' to recognise the common humanity that they share with the disabled, particularly with those who are considered to be 'slow' or who 'behave inappropriately'. The assumption that the 'handicapped' (to use the terminology of the past) were social rejects and should be cared for in asylums and institutions, which provided permanent segregation, has left its mark (Cole, 1989; Tilstone *et al.* 2000; Brigham *et al.* 2000). Their legacy has been the minimising of meaningful experiences and the reduction of expectations.

Despite the progress towards inclusive education, and full participation in society for a range of pupils with disabilities, the inclusion of those with complex needs or with severe challenging behaviours has been painfully slow. Full participation means active involvement in the community, as opposed to the passive acceptance of a system that has been made available to them or has been imposed on them (Tilstone *et al.* 1998). Inclusive International, an organisation largely run by people with disabilities, takes a broad definition of inclusion that goes beyond education and states that it is 'the opportunity for persons with a disability to participate fully in all educational, employment, consumer, recreational, community, and domestic activities that typify everyday life' (Tilstone *et al.* 1998, p. 16).

Research undertaken in the 1950s confirmed that some disabilities are easier for society to accept than others and that it is possible to construct a hierarchy of disability (Kvaraceus 1956). In the main, UK society finds those with hidden impairments, together with the visually impaired or the blind, as being the most acceptable; and, certainly, these pupils were the ones who were first included in mainstream education. The push for access to buildings and the legislation supporting it has led to greater acceptance of the physically disabled, as long as they are not facially disfigured. As a society we are conditioned to the Hollywood model of beauty (slim and perfectly formed), but it is often facial appearance that determines our response. Unusual facial features due to genetic abnormalities or neurological damage can result in negative attitudes, and the aetiology (not the essential humanness) becomes the focus; research into the unusual facial appearance of schoolchildren shows that embarrassed reactions from other children result in staring, teasing, bullying and name calling (Frances 2000).

We also tend to draw inferences about a person based on a single prominent characteristic, which Wright (1974) termed the 'spread phenomenon'. People who are perceived as 'slow' or who behave 'inappropriately' are often labelled and stigmatised. Many of us can remember the effects of being called 'thick', 'stupid', 'an idiot' or 'hopeless' at some point in our lives, but to be perpetually referred to in this way is a constant reminder of personal inadequacy, which reinforces feelings of failure and rejection in an adult or a child (Tilstone and Visser 1996).

Why attitudes need to change

The stereotypical images and labels that are a form of public degradation are hard to eradicate, and there is an obligation on the part of every member of society to press for access to an inclusive society in order that *all* people, including those with learning difficulties, can be included. Mittler (2000) makes no bones about the obligations of schools when he states (p. 189): 'Schools are societies' agents for the socialisation of its young.' As such, they have a commitment to demonstrate how to value diversity and dissimilarity, and they should be the training ground for a people-oriented society that respects both differences and the dignity of all human beings. Schools have a duty, therefore, to challenge negative attitudes and, consequently, changing contrary attitudes must become a part of their role.

Where do we start?

In order to affect change, it is important to understand *what* it is we are changing. What *is* an attitude ? The following definitions suggest that it consists of cognitive, affective and behavioural components that interact with each other:

- a mental view or disposition, especially as it indicates opinion or allegiance (*Collins English Dictionary* 1991) ;
- settled behaviour or manner of acting as representative of feeling or opinion (*Shorter Oxford English Dictionary* 1983);
- a habitual mode of thought or feeling (*The Chambers Dictionary* 1993).

Put simply, our feelings in the presence of someone with an obvious impairment, or who may not be acting in a conventional way, may be irrational and often fearful; our response is often withdrawal.

McConkey (1991) reminds us that such reactions are rarely based on first-hand experience, and that around three-quarters of the population had, in the early 1990s, never met a person with severe learning difficulties. Since then, many more people with severe learning difficulties are living in the community, but there may be limited opportunities for natural interactions. For those who need support, journeys into the places where *sustained* contact with the general public is possible relies on the good will of the professionals involved. Although most children with complex needs live either at home or in homes in their locality, it is likely that they still have most contact with other children with similar needs. When they meet other children in the vicinity, it is not uncommon for them to be victimised and bullied (Mencap 1999).

An analysis of ways in which attitudes are formed shows that they are not only acquired by each and every individual as a result of personal experiences, but they are also strongly influenced by the feelings, reactions and beliefs of the past – and, consequently, unless challenged, they are handed down from generation to generation. The tales from inmates of the mental-handicap hospitals of the 1960s, and the fact the children with learning difficulties did not enter the education system until 1971, have contributed to the fear and prejudice surrounding them.

In order to change perceptions and views, it is vitally important to learn from research. The pioneer in this area is McConkey, who has rigorously and systematically explored ways in which the public can become better informed and involved in the inclusion of people with learning difficulties in their communities (McConkey 1996, 1994, 1991 and 1987; McConkey and McCormick 1983; and McConkey *et al.* 1993). McConkey's work indicates that any attempt to prepare communities or groups to accept others whom they perceive as different will have positive effects, and that positive experiences shape positive attitudes. He also stresses that there are certain key elements in bringing about attitudinal change: planned personal contact; interesting and relevant information; and multimedia presentations.

McConkey's work has encouraged people with learning disabilities to give their views on *who* needs educating about disability and *how*. The results of his workshops and other initiatives are vitally important if we are serious about ensuring that people with learning difficulties are to become valued members of society. Not surprisingly, the workshop participants stressed that anyone who has not been involved with a person with a disability needs to be educated, and gave the following groups a special mention (see McConkey 1994):

- influential people, MPs and councillors;
- school kids, pre-schoolers, students and teachers;
- DSS people;
- police officers;
- social workers and community workers;
- doctors, nurses and others in the medical profession;
- bus companies;
- licensed victuallers' associations;
- shop owners (because of access problems);
- local residents and communities;
- planners and architects;
- potential employers;
- people in the media and newspapers, including children's TV presenters;
- staff in services 'who don't listen to you'.

So where do we start? Certainly not by trying to change the whole world immediately, but by adopting policies and practices that are possible and practicable. I would suggest that we need to:

- acknowledge that attitudinal change is vital if people with learning difficulties – particularly those with complex needs and who exhibit unusual behaviours – are to become part of the social organisation of society;
- recognise that schools have an obligation to work on changing attitudes as an activity in its own right;
- ensure that such work needs to be undertaken in a structured and systematic way and therefore must become a major part of the policy, administration and curriculum of a school;
- ensure that pupils with learning difficulties are a valued part of the organisation of a school, are listened to and consulted, and are able to influence decisions about their school's management and organisation;
- work from the evidence already available from research;
- work on aspects that are feasible, and are already part of the working practices of a school;
- monitor and evaluate the work.

Although all these needs are considered in this chapter, it is important to pay particular attention to the opportunities that already exist in mainstream and special schools and that can contribute to changes in attitudes in the community – in other words, to build on best practice.

Making the most of opportunities: inclusive education

The inclusion of pupils with special educational needs into mainstream education is now well established as a goal within UK legislation. It began with the Warnock Report (DES 1978) and the Education Act 1981, and it has been continued through recent documents from the DfEE (DfEE 1997a, 1997b, 1998 and 1999). In theory, there is now a greater commitment to the inclusion of children with the full range of disabilities in mainstream education and, in practice, more pupils with special educational needs are being educated in mainstream schools each year.

There is a general acceptance by teachers and other professionals of the humanistic and social arguments for inclusion, but in the main the children who have been included are those at the top of Kvaraceus's (1956) hierarchical list. The inclusion of pupils with complex needs (including those with severe and profound learning difficulties and behaviours, which challenge the system) is still proving problematical, although there may always, for sound educational reasons, be a small proportion of children who will need the protection of a sheltered environment. Nevertheless many children are at present excluded from mainstream due to fear and prejudice – and, if we are serious about people with learning difficulties becoming a truly valued part of the social organisation of society, both special schools and mainstream schools must make greater attempts to break down the barriers to interaction and acceptance.

McConkey's research shows that *any* attempt to prepare communities or groups to accept others whom they perceive as different will have a positive effect (McConkey 1996). Teachers are part of society, and great strides have been made to help them to become more confident in the teaching of pupils with diverse needs. The addition of the important inclusion statement in the primary and secondary teachers' handbooks and the 'subject orders' of the new National Curriculum (DfEE/QCA 1999a and 1999b) is a breakthrough in making the curriculum more flexible and manageable for pupils with a whole range of disabilities. That inclusion statement sets down that there are three essential principles to developing a more inclusive curriculum: setting suitable learning challenges; responding to pupils' diverse needs; and overcoming potential barriers to learning and assessment for individual pupils. Together with the long awaited non-statutory curriculum guidelines, entitled *Planning, Teaching and Assessing the Curriculum for Pupils with Learning Difficulties* (DfEE/QCA 2001), the documents support staff in examining their practices in order to ensure that they are enabling pupils with complex needs to play a full part in every aspect of the educational system.

Alongside these UK Government initiatives is the DfEE's involvement in the publication and distribution of the *Index for Inclusion* (CSIE 2000). The *Index* is a tool that schools can use to develop inclusive practices through the process of self-assessment. It contains three dimensions: creating inclusive cultures; producing inclusive policies; and evolving inclusive practice. These are interlinked and are important features in the changing of attitudes. The indicators and questions set for each dimension can be used to explore shared values between staff and pupils and to establish a culture of inclusion beyond the confines of a school. If used sensitively in conjunction with a systematic recording system, the *Index* could accelerate attitudinal change.

What is missing in the *Index* – and, indeed, in many books written about the practice of inclusion – is the need to recognise that, before entering a school, ordinary pupils may have had little contact with pupils with the more severe difficulties in learning. When pupils with complex needs are included in any way in mainstream education, name-calling and feelings of isolation are often recorded by those who can articulate their concerns. As Shaw quotes (1998, p. 79):

'They would say I was a baby and I was in a pram and things because I was in a wheelchair. I told them to shut up and I told the teacher and they stopped it. They were not used to seeing people in wheelchairs in the school and they didn't really think about what they were saying.'

The pupil quoted above was one of the lucky ones because a solution was found. Less articulate and less confident children with greater difficulties in learning and communication may find contact with their mainstream peers a painful and degrading ongoing experience.

After the introduction of the Warnock Report, head teachers wrote about *preparing* pupils to accept others. The Warnock Committee's view of 'education for all' was, of course, based on a notion of integration in which children were placed in ordinary schools in order to share the facilities and curriculum of their mainstream peers. The process of inclusion, based on concepts of equal opportunities and humanistic philosophy, requires both mainstream and special schools to work together to develop positive relationships in order to enable all learners to grow into adults who can participate fully in all aspects of society. It is often assumed that this aim is achieved by osmosis; and, consequently, the preparation of pupils to accept those with a disability or learning difficulty as an ingredient in the development of positive relationships is forgotten.

Developing positive attitudes is likely to be most effective if ordinary children are introduced at an early age to those with learning difficulties. They are the ones whose attitudes, in the long term, will be instrumental in creating the future for people with learning difficulties. Happily, nursery schools and units, day nurseries, playgroups and day-care services are including more children with learning difficulties and the pre-school years are proving a firm base for their acceptance in society.

It is, however, worth challenging perceptions at any age, and we can learn much from the participatory schemes between mainstream and special schools that have proved a powerful and efficient way of developing positive attitudes through shared activities and interactions. Lindoe (in Carpenter *et al.* 1991), Lewis (1995), Beveridge (1996), and Shelvin and O'Moore (1999 and 2000) show that attitudinal change can be accelerated by encouraging shared activity based on common interests.

Shelvin's work has involved setting up structured schemes known as 'Fast Friend' programmes, in which thousands of pupils from mainstream and special schools across Ireland have participated in regular timetabled class sessions. Shelvin and his colleagues have accessed the social and educational benefits for all the children involved to date, and the work shows gains for all. Of importance is the emotional responses of mainstream peers, which are consistent with reports of other work in this area (Biklen *et al.* 1989; Peck *et al.* 1990). All show what the latter researchers call (p. 33) a 'reduced fear of human difference'. Through the scheme, mainstream pupils have begun to recognise a common humanity with those with complex needs.

In Lindoe's earlier link-scheme studies, a mainstream pupil and a pupil with SLD from a special school were encouraged to work together if they had a shared enthusiasm for a subject or an activity; and, as part of a planned programme, they were allowed, either formally or informally, to develop the interest together. Simply sharing an interest may, however, result in the domination of the activity by the mainstream pupil, and 'learned helplessness' by the pupil with learning difficulties (Lewis 1995). Using the interest as the basis for initial contact, it is important to ensure that the power-base is more evenly weighted, and that the pupil with learning difficulties, either alone or with his or her classmates, is given every opportunity to take the lead in activities.

One of the important elements in attitudinal change, which McConkey (1994) identifies, is that of giving information. Lindoe (in Carpenter *et al.* 1991) has alerted us to the importance of not only giving mainstream children basic information on disability as part of the preparation for link schemes, but allowing them to take part in 'sanctioned staring'. By showing video films of children who are physically different, or whose behaviour indicates slowness, she encouraged the mainstream children to ask questions and to articulate the negative feelings that surround physical and facial 'difference'. Using a simple questionnaire at the beginning and at various stages throughout the project, Lindoe was able to record the positive changes that occurred.

Making the most of opportunities: self-advocacy

People with learning difficulties are their own best advocates and are powerful agents for the changing of attitudes. They need, however, to acquire the skills and confidence to enable them to 'speak for themselves'. The components of self-advocacy include: choosing; decision-making; problem-solving; interacting and communicating with others; listening; being assertive without aggression; and taking responsibilities (see also Mittler's Chapter 23 in this book). These components are now recognised as skills that *all* pupils should acquire and are embedded in the subjects of the National Curriculum, particularly in citizenship and within the framework for PSHE (DfEE/QCA 1999a and 1999b). The key skills of communication; the application of number; information technology; working with others; and improving one's own learning and performance are recognised skills that advance performance, not only in education but in all aspects of work and life. Other priority skills such as those of learning to be organised, study skills, and managing one's own behaviour and emotions are also recognised as being important for pupils with learning difficulties (DfEE/QCA 2001). In using these documents to implement, plan and develop the curriculum, staff will be providing the foundations for the development of self-advocacy skills in their pupils.

These skills are also fundamental to early-intervention approaches, such as High Scope, where a child has the opportunity to exert control over both the learning situation and the teacher (Weikart 1989). They, as well as the interactive approaches of Coupe O'Kane and Smith (1994) and Collis and Lacey (1996), are being widely used in mainstream and special schools for pupils with learning difficulties. Nind and Hewett's intensive approach with children who are either at an early stage of development or whose behaviour challenges the school system is an imaginative attempt to encourage children to actively become their own advocates in the learning process (Nind and Hewett 1994; Hewett and Nind 1998).

Although the curriculum content and teaching approaches are of vital importance, the ethos and attitude of each school are also crucial in encouraging the empowerment of all of its pupils. Embedded in the notion of empowerment is the school's promotion of the feelings of self-worth in all of its pupils and the respect that the staff show for each other and their daily valuation of their pupils. Showing respect and value is well demonstrated by the work of Cleves school, which, in order to ensure such an outcome, has devised checklists with pupils to allow them and the staff to monitor their own performances (Alderson 1999). One of the elements to be monitored is the language that is used to describe and talk *to,* and *about,* the pupils. Language is powerful and can be used both wittingly and unwittingly to suppress and devalue children (Corbett 1996; Tilstone *et al.* 2000). Self-advocacy and self-esteem are interlinked and their development will be inhibited if labels are used – albeit unintentionally – in classrooms and staff rooms as a shorthand to point out children's shortcomings, or if 'what they cannot do' is constantly referred to in reports, in prerequisites for IEPs, or in other school and classroom documents. Describing someone as 'a wheelchair user' is much more likely to promote self-advocacy than being referred to as 'confined to a wheelchair'!

In addition, Alderson (1999) demonstrates the importance of partnership with pupils by encouraging children with learning difficulties to make a contribution to the running of the school, the formulation of school rules, and to the development of all major policies. Such a position is in keeping with the consultation document on the revised SEN Code of Practice (DfEE 2000), in which pupil participation is a central issue whereby pupils should be encouraged to become partners in every aspect of school life, including their own statutory assessments. This position is developed by Mortimer (2000), whose simple books are designed to help even very young children to take part in the assessment of their special educational needs. Jelly *et al.* (2000) also undertook research into pupil participation in seven special schools and units for a wide range of pupils with special educational needs, and those authors have recorded a comprehensive list of initiatives. In addition to the involvement of pupils in IEPs and the setting of personal targets, they detail (Jelly *et al.* 2000, p. 9) the preparation required to encourage pupils to actively participate in annual reviews and student/school councils.

Once given the tools to speak for themselves – as McConkey's research shows – pupils with learning difficulties have much to tell us that should be used at the micro level of changing local attitudes and at the macro level of influencing governments. In 1992, for example, Barb Goode, a Canadian, became the first person with learning difficulties to address the General Assembly of the United Nations. Her speech centred on the importance of pushing forward the rights of those with learning difficulties in order that they could take their place as equal citizens, living and working in their own communities (Ward 1995). Since then, there have been many examples of pupils and young people with learning difficulties becoming their own self-advocates, including Greg Sylvester, the athlete with Down's syndrome who carried the Olympic torch in Auckland, New Zealand, on its way to the Sydney 2000 Olympic Games.

Making the most of opportunities: promoting positive images

Every school has a reputation in the community. Unfortunately, as Mittler (2000) points out, all too often the reputation is based on league-table results. Schools, however, have many opportunities to ensure that positive messages and images are given to parents and to the general public on their work and on their pupils. A home–school policy is not a legal requirement but partnerships with parents are aspects of school life that are evaluated by OFSTED inspectors and, consequently, most schools have written proposals on working with parents.

'Working with parents' entails the provision of information; newsletters; reports of pupils' progress and home–school diaries, all of which are designed to communicate vital information. It is likely that the messages will generate dignity and respect, but it is also essential that the information is available to the local community. One way is through the school prospectus, yet Copeland (1992) has consistently found that the meanings conveyed by pictures and words are far from clear. His analysis of a range of prospectuses from special and mainstream schools shows that, in general, negative images of special educational needs are portrayed; there is a lack of clarity about schools' policies and procedures on special needs; and technical terms are overused. Such a situation is more likely to produce uncertainty and apprehension than to eradicate them.

As stereotypes and prejudices are socially learned, the media have a great influence on attitudes to people with learning disabilities (Philpot 1995). Fortunately, there has been a change in the way that people with difficulties in learning are portrayed, and TV programmes are beginning to employ people with learning difficulties as actors and presenters in their own right. Of concern, however, are the messages conveyed by local newspapers on the teaching and learning taking place in schools, particularly for those pupils with complex needs. Schools often contact newspapers to publicise fund-raising activities, to celebrate successes or to emphasise special events, but unfortunately the words and pictures used to make a 'good story' can give the 'wrong messages'. Journalists are unlikely to be any better informed than the general public, and sensational stories sell papers. Nevertheless, the media are a powerful influence and, as a consequence, a school's policy on changing attitudes should include sections on ways of helping the media to present children with learning difficulties through positive images.

As a former journalist, Shearer (1996) emphasises the importance of showing children with learning difficulties in normal environments (not just in specialised environments such as multisensory rooms); interacting with other children (with and without learning difficulties); engaged in activities (rather than just smiling at the camera); and speaking for themselves.

Structured attitudinal change: policy

Schools must be driven by policies that outline their philosophy and the aims of their work and, as Byers and Rose point out (1996, p. 16): 'Policies should further be regarded as a means of communicating the purpose of the school to those who have a vested interest: pupils, teachers, parents and the local community.'

Schools will have policies in place that deal with the ethos of the school, with the teaching and learning that is undertaken, with inclusive practices, and with working with parents and the community. The building blocks are in place, but how many of these policies clearly explain how a particular school is going to fulfil a role of accelerating attitudinal change within society? If the vision that 'persons with a disability are to participate fully in all educational, employment, consumer, recreational, community, and domestic activities that typify everyday life' (Tilstone *et al.* 1998, p. 16), including those with complex needs, is to become more than rhetoric, the importance of changing entrenched attitudes must not be underestimated. It is some 30 years since these pupils became part of education; will it take another 30 years for them to play their full part in society?

References

Alderson, P. (eds) (1999) *Learning and Inclusion: the Cleves School Experience*. London: David Fulton Publishers.

Beveridge, S. (1996) 'Experiences of an integration link scheme: the perspectives of pupils with severe learning difficulties and their mainstream peers', *British Journal of Learning Disabilities* 24, 9–19.

Biklen, D. *et al.* (1989) 'Beyond obligation: students' relationships with each other in integrated classes', in Lipsky, D. K. and Gartner A. (eds) *Beyond Separate Education: Quality Education for All*. Baltimore. USA: Paul H. Brookes.

Brigham, L. *et al.* (2000) *Crossing Boundaries: Change and Continuity in the History of Learning Disabilities*. Kidderminster: BILD.

Byers, R. and Rose, R. (1996) *Planning the Curriculum for Pupils with Special Educational Needs*. London: David Fulton Publishers.

Carpenter, B. *et al.* (1991) 'Changing attitudes', in C. Tilstone (ed.) *Teaching Pupils with Severe Learning Difficulties*. London: David Fulton Publishers.

Cole, T. (1989) *Apart or a Part? Integration and the Growth of British Special Education*. Milton Keynes: Open University Press.

Collis, M. and Lacey, P. (1996) *Interactive Approaches to Teaching*. London: David Fulton Publishers.

Copeland, L. (1994) 'Special education needs and the issue of the School Prospectus', *British Journal of Special Education* **21**(4), 77–9.

Corbett, J. (1996) *Bad-Mouthing the Language of Special Needs*. London: Falmer Press.

Coupe O'Kane, J. and Smith, E. (eds) (1994) *Taking Control: Enabling Pupils with Learning Difficulties*. London: David Fulton Publishers.

CSIE (2000) *Index for Inclusion: Developing Learning and Participation in Schools*. Bristol: CSIE; and London: DfEE.

DfEE (1997a) *Excellence in Schools*. London: DfEE.

DfEE (1997b) *Excellence for All Children*. London: DfEE.

DfEE (1998) *Meeting Special Needs: a Programme for Action*. London: DfEE

DfEE (1999) *From Exclusion to Inclusion; Report of the Disability Task Force*, London: DfEE.

DfEE (2000) *SEN Code of Practice on the Identification and Assessment of Pupils with Special Educational Needs* (consultation document). London: DfEE.

DfEE/QCA (1999a) *The National Curriculum Handbook for Primary Teachers in England*. London: HMSO.

DfEE/QCA (1999b) *The National Curriculum Handbook for Secondary Teachers in England*. London: HMSO.

DfEE/QCA (2001) *Planning, Teaching And Assessing The Curriculum for Pupils with Learning Difficulties*. London: QCA.

DES (1978) *Special Educational Needs: Report of the Committee of Enquiry into the Education of Handicapped Children and Young People* (The Warnock Report). London: HMSO.

Frances, J. (2000) 'Providing effective support in school when a child has a disfigured appearance: the work of the Changing Faces School Service'. *Support for Learning* **15**(4), 177–82.

Hewett, D. and Nind, M. (1998) *Interaction in Action*. London: David Fulton Publishers.

Jelly, M. *et al.* (2000) *Involving Pupils in Practice*. London: David Fulton Publishers.

Kvaraceus, W. C. (1956) 'Acceptance: rejection and exceptionality', *Exceptional Children*, 328–33

Lewis, A. (1995) *Children's Understanding of Disability*. London: Routledge.

Lindqvist, E. (1995) 'Europe should take the lead', *Helioscope* **6** (Winter), 2.

McConkey, R. (1987) *Who Cares? Community Involvement and Handicapped People*. London: Souvenir Press.

McConkey, R. (1991) 'Changing the public's perception of mental handicap', in Segal, S. and Varma, V. (eds) *Prospects for People with Learning Difficulties*. London: David Fulton Publishers.

McConkey, R. (1994) *Innovations in Educating Communities about Disabilities*. Chorley: Lisieux Hall Publications.

McConkey, R. (1996) 'Seen through a glass darkly: modifying public attitudes', in Mittler, P. and Sinason, V. (eds.) *Changing Policy and Practice for People with Learning Disabilities*. London: Cassell.

McConkey, R. and McCormack, B. (1983) *Breaking Barriers: Educating People about Disability*. London: Souvenir Press.

McConkey, R. *et al.* (1993) 'Neighbours' reactions to community services: contrasts before and after services open in their locality', *Mental Handicap Research* 2, 131–41.

Mason, M. and Reiser, R. (1994) *Altogether Better*. London; Charity Products.

Mencap. (1999) *Living in Fear*. London: Mencap.

Mittler, P. (2000) *Working Towards Inclusive Education: Social Contexts*. London: David Fulton Publishers.

Mortimer, H. (2000) *Taking Part: Helping Young Children to Take Part in a Statutory Assessment of their Special Educational Needs*. Lichfield: QED.

Nind, M. and Hewett, D. (1994) *Access to Communication*. London: David Fulton Publishers.

Oliver, M (1996) *Understanding Disability from Theory to Practice*. Basingstoke: Macmillan.

Peck, C. *et al*. (1990) 'Some benefits non-handicapped adolescents perceive for themselves from their social relationships with peers who have severe handicaps', *JASH (Journal of the Association for Persons with Severe Handicaps)* **15**(4), 241–9.

Philpot, T. (ed.) (1995) 'What the papers say: media images -of people with learning difficulties', in Roffey, S. *et al* .(1994) *Young Friends: Schools and Friendship*. London: Cassell.

Shaw, L. (1998) 'Children's experience of school' in C. Robinson and K. Stalker (eds) *Growing Up With Disability*. London: Jessica Kingsley.

Shearer, A. (1996) 'Think positive! Advice on presenting people with mental handicap', in Mittler. P. and Sinason, V. (eds) *Changing Policy and Practice for People with Learning Disabilities*. London: Cassell.

Shelvin, M. and O'Moore, A. (1999) 'Schools' link programme; enabling strangers to meet', *REACH (Journal of Special Needs Education in Ireland)* **12**(2), 102–9.

Shelvin, M. and O'Moore, A. (2000) 'Creating opportunities for contact between mainstream pupils and their counterparts with learning difficulties', *British Journal of Special Education* **27**(1), 29–34.

Tilstone, C. and Visser, J. (1996) 'Learning difficulties', in Varma, V. (ed.) *Coping with Children in Stress*, Aldershot. Hampshire: Ashgate Publishing.

Tilstone, C. *et al*. (eds) (1998) *Promoting Inclusive Practice*. London: Routledge.

Tilstone, C. *et al*. (2000) *Pupils with Learning Difficulties in Mainstream Schools*. London: David Fulton Publishers.

Walsh, P. N. and Shelvin, M. (1991) *Fast Friends*. Dublin, Ireland: St. Michael's House Research.

Ward, L. (1995) 'Equal citizens! Current issues for people with learning difficulties and their allies', in Philpot, T. and Ward, L., (eds) *Values and Visions: Changing Ideas in Services for People with Learning Difficulties*. Oxford: Butterworth Heinemann.

Weikart, D. P. (1989) 'The High/Scope curriculum in practice', *The High/Scope Project: Perspectives* 40. Exeter: University of Exeter, School of Education.

Wright, B. A. (1974) 'An analysis of attitude, dynamics and effects', *The New Outlook for the Blind*. 68, 108–18.

Chapter 23

Preparing for Self-Advocacy

Peter Mittler

People with intellectual impairments have, in my lifetime, gone from 'feeble-minded patients' to empowered agents of social change. They work to make the world a better place not just for themselves but for the rest of us as well.

(Dybwad 1996, p. 16)

The challenge of self-advocacy

The self-advocacy movement among young people with learning disabilities has become a force to be reckoned with and is growing stronger all the time. How, then, can schools prepare young people for adult life by helping them to develop the skills and confidence to speak for themselves, to be self-assertive – and even to be militant when this is necessary? How can they prepare them to become 'empowered agents of social change'?

Traditionally, much emphasis has been given by special schools to equipping young people with learning disabilities with the skills that they will need so as to live and work in the community – communication, money, shopping, budgeting and public transport, among others. More emphasis has recently been given to personal and social education and to issues concerned with personal and sexual relationships and the prevention of abuse. These are all essential skills that need to be nurtured in partnership with teachers, parents and the young people themselves.

But this is not enough. We need to take account of the initiatives that young people themselves have taken to shape their own future, what they have said about their schooling, and their own rights and aspirations to achieve independence and autonomy. The frustrations and aspirations experienced by young people have found expression in the growth of People First and other organisations of people with learning disabilities. The self-advocacy movement reflects their determination and their ability to find a voice.

Disabled young people have much in common with other minorities, such as those disadvantaged by poverty, chronic ill-health, old age, membership of an ethnic minority group or culture, or by the interaction of any or all of these with the additional discrimination that arises from gender. Are we making our students aware of these potential allies in the fight for rights and for more accessible environments?

Quality of life in the community

In thinking about how schools can support young people in speaking for themselves, and in joining with others who want to do so, teachers might make contact with former students and talk with members of their household or family to try to experience something of the quality of their day-to-day lives.

They may be surprised by how well many of their former students have developed since leaving school. A few will be living in ordinary houses with support tailored to their individual needs, perhaps in full-time supported or sheltered employment. Increasing numbers are attending further education colleges, at least on a part-time basis (Johnstone 1995). Many who had not acquired literacy skills before leaving school will have learned to read competently. A few will have formed stable long-term relationships, and some will have married or become parents.

But they will also be depressed by the paucity of service provision for young adults in most areas (Mittler and Sinason 1996). Many will still be attending day centres with poor staffing ratios and little or no possibility of continuing with the learning programmes initiated at school. Some will be living with parents who are becoming increasingly frail and anxious about the future. Some of the residents of group homes or sheltered housing schemes are leading lonely and isolated lives, and sometimes are victimised, exploited and abused by their neighbours (Flynn 1988).

Teachers in search of their ex-students will also find that nearly all are living in serious poverty. Most of their income from welfare benefits will be deducted to contribute directly or indirectly to living or service costs, leaving them with little or no money of their own. If they are attending day services, they are likely to receive between £2 and £4 a week – rates that have hardly changed for 20 years – though some will receive even less or be charged for the service. A few will have fallen victim to a criminal justice system that is not responsive to their needs and will have been punished for crimes that they did not commit (Clare and Murphy 1998; Edwards 1998).

Underestimation as a handicap

Young people leaving school are likely to encounter major obstacles to their participation in society over and above any difficulties arising directly from their disability. Perhaps the biggest single obstacle is the continuous pervasive underestimation of their abilities by society and its representatives and by the public at large. Even parents and professionals with many years of experience are in danger of such underestimation, believing it to be in the best interests of the young person 'to be realistic' and 'not to expect too much'. Such sentiments, however well-meaning, need to be challenged, not least by the young people concerned, because they act as a self-fulfilling prophecy and thus create further underestimation.

At the age of 16, Tracey Samutt, an actress with Down's syndrome and known throughout Australia for her starring role in a soap opera, told an audience of special educators (Samutt 1995):

> People should set higher goals and maybe they would be surprised by what we can do. ... I think I could do better if I was pushed a bit more, but the teachers are afraid I might fail. If I did something wrong, it was not because I made a mistake but because I had [Down's] Syndrome. ... I can get there. I might need more time; I might need repetition. But once I've got it, I've got it for life.

One way to combat underestimation by the general public as well as by professionals and parents is to publicise examples of outstanding achievement at all levels. Who would have predicted 30 years ago that the time would come when young people with Down's syndrome or those labelled as having severe learning difficulties would not only complete five years of secondary education in an ordinary class of a comprehensive school but would achieve several General Certificate of Secondary Education (GCSE) passes and later hold down a full-time job, live independently, get married – and even address the United Nations General Assembly?

These examples may, at least for the present, be exceptional; but they are real, not token, achievements. They raise questions about how many more individuals are capable of beating prediction. Likewise, teachers and schools could ask themselves whether there are students in their charge now whose abilities may be being underestimated?

Origins of the self-advocacy movement

As early as 1971, people with learning disabilities held their first residential conferences for people with learning disabilities, supported by the Campaign for the Mentally Handicapped (now Values into Action; Whittaker 1996). By the early 1980s, they were speaking at national and international conferences.

Student committees were established in more than a quarter of all Adult Training Centres in the United Kingdom. By 1988, the proportion was over one-half (Crawley 1988). Some of these committees persuaded social-services managers to change the name of their centre from Adult Training Centre to Social Education Centre and to refer to their membership as 'students' or 'service users' rather than 'trainees'. Others came into conflict with their managers – e.g. in applying (successfully) to join the National Union of Students.

Williams and Shoultz (1982, 1991) have traced the origins of self-advocacy movements in Sweden, Australia, the USA and the United Kingdom. Later accounts of developments in the UK are available in Flynn and Ward (1991), Whittaker (1996), Ramcharan *et al.* (1997) and Ward (1998). In the USA, strong People First organisations have been set up in most states, but there is also a national organisation that has run international conferences for self-advocates.

The self-advocacy movement affirms the rights of disabled persons to enjoy the same basic human rights as their fellow citizens. It has developed in reaction to the obstacles placed in the way of disabled people in expressing choice and self-determination. The movement can be seen as an expression of the struggle to redress the gross power imbalance between professionals and service users. This is potentially greater and more damaging to people with learning disabilities than most others. It also renders them particularly vulnerable to well-meaning and experienced professionals who claim to understand their needs and, in the light of this assumption, make decisions on their behalf. This powerlessness also makes them particularly vulnerable to oppressive and abusive practices, including repeated sexual abuse and the emotional abuse that springs from neglecting ordinary human needs for personal relationships and for the expression of feelings.

More recently, organisations of disabled people have voiced a fundamental objection to the principle of normalisation. They are critical of well-meaning attempts to help them fit into society and have insisted instead on their 'right to be different' (e.g. Walmsley and Downer 1997). Organisations of disabled people argue that society should value and cater for diversity and that its laws and institutions should respond more fully to the needs of all its citizens, not just those who happen to constitute the majority. This position is also taken by organisations representing ethnic minorities who reject the assumption that they should assimilate the values and norms of the majority. In the same way, the deaf community insists on the right to its own culture and its own language.

Self-advocates, working as individuals, in small groups and at national and international levels, have fought – and are still fighting – to achieve a number of goals. An issue of *Mental Retardation* includes articles by three self-advocates that reflect the need to be heard and valued, and the right to be consulted on all decisions affecting their lives (Monroe 1996; Pacht 1996; Ward 1996). In the United Kingdom, service users are increasingly involved in the selection of staff, in the evaluation of services and in quality-assurance procedures (Kroese *et al.* 1998). They have produced training materials to help other self-advocacy groups and have acted as consultants and trainers (Ward 1998). Others are carrying out their own research and are rejecting the role and status of 'subjects' in the research of academics and professionals (Minkes *et al.* 1995).

Self-advocates have also been a powerful voice on issues of labelling and terminology. In Canada, they were the moving force that led to the change of name from Canadian Association for Mental Retardation to Canadian Association for Community Living. In the UK, they campaigned successfully against the MENCAP 'little Stephen' logo and against negative and degrading fund-raising images.

There is now a wealth of published material on the development of the self-advocacy movement and on the achievements and views of individual self-advocates. Dybwad and Hersani (1996) have brought together a comprehensive worldwide account of the progress of the self-advocacy movement, using the voices of people with learning disabilities themselves and drawing examples from different countries and settings.

Self-advocates have also played an increasingly influential and powerful role in international organisations such as Inclusion International (formerly the International League of Societies for Persons with Mental Handicap). Since 1982, self-advocates have attended international conferences, increasingly as ordinary participants rather than 'special groups', and they have worked together to articulate a clear vision of rights and responsibilities. In 1994, the self-advocacy committee of Inclusion International completed work on a 40–page document entitled, *The Beliefs, Values and Principles of Self-advocacy*. The following are the headings, which are expanded and discussed in the text (Inclusion International 1994):

- *beliefs and values* (things of the heart that you believe in):
  - being a person first;
  - being able to make our own decisions;
  - believing in my value as a person;
  - having other people believe in you as a person;
- *principles* (guidelines that we follow in making decisions):
  - empowerment (to give control to a person so they can make their own decisions);
  - equal opportunity (a situation in which it is possible for you to do something you want to do);
  - non-labelling;
  - learning and living together – e.g. as children, we have the right to support to attend our local school, regardless of our disability, and to grow up with other children.

The core components of self-advocacy have been summarised as follows (Further Education Unit (FEU) 1990):

- being able to express thoughts and feelings with assertiveness, if necessary;
- being able to make choices and decisions;
- having clear knowledge and information about rights;
- being able to make changes.

Griffiths (1994) lists the essential elements of successful self-advocacy practice. These include:

- an understanding of choice;
- a feeling of being regarded;
- a better understanding of the world, its possibilities and difficulties;
- a feeling of self-worth;
- the development of skills and competencies;
- competence in risk-taking;
- a feeling of safety which makes risk-taking possible;
- a feeling of confidence;
- a feeling of being encouraged and supported as they develop towards autonomy.

How, then, can the foundations for the principles and practice for successful self-advocacy be laid in schools? The next section outlines some thought in this regard.

Implications for schools

The remainder of this chapter summarises some of the strategies and opportunities for incorporating the curricular aims and activities that, to a greater or lesser degree, are designed to foster skills and experience underlying self-advocacy both now and in the future. Many of these are already elements of good practice. Volumes edited by Coupe O'Kane and Smith (1994) and Garner and Sandow (1995) provide a radical rationale for self-advocacy in schools, as well as examples of good practice.

Towards a new curriculum

The present time is an opportune moment to reconceptualise curriculum priorities. We need to ask questions concerning the extent to which existing practice should be modified to support students in acquiring and using the knowledge, skills, attitudes and understanding that they will need as self-advocates in the community. Fortunately, developments in professional practice over the past decade or so, both in mainstream and in special schools, are at least in part consistent with these aims.

The case for more attention to preparation for self-advocacy is not merely a plea for more time on the timetable. Personal, social and health education (PSHE) and citizenship are much more than 'another subject' (Tyne 1996). The way in which these issues are addressed by a school can have a powerful impact on the development of self-awareness and provide firm foundations for empowerment and self-advocacy.

Despite the inexorable demands of the National Curriculum, and politicians' and pundits' obsession with 'standards', the past decade has seen a greater emphasis on more holistic pupil-centred approaches in special schools. Although the original National Curriculum, with its emphasis on subjects, attainment targets and national assessment, was at first seen as a retrograde step, teachers have successfully developed innovative methods of teaching that combine the best elements of an objectives-based approach with a regime that tries to develop relevant individualised plans (Farrell 1997).

The earlier Dearing review of the National Curriculum (SCAA 1993) prompted a reconsideration of priorities and, in theory at least, released the equivalent of a day a week for other activities. Moreover, students over 16 are not obliged to follow the National Curriculum. The Dearing review gave scope for more flexibility to relate the programmes of study and the assessment arrangements to the needs of individual pupils and provided time and freedom to design school experiences accordingly.

A mass of evidence is now available that reflects the attempts of teachers to develop a 'broad and balanced curriculum which meets the individual needs of pupils' and to which they are entitled by law. The results of this work are summarised in the present volume and its predecessor (Ashdown *et al.* 1991) and elsewhere (National Curriculum Council 1992; Rose *et al.* 1996; Sebba *et al.* 1993; Tilstone 1991).

The work reported in these books was carried out at a time of crisis for the whole of education, and for special needs education in particular. Although most schools tried to strike a sensible balance between combining 'the best of the old' with the 'best of the new', the effort and energy required to keep pace with constant innovation have left many schools exhausted and eager for a period of stability. A recent study of curriculum development in 12 special schools (Halpin and Lewis 1996) concludes:

> In various ways, the National Curriculum is interpreted as either irrelevant to the special school context or is accepted at the level of rhetoric while making minimal impact on practice (as in the minimal use made of cross-curricular strategies by some schools).

In a survey of 75 special schools catering for over 4,000 pupils with SLD, Male (1997) reports the views of the majority of head teachers that 'the National Curriculum is clearly not meeting the needs or recognising the achievements of pupils with PMLDs; neither is it recognising what *is* being accomplished by all those who work with them'. The questionnaires for this research were distributed in the summer of 1995, shortly before the publication of the guidance on planning the curriculum for pupils with PMLD published by SCAA (1996).

Curriculum 2000

In revising the National Curriculum for September 2000, the Qualifications and Curriculum Authority has learned the lessons of the past by ensuring that special-needs issues were built into the foundations from the outset and reflected in every subject area and at all key stages. This process was reinforced by a clear Parliamentary commitment to the principle of inclusion. This in turn is an expression of wider policies concerned with social justice and reducing the impact of poverty and exclusion.

The Secretary of State's introduction to *Curriculum 2000* (DfEE 1999a) includes a substantial section headed 'General statement on inclusion', which refers to three principles to which teachers 'are required to have regard' in planning and teaching the National Curriculum. Each of these is developed in some detail:

- setting suitable learning challenges;
- responding to the diverse needs pupils bring to their learning;
- overcoming potential barriers to learning and assessment for individuals or groups.

PSHE and citizenship

The new curriculum provides a framework for PSHE and citizenship throughout all key stages. The QCA (1999) proposals set out (p. 12) a learning framework across the key stages to enable schools to:

- promote their pupils' personal and social development (PSD), including their health and well-being, effectively;
- develop pupils' knowledge and understanding of their roles and responsibilities as active citizens in a modern democracy;
- equip them with the values, skills and knowledge to deal with the difficult moral and social questions they face.

The proposals 'recognise the contribution that PHSE and citizenship can make to combating racism and promoting equal opportunities through teaching about fairness, justice, rights and responsibilities and through developing an understanding and appreciation of diversity' (QCA 1999, p. 13).

These aims could hardly be more relevant to pupils with special educational needs in general and learning disabilities in particular. At one level, the pupils themselves will benefit if the next generation of citizens has a clearer understanding of issues concerned with social justice and human rights. A much more direct and immediate impact reflects the day-to-day experience of people with learning disabilities themselves, since all too often they are the victims of denial of human rights and of unfairness and injustice.

In *Redefining the Whole Curriculum for Pupils with Learning Difficulties*, Sebba *et al.* (1993) had already made a strong case for PSD permeating all aspects of the work of schools, both mainstream and special. They saw PSD as concerned with the development of personal autonomy and self-determination, rather than with the acquisition of skills in themselves. Planning a PSD curriculum involves a reconsideration of the nature of the power relationship between teacher and pupil and the extent to which the aims of schooling should be concerned with 'empowerment and liberation rather than remediation and normalisation'. The aim is to foster environments that reduce dependency and remove practices that disempower pupils (see also Byers 1998).

Their arguments represent a radical departure from current special-needs theory and practice. But seen from the perspective of the community of adult disabled people, they have a familiar ring because they are couched in the language of disability rights. This is the language that young people are hearing, learning and using. It seems appropriate that teachers should support them in doing so.

Aims concerned with opportunities for choice, decision-making and empowerment can be woven into the life of the school and all its activities. Even so, some activities lend themselves particularly well to this aim.

Consulting the pupil

Both the Children Act 1989 and the *Code of Practice on the Identification and Assessment of SEN* (DFE 1994) emphasise the importance of listening to the views of children and young people and giving them the fullest possible opportunity to take part in discussions and decision-making concerning their education and key issues in their life. In fact, encouragement to do this was already explicitly provided in Department of Education and Science Circular 1/83 concerned with the implementation of the Education Act 1981. This stated that the principle of partnership with pupils was as important as that of partnership with parents. Nevertheless, research on the implementation of the 1981 Act indicated that such practice was extremely rare (Goacher *et al.* 1988).

Records of Achievement

Records of Achievement are intended to celebrate all aspects of achievement and are much more than a summative record of educational attainments. They provide a rich source of evidence about a pupil's interests and hobbies, both inside and outside school. Above all, pupil involvement in developing Records of Achievement lies at the heart of the whole process.

Despite lukewarm support from the Conservative Government in the early 1990s, Records of Achievement were developed in secondary and special schools and are now widely used in primary schools as well. Lawson (1996) provides a useful summary of their origins and development in special schools and demonstrates how they reflect a more holistic approach to formative assessment than those required by the Education Reform Act 1988 or by the Dearing modifications. Parker (1994) describes in some detail the development of Records of Achievement initiatives in the West Midlands in general and in one special school in particular.

Key features of the Record of Achievement are summarised by Lawson (1996) as follows:

- assessment is an ongoing process;
- only success is recognised;
- all experiences are important;
- the process is participative;
- the Record of Achievement enhances learning;
- it provides evidence rather than judgement;
- ownership lies with the pupil.

SEN Code of Practice

Developments since the early 1980s, including Records of Achievement, have created a more favourable climate for the involvement of pupils in their own learning. Therefore, it was hoped that research on a SEN Code of Practice would provide evidence that pupils with learning difficulties were being consulted at all five stages of the Code.

The case for pupil involvement was well stated in the Code (DFE 1994, paras 2.34–2.37):

> The effectiveness of any assessment and intervention will be influenced by the involvement and interest of the young person concerned. The benefits are:
> - practical: children have important and relevant information. Their support is crucial to the effective implementation of any individual educational programme;
> - principle: children have a right to be heard. They should be encouraged to participate in decision-making about provision to meet their SEN;
>
> Schools should consider how they can:
> - involve pupils in decision-making processes;
> - determine the pupil's level of participation, taking into account approaches to assessment and intervention which are suitable for his or her age, ability and past experiences;
> - record pupils' views in identifying their difficulties, setting goals, agreeing a development strategy, monitoring and reviewing progress;
> - involve pupils in determining individual educational plans.

Unfortunately, research on the Code of Practice suggests that neither mainstream nor special schools have gone very far in implementing this advice. The OFSTED (1999) national review of special schools, secure units and pupil referral units in England in the period 1994–8, while recognising significant improvements in teaching and learning over this period, found marked weaknesses in assessment and recording of pupils' progress, though SLD schools 'demonstrated best practice overall' (p. 52). In particular, 'a very small number of schools involved pupils in self-assessment that contributed significantly to the overall assessment process'. The work of Greenside School in Hertfordshire was commended (p. 55):

> 'Where possible, self assessment is encouraged and some pupils are able to appraise their own progress. This information is appropriately included in annual reviews and transition reviews which are attended by the pupils, parents and professionals.

Rose *et al.* (1996) published an early survey of LEAs in England and reported that few 'were seen to have recognised the significance of this part of the Code and most were unable to identify schools in which they could affirm good practice related to this area'. Information was obtained from 41 mainstream and special schools selected by LEAs, 10 of the latter catering for pupils with SLD. The questions focused on three aspects of pupil involvement:

- *setting of learning targets*: this took place in around 40 per cent of SLD schools, compared with all the schools for children with moderate learning difficulties and most mainstream schools;
- *assessing their own progress*: this took place in 40 per cent of SLD schools, and very similar percentages were found in other types of school;
- *reporting achievements and experiences*: this was found in 30 per cent of SLD schools, compared with 83 per cent of MLD schools, 25 per cent of schools for children with emotional and behavioural difficulties (EBD), and 59 per cent of mainstream schools.

Building on these findings, Rose *et al.* (1999) report a detailed study of a piece of action research carried out in one school (Watling View, St Albans) in partnership with Nene University College, Northampton. The resulting paper provides a detailed account of the problems, processes and problem-solving strategies that took place over a period of months in involving 30 pupils, aged 12–19 years, in setting their own achievement targets.

An early finding from the project was that while some pupils were able to respond positively with appropriate support, others needed to be taught the relevant cognitive skills on a one-to-one basis. These skills were identified as:

- negotiation;
- self-knowledge and recognition of their own potential;
- prediction skills, including concepts of time.

Each of these was broken down into smaller units to form a pupil profile that acted as a basis for a teaching programme to support pupils in acquiring the skills necessary to take part in target-setting. Some examples of the 13 skills listed under negotiation (Rose *et al.* 1999, p. 223) include:

- can state an opinion with confidence;
- expresses personal feelings and needs;

- achieves a good balance between listening and responding;
- has well-developed skills of refusal.

The UK Government's proposals for revision of the SEN Code of Practice include a commitment to 'strengthen the guidance in the Code to encourage LEAs and schools to seek and take account of the child's views throughout the SEN process'. In addition, the Programme of Action includes a commitment 'to amend regulations to place the SEN Tribunal under a duty to have regard to the views of the child, where these can be ascertained' (DfEE 1999b). The Action Plan also suggests that 'some LEAs may wish to experiment with fora in which children with SEN, or with disabilities, have an opportunity to meet local policy-makers (DfEE 1998).

Individual Educational Plans, annual reviews and transition planning

The involvement of pupils in the process of IEP development, in the annual review and most importantly in the transition process is particularly vital. If such involvement is to be genuine and not tokenistic, a long period of preparation and successful participation in discussion and decision-making is essential. Everything depends, therefore, on the pupil participation policy of the school as a whole and on the nature and quality of the opportunities that have been available to students over a period of years.

Here again, the Code of Practice is quite explicit (DFE 1994, para. 6.15):

> Wherever possible, pupils should be actively involved in the review process, including all or part of the review meeting and should be encouraged to give their views of their progress during the previous year; discuss any difficulties encountered; and share their hopes and aspirations for the future.
> Effective arrangements for transition will involve young people themselves addressing issues of:
> - personal development;
> - self-advocacy;
> - the development of a positive self-image;
> - the growth of personal autonomy and the acquisition of independent living skills.

Despite this, the OFSTED review of special school practice states (OFSTED 1999, p. 57):

> Few schools progressed to the level of involving pupils in the setting and review of IEP targets, although this was slightly more common in annual reviews. Where pupils were involved, the sense of involvement and partnership was beneficial and pupils were especially well motivated to achieve the targets. This practice is worthy of wider adoption.

Intensive interaction

'Intensive interaction' is the generic name given to a style of teaching that emphasises the centrality of the pupil–teacher relationship. The main proponents of this approach are Nind and Hewett (e.g. 1994). In behavioural strategies, the teacher is held to be firmly in control of what is to be taught, and defines the steps to acquisition and the reward system to be used. In comparison, intensive interaction can follow leads provided by the child. Put simply, the emphasis is on process as much as product. Thus (Nind and Hewett 1994, pp. 14, 16)

> Much consideration is given to the learning environment and to the stimulation which is offered but what happens will depend very much on the student, following his/her interests and lead.

In this way, the teaching is seen less as technology and more as art ... the emphasis is on the exploring, the doing, the discovery. It is the understandings that come as part of this active process that the teacher aims to promote.

Intensive Interaction is concerned with negotiation and participation, as opposed to dominance and compliance. Part of valuing the learner on an equal basis is not imposing on him/her our agenda for action, our style and pace of working and our needs.

Turn-taking

A number of researchers studying interactions between mothers and new-born or very young babies have detected patterns of timing and synchronisation in which mother and baby appear to wait for pauses before taking their turn in the interaction. Studies along these lines have been carried out with infants with Down's syndrome and with young children with profound and multiple impairments.

Goldbart (1988) and Harris and Wimpory (1992) provide useful discussions of the implications of this and related research for classroom practice. Here again, the focus is on the style and nature of adult-child interaction and the opportunities that it provides for facilitating successful communication. (See also Coupe O'Kane and Goldbart (1998) and Harris (1994) for a fuller elaboration of these ideas.)

Children controlling their environment

In working with pupils with profound and multiple impairments, it is important to provide them with opportunities to control features of their environment. By this means they learn that certain actions on their part invariably trigger a particular response – an early example of empowerment!

With or without the use of information technology and microelectronics, it is possible to design environments that will be responsive to sounds or movements made by a child, which will in turn trigger a specific response. This has implications for the design of multisensory environments; instead of – or in addition to – providing sensory stimulation, opportunities should be available for children to control aspects of their environment through their own actions. Barber (1994) and Wilkinson (1994) provide detailed accounts of how this can be done.

Elsewhere, Wilkinson (1995) reports a telling example of ways in which the use of drama can enable students with profound and multiple learning difficulties to acquire a 'voice' of their own and to be in control. The drama involves hand-held placards, character representations, speech synthesisers and the use of the pupils' own voices where possible. Similarly, Bowen (1997) illustrates how the use of stories can help to develop pupils' skills in argument and decision-making – for example, in relation to their experience of bullying. She also refers to soap operas, pictures that tell a story, magazine and newspaper articles, plays and videos.

Dealing with the unexpected

Goldbart (1988) argues that a 'well run classroom' is not a good place to learn to communicate or to affect your environment because everything happens in an orderly, systematic and predictable way. She provides examples of a variety of 'arranged' unpredictable events that required action and initiative on the part of the child – a form of teaching by sabotage. These included breaking the tips off classroom pencils, taking the refills out of biro pens, removing the middle screw from scissors, handing round an empty biscuit tin, and asking a student to pour drinks for others from an empty jug. In the same vein, Gunton (1995) records the reactions of a group of children sitting down to school lunch at a table lacking knifes and forks, which the class monitor had forgotten to lay. Despite the monitor fetching her own cutlery from a nearby table, and the children also seeing an example of another pupil, it was a long time before other children followed their example, the last to do so having to be told to do so before bursting into tears. More recently, Coupe O'Kane and Goldbart (1998) provide a more detailed discussion of such approaches in the context of teaching language and communication skills through shared attention and joint action routines.

Opportunities for choice and decision-making

Most schools now try to ensure that opportunities for exercising choice are an integral part of the everyday experience of all pupils, including those with profound and multiple impairments. Numerous opportunities occur in the course of ordinary routines to present pupils with simple choices – between two toys, milk or juice, blue or red sweater, story now or later – but gradually extending to more complex choices between activities, games, companions or teachers. As an aid, a short videotape of ordinary classroom activities could indicate how many opportunities for choice were naturally available or were presented by adults or other children, how many pupils were and were not offered such opportunities, and how adults and other pupils reacted to such choices as were made.

Gunton (1990) developed some detailed principles and guidelines on ways in which SLD schools could foster the development of self-advocacy skills. The following is an extract from the 'general philosophy' introduction; in other sections she makes specific suggestions for ways in which opportunities for choice and decision-making can be given to children with PMLD and very limited communication skills in other curriculum areas, such as language and communication, music, drama, dance, physical education and games. Gunton (1990) suggests:

> Pupils should be treated with respect and dignity at all times. No one should be discussed or spoken about as if they were not there.
>
> Aim to provide choice whenever you can. Introduce option afternoons if you haven't already got them. Try to give choices within each lesson – choice of partner, choice of activity, choice of teacher. Don't end up with an identical object for each child at the end of the lesson. Encourage individuality.
>
> Ask the child to make decisions – and act on them.
>
> Reasons should always be given to and asked from a pupil.
>
> Pupils should be given every opportunity to learn that actions have consequences and that they should be able to question another's actions and explain their own.
>
> The pupil should be asked for his/her opinion whenever possible.
>
> The fact that one's opinion is sought and acted upon helps to promote self esteem. Imagine how it would feel if no one ever consulted you about anything. Discuss feelings, preferences, whenever you can. Let pupils know you are interested in their opinions, that they matter.
>
> Pupils should be involved wherever possible. Decisions involving pupils should be made by them if at all possible. Ask them if they would prefer a disco or a film at the end of term; hot

dogs or beef burgers at the fête; where would be the best place for the new fish tank; should they have fish or terrapins?

Pupils should be allowed to make mistakes.

Pupils should be involved in the school organisation.

The school is there for the benefit of the children and their parents. Pupils should feel that the school is theirs and that they have a say in what goes on and what goes where. Where shall we put this display? Which flowers shall we buy for the entrance? What colour curtains, cushions?

Pupils should be given the skills to make decisions.

Carefully graded decision-making should be part of every child's programme – no matter how limited their ability.

Every member of staff, every student and every volunteer should have the philosophy of self-advocacy, choice and decision-making explained to them.

Every parent should be told that this is the philosophy of the school.

Parents sometimes need help and encouragement to allow their child to experiment and take risks. They need to be assured that their worries and desires will be taken into account and that they will always be welcomed and kept informed.

Griffiths (1994) provides a detailed checklist adapted from the FEU (1990) document *Developing Self-advocacy Skills for People with Disabilities and Learning Difficulties*. The checklist is too long to reproduce in full, but one section headed 'Negotiation and Choice' is particularly relevant in the present context.

Are young people always consulted about such basic matters as being touched, lifted or being taken somewhere else if they are in a wheelchair?

At the start of a session, do staff seek to gain the young peoples' consent to the content and method of teaching?

Is it genuinely acceptable for young people to say 'no'?

Is it accepted that young people may have legitimate criticism of a member of staff?

Can programmes be changed at a young person's request?

Is there always a choice of activities within sessions?

Is there alternative provision for young people who want to opt out of a session?

Is one to one guidance and counselling available?

Are there staff guidelines about when to insist that a young person abides by a contract that he or she has made?

Is there a policy of gaining young peoples' consent to behaviour modification programmes if that is at all possible?

Gunton (1990) also poses some searching questions that are relevant to both teachers and parents of young people with learning difficulties: 'Are you skipping adolescence?' and 'Are you expecting young people with SLD to move straight from childhood to sensible middle age?' These questions are prompted by the following observations, all too familiar to those who have ever shared a home with one or more teenagers. Most adolescents do not:

- dust;
- make sponge cakes or apple pie;
- wear 'sensible clothes';
- go to bed early (or get up at a 'normal time');
- behave well towards adults;
- do what they are told without arguing;
- eat sensibly;
- plan carefully;
- keep their cupboards, drawers and rooms tidy;
- behave in an exemplary way towards the other sex.

A glance at some current 'social education' or 'social skills' programmes would no doubt add to the list.

Student committees

Many special schools have established a student committee (Winup 1994). The nature and quality of teacher support and teacher 'presence' varies considerably from school to school and over a period of time. Some committees concern themselves with relatively minor issues; others have a considerable impact on the life of the school – e.g. the policy on visitors entering the classroom, talking about pupils in their presence, access to records. Whatever is discussed, it is important that students should feel that these meetings are not just a 'talking shop' and that action is taken where it is agreed to be necessary and follow-up action can be taken.

Students learn valuable committee and negotiating skills from membership of such committees – e.g. setting and keeping to an agenda, taking turns, waiting for others to have their say, not interrupting, speaking through the chair, accepting majority decisions, not 'hogging the floor', as well as techniques of persuasion and argument.

Working with families

Inevitably, providing opportunities for choice and decision-making for school-age pupils reduces the 'authority' and control of the teacher and brings the risk of resentment or conflict. In particular, tensions may arise when teachers, parents and the pupil have different priorities about what should be taught. This may include readiness to go out alone, embark on a sexual relationship, live independently, or get a job.

Because families have their own agendas and concerns, no school-based programme of preparation for advocacy, however well planned and delivered, can hope to succeed without the collaboration and participation of the family. Helping young people to become autonomous adults – to express their opinions and, where necessary, to insist on them to the point of refusal or militancy – makes it necessary for the family to be involved in the initial planning. This allows teachers and family members to anticipate difficulties and work together from the outset. This is perhaps the most sensitive area for discussion between parents and teachers (Mittler 1996).

Developing school policies

Byers (1998) emphasises the importance of a clear school policy on PSD. He provides a full summative discussion of the issues and follows this with some useful guidelines to enable schools to develop and monitor such a policy. A few selected extracts are given by way of example.

Ethos, spirit and atmosphere
A school should consider the following questions in relation to this topic:

- What sort of a society do we imagine school leavers will join?
- How do schools find out about the kinds of futures leavers face?
- Does the school have:
  – pupil/student councils and committees
  – access for learners to setting targets in the school development plan
  – representation for service users and/or advocacy groups on the governing body?

Meeting individual needs
Schools should consider the following question for meeting individual needs:

- How are individual pupils involved in the process of identifying their own strengths and difficulties, setting their own targets, creating strategies for intervention and implementation?

Observation, recording, assessment reporting and accreditation
Here are two questions in relation to this topic:

- How are pupils involved in assessment, record keeping, monitoring progress, review of plans and procedures for reporting?
- Do accreditation and Records of Achievement encompass a range of nationally validated forms of accreditation, including progress files, relating to a range of whole curriculum issues?

Conclusions

Young people with learning disabilities are part of a worldwide movement of self-advocacy, emancipation and 'liberation', initiated by disabled people themselves. They are not content any longer to have others speak on their behalf – whether they be parents, professionals, politicians or leaders of voluntary organisations. They are highly critical of society's low expectations of their capacity to learn and they insist on their rights to be treated as fellow citizens, with the same rights to have their needs met as any one else.

It is precisely because they are now living in less-segregated environments that they will have daily experience of discrimination and various forms of abuse and exploitation. They are also likely to lead lives characterised by loneliness and poverty and to lack the means to have access to community leisure and recreational facilities. They may be denied access to certain places of entertainment because of their disability and are at risk of being accused and found guilty of offences they have not committed. In general, their quality of life is likely to be poor.

It follows that young people need to be helped to fend for themselves in environments that may be lonely or hostile. In this context, self-advocacy provides not only a foundation for assertiveness but also a means of support and empowerment from others. This process needs to begin in school. It must also take place in the closest possible partnership with parents and with the young people themselves.

References

Ashdown, R., *et al.* (eds) (1991) *The Curriculum Challenge: Access to the National Curriculum for Pupils with Learning Difficulties.* London: Falmer Publishing.

Barber, M. (1994) 'Contingency awareness: putting research into the classroom', in Coupe O'Kane, J. and Smith, B. (eds) *Taking Control: Enabling People with Learning Difficulties.* London: David Fulton Publishers.

Bowen, M. (1997) 'Learning to make decisions', *SLD Experience,* spring, 12–13.

Byers, R. (1998) 'Personal and social development', in Tilstone, C. *et al.* (eds) *Promoting Inclusive Practice.* London: Routledge.

Clare, I. C. and Murphy, G. (1998) 'Working with offenders or alleged offenders with intellectual disabilities', in Emerson, E. *et al.* (eds) *Clinical Psychology and People with Intellectual Disabilities.* Chichester: Wiley.

Coupe O'Kane, J. and Goldbart, J. (1998) *Communication before Speech: Development and Assessment,* 2nd edn. London: David Fulton Publishers.

Coupe O'Kane, J. and Smith, B. (eds) (1994) *Taking Control: Enabling People with Learning Difficulties.* London: David Fulton Publishers.

Crawley, B. (1988) *The Growing Voice: A Survey of Self-advocacy Groups in Adult Training Centres and Hospitals in Great Britain.* London: Campaign for People with Mental Handicap.

DFE (1994) *Code of Practice on the Identification and Assessment of Special Educational Needs.* London: HMSO.

DfEE (1998) *Meeting Special Educational Needs: A Programme of Action.* London: DfEE.

DfEE (1999a) *The National Curriculum: Secretary of State's Proposals.* London: DfEE/The Stationery Office.

DfEE (1999b) *Consultation document on the proposed revision of the SEN Code of Practice.* London: DfEE.

Dybwad, G. (1996) 'Setting the stage historically', in Dybwad, G. and Hersani, H. (eds) *New Voices: Self-advocacy by People with Disabilities.* Baltimore, MD: Brookline Press.

Dybwad, G. and Hersani, H. (eds) (1996) *New Voices: Self-advocacy by People with Disabilities.* Baltimore. MD: Brookline Press.

Edwards, W. J. (1998) 'Learning disabilities and the criminal justice system'. Paper presented to British Institute of Learning Disabilities, Eastbourne.

Farrell, P. (1997) *The Education of Children with Learning Difficulties.* London: Cassell.

FEU (1990) *Developing Self-advocacy Skills with People with Disabilities.* London: FEU.

Flynn, M. (1988) *Independent Living for Adults with Mental Handicap.* London: Cassell.

Flynn, M. and Ward, L. (1991) 'We can change the future: self and citizen advocacy, in Segal, S. and Varma, V. (eds) *Prospects for People with Learning Difficulties.* London: David Fulton Publishers.

Garner, P. and Sandow, S. (eds.) (1995) *Advocacy, Self-advocacy and Special Needs.* London: David Fulton Publishers.

Goacher, B. *et al* . (1988) *Policy and Provision for Special Educational Needs.* London: Cassell.

Goldbart, J. (1988) 'Re-examining the development of early communication', in Coupe O'Kane, J. and Goldbart, J. (eds) *Communication Before Speech.* London: Croom Helm.

Griffiths, M. (1994) *Transition to Adulthood: The Role of Education for Young People with Severe Learning Difficulties.* London: David Fulton Publishers.

Gunton, P. (1990) 'Encouraging self-advocacy at an early age'. Dissertation submitted to Cambridge University Institute of Education.

Gunton, P. (1995) 'Draw back the blinds', *National Association for the Prevention of Child Abuse in Children Bulletin,* June, 3–5.

Halpin, D. and Lewis, A. (1996) 'The impact of the National Curriculum on twelve special schools', *European Journal of Special Needs Education* **11**, 95–105.

Harris, J. (1994) 'Language, communication and personal power: a developmental perspective', in Coupe O'Kane, J. and Smith, B. (eds) *Taking Control: Enabling People with Learning Difficulties*. London: David Fulton Publishers.

Harris, J. and Wimpory, D. (1992) *Get Kids Talking*. Kidderminster: British Institute for Learning Disabilities.

Inclusion International (1994) *The Beliefs, Values and Principles of Self-advocacy*. Washington, DC: Inclusion International.

Johnstone, D. (1995) *Further Opportunities*. London: Cassell.

Kroese, B. S. *et al.* (1998) 'Consumers with intellectual disabilities as service evaluators', *Journal of Applied Research in Intellectual Disabilities* 11, 116–28.

Lawson, H. (1996) 'Exploring the relationship between teaching, assessment and research methodology: an inquiry into pupil involvement with pupils who experience severe learning difficulties'. Unpublished Ph.D. thesis, University of East Anglia.

Male, D. (1997) 'Who goes to SLD schools?', *Journal of Applied Research in Intellectual Disabilities* 9, 307–23.

Minkes, J., Townsley, R., Weston, C. and Williams, C. (1995) 'Having a voice: involving people with learning difficulties in research', *British Journal of Learning Disabilities* 23, 94–8.

Mittler, P. (1996) 'Laying the foundations for self-advocacy', in Coupe O'Kane, J. and Goldbart, J. (eds) *Whose Choice? Contentious Issues in the Lives of People with Learning Disabilities*. London: David Fulton Publishers.

Mittler, P. and Sinason, V. (eds) (1996) *Changing Policy and Practice for People with Learning Difficulties*. London: Cassell.

Monroe, T. J. (1996) 'We need to educate the professionals', *Mental Retardation* 34, 122–3.

NCC (1992) *The National Curriculum and Pupils with Severe Learning Difficulties*. London: SCAA.

Nind, M. and Hewett, D. (1994) *Access to Communication: Developing the Basics of Communication with People with Severe Learning Difficulties through Intensive Interaction*.London: David Fulton Publishers.

OFSTED (1999) *Special Education 1994–1998: A Review of Special Schools, Secure Units and Pupil Referral Units in England*. London: The Stationery Office.

Pacht, H. (1996) 'My thoughts: self-advocacy, professional organisations and the public', *Mental Retardation* 34, 123–4.

Parker, S. (1994) 'Taking control with the help of the technical and vocational education initiative and Records of Achievement', in Coupe O'Kane, J. and Smith, B. (eds) *Taking Control: Enabling People with Learning Difficulties*. London: David Fulton Publishers.

QCA (1999) *The Review of the National Curriculum in England: The Secretary of State's Proposals*. London: QCA/DfEE.

Ramcharan, P. *et al.* (eds) (1997) *Empowerment in Everyday Life: Learning Disabilities*. London: Jessica Kingsley.

Rose, R. (1999) 'The involvement of pupils with severe learning difficulties as decision makers in respect of their own learning needs', *Westminster Studies in Education*. (in press).

Rose, R., Fletcher, W. and Goodwin, G. (1999) 'Pupils with severe learning difficulties as personal target setters', *British Journal of Special Education*, 26, 220–6.

Rose, R. *et al.* (1996) 'Promoting the greater involvement of pupils with special needs in the management of their own assessment and learning processes', *British Journal of Special Education* 23, 166–71.

Rose, R. *et al.* (1996) *Implementing the Whole Curriculum for People with Learning Difficulties*. London: David Fulton Publishers.

Samutt, T. (1995) Address to Australian Association of Special Education (July), Darwin, Australia.

SCAA (1993) *The National Curriculum and its Assessment* (Final Report). London: SCAA.

SCAA (1996) *Planning the Curriculum for Pupils with Profound and Multiple Learning Difficulties*. London: SCAA.

Sebba, J. *et al.* (1993) *Redefining the Whole Curriculum for Pupils with Learning Difficulties*. London: David Fulton Publishers.

Tilstone, C. (1991) *Teaching Pupils with Severe Learning Difficulties: Practical Approaches*. London: David Fulton Publishers.

Tyne, J. (1996) 'Advocacy: not just another subject', in Rose, R. *et al*. (eds) *Implementing the Whole Curriculum for People with Learning Difficulties*. London: David Fulton Publishers.

Walmsley, J. and Downer, J. (1997) 'Shouting the loudest: self-advocacy, power and diversity', in Ramcharan, P. Èet al. (eds) *Empowerment in Everyday Life: Learning Disabilities*. London: Jessica Kingsley.

Ward, L. (ed.) (1998) *Innovations in Advocacy and Empowerment for People with Intellectual Disabilities*. Chorley, Lancs.: Lisieux Hall Publications.

Ward, N. (1996) 'Supporting self-advocacy in national organisations: our role and yours', *Mental Retardation* 34, 121–2.

Whittaker, A. (1996) 'The fight for self-advocacy', in Mittler, P. and Sinason, V. (eds) *Changing Policy and Practice for People with Learning Difficulties*. London: Cassell.

Wilkinson, C. (1994) 'Teaching pupils with profound and multiple learning difficulties', in Coupe O'Kane, J. and Smith, B. (eds) (1994) *Taking Control: Enabling People with Learning Difficulties*. London: David Fulton Publishers.

Wilkinson, C. (1995) Self-advocacy through drama, *PMLD Link* 23, 11–14.

Williams, P. and Schultz, B. (1982 and 1991) *We Can Change the Future*. London: Souvenir Press.

Winup, K. (1994) 'The role of a student committee in promotion of independence among school leavers', in Coupe O'Kane, J. and Smith, B. (eds) *Taking Control: Enabling People with Learning Difficulties*. London: David Fulton Publishers.

Glossary

Attainment targets (AT) Objectives for each core and foundation subject of the National Curriculum. Attainment targets define the expected standards of pupil performance in terms of eight level descriptions and 'exceptional performance'. The expectation is that the majority of pupils will move up through the level descriptions as they grow older and make progress.

Code of Practice (on the identification and assessment of special educational needs) This code gives practical guidance to local education authorities and the governing bodies of schools on the discharge of their functions in relation to statemented and non-statemented pupils with special educational needs.

Core subjects English, mathematics and science within the National Curriculum.

Cross-curricular elements These run across the whole National Curriculum and are not confined to one subject. They cover **dimensions** (e.g. equal opportunities), **themes** (e.g. health education) and **key skills** (e.g. communication).

Department for Education and Employment (DfEE) Central Government department with duties and responsibilities relating to the provision of education in schools in England. Formerly known as the **Department for Education (DFE)**, and as the **Department of Education and Science (DES)** prior to that. From June 2001 this becomes the **Department for Education and Skills (DFES).**

Differentiation The matching of work to the differing capabilities of individuals or groups of pupils in order to extend their learning.

Disapplication A school can propose that a particular pupil should not study all the compulsory National Curriculum subjects so that they can take part in an individualised programme of education. For pupils with a statement of special educational needs, disapplications should be recorded in the statement.

Foundation subjects Usually taken to refer to design and technology, information and communication technology (ICT), geography, history, physical education, modern foreign languages, music and art. Strictly speaking English, mathematics and science are both core and foundation subjects.

Individual Education Plan (IEP) Pupils with special educational needs, at whatever stage in the process of assessment recommended by the Code of Practice, should have an IEP that identifies the nature of the child's learning difficulties, action to be taken, staff involved, specific programmes and resources, targets to be achieved within a given timescale, monitoring, assessment and review arrangements and other information. IEPs are usually reviewed two or three times per year.

Inclusion One of the aims of the Government is that, as far as possible, schools should teach all pupils the National Curriculum, whatever their needs. There are many different definitions of inclusion offered by writers, but the main emphasis of educationists is upon developing inclusive education practices and provision in mainstream schools and colleges.

INSET In-service education and training, often called **continuing professional development**.

Key stages The periods in each pupil's education to which the elements of the National Curriculum apply. They are: Key Stage 1, beginning of compulsory education to age 7 years; Key Stage 2, 7–11 years; Key Stage 3, 11–14 years; Key Stage 4, 14 years until the end of compulsory education. The equivalent year-groups are Years 1 and 2; Years 3–6; Years 7–9; Years 10 and 11 respectively. Also recognised as important stages of education are the Foundation Stage for children aged 3–5 years, including children in the Reception Year, and the Post-16 stage for students aged from 16 to 19 years.

Learning difficulties This book deals mainly with pupils with **profound, severe** or **moderate learning difficulties**. Their learning difficulties result from a degree of intellectual impairment, often of organic origin but compounded by social and environmental factors. These pupils are a minority of the pupil population – perhaps about 2 per cent. Many other children experience milder learning difficulties.

Local Education Authority (LEA) Parliament has given a number of duties relating to the provision of schools and an appropriate education for all children to these local elected bodies and a range of powers to enable them to carry out these duties. Some of these powers and duties are delegated to the governing bodies of schools, which are made up of LEA-appointed people, elected representatives of staff and parents, and local community representatives.

Level descriptions In each National Curriculum subject there are eight level descriptions per attainment target. Level descriptions indicate the types and range of performance that a pupil is expected to demonstrate for each level. They are used to make summative judgements about a pupil's performance at the end of a key stage. The National Curriculum levels are not used for assessment at Key Stage 4.

Local Management of Schools (LMS), Local Management of Special Schools (LMSS) The arrangements by which local education authorities delegate to the governing bodies of individual schools responsibility for the management of their budget share and other aspects of school management.

National Curriculum The core and foundation subjects and their associated attainment targets and programmes of study.

National Curriculum Council (NCC) Former advisory body on aspects of the curriculum in schools. Its functions were taken over by the SCAA in October 1993.

Office for Standards in Education (OFSTED) A non-ministerial UK government department that has responsibility for the inspection of all schools in England. The professional arm is formed by **Her Majesty's Inspectors (HMI)**.

'P'-levels In 1998, the Department for Education and Employment and the Qualifications and Curriculum Authority produced eight level descriptions for each attainment target in English and mathematics, leading up to Level 1 of the National Curriculum. The levels are framed in terms of performance criteria that indicate how much a pupil knows, understands and can do. See **Level descriptions** above. The so-called 'P'-levels were introduced as objective measurements of attainment of pupils who typically achieve below Level 1. They are used to support school target-setting (rather than individual pupil target-setting) as part of the process of school improvement. Similar level descriptions were introduced at the same time for aspects of personal and social development. These have been replaced by P-Levels for science subsequently.

Performance descriptions. In 2001, performance descriptions of the attainment of pupils working towards Level 1 of the National Curriculum developed for all National Curriculum subjects plus PSHE and citizenship and religious education. These were developed for the purpose of demonstrating pupil progress rather than target-setting for school improvement.

Programmes of Study (PoS) The programmes of study set out the minimum statutory entitlement to the knowledge, understanding and skills for each National Curriculum subject and at each key stage.

Qualifications and Curriculum Authority (QCA) The current advisory body on all aspects of the curriculum and its assessment in schools, as well as examinations.

School Examination and Assessment Council (SEAC) Former advisory body on all aspects of examinations and assessment in schools. Its functions were taken over by the SCAA in October 1993.

School Curriculum and Assessment Authority (SCAA) Successor advisory body to SEAC on all aspects of the curriculum and its assessment in schools, as well as examinations. Its functions were taken over by the QCA in 1996.

Special educational needs (SEN) Referring to pupils who, for a variety of intellectual, physical, social, sensory, psychological or emotional reasons, experience learning difficulties that are significantly greater than those experienced by the majority of pupils of the same age.

Special support assistants Non-teaching staff who assist teachers, usually within the classroom. Typically, they are also called **teaching assistants** or **learning support assistants (LSAs)**.

Standard Assessment Tasks (SATs) These may also be called **Standard National Tests**. They are externally prescribed National Curriculum assessments administered to pupils in the final year of a key stage. The methods of assessment vary depending on the subject and key stage.

Statements (of Special Educational Needs) Statements of special educational needs are provided under the terms of the Education Act 1993 to ensure appropriate provision for pupils formally assessed as having special educational needs.

Statutory order or Order A statutory instrument that enables the provisions of an Act of Parliament to be augmented or updated. Each National Curriculum subject has its related statutory order.

Teacher Training Agency An advisory body on many aspects of teacher recruitment and training. It has been instrumental in developing and disseminating national standards for subject leaders, head teachers, special educational needs specialist teachers, and other school professionals.

Whole curriculum The curriculum of a school incorporating the basic curriculum and all other curricular provision deemed appropriate by the school.

Author index

Subject index

Lightning Source UK Ltd.
Milton Keynes UK
11 July 2010

156852UK00005B/2/A

60 4152934 0

9 781853 466762